BARRIO RISING

The publisher gratefully acknowledges the generous support of the Humanities Endowment Fund of the University of California Press Foundation.

BARRIO RISING

URBAN POPULAR POLITICS AND THE
MAKING OF MODERN VENEZUELA

Alejandro Velasco

 UNIVERSITY OF CALIFORNIA PRESS

University of California Press, one of the most distinguished
university presses in the United States, enriches lives around the
world by advancing scholarship in the humanities, social sciences,
and natural sciences. Its activities are supported by the UC Press
Foundation and by philanthropic contributions from individuals
and institutions. For more information, visit www.ucpress.edu.

University of California Press
Oakland, California

Library of Congress Cataloging-in-Publication Data

Velasco, Alejandro, 1978– author.
  Barrio rising : urban popular politics and the making of modern
  Venezuela / Alejandro Velasco.
      pages cm
  Includes bibliographical references and index.
    ISBN 978-0-520-28331-2 (cloth : alk. paper) — ISBN 978-0-520-
  28332-9 (pbk. : alk. paper) — ISBN 978-0-520-95918-7 (ebook)
      1. Political participation—Venezuela—Caracas. 2. City planning—
  Political aspects—Venezuela—Caracas. 3. Squatters—Political
  activity—Venezuela—Caracas. 4. Venezuela—Politics and govern-
  ment—20th century. I. Title.
    F2341.C257V45 2015
    987.06′3—dc23   2015006420

Manufactured in the United States of America

24 23 22 21 20 19 18 17 16 15
10 9 8 7 6 5 4 3 2 1

In keeping with a commitment to support environmentally responsible
and sustainable printing practices, UC Press has printed this book on
Natures Natural, a fiber that contains 30% post-consumer waste and
meets the minimum requirements of ANSI/NISO z39.48–1992 (R 1997)
(Permanence of Paper).

CONTENTS

ILLUSTRATIONS

PREFACE

In late July 2014 authorities in Venezuela began to relocate over 3,000 men, women, and children from the downtown Caracas slum where they had lived since 2007 into newly built government housing on the city's outskirts.[1] It was the kind of news that hardly ever registers. After all, slums are staples of urban landscapes across the globe, housing nearly one billion of the world's poorest and least visible people.[2] And as slums proliferate so too do efforts to eradicate them, often by force, usually in the name of modernity, renewal, or of a euphemistic "beautification" that seems again and again to leave those already vulnerable in conditions far worse than before.[3]

Yet news of this particular eviction in Venezuela's capital spread worldwide. Reuters and the Associated Press highlighted the item in their wire. From there, hundreds of outlets picked up the story.[4] In the United States the *New Yorker* magazine and National Public Radio ran features.[5] So did the *Guardian*, the *Daily Mail*, and the BBC in England;[6] major newspapers in Argentina, Brazil, and Colombia offered readers full accounts of the move.[7] The news even rippled as far away as Australia and China where the Guoji Zaixian radio service headlined: "Venezuela military police sweep landmark slum, hundreds of poor 'move to new homes.'"[8]

In fact, this was no ordinary slum. In September 2007 a group of men and women in search of a place to live broke through the ground-floor fence of a half-finished 45-story skyscraper in the heart of Caracas's financial district and claimed the building as their own.[9] It had been over a decade since the tower had seen any signs of life. In 1994, after a financial meltdown left

Venezuela's economy in shambles, construction halted on banker David Brillembourg's dream of a site that would be "Venezuela's answer to Wall Street." So it lay abandoned for years, a rusting shell of a building memorializing an era of reckless private investment that helped push millions into poverty. Then Venezuela's political landscape shifted. Hugo Chávez, a former army commander who had led a failed coup attempt in 1992, swept into the presidency in 1998 promising to usher in a revolution where the country's poor would take center stage, eventually calling it "twenty-first-century socialism." But after years of waiting for long-promised housing, hundreds of families resolved to make real Chávez's claims of a future in which they held power, breaking into and then squatting in Brillembourg's abandoned skyscraper, and in the process giving rise to "the world's tallest slum." For most it was simply *la Torre de David* [the Tower of David].[10]

Over the next seven years, the story of a skyscraper built to symbolize an era of capitalist ambition, then abandoned, then forcibly occupied by citizens at large in the midst of a socialist revolution captivated journalists, architects, and academics. Their accounts varied wildly. For some the Tower became a last resort for the desperate, hated by society, a conundrum for the government.[11] Those who managed an existence in its bowels did so lacking running water, sewer lines, elevators, and even walls. Unsupervised children fell to their deaths by accident; wayward adults by design. Others saw it as a den of drugs, rape, and violence, "a byword for everything that is wrong with [Venezuela]." Wrote the *New Yorker's* Jon Lee Anderson: "Caracas is a failed city, and the Tower of David is perhaps the ultimate symbol of that failure."[12] The U.S. television drama *Homeland* even featured a fictional representation of the Tower in its storyline, billing it as a lawless haven for murderers and terrorists where police dared not enter.[13]

But when stripped of hyperbole and dramatic license, for others, including its residents, the Tower and the life they crafted for themselves stood not for violence but for popular ingenuity and even hope, precarious and sometimes dangerous, to be sure, but also stable and removed from the most extreme perils of poverty.[14] To the hundreds of homes fashioned inside the building were also added shops, beauty salons, Internet cafes, sports facilities, and churches, all governed by "a set of written rules established by the community."[15] Architects at the firm Urban Think Tank upheld "the settlement as a font of lessons on how to adapt broken cities to the millions who flock to them," exhibiting designs, photographs, and a documentary about the Tower to much acclaim at the Thirteenth International Architecture Biennale, in Venice, in 2012.[16] Anthropologist Gastón Gordillo, studying what he called "the rubble of elite architectural forms" left over when grand designs go awry, wrote of the Tower's inhabitants: "They have ... appropriated a node of rubble and turned it into something else: a home they feel attached to."[17]

Yet for all the attention the Tower and its residents mustered, in print or film or web traffic, the most remarkable feature of all went unremarked: this phenomenon had happened before. Not somewhere else in the world, or even elsewhere in Latin America, but in Caracas, in fact just over a mile from where the Tower of David stood.

In January 1958 thousands of apartments lay vacant in still-unfinished fifteen-story superblocks built by the dictatorship of Marcos Pérez Jiménez to house the city's poor. It was his grand plan for a modern Venezuela where sleek high-rises would replace ramshackle *barrios*—slums in Venezuelan parlance—and turn a long-chaotic Caracas into a model of order and progress, no matter who or what stood in his way. He built them in the heart of the capital for all to marvel. In time, his uncompromising vision spawned calls for his ouster, and on 23 January 1958 a group of military officers and civilians, buoyed by the public at large, overthrew Pérez Jiménez and promised to usher in a democratic revolution. As word spread, twenty thousand people across Caracas and its surroundings rushed to the empty superblocks. Two days later, they had occupied every vacant apartment in sight, 3,000 in all.

Once a symbol of dictatorship, the dozens of high-rises Pérez Jiménez ordered built in downtown Caracas now stood as an emblem of the revolutionary fervor that overthrew him; their new inhabitants even took as the neighborhood's name the date of his ouster: *23 de Enero* (23rd of January). But it was hardly good news for the new government, suddenly responsible not just for completing but for administering the signature project of the previous regime, now packed with tens of thousands of squatters. Staggering operating costs coupled with the new government's general disdain for the deposed dictator's brand of urban planning gradually caused living conditions to deteriorate, generating deep friction that often manifested itself in violent protest. Meanwhile leftist guerrillas in pursuit of state power took advantage of the neighborhood's location to launch attacks on the government. Eventually the 23 de Enero came to be seen as a lawless place, a tangle of high-rise slums amid new slums that rose up around the superblocks. For many it seemed to mark a failure of two regimes: the one that built it and the one that inherited it.

But the men and women who took up residence in the neighborhood had laid claim not just to physical space but to the promise of a more inclusive, more responsive, more democratic society. From their perch overlooking downtown Caracas, they continued to hold the government to account through a variety of means available to them. At times they took to the polls, less to support those in power than to uphold a key tool of democratic citizenship—the vote. At times they took to the streets, not to seek anyone's ouster but to demand solutions to their grievances and, more significantly, a greater say in the political system. In the process, they fashioned a space—and an understanding of democracy—at once part of the state and outside of it, at once deeply bound to the underpinnings of the political project but also, by their actions and by their very existence, sharply critical of it.

The parallels between the 23 de Enero and the Tower of David are thus striking; that not a single story made mention of it, domestically or abroad, is less so. Venezuela's past remains caught in what anthropologist Fernando Coronil has called "a collective amnesia that envelops the dominant memorialization of Venezuela's history." Induced by illusions of limitless wealth fueled by oil booms, successive governments and their analysts over the last hundred years in Venezuela—whether dictatorial or democratic, socialist or capitalist, modernist or provincial—have taken to "manufacturing collective fantasies of progress" in which vast state spending "casts its spell over audience and performers alike. As a 'magnanimous sorcerer,'" continues Coronil, "the state seizes its subjects by inducing a condition or state of being receptive to its illusions—a magical state."[18] In this sense, for political elites survival relies on perpetuating an ever more dazzling vision of the future with ever more spectacular displays of power in the present. But as there are oil booms there are also oil busts, ensuring that over time the breach between future and present will expand unsustainably. Reaping the benefits of a spectacular present unable to keep pace with a magical future therefore requires eliminating memories of a well-trod past, lest the memory of that past expose the precariousness of a magical future.

At the same time, and much as happened with the 23 de Enero, the Tower of David and the wildly contradictory interpretations it spawned call attention to another key but less familiar feature of Venezuela's political nature: absent history, hysteria reigns. Haunted by failures past, yet unable to contend with them so as to maintain the plausible illusion of a magical future, the precarious present becomes a site of urgent but unstated anticipation, of immediate gratification or punishment. Writes Venezuelan novelist Federico Vegas: "A historian says hysteria is like a platform where everything that happens to us bounces back, preventing what we live through from becoming experience. This means we are constantly on the surface, never reaching deeper, never gazing inward, unable to link our past to the history of man on earth." Unmoored from any sense of history that might offer lessons or comfort in moments of crisis, anxieties are met not with nuance but with hyperbole: at hand is always either utopia or apocalypse, nothing in between. "We therefore have in Venezuela," offers Vegas, "a hysterical country subject to infernal repetition."[19]

Today, from the rooftops of the 23 de Enero it is easy to spot the Tower of David just over a mile away due west. It is a short distance as the crow flies, but embedded in that space is a history marked more by continuities than by ruptures, nevertheless masked and distorted by layers of amnesia and hysteria. What the Tower of David represents is a small-scale version of what the men and women who occupied thousands of vacant apartments here fifty years before undertook, in search of better lives for themselves and for their families, drawing on a revolutionary discourse that held the promise of greater participation, of greater democracy. This book tells that story.

ACKNOWLEDGMENTS

Deep down, *Barrio Rising* is an effort to grapple with the roots and legacies of a massacre that dramatically informed my upbringing in Caracas. In February 1989 mass protests over neoliberal economic reforms rocked the capital, claiming hundreds of lives after the government unleashed unprecedented repression to regain control. Coming of age after what became known as the *Caracazo* was for many in my generation a watershed that set off a period of daily protests, failed coups, and economic collapse. For my family it also meant leaving Venezuela in the mid-1990s. In this sense my parents, Álvaro Velasco and Astrid Cañete, deserve my first thanks. Their doubtlessly difficult decision provided me with more stability than I might have found at home, and set me on the path that would ultimately allow me to return to Venezuela to help make sense of the history that occasioned our departure. I suspect it was not a path they imagined for me; I know it has brought them heartache. For their unflinching support, for me and for this book, I am grateful.

That path might have led to somewhere else entirely had it not been for the mentorship I received as an undergraduate at Boston College. David Quigley sparked my interest in the interplay of urban life and democracy; Deborah Levenson, in the sophistication and commitment required to do oral history, especially among those whose voices are rarely heard. Both deeply inform this book, as does Fr. Donald MacMillans's dedication to social justice in the Jesuit tradition. They were also the first to suggest I consider graduate school, and gave generously of their time to help me get there, as did Kelly Wise, Clement

White, and Alexandra Cornelius at the Institute for the Recruitment of Teachers, in Andover, Massachusetts.

I was fortunate to arrive in the PhD Program at Duke University's History Department while Greg Grandin was still there. His guidance and commitment to politically informed scholarship gave me an early sense of what historical analysis can and should be. So did the insights and training of Charles Payne, Susan Thorne, Barry Gaspar, Bill Reddy, and Gunther Peck. Jocelyn Olcott's brilliant analytic eye around questions of gender, citizenship, and revolution enriched my thinking and honed my research—while her wit and banter reminded me to find humor where possible. Beyond Duke's History Department, the Center for Latin American and Caribbean Studies (CLACS) nurtured a community of scholars in anthropology, political science, and literature that helped shape the interdisciplinary foundations of this book. Natalie Hartman, Bonnie McManus, and Jenny Williams made of CLACS the sort of place where ideas flowed freely among colleagues at Duke and the University of North Carolina Chapel Hill.

The Duke CLACS also provided early funding support for my research. A summer 2002 travel grant took me to Caracas during the fallout from a failed coup that just weeks earlier temporarily ousted President Hugo Chávez. The April coup pitted organized business groups, trade unions, and a largely middle-class civil society against urban popular sectors that made up the core of Chávez supporters. For forty-eight hours Chávez was held under arrest, and an interim president from the ranks of the business elite was sworn in with U.S. support. In a dramatic turn of events, a multitude including thousands of residents from the 23 de Enero braved a media blackout and surrounded the Presidential Palace, located a short distance away, helping to bring about Chávez's reinstatement. In casual conversations with 23 de Enero residents about their memories of the April events, I began to imagine that a grassroots study of this key neighborhood in Caracas could provide a new understanding of the development of urban popular politics in Venezuela.

A generous International Dissertation Research Fellowship from the Social Science Research Council (SSRC) supported a fourteen-month stay in Caracas in 2004–2005. While there, the archival staffs of the Universidad Central de Venezuela (UCV), the then Instituto Nacional de la Vivienda, the Archivo Audiovisual de la Nación, and the Archivo El Nacional diligently attended to my requests and offered their expertise. An Albert J. Beveridge Grant from the American Historical Association funded travel to Costa Rica to work at the Inter-American Court of Human Rights (IACHR) library in San José, Costa Rica, to consult the *Caracazo* case files. At the UCV's Centro de Estudios del Desarrollo in Caracas where I was a Visiting Scholar, I began to generate the outlines of what became this book. All the while Andreina Velasco ably and quickly transcribed dozens of interviews, helping to move my research along.

The greatest influence on this book, of course, are the people of the 23 de Enero. The community that welcomed me there had every reason to be skeptical, or at least tired, of another U.S.-based researcher asking probing questions about their lives and politics. Over time they gained confidence that my commitment to learning about their neighborhood's history was serious, not episodic. As a result, more and more women, men, and youth granted me entry into their living rooms, domino games, offices, and memories. Their patience and generosity seemed boundless, especially as I pressed them to move beyond familiar narratives, to consider contradictions in their testimonies, or to revisit moments long-since forgotten. To all of them, my deepest thanks. But I owe particular debts of gratitude to Omar Machado, Gustavo Borges, Ravín Sánchez, Priscilla Carrero, Lisandro Pérez, Lourdes Quintero, Juan Contreras, and the Santana family for the many hours they spent with me during the year I lived in their neighborhood. Each reflected different strands of a larger history of social and political activism in the neighborhood. We did not always share the same interpretations of that past, but by engaging and debating with me and with one another they offered a glimpse into the vibrancy that has long shaped life in *el veintitrés*. If this book captures even a small part of that spirit, it will have proven worthwhile.

Many critics have offered helpful feedback at crucial stages. I am thankful to Nicole Stahlman, Jason Seawright, and Eric Hershberg for stimulating conversations during an SSRC Fellows Conference in 2005. The Latin American Labor History Conference at Duke remains a preeminent site for fierce debate; over the years Anne Farnsworth-Alvear, Joan Bak, Thomas Klubock, Pete Sigal, Jeff Gould, and Daniel James took turns pushing me to clarify my thinking and my writing. I owe special thanks to Mark Healey who has made his keen mind, students, and institutional spaces available to me, from the University of California, Berkeley, to the University of Connecticut, Storrs (and a brief sojourn in Mendoza), to share my work and ideas. I am also grateful to Gil Joseph for generously hosting me at Yale at various times. While I was a Five College Fellow at Hampshire

College in 2006–2007, Frank Holmquist and Margaret Cerullo read and commented on early drafts of this work, and John Drabinski, Christina Hanhardt, and Omar Dahi provided both intellectual stimulation and, more important, friendship. To Omar and to Cora Fernández Anderson, especially, *shukran* and *mil gracias*. During my stay in Amherst, Sonia Álvarez, Jeffrey Rubin, Gianpaolo Baiocchi, Millie Thayer, and Agustín Lao Montes welcomed me into their community of Latin Americanists at the University of Massachusetts, for which I remain grateful.

Throughout I have benefitted from the work, feedback, and support of Venezuela experts, here and there, especially Fernando Coronil, Julie Skurksi, Margarita López Maya, Daniel Levine, Miguel Tinker Salas, and Javier Corrales. Steve Ellner's encyclopedic knowledge of modern Venezuelan history and politics has saved me from errors both factual and conceptual. David Smilde deserves special thanks, for believing in the promise of this project when it was just gestating, then supporting it and me, intellectually and emotionally, every step of the way. It is kindness I can never fully repay (though I hope a *polarcita* may help). More recently, Sujatha Fernandes, George Ciccariello-Maher, Olga González-Silen, Naomi Schiller, Luis Duno Gottberg, Robert Samet, Rebecca Hanson, Gabriel Hetland, Jonathan Weinstock Rodrigo, and Verónica Zubillaga have inspired me in their commitment to study the political life and history of Venezuela's popular sectors. Their work offers hope that, whatever else may happen, future research on Venezuela will no longer be limited to elites and institutions, but will instead have to engage seriously with new actors and voices among the poor and working class.

An amazing stroke of good luck landed me at New York University (NYU), where I have met with far more support—institutional, financial, intellectual—than any Assistant Professor should reasonably expect. In the History Department, Greg Grandin, Barbara Weinstein, and Sinclair Thomson, as well as their students Josh Frens-String, Marcio Siwi, Natan Zeichner, and Christy Thornton have offered feedback and encouragement at crucial moments. At the Center for Latin American and Caribbean Studies, Ada Ferrer, Jill Lane, and Amalia Córdova have created a stimulating academic environment in which to share projects, as well as granted me Title VI funds that allowed me to return to Venezuela in 2012 to complete additional research for the book.

But it is at NYU's Gallatin School of Individualized Study, my academic home, where my thinking and scholarship have most grown, sharpening this book and so much more. My debts to Stephen Duncombe, George Shulman, Stacy Pies, Lisa Goldfarb, Ali Mirsepassi, and Kim Phillips-Fein are too great to detail; I know they will understand. I am especially grateful to Dean Susanne Wofford for her generous support of junior faculty and of my work in particular, including through two Faculty Research Awards. To Pat McCreery, Celeste Orangers, Mary Witty, Rachel Plutzer, and Theresa Anderson: for your logistical help (and patience), thank you. Above all, I have been privileged to work with Gallatin's remarkable students. Their intellectual curiosity and impatience with injustice are a constant inspiration to redouble my commitments to engaged scholarship. Maggie Carter, Rick Stern, Thomaz Marcondes, Emma Young, Renée Schomp, Lauren Wilfong, Helen Isaac, Joshua Lieberman, and Mira Chernick in particular—you make me proud. And for ably assisting my research with patience and care, I am especially grateful to Julia Burnell.

My students are a regular reminder that for ideas to flourish they require a lively community of peers committed to thrashing ideas about fearlessly. While I was at Duke, I found that community in Linda Rupert, Phil Rubio, Silvermoon, Dan Golonka, Gonzalo Lamana, David Carlson, Joshua Nadel, and James Palmer, and especially in Ivonne Wallace Fuentes, Tom Rogers, and Jody Pavilack, whose scholarship and camaraderie remain deeply inspiring. More recently, Bryan Pitts, Elizabeth Shezko, Katharine French-Fuller, and Kristen Wintersteen, have read and commented on parts of this book. Their generosity in helping a student they barely knew speaks to the strengths of the graduate community of Latin Americanists at Duke, one that I had the privilege to become reacquainted with while presenting this manuscript in full for feedback in 2013. In particular I thank David Romine, Vanessa Freije, Yuridia Ramírez, Paola Reyes, Anne Phillips, Christina Davidson, Caroline Garriot, and Corinna Zeltsman for their comments.

The continuing strength of Duke's Latin American History community is the work of John French. Early in our collaboration John wrote on a paper where I first showed interest in exploring the modern history of Venezuelan popular politics: "Your work is important." It was a vote of confidence illustrating John's abiding sense that as historians, our work matters. And to make it matter requires responsibility and commitment that extends beyond the archives and reflects a life lived at the service of critical thought. Over the years this dynamic has informed every one of our exchanges. John will always have my gratitude for teaching me that history, as the social historian Marc Bloch put it, is a craft more than a discipline.

At the University of California Press, Kate Marshall's enthusiasm for this project was clear from our first meeting, and her keen editorial eye sharpened the book's style and argument. So did the detailed reports by the Press's reviewers and, more recently, Juan Quintana's meticulous copyediting. I am grateful to them, and to Stacy Eisenstark, Rose Vekony, and Ryan Furtkamp, as well as to Susan Storch for her indexing talents, and to Ben Pease, whose beautiful maps will make navigating the complex social and geographic terrain of Caracas and the 23 de Enero far easier for readers.

Jan, Paul, and Elizabeth French deserve special recognition for bearing with me as I made extraordinary demands on John's time and energy. Their patience speaks volumes to the bonds of love that sustain any long-term project. Over the years it has taken to finish this book, I have drawn on such bonds from Estela de la Hoz, Rick and Liz Kenney, Mario and Mónica Umaña, and especially George, Janet, and Julie Paradis, who welcomed me warmly into their home and their extended family when Aimée Paradis Velasco and I first met in college. Through long stretches of separation, Aimée and I continued to find inspiration in each other, and from there came the greatest thrill of our lives: our daughters Isabel and Sofia—your boundless energy and curiosity have kept me from forgetting to live outside this book; I can't wait to see (and read) what books life has in store for you. *Las amo.*

A History of Place and Nation

This is a book about popular politics in Venezuela in the forty years before Hugo Chávez's election as president. It offers the long history of how the urban working poor—in fragmented and often contradictory ways—became the most important political constituency in contemporary Venezuela. It is a book that explores how and why people often excluded in ways formal and informal from the exercise of politics understand and experience democracy not merely as elections, but also as a political order that allows for dynamic, participatory action, not always bound by rules, laws, and institutions. In short, it is a book about how democracy happened—and continues to happen—everyday, on the streets of Venezuela.

Much about the way this democracy came to be is visible from the roof of Block 7 (fig. 1), in the heart of the 23 de Enero neighborhood (23rd of January; pronounced *vain-tee-TRESS deh uh-NEH-roh*). By any measure, standing here can be overwhelming. In part it's the sense of danger. There is no railing or fence, nothing except a knee-high barrier on the building's edge, to prevent a fatal fifteen-story fall. In part it's the sense of scale. From here, atop a hill overlooking downtown Caracas, the whole of Venezuela's capital opens up, ten miles from west to east, with the coastal Cordillera lining the valley's north like a massive sentinel. Closer, barely 80 yards away, stands an identical fifteen-story building, 150-units strong. It is one of dozens of so-called "superblocks" rising all around, rectangular, evenly spaced—like giant sideways dominoes ready to tumble.

More than size or vertigo, it is the sense of history that overwhelms. From the roof of Block 7 it is easy to see the broad sweep of modern Venezuelan

FIGURE I. 23 de Enero neighborhood, looking north from the roof of Block 7 in Monte Piedad. (2014 photo by the author)

history on dramatic display (maps 1–3). Some of this history is well known. It is in places like the Miraflores Presidential Palace, nestled amid lush trees just half a mile northeast. From here, in the mid-1950s, a military dictatorship looked out onto the hillside where Block 7 currently stands and saw slums dating back decades. Flush with oil wealth and resolving to bring order to the capital—and the nation—authorities moved to raze all vestiges of that past and build in its place modern high-rises to house the city's working class. It was among the largest public housing projects of its kind in Latin America, built conspicuously in the heart of the nation's capital as a symbol of the new Venezuela. And it bore the name 2 de Diciembre (2nd of December; pronounced *dos deh dee-SIEM-breh*), the date in 1952 when the dictatorship of General Marcos Pérez Jiménez cemented its rule.

But on 23 January 1958, residents of the 2 de Diciembre neighborhood flooded Avenida Sucre, just at the bottom of the hill from Block 7, and from there walked the short distance to Miraflores. They went to show their support for the ouster of the Pérez Jiménez dictatorship by a group of civilians and

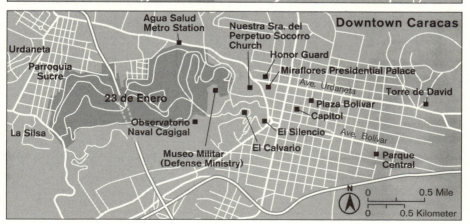

MAPS 1–3. Venezuela and the Americas; Caracas; downtown Caracas. (Cartography by Ben Pease)

military officers promising a new era of democratic government, one in which their votes would count and their voices would be heard. In turn, residents renamed their neighborhood 23 de Enero, linking it in name and in spirit with the fortunes of the infant democracy. Over the next thirty years, broad-based political parties traded power through competitive elections. Meanwhile, power-sharing pacts between political leaders, trade unions, and economic elites brought a level of stability under representative government unheard of in a region languishing in dictatorships and civil wars. Like the "superblocks" themselves, then, one history seen from the roof of Block 7 is made up of solid structures and formal institutions, of grand projects of a well-ordered society with dreams of a strong, stable democracy.

But there is another history on display, just as visible from here, yet largely untold. This history rises from the spaces between the superblocks, in dense webs of *ranchos*—improvised shacks—that surfaced in the months and years after 1958, as people in search of opportunity settled in new slums, no longer the targets of a modernizing dictatorship. Seen from Block 7 these ranchos and the *barrios* they make up—long since incorporated, sometimes uneasily, into the larger neighborhood—occupy what seems like every crevice of the landscape where buildings didn't already stand by 1958.

This other history also rises in places like Blocks 54, 55, and 56, just west of here, difficult to distinguish against the backdrop of tightly packed ranchos that surround them. These are the last superblocks ever built in Venezuela, completed several months after the fall of the Pérez Jiménez dictatorship. In January 1959, just three weeks after triumphantly entering Havana to usher in the Cuban Revolution, Fidel Castro visited Caracas and the 23 de Enero neighborhood. He brought a message of gratitude for the example Venezuelans had set a year earlier on the date after which the neighborhood was named. In response, residents named the sector Sierra Maestra (map 4), in honor of the mountain stronghold in Cuba from which Castro had launched his guerrilla campaign.

Just a few years later, as the promise of representative democracy gave way to bitter struggles over just whom and what that democracy should represent, guerrilla war came to Venezuela. It did so in places like Block 1, which stands exposed on a hill north of Block 7, directly overlooking Avenida Sucre. In the 1960s, armed insurgents took to the roof of Block 1 to engage government forces in the streets below. By the 1970s the insurgency had been defeated, but battles over the limits and possibilities of democratic government continued in places like the rotary in Block 7, a strategic nexus between several neighborhood sectors. While everyday challenges, from rising crime to water shortages to faulty trash collection, made life in the 23 de Enero a daily slog, residents again and again set up roadblocks at this rotary to demand the attention of increasingly unresponsive officials. By the 1980s severe economic crises made their problems more acute, and government even less accountable. In response residents more and more took matters into their own hands. In barrios like Arbolitos, just west of Block 7, self-defense brigades such as the one known as La Piedrita organized to fight a raging drug trade while at the same time raising political awareness among neighbors through murals and street art. Many of these murals are easily spotted from the roof of Block 7.

Then, in 1989, the mounting pressures of a democratic government that had grown alienated from its citizens came to a head, and places like Block 22, easily seen to the northwest from Block 7, were among the ones to bear the brunt. In late February of that year newly elected President Carlos Andrés Pérez went back on promises he had made on the campaign trail and implemented a severe austerity program to avert economic collapse. From the barrios of Caracas—places like the 23 de Enero—people descended onto the streets to protest. The government responded with unparalleled repression; in a matter of days, hundreds lay massacred, many of them left to rot in mass graves. The civil unrest and government countermeasures surrounding these events came to be known as the *Caracazo*. Because of its strategic location, and its previous history as a hotbed of guerrilla insurgency, the 23 de Enero was the site of especially acute violence from army units deployed to restore order. In Block 22, overlooking Avenida Sucre, residents endured such intense gunfire from troops stationed below that today it is still easy to make out the spray of bullets on its walls.

While the scars of Block 22 are a reminder of how the promise of democracy ushered in on the date in 1958 after which the 23 de Enero was named came to die, the Museo Militar (Military Museum) is a reminder of a new set of promises that would rise in its wake. A nineteenth-century castle so close to the east of Block 7 that a strong arm might reach it with a rock, this is the place from where in the predawn hours of 4 February 1992 troops loyal to Lieutenant Colonel Hugo Chávez staged a coup against what by then had become a broadly unpopular political system. The coup failed, but the discontent it revealed, and the expectations for far-reaching changes that it unleashed, eventually helped Chávez win Venezuela's presidency in 1998 under a banner of Bolivarian

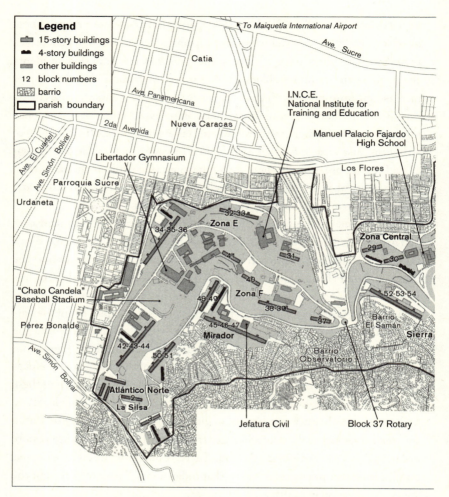

MAP 4. 23 de Enero (2000 Map). (Alcaldía de Caracas; cartography by Ben Pease)

Revolution that promised to found Venezuela anew and give greater voice and political power to the same popular sectors that had found themselves excluded from the political project begun on 23 January 1958, the people from places like the 23 de Enero. Today, this is where Chávez lies entombed, in the bowels of the Museo Militar, a stone's throw from Block 7.

In ways literal and figurative, then, the 23 de Enero and its residents stand at the center of social and political life in Venezuela, as they have since the

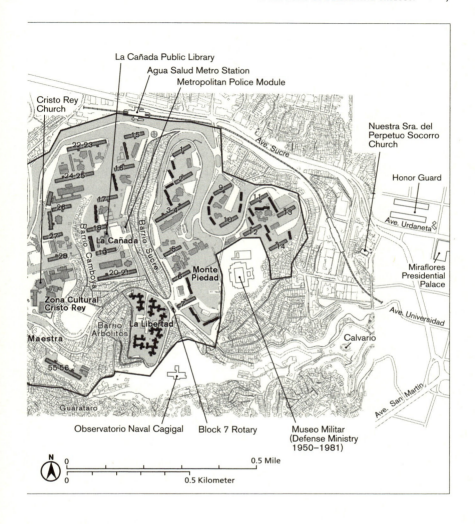

La Cañada Public Library
Agua Salud Metro Station
Metropolitan Police Module

Cristo Rey Church

Nuestra Sra. del Perpetuo Socorro Church

Ave. Sucre

22-23
24-25
26
27
28
15
1.6
1.7
18
19
20-21
1

2
3-4
5
6
6
9
10
11
12
13
14

Honor Guard
Ave. Urdaneta

Miraflores Presidential Palace

Ave. Universidad

Barrio Camboya
Barrio Sucre
La Cañada
Monte Piedad

Zona Cultural Cristo Rey

Maestra
Barrio Arbolitos
La Libertad

Calvario

Ave. San Martin

55-56

Guarataro

Observatorio Naval Cagigal   Block 7 Rotary   Museo Militar (Defense Ministry 1950–1981)

N

0   0.5 Mile

0   0.5 Kilometer

neighborhood's founding nearly 60 years ago, their evolution mirroring that of the nation as a whole. "To speak of the 23 de Enero," wrote one major newspaper in 2002, "is to invoke the democratic spirit of the nation."[1] But like the landscape visible from Block 7, this democratic spirit is riven and complex. It is marked not by any one history but by many in sometimes tense interaction, by the interplay of formal and informal structures, of dramatically differing visions of the nation's future. It reflects the history of modernizing dictatorships and democratic governments and revolutionary projects. It is a history of barrios and high-rises. It is the history of a neighborhood, and of a nation. Welcome to *el veintitrés*.[2]

VENEZUELAN COUNTERPOINT: THE STREET AND THE BALLOT

There is a counterpoint driving Venezuelan democracy, and this book. It is the counterpoint of popular protest and electoral politics, two strands of political action often seen as contradictory and zero-sum: the stronger the latter, the weaker the former, and vice versa. In representative systems of government, according to mainstream political theory going back centuries, the chief aim of the vote is to steer the will of the electorate away from the streets, where the passions of the mob rule, and into institutions where reason, procedure, and civility can prevail among varied interests to make policy in the public good. Where popular protest is either present or predominates, it is evidence of a breakdown in the institutions of democracy. By contrast, where popular protest is absent or minimal, this is evidence that democratic institutions enjoy enough legitimacy and support to channel social tensions successfully.[3]

For decades, Venezuelan democracy was seen—praised at first, later maligned—in precisely these terms. After 1958, and especially after the defeat of guerrilla insurgents in the 1960s, most observers and analysts understood Venezuelan democracy to derive its durability from the skillful exercise of politics by enlightened, socially conscious statesmen who had found ways to channel social tensions into broadly inclusive political parties and state institutions.[4] Underwritten by the effective management of the nation's oil wealth, the political system they crafted seemed to represent the interests of competing sectors of the population, which again and again proved their support by participating massively in periodic competitive elections. Against the backdrop of military rule and bloody civil wars that filled Latin America's political landscape in the 1970s, Venezuela's high-turnout elections and relative absence of social conflict made its representative system an exception, the envy of the region, a model democracy for others to admire.[5]

Yet, beginning in the 1980s, Venezuela's economy took a dive as once-booming oil prices collapsed. As inflation, recession, capital flight, and poverty skyrocketed, alternative readings of Venezuelan democracy now suggested that the centralization of power around strong leaders, once held as the reason for

Venezuela's vaunted stability, had in fact cemented an "elite political culture . . . that shut out new players."[6] But the seemingly skillful exercise of consensus politics had nevertheless contrived for decades to keep social tensions in check, and political leaders pushed through dramatic economic reforms under the plausible assumption that the pact between the government and its people was sufficiently elastic, having been forged over three decades of widely praised representative democracy, to withstand the pressures of deep crisis.[7]

But the *Caracazo* exposed these political leaders' profound misreading of the limits of elasticity, as well as their deep disconnect with the urban poor, who took to the streets and fell victims to a massacre. When corruption scandals, attempted military coups, street demonstrations, a presidential impeachment, and banking crises followed the 1989 protest, analysts began to speak of the crisis of Venezuela's democracy as inevitable.[8] Some went further, suggesting that the economic and political tensions expressed in daily street protests throughout the 1990s in fact resulted from irrational popular sectors acting against the better judgment of reform-minded politicians who well understood that Venezuela was far from infinitely wealthy, even if urban masses did not.[9] Focusing on questions of institutional decay, adjustment, or survival, this dominant approach was unable to take seriously the popular sectors to which society had been blind. Wrote anthropologist Fernando Coronil: "After thirty years of stability supported by oil income and the parties' control over popular sectors, these leaders believed that *el pueblo* was incapable of independent action."[10]

In fact, just as it had acted on 23 January 1958, *el pueblo* was far from passive in the years that followed. Instead, it actively participated in debates over what type of democracy would take shape in Venezuela. Over the years, Venezuelans—more and more concentrated in urban spaces—developed an expansive understanding of democracy that combined institutional and noninstitutional, formal and informal, legal and illegal practices in their dealings with the state as they sought accountability and greater inclusion. And yet, these popular understandings of democracy chafe against revolutionary designs in the Chávez era that claim a general rejection of representative democracy by urban popular sectors, in favor of revolutionary socialism.[11] Both accounts—the one presuming co-optation by and compliance with the state, and the other suggesting broad repudiation of representative democracy—are marked by an episodic view of history that splits pre-1989 Venezuela from post-1989 Venezuela, leaving local histories of social and political organizing and mobilization unexamined, and thereby marginalizing the complex and contradictory ways in which popular sectors have long engaged with the state, both before and during the Chávez era.

Nowhere was this complexity more dramatic than at the 23 de Enero. For forty years, residents there had fervently believed in the promise of democratic governance, since they had helped to found it by taking to the streets on the date after which their neighborhood was named. In the years after 1958, however, as the contours of Venezuelan democracy took shape, residents of the 23 de Enero forged a contradictory relationship with a state from which they felt increasingly estranged despite its growing presence in their lives. The 23 de Enero's symbolism and proximity to national centers of power—the Presidential Palace, Congress, the Defense Ministry—fueled intense co-optation efforts; over time, sprawling partisan networks emerged throughout the neighborhood. Alliances were formed and debated over the allocation of state resources. Meanwhile, residents flocked to the polls, at first opting for outside candidates and underdogs, and later supporting mainstream parties of the era. In the process they crafted an understanding of the vote as a powerful weapon in a broad arsenal of political action, which they came to understand as the pillar of democratic life.

Yet when formal democratic processes failed to reap benefits for the community, residents mobilized—often contentiously—drawing media attention around forms of collective action that moved in and out of the terrain of formal politics. In the 1960s, some residents took up arms to protest the exclusion of leftist parties from the political arena; in the 1970s, others set up roadblocks to call attention to water shortages; and, in the 1980s, neighbors hijacked public service vehicles to underscore growing state inefficiency at a time of economic crisis. Refusing to accept a narrow formulation of "democratic participation," residents of the 23 de Enero protested and fought the state because, for them, what was at stake was nothing less than Venezuela's "democratic revolution," the same revolution that had been ushered in on the date that the name of their neighborhood commemorated. Through informal political processes, residents upheld democratic principles by holding the state accountable for its responsibilities to the electorate. In this way, popular protest and electoral politics became complementary rather than antagonistic pieces of a democratic equation, coming eventually to characterize the tenor of politics in modern Venezuela in particular, and more broadly in Latin America as a whole.

INFORMAL DEMOCRACY IN LATIN AMERICA

Democratic theory tends to view the relationship between popular protest and electoral politics as antagonistic. But the case is different for students of urban Latin America. For some, intertwined processes of rapid urbanization and the advent of mass electoral politics in the early and mid-twentieth century turned Latin American cities into incubators of radical movements that sought access to state resources and the reconfiguration of social and political relations, where a mass urban electorate stood at the center. Dense populations, new forms of mass communication and transport, and the physical proximity to state institutions meant that cities were ripe for the mobilization of newly enfranchised popular sectors, whose rapidly swelling numbers and demands clashed with the entrenched power of traditional elites in often violent ways, whether that violence was purveyed by the state or by the people.[12]

Beyond spectacular displays of constituent power, whether viewed as riotous or radical, others have observed how urban popular sectors' signature demands for housing, for public services, and for the legalization of living arrangements were more likely to result in appeals to the state than in calls for its overthrow or dramatic reconstitution. The outcome was often political co-optation. As new political leaders found electoral constituencies among urban sectors seeking representation in newly democratic contexts, the resulting clientelist relationships—based on the exchange of votes and political support for goods and favors—came to define urban popular politics, depriving urban movements of far-reaching political impact. The local nature of urban popular sectors' demands tended to limit their potential scope.[13]

Recent historical literature notes how urban popular sectors' relationship to electoral politics more often transcended populist dependency or clientelist co-optation, even if it rarely resulted in radical mobilization. Electoral opportunities dramatically expanded the scope of demands by providing urban popular sectors with new avenues for mobilization, turning the electoral process into another, often effective, means of achieving dual goals of political participation and social inclusion.[14] In her study of *favelados* (residents of Brazilian slums, or *favelas*) fighting legal, political, and social exclusion in midcentury Rio de Janeiro, Brodwyn Fischer shows that a return to electoral politics "allowed for significant strategic innovations" that included the use of both "a whole range of pacific tactics," such as interfacing with political parties, and more-direct public pressure, such as "open resistance" to state eviction efforts. Though the *favelados* were ultimately unsuccessful in securing formal legal rights to their homes, the experience left them "anchored to the city by the combined weight of community resistance, populist politics, and scarcely viable alternatives," powerfully showcasing the dynamic nature of urban popular politics.[15]

While historians continue to uncover a rich tapestry of political action among sectors once considered passive and easy to manipulate politically, new theoretical work has focused on the dynamic interplay between radicalism and dependency, legality and illegality, among urban popular sectors in democratic contexts. James Holston argues that the urban poor in the periphery of São Paulo, Brazil, inhabit a liminal space—they possess formal participatory rights in democracy, but at the same time live under conditions of practical exclusion. This results in democratic disjunctions, or "contradictions between forms of government and practices of citizens, simultaneous expansions and erosions of rights, and other contradictions [that] characterize modern citizenship everywhere." These disjunctions enter political life as popular sectors participate in "a system of stratagem and bureaucratic complication deployed by both state and subject to obfuscate problems, neutralize opponents, and, above all, legalize the illegal." The result, Holston argues, is an "insurgent citizenship" that transforms the challenges of urban popular life into a new terrain of political opportunity, in turn helping to close the gap between democracy as aspiration and democracy as lived in the everyday.[16]

Barrio Rising engages a literature that identifies the blend of institutional and extra-institutional mobilization characteristic of urban popular politics not as exceptional, but rather as an essential element of democratic life.[17] As Enrique Peruzzoti has argued, where the ability of states to respond to citizen demands is weak or intermittent, this form of mobilization that "employs both institutional and non-institutional tools" serves a crucial democratic function of "social accountability," exerting pressure on government outside traditional mechanisms for articulating demands, seeking solutions, and redressing grievances.[18] In turn, this strategic interplay of institutional and noninstitutional tools rises from long-standing processes of uneven urbanization, where the boundaries between formal and informal housing, labor, and social life, like the boundaries between formal institutions and informal political practices, are fluid as a matter of course. This type of urbanization, writes Brodwyn Fischer, "demands . . . that we recognize that Latin American cities are defined rather than deformed by the dynamic intersection of formal and informal urbanity."[19]

And yet, the case of the 23 de Enero is unusual. Unlike most examples examined by scholarship on urban movements, this neighborhood was not peripheral. To the contrary, the neighborhood and its residents stood at the spatial and symbolic heart of the nation. Their centrality helped to turn local issues into national issues through spectacular displays of constituent power— whether hijacking state vehicles, engaging in guerrilla war, or taking to the polls en masse. In this sense, it was not physical and political exclusion that informed insurgent forms of citizenship. Instead, it was a process of signifying and re-signifying an already highly charged urban space during times of political and economic transition that created fissures, and opportunities, for popular expressions of democracy. Likewise, the neighborhood became an amalgam of formal and informal housing, of *barrios* and high-rises, of renters and squatters, ensuring that, like the physical environment itself, this process was in constant flux, never fully gestating but instead existing in a liminal state that over time helped to forge an expansive definition of democracy, one that upheld the interplay of formal electoral politics with contentious and often illegal protest as a legitimate and even necessary form of everyday political practice. Seen in this light, urban popular protest that straddles legal and extralegal, institutional and noninstitutional means may be read as the radical realization of the promise of democratic participation, accountability, and citizenship.[20]

STRUCTURE AND SCOPE

Seven chapters make up this book. They trace intersecting histories—of the 23 de Enero neighborhood on one hand, and of the Venezuelan state on the other, as each responded to critical moments in the nation's political evolution in the last half century.[21] These intersections of local and national histories reflect larger patterns that helped shape the relationship between Venezuela's government and its citizens, patterns that reveal how urban popular sectors came to understand the promises and shortcomings of Venezuela's political system, and in the process developed their own sense of what democracy should be and do.

Part One of the book, "Landscapes of Opportunity," surveys the physical and political terrain that gave rise both to the housing project and to the political projects to which the neighborhood became linked: dictatorship and democracy. Between the 1930s and the 1960s, Venezuela underwent a rapid and dramatic transformation from a provincial country into an urban nation, and Caracas was the canvas on which elites and popular sectors alike projected their aspirations for that nation, presenting each with opportunities to experiment with new forms of social organization and political mobilization. Chapter 1, "Dictatorship's Blocks," focuses on the early life of what became the 23 de Enero neighborhood. It considers how and why high-rise urbanism came to inform dictator Marcos Pérez Jiménez's vision for a Venezuela where the visible poverty of slums gripping the capital's hillsides would be no more, and in turn, how those who came to live in the structures he imagined as the symbols of a new Venezuela responded to life in the superblocks. Often grateful for the new, modern facilities, but also feeling trapped by the strict social controls that were, in the end, the dictatorship's major aim for its public housing projects, residents came to hold an ambiguous view both of their new homes and of the political regime that gave rise to them.

What came of this ambiguity in the days, weeks, and months that immediately followed Pérez Jiménez's overthrow on 23 January 1958, is the subject of Chapter 2, "Democracy's Projects." While political elites celebrated the moment as a "democratic revolution," exactly what direction that democracy would take remained far from certain. More immediately, over half of the buildings in the newly renamed 23 de Enero project lay vacant on the day of Pérez Jiménez's overthrow, leading to the frantic occupation of thousands of apartments in two days' time by popular sectors from throughout Caracas and even the country's interior. Once all apartments were gone, new arrivals began settling in the spaces between the superblocks, resurrecting the very ranchos the housing project aimed to eradicate. But more than physical space, what these new arrivals were seizing was the opportunity of a moment of uncertain transition, an opportunity that residents relocated during Pérez Jiménez's rule also seized to make demands long muted under the dictatorship. In the process, a neighborhood designed to homogenize space and social relations was transformed into a deeply complex landscape where old and new residents, apartment dwellers and rancho inhabitants, coexisted, sometimes uneasily. In turn, they shaped new needs, identities, and forms of mobilization against the backdrop of a political system also very much in gestation.

How this deeply riven social landscape shaped a new set of political expectations and relations between residents and the emerging political system is the subject of Part Two, "Paths to Democracy." Following the 1958 revolution, residents of the 23 de Enero neighborhood emerged well aware of their newfound significance as a key constituency, particularly in what was now billed as an electoral democracy. Again and again, they flocked to the polls, supporting candidates who promised to make urban popular sectors the center of politics. And, again and again, these candidates lost, the elections instead bringing to power presidents who shifted policy and resources decidedly away from Caracas, and from their neighborhood. Through the 1960s, most residents expressed their dissatisfaction at the ballot box. Others took up weapons in a bid to seize state power outright, turning the neighborhood into a hotbed of insurgent and counterinsurgent conflict. And as infrastructure problems grew more acute, daily life became a bitter struggle for most residents. Still, though deeply disenchanted with both insurgents and the major parties in power, they continued to hold on to the promise of responsive, accountable government rooted in the vote, such as had informed the earliest days of transition in 1958.

While Part Two (Chapters 3–4) considers the range of opportunities seized and squandered as Venezuela moved from a rural to an urban nation, and as residents of the 23 de Enero moved from dictatorship to democracy, Part Three, "Streets of Protest" (Chapters 5–7), examines how, following the 1960s era of guerrilla war and in the context of a now-consolidated party system, elites and urban popular sectors experimented with new discourses and forms of mobilization in order to reclaim the early promises of democratic revolution. Chapter 5, "Water, Women, and Protest," follows residents of the 23 de Enero as they once again took up the tradition of street protest in the pursuit of local demands that had informed their organizing and mobilization in 1958. The military defeat of Venezuela's guerrilla movement gave way in the 1970s to a period of community organizing around local needs and demands that had gone ignored for much of the 1960s. Though widespread, residents' protests proved unable to secure significant attention and improvements from the government, even as an investment spree fueled by petrodollars set in by mid-decade.

Instead, residents found ways to bring together once-disparate strands of local organizing during a highly publicized series of hijackings of garbage trucks and other public service vehicles between 1981 and 1982. Chapter 6, "A Weapon as Powerful as the Vote," details this protest and its outcomes. The protest brought together what had been dueling strands of local politics: on one hand, radical tactics forged in the fray of unpopular guerrilla war in the 1960s and passed down to a younger generation of activists; on the other hand, a community-oriented ethos that marked the 1970s era of organizing around basic needs. Residents also took advantage of a new discourse and practice of electoral accountability from key figures in Venezuela's government as they attempted to reform from within. Ultimately, the hijackings redefined the boundaries of legitimate protest, and in the process helped to recalibrate popular expectations of democracy and of democratic citizenship as an interplay of street action and the vote, in so doing rendering government more accountable to the electorate.

But as economic crisis deepened, the government experimented with structural adjustment throughout the 1980s in areas that most affected urban popular sectors—public services, public housing, and local governance. In each of these areas, efforts at "unloading" former public ventures by calling upon financial exigency and personal responsibility were met with significant operational problems, in turn shaping what popular sectors came to expect from neoliberal reform. In the 23 de Enero, the government moved to turn over responsibility for the neighborhood to residents themselves, transforming the buildings from public housing to hastily established condominiums. For some, it meant an opportunity to finally take control over their own affairs, even if it came with significant challenges—as local leaders discovered, organizing to make demands of the government was far different from organizing to make demands of their neighbors. For others, though, this was a thinly veiled government effort to finally rid itself of the costs—financial and otherwise—of a neighborhood that had long proved a thorn in its side.

Yet nothing prepared residents of 23 de Enero for what came once officials embraced neoliberalism in earnest in 1989. The final chapter, "Killing Democracy's Promise," revisits the *Caracazo* massacre and its consequences for Venezuelan politics and history in the context of the decades-long relationship established between residents of the neighborhood and the Venezuelan state.[22] Following the pattern of the book as a whole, this chapter offers a detailed local history of the events as they unfolded in the 23 de Enero neighborhood, drawing both on oral accounts and on previously untapped documents from the Inter-American Court of Human Rights, which in 1999 ruled that Venezuela's government had indeed perpetrated a massacre. And it was a massacre, though not just of people but also of expectations: as state officials expressed surprise at the response of urban popular sectors they could no longer claim to understand, these sectors, too, were shocked by the response of state that they could no longer plausibly view as representative. In the vacuum, they would seek other political opportunities for fulfilling the promise of democracy, as they had come to understand it.

How well did Hugo Chávez's Bolivarian Revolution reflect popular understandings of democracy? Much in the same way that Venezuelan political elites before Chávez marginalized histories of local organizing and mobilization, *chavista* narratives that upheld the *Caracazo* as the beginning of an era of popular political awakening would follow in the same tradition. And unsurprisingly, the 23 de Enero and its residents once again stood as centers of conflicting support for and dissent from the Bolivarian Revolution's underlying promises of greater participation, combining, as they long had, both street protest and the vote to reflect their own vision of democracy. Understanding how these continuing tensions between government and urban popular sectors build upon legacies of political action neither beholden nor opposed to Venezuela's state, is the final aim of *Barrio Rising*.[23]

All told, this book follows residents of Venezuela's largest urban housing project for forty years, through the rise, consolidation, and crisis of a political system once thought resilient. It considers when, why, and how residents of the 23 de Enero neighborhood engaged with the state since the onset of democracy in 1958, and with what consequences for the development of democracy in Venezuela in particular and Latin America more broadly. This book neither assumes the co-optation of popular sectors during the years before the *Caracazo*, nor does it see the *Caracazo* as an eruption of the poor and their subsequent politicization under Chávez as a sudden awakening. Instead, it argues that the 23 de Enero neighborhood constituted an actively politicized sector of the urban population that asserted its power as a growing population whose strategic location, symbolic charge, and expanding votes allowed them to make demands upon the state in ways that contested the boundaries of formal politics, all in the name of achieving meaningful integration into a political project founded on the date that gave the neighborhood its name. Ultimately, it sheds light on the counterpoint of street protest and electoral politics that over the course of decades shaped popular understandings of democracy that live on today.

PART ONE

Landscapes of Opportunity

CHAPTER I

Dictatorship's Blocks

The Battle for the New Urban Venezuela

By all accounts, the 2 de Diciembre housing project cut an imposing figure on the Caracas landscape: thirteen residential buildings, each fifteen stories tall and containing 150 identical apartments, with only a seemingly random patchwork of colors breaking the monotony of concrete (fig. 2). The so-called superblocks rose from the hills overlooking the Presidential Palace, Defense Ministry, Congress, and National Cathedral, in an area where just months before had stood growing slums. When finished, the 2 de Diciembre project would consist of 56 superblocks and 42 four-story blocks, planned in addition to new schools, parks, athletic facilities, roads, and commercial strips. It was to become one of Latin America's largest public housing projects, capable of housing seventy thousand working-class residents while promising to remake Caracas, and the nation.[1] And it was brought to initial fruition on the third anniversary of the 2 December 1952 coup that cemented the rule of its founder, General Marcos Pérez Jiménez.

Of all the public works built during Pérez Jiménez's dictatorship—a period of such frenzied construction that some have dubbed it "the bulldozer years"[2]—the 2 de Diciembre housing project stood out as the most emblematic of his efforts to provide for Venezuela's rapidly urbanizing working classes a central place in the nation's body politic. Official photos of the inauguration told as much, showing Pérez Jiménez surveying the superblocks with crowds of ministers, soldiers, and onlookers flanking him, all of them dwarfed by imposing high-rises. Almost everything about the 2 de Diciembre signaled the symbolic and unmistakable ambition of Pérez Jiménez's "New National Ideal." Razing

FIGURE 2. In this east-to-west aerial view from 1955, the newly completed Phase One of Unidad Residencial 2 de Diciembre stands out, consisting of Blocks 1 through 14 of Monte Piedad. In the background, pending demolition, are densely populated areas in what would become the Zona Central and Zona Oeste. Further west are the Pro-Patria superblocks. (Hamilton Wright)

slums as well as historic neighborhoods, Pérez Jiménez cleaned the slate of Venezuela's provincial past to make way for its urban future. In their clean lines and angular shapes, the superblocks—neatly arranged one behind the other—marked the triumph of order over the chaos that had increasingly characterized Caracas's unplanned growth. In its name and location, situated by the major symbols of social and political power—the presidency, the legislature, the military, and the church—the neighborhood and its working-class population represented the popular foundations of Pérez Jiménez's government. Here, in short, was the "material expression" of *perezjimenismo*.[3]

For Inés Oliveira the superblocks represented "a whole new way of life." When she was 15 and her family arrived in Block 12 of the La Cañada sector of the 2 de Diciembre, they were typical of Caracas's urban poor, forcibly moved from the crammed improvised housing that precariously hugged Caracas hillsides. Like many others, they left for their new home the night bulldozers razed what remained of their old zinc-roofed rancho. Fifty years later, Oliveira still recalled the exuberance of early life in the superblocks: "That for us was like a mansion. You know the conditions we poor people lived in? When we learned we were to be moved, no one slept from the happiness, the joy of it all. No more cockroaches, no more outhouses. . . . My parents were ecstatic." Despite the dust and the tight quarters (two bedrooms for eight people) that greeted them in their new thirteenth-floor apartment, Oliveira stressed, "that was so beautiful. . . . If Pérez Jiménez hadn't left, well, if he hadn't been overthrown, there would be no ranchos in Caracas, because he dreamed of a beautiful Venezuela."[4] So it was striking that Oliveira was among those who took to the streets to celebrate Pérez Jiménez's ouster.

At dawn on 23 January 1958, just weeks after workers laid the final slab on the neighborhood's third and largest construction phase, Pérez Jiménez fled Venezuela on a plane bound for the Dominican Republic. His departure followed a volatile month that began with a failed coup attempt on New Year's Day, several cabinet shuffles, an indefinite national strike, and violent street clashes between state security forces and Caracas residents. Finally, on 23 January, a junta composed of young military officers formally seized power in the vacuum left by Pérez Jiménez's departure. As Oliveira remembers it, at seventeen years old the self-admitted *saltamonte*[5] "was one of those who shouted, ran through the streets, and got on a truck and yelled 'Down with the government! Down with the government!'" The ten-year dictatorship was over.

Oliveira's participation in the events of 23 January reveals the ambivalent relationship between Pérez Jiménez and residents of the superblocks he built to make concrete his government's vision for Venezuela. No doubt the passage of time helps wash the past in comfortable shades. But Oliveira's testimony reflects a complex, conflicted set of memories and emotions: a spirited appreciation for the man whose ouster she supported. In memorializations that followed Pérez Jiménez's ouster, these complexities were largely lost. Returning from exile, political figures now cast Oliveira and others taking to the streets that day as central players in a narrative of popular insurrection by a people unwilling to accept tyranny in exchange for concrete goods, and ready to support the promise of a democratic government, however ill-defined that promise remained. In press accounts, the neighborhood that once stood at the literal and figurative center of Pérez Jiménez's regime was now a backdrop to the coup. Press photos of the superblocks he had inaugurated with high fanfare just two years earlier now portrayed the site as emblematic of his downfall, high-rises dwarfing the crowds and tanks gathered in front of the Presidential Palace below. The very neighborhood that was founded as the symbol of Pérez Jiménez's new Venezuela turned on him to forge a new and again deeply symbolic connection with the national government. Henceforth, the 2 de Diciembre would be known as the 23 de Enero.

This chapter examines the complex social foundations of a neighborhood conceived, planned, and built to link urban popular sectors to the modern Venezuela state. Where at first the hundreds of photos that graced government publications, architecture journals, and press reports offered a gleaming portrait of a government committed to the wellbeing of its urban underclass, following Pérez Jiménez's ouster those same photos seemed more significant for what they lacked than for what they showed: scarcely any people. The buildings stood as monuments of political achievement, more to be admired than inhabited. This was perhaps the most revealing symbolic tie to Pérez Jiménez's government: whether grateful for their new housing or indignant at the dictatorship that made it possible, the opinions of people like Inés Oliveira and the thousands of others moved to the blocks hardly mattered. Symbols of the regime's popular foundations on the one hand, but effectively cast aside on the other, residents of the 2 de Diciembre held a contradictory place in the national imagination. This dynamic would become a central feature of the relationship between state and urban popular sectors in modern Venezuela, one that would follow from one regime to the next.

VENEZUELA'S "GREAT URBAN REVOLUTION"

"You have to keep in mind," says Juan Martínez to help explain conflicting attitudes toward Pérez Jiménez by residents of the 2 de Diciembre, "that we were in a dictatorship."[6] And a particular kind of dictatorship, one that, after several decades of failed attempts by various governments to harness economic prosperity into concerted state policy, had turned oil wealth into massive construction projects aimed at moving Venezuela away from its provincial past and toward a modern and urban-based future. Martínez, a father of three, was in his twenties when he first arrived in Block 4 in the neighborhood's Monte Piedad sector, part of the first of three phases of the project. He had come to Caracas as a child in 1935, seeking work opportunities in the capital following the death of Dictator Juan Vicente Gómez after 27 years in power. The Caracas that Martínez found was a city long held back by Gómez's provincial proclivities, though nevertheless on the cusp of dramatic transformation. Twenty years prior, a handful of oil wells had begun to sprout in Venezuela's arid northwestern plains, where petroleum seeped freely from the ground. Shell had installed Venezuela's first oil rig in 1914. But in the first decade of Gómez's dictatorship, Venezuela's economy remained tied to the fortunes of a coffee crop that since the 1830s had been a reliable if financially lackluster staple export.[7] That Gómez's own power base hailed from Venezuela's coffee-rich southwestern Andes inhibited any serious changes to national economic policy.

But the post-World War I economic boom and the burgeoning prominence of internal combustion engines in Europe and the United States created a demand for oil that Gómez shrewdly exploited in negotiating land concessions and leases with British and North American corporations. By 1928, oil exports equaled three times the combined worth of all other Venezuelan exports, exploding from an annual production of 490,000 barrels in 1920, to 140 million in 1930.[8] To appease coffee-planting elites, Gómez distributed revenues from oil concessions and rents through lucrative bribes; to check challenges from regions poorly favored under his "patriarchal autocracy," Gómez professionalized, modernized, and expanded the military, constructed Venezuela's first interregional road system, dispersed trusted Andean lieutenants throughout the national territory to enforce his orders, and made fast use of a vast network of spies that infiltrated all sectors of social life.[9]

In this climate, Gómez relocated Venezuela's capital to Maracay, a sleepy provincial city 60 miles west of Caracas. It was a personal choice born in part of his antagonism toward the Caracas elite—whom he regarded as a nuisance rather than a threat to his rule—and in part as a strategic play meant to subvert Caracas's growing prominence through a policy of neglect.[10] Distrust for Caracas and its elites exposed deeper misgivings about urban life and culture, which Gómez viewed as "potentially revolutionary."[11] Yet, during the 1920s Caracas grew in political importance and size, an unintended result of the shift toward an oil-based economy. For one, the explosive growth of the oil industry replaced investment in coffee, depressing traditional coffee-growing regions and sparking peasant migration to cities.[12] As the nation's major urban hub, Caracas proved a desirable destination for oil executives and became home to the industry's corporate offices, while rural migrants found work in the growing service sector of the city.[13] From 1920 to 1930 Caracas's population nearly doubled, from 92,000 to about 175,000 residents. By the time of Gómez's death in 1935, 260,000 people lived in the city.[14] Despite Gómez's efforts, then, the 1920s had set the stage for "Venezuela's great urban revolution."[15]

Still, even with efforts to institutionalize urban planning in the interwar years—for instance through the founding of a *Dirección de Urbanismo* (Urbanism Directorate) in 1938 and the unveiling of a *Plan Monumental de Caracas* (Caracas Master Plan) in 1939—early urbanization in Venezuela was more of a rudderless revolution. In the wake of Gómez's death political and economic elites agreed that Caracas would be Venezuela's main urban hub. And while they had formed part of the Gómez regime, neither of his immediate successors, Eleazar López Contreras (president 1935–1941) or Isaías Medina Angarita (president 1941–1945) shared Gómez's fear of urbanization. Instead they looked to exploit the capital's strategic "proximity to the centers of the civilized world" vis-à-vis other would-be South American competitors: Rio de Janeiro, São Paulo, Buenos Aires, Lima, and Bogotá.[16] Yet neither commanded Gómez's power, ensuring that during this period the growth of Caracas would be debated in national politics rather than imposed by force.

For their part, the traditional elites of Caracas were committed Francophiles, and had been since the late nineteenth century, when President Antonio Guzmán Blanco had tried to turn the capital into a tropical Paris.[17] They favored investing oil revenue into building an ornate city that would mirror Parisian grandeur, envisioning broad tree-lined boulevards linking multiple city centers, where residential and commercial life would coexist. The city's emerging middle class also voiced a vision for their city. Made up largely of oil industry technocrats and engineers who identified with British and North American utilitarian planning methods, these new, modern middle classes emphasized the need to create a sense of urban discipline along axes of work, leisure, and sanitation, with a strong and unmistakable business hub.[18]

As planning debates unfolded, the population of Caracas continued to grow through the mid-1940s, drawing both from internal migration to the city and from postwar immigration from Europe. In the 1941 census, roughly 39% of Venezuela's population lived in cities. By 1950 that number had grown to 54%, marking the first time more Venezuelans lived in cities than in the countryside. As the country's largest city, Caracas experienced the greatest growth: by 1950 the population in the capital had risen to nearly 700,000, up from 500,000 in 1945.[19] But an official plan to guide Caracas's growth remained elusive. More and more, elites and middle-class sectors abandoned a city center that was becoming increasingly chaotic—the narrow colonial-era streets now filled with ever-expanding squatter settlements—establishing new communities in the old coffee estates to the east.[20] Rapid densification and increased segregation thus came to define the human and political geography of midcentury Caracas.

As the country's population changed, so did its politics. This period of major urban growth coincided with a short-lived period of democracy when the political party *Acción Democrática* (Democratic Action) rose to power in 1945, affecting Caracas's social and political life for several decades. Founded in 1941 as a social-democratic alternative to the *Partido Comunista de Venezuela* (Venezuelan Communist Party), the leaders of Acción Democrática (AD) cut their political teeth under the Gómez regime. They drew on nationalist, anti-imperialist discourse to decry the dictator's concessions of Venezuelan subsoil to U.S. and European interests. They denounced the failure of the Gómez regime to distribute oil wealth across economic sectors, instead dividing the spoils among those in his milieu. But while AD differed with Gómez, the party shared the dictator's popular foundation in the countryside, taking up "Bread, Land, and Labor" as its banner and seeking to vindicate the peasantry through agrarian reform financed by redistributed oil revenues.

In 1945, AD leaders joined with a group of military officers to stage a coup and seize power, laying the groundwork for Venezuela's first popular elections. In the meantime, interim President and AD founder Rómulo Betancourt moved to "sow the oil" nationally, mandating a 50/50 revenue-sharing agreement with foreign oil companies and seeking to diversify Venezuela's economy by jump-starting long-abandoned agrarian sectors. In the process, AD cemented its support among the rural peasantry, still Venezuela's largest constituency in 1946: that year AD took 78% of the vote in Constituent Assembly elections, the nation's first contest conducted by universal suffrage; and in 1947, AD candidate Rómulo Gallegos won 74% of 1.2 million votes cast, to become Venezuela's first popularly elected president.[21]

In practice, Acción Democrática's focus on wealth distribution to the rural peasantry meant diverting already-limited resources and attention away from urbanization plans and projects in Caracas.[22] Yet migration statistics showed that the prominence of urban popular sectors continued to grow. In November

1948, Colonel Marcos Pérez Jiménez and a cadre of midlevel military officers overthrew Gallegos in a bloodless coup centered in Caracas. What the coup revealed was a striking contradiction of Venezuela's first democratic experiment: a popular government, elected by an astonishing margin just nine months before, was overthrown without popular resistance.[23] Whereas AD had largely overlooked the political opportunities offered by the country's growing urban base, the new junta would channel oil wealth and state attention toward urban hubs, Caracas in particular. In doing so, the junta would powerfully show how urbanization had significantly shaped the future of national politics.[24]

TARGETING THE URBAN LABYRINTH

Juan Martínez, who had moved to Caracas in 1935 at the dawn of Venezuela's urban revolution, came of age during a period characterized by shifting dictatorships and hectic growth. In 1948 he took a construction job and settled with his new bride in the Tiro al Blanco barrio at the foot of the mountain known as El Ávila, in north-central Caracas.[25] It was a neighborhood that well encapsulated Caracas's explosive growth in the 1930s and 1940s: a community made up mainly of provincial migrants. "[We started] with cardboard and zinc roofs," recalled neighborhood resident Francisco Suárez, a child at the time.[26] But as time went on "and a little money started coming in, we bought [cinder] blocks," eventually building, block by block, a four-bedroom, two-bathroom home for their seven-person family. Other houses in the community were two stories tall and had real foundations, according to Suárez—"and there were also red-tiled colonial houses." The Tiro al Blanco of Suárez's memory—a heterogeneous neighborhood—mirrored how the new military government that took power in 1948 saw Caracas: as a mix of traditional poor rancho housing amid more-sophisticated and -hygienic developments. For housing authorities, even a makeshift rancho could be seen as "part of a neighborhood," a community and constituency with political power.[27]

Uncertainty about the new junta moved citizens in communities like Tiro al Blanco to organize. In 1948, the year Martínez settled in the neighborhood, he helped publish a weekly paper—*Laberinto*—billed as the "organ of the barrio" (fig. 3). Local business advertisements sponsored the publication and community members provided the content, everything from new features to literary fiction. In its inaugural issue, published on 30 April 1949, *Laberinto* included a story about local infrastructure needs, with a particular focus on

FIGURE 3. 14 May 1949 issue of *Laberinto*, an independent biweekly newsletter published by residents of the Tiro al Blanco neighborhood, currently known as Simón Rodríguez, in north Caracas. Among the contents: Barrio needs, literary page, and a profile of a local young woman. (Courtesy Juan Martínez)

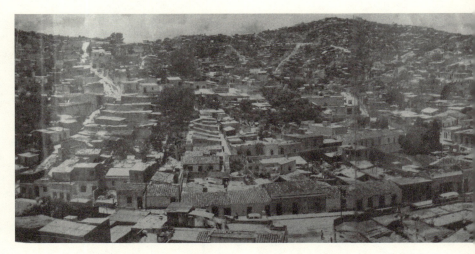

FIGURE 4. La Cañada as seen from Avenida Sucre in 1950: paved roads, red-tiled roofs, solid structures. Five years later, all would be razed to make way for Phase Two of the 2 de Diciembre. (Banco Obrero)

water. Poetry, birthday announcements, the first installment of a serial murder-mystery novel, and a profile and interview with a local *muchacha* from the community rounded out the issue. Later issues focused on initiatives organized through neighborhood associations in Tiro al Blanco. For example, a front-page article chronicled the formation of "water brigades," made up of community members, to help ferry water from the area's only spigot to individual houses, especially for those unable to make the trek.

Laberinto chronicles the emergence of a community consciousness among the urban poor of a booming city. Its pages tell the history of how local residents organized in order to attend to the needs of their community. It also reveals how daily life in the barrio built a sense of local solidarity and a unique neighborhood identity. It is a solidarity that many former residents still remember with great nostalgia. Francisco Suárez, for example, recalled how the community helped a young couple arriving from the interior erect a house in a small lot in Tiro al Blanco. Similarly, Rafael Gutiérrez—who grew up in the La Cañada neighborhood just southeast of the Presidential Palace— remembered how "there was always someone" who looked after, and occasionally scolded, neighborhood youth on behalf of other parents. "There was no [formal] organization," he observes, "but there was unity . . . and respect, a lot of respect."

In addition to recalling a sense of community in the barrio, many also remember how invested community members were in the development of stable, beautiful homes. Rafael Gutiérrez's own family, he recounts, lived in a "very, very good house," explaining that "people back then worried about building properly." Mireya Maldonado, who also spent her youth in La Cañada before her family moved to the 2 de Diciembre, likewise described the neighborhood as filled with "good houses with foundations, pretty houses."[28] According to some, structures like La Cañada's iconic church proved so sturdy that they required dynamite to level (fig. 4).[29]

It is of course difficult to confirm these testimonies. But they are significant for illustrating the gap between how residents and the government described working-class neighborhoods in the years immediately prior to the construction of the 2 de Diciembre. Martínez, Suárez, Maldonado, Gutiérrez, and thousands of others in Caracas's barrios recall neighborhoods with budding infrastructure and a community commitment to improve. What Pérez Jiménez and the military junta that took power in 1948 saw, however, were slums and obstacles to the city's progress toward modernity. For the junta, the same urban migration flows that had helped to generate explosive population growth in Caracas, coupled with grandly conceived but poorly implemented plans for the city in the preceding decades,[30] had littered the capital with thousands of what government publications called "miserable ranchos" in and around the city hillsides, "generally [consisting of] one cardboard-walled room, wooden planks, and a zinc roof."[31] In fact, between 1941 and 1950, according to the census, the number of ranchos in Caracas had climbed from fourteen thousand to over twenty-eight thousand, fully 25% of Caracas households. Analyzing these trends, a team of planners and architects concluded in 1957 that Venezuela would need to build 78,500 residences per year for a period of twenty years in order to keep pace with existing housing shortages and projected housing needs.[32]

These were staggering figures. For the junta, they offered an opportunity—one largely missed by the Acción Democrática leaders they had overthrown—to cement a popular base by attending to the needs of a growing urban population, especially around housing. Revisiting 1930s planning debates centered on Caracas, junta leaders favored functionalist schemes that promised "to mold and discipline the social body," especially among working-class sectors in a capital whose rapid growth they embraced as a sign of progress and modernity.[33] In 1951, they charged the Banco Obrero (Workers' Bank) with developing a four-year National Housing Plan, Venezuela's first effort to resolve its housing deficit.[34] The growth of the Banco Obrero (BO) mirrored Venezuela's urban boom. Its primary function since its founding by Juan Vicente Gómez in 1928 was to develop affordable housing solutions for the nation's working classes by building, adjudicating, and managing properties. Its first ventures during the Gómez regime were small in scope and scale, and focused mainly in the outskirts rather than in cities proper. In the 1930s, as elites debated the future shape of Caracas, the BO made only minor interventions in housing construction in the capital. But by the early 1940s, as Caracas's population began to explode, the BO launched a concerted effort to attend to the housing needs of the growing urban working class.[35]

In 1941 the Banco Obrero tapped Carlos Raúl Villanueva, then a rising star in Venezuelan architecture, to remodel El Silencio—"one of the worst areas of Caracas at the time, full of hovels and dangerous centers of vice"—into a residential complex of 850 working-class apartments and 400 commercial spaces.[36] Villanueva's design boldly combined neoclassical, neo-Renaissance, and art deco styles into several four- and seven-story building blocks. But El Silencio's key innovation lay in its view of the social function of the built environment. Villanueva's design "introduced to Venezuela the new concept of spatial organization with the function of grouping families around a central recreational space to facilitate a more intense community life."[37]

FIGURE 5. 1952 pamphlet trumpeting "The Battle against the Rancho." The caption at right reads: "This is how the first rancho was born. Built on the side of any which hill. In the middle—an ironic sign presumably for a client—an offer to sell, of doubtful spelling. Then came others. Built with boards [*tablas*], from which the original name of the barrio came [known as *Ciudad Tablitas*], they formed the first cluster of settlements." (Banco Obrero)

By 1946, BO called on Villanueva to help lead its new Taller de Arquitectura del Banco Obrero (Architecture Workshop, TABO), aimed at generating ideas and projects to help tackle Venezuela's housing shortage, especially in urban areas in Caracas and beyond. Though more aspirational than operational at its outset, TABO's creation in the 1940s points to the slow but growing importance of urban housing development in the interwar years, which would reach its zenith under the military rule that followed the 1948 overthrow of Acción Democrática.[38] It was through TABO that the new junta turned its attention to urban Venezuela and its growing capital city after 1948; in turn, TABO leaders led the charge against unplanned growth and the perils it represented for a modern nation. As a TABO technical report on the issue stressed in 1954, "housing construction in [working-class barrios has] been completely anarchic and in many cases clandestine," amounting to an imminent "threat" against "morals, health, and safety."[39] The junta agreed, declaring a "battle against ranchos" (fig. 5) and selecting two slums for eradication and reconstruction, aiming to transform them into models for what a new Caracas would offer its burgeoning working classes.

The result was "a new world for Venezuelan workers" as two housing complexes were built in Caracas: Urdaneta, west of the city, and Pedro Camejo, in the north.[40] Unlike El Silencio, built ten years before with both function and aesthetics in mind, Villanueva's new housing blocks were purely functional. They contained over 2,100 apartments in four-story blocks and single-story row units, and were equipped with sewer and electricity lines, roads, commercial space, schools, parking facilities, and recreational grounds.[41] It was the community new and whole, pointing the way to a rational, scientific approach to urban planning. Together, Urdaneta and Pedro Camejo constituted "a positive conquest in the program of social action under way in Venezuela for the working classes," and promotional pamphlets declared the two projects nothing short of victories in the battle against ranchos.[42] More broadly, this battle was also a social one, stressing "modesty," "sobriety," "hygiene," and "good taste" for the new residents. All told, "new habits, new experiences, and better opportunities to join modern social life, [were] now open to the Venezuelan worker as he [became] owner of hygienic and comfortable housing."[43]

The junta's attention both to the social and the spatial functions of working-class housing was not, however, a resounding success for working-class people. Yes, the government needed to respond to Caracas's growing housing crisis quickly and efficiently. And they were eager to attend to the needs of the urban working class, weaving them as never before into the fold of a modern Venezuela. But the urban working class was not new to Caracas. Existing popular-sector communities fit in poorly with the junta's totalizing vision of a modern Venezuela when they were seen as being born not of planning but of circumstance. What the new functionalism of government housing projects provided was a uniform experience of modernity, one in stark tension with the socially complex, physically heterogeneous spaces that characterized many of the capital's existing barrios.

For these communities, the tensions were "eminently political," as Juan Martínez understood. "There came a time when the dictatorship, even though [*Laberinto*] was just a little sheet, a simple little sheet, that came out weekly, they told us we couldn't publish it unless they saw in advance what it was going to say; and this was a newspaper that only this community saw!"[44] But it was not difficult to see why such "a simple little sheet" might rankle a government bent on modernizing the city. *Laberinto*'s focus on local infrastructure needs was a constant reminder of the chaotic origins of many of the city's working-class barrios. And the circular's promotion of a collective identity among neighbors based on those needs challenged their ability "to join modern social life," where basic necessities should be taken for granted. If eliminating the city's frenzied past and habits meant sacrificing the vibrancy of existing community life, such was the price of a modern, ordered future.

A SHOWCASE OF IDEALS, A CAGE OF EXPECTATIONS

"The first time I walked into this apartment I felt like I was in a cage unable to fly," remembers Francisco Suárez, nine years old at the time. "My house [in Tiro al Blanco] had a yard where I played with marbles, with a kite, with a top. When I got [to the 2 de Diciembre] I felt like I was in an alley with no exit. . . . We lived at that time as though caged."[45] By late April 1956, Tiro al Blanco was no more. In a little over two months Banco Obrero demolition crews, working alongside military personnel, razed the neighborhood to the ground. For some it was an opportunity to demand monetary compensation for their homes to invest in new properties. Others boarded trucks and traveled across town to the new superblocks where, as former residents of the now defunct Tiro al Blanco, they would become the first tenants of Unidad Residencial 2 de Diciembre. Suárez's recollections of arriving in the 2 de diciembre likely accentuated his sense of entrapment as a child. But the fact that his negative memory lingered over the course of decades reveals a major contrast between the ideals that underpinned the project's design and construction, and the way in which some residents came to experience, and remember, the new neighborhood.

The first years of the junta brought unprecedented national attention to urban planning and housing shortages. Those efforts would reach new heights under the rule of Marcos Pérez Jiménez. After maneuvering for four years to sideline rivals in the military junta he helped run, in 1952 Pérez Jiménez looked to consolidate power and grant his rule legitimacy by calling for a new constitution, drafted by representatives elected by way of Venezuela's first popular vote since 1947. Set for 1 December 1952 and billed by his supporters as a proxy referendum on Pérez Jiménez's presidential ambitions, the elections revealed instead what historian Ramón Velásquez has called Venezuelans' "confidence in the vote as a weapon."[46] Voters flocked to the polls: 1.8 million of them, half a million more than in 1947. It was an especially surprising, and troublesome, turnout for Pérez Jiménez, who expected the kind of low participation that might have facilitated electoral fraud if necessary. Instead, as radio stations prepared to announce the defeat of his *Frente Electoral Independiente* (Independent Electoral Front, or FEI) party, Pérez Jiménez shut down broadcasts and strong-armed election authorities into announcing manufactured results awarding FEI an overwhelming majority over center-left *Unión Republicana Democrática* party (Republican Democratic Union, or URD, founded in 1945) and the center-right *Comité de Organización Política Electoral Independiente* (Committee for Independent Electoral Political Organization, or COPEI, founded in 1946).[47] On December 2, a handpicked electoral board formalized the new electoral results granting Pérez Jiménez, at last, undisputed power over Venezuela.[48]

Losing at the national level may have surprised Pérez Jiménez. But losing in Caracas was especially remarkable, and among popular sectors, even more so. After all, these were the areas where the junta had invested most of its efforts at modernization. It was also where "FEI had undertaken an intense co-optation campaign and had distributed cash, blankets, and zinc boards hand over fist."[49] For the new undisputed President, the results offered a valuable if seemingly contradictory lesson: ridding Caracas of slums and moving their inhabitants to modern housing might be in the popular interest, but it would not ensure popular support. To modernize Caracas, and all of Venezuela, he would need to push through his vision with no expectation of popular support. As he noted years later: "There must be a leader who shows the way without being perturbed by the necessity of winning demagogic popularity."[50]

But even if his words indicated "no intention of trying to become a popular politician," Pérez Jiménez's policies revealed a project aimed at improving the lives of most Venezuelans.[51] In the five years following his 2 December 1952 coup, Pérez Jiménez undertook the most expansive, expensive, and ambitious public works campaign in Venezuelan history, combining private investment and state spending in a plan that he would formally call the "Nuevo Ideal Nacional" (New National Ideal, or NIN). In development since before his 1952 coup,[52] but officially unveiled in 1955, the NIN aimed to "rationally transform the physical environment and improve the moral, intellectual, and material conditions of the nation's inhabitants."[53] It was a sweeping vision for a new Venezuela. Fueling it were nearly US$550 million—US$(2014)5 billion, adjusted for inflation—in annual revenues derived almost exclusively from the shared profits of oil exports. Like regimes before, that of Pérez Jiménez would promote development across the nation—notably through highways, agricultural development, and investments in steel and chemical industries. But unlike with prior governments, it would be Caracas—Venezuela's "national show window"—where the new Venezuela would rise.[54]

FIGURE 6. On 2 December 1955, surrounded by ministers and onlookers, General Marcos Pérez Jiménez (fourth in uniform from left) inspects newly completed buildings in Monte Piedad, formally inaugurating Venezuela's New National Ideal. (Archivo Audiovisual de la Nación)

Already, public housing construction in the preceding years had spurred continued migration to Caracas. By 1955, the capital reached one million inhabitants, doubling its population over the previous decade. Many had come from Europe, part of the 373,000 people who immigrated to Venezuela after World War II.[55] New neighborhoods such as Pedro Camejo and Urdaneta, as large and innovative as they were, proved insufficient to house the new arrivals. Pérez Jiménez's New National Ideal, by contrast, promised ambitious solutions that would not only keep pace with growing housing demands, but eliminate housing deficits altogether. On the third anniversary of his 2 December 1955 coup, just two months after formally unveiling his NIN, Pérez Jiménez stood at the foot of the new 2 de Diciembre housing project amid crowds of onlookers and stared at his vision grandly realized (fig. 6).

It was the first stage of a planned four-stage project, conceived to settle the rancho issue once and for all by incorporating several urban housing solutions the Banco Obrero had experimented with over the previous five years. Like

Pedro Camejo and Urdaneta, the 2 de Diciembre aimed to build not just housing but a fully integrated community with support systems such as schools,
parks, and commercial areas. But unlike previous working-class housing projects—characterized by high-density, low-altitude buildings—the centerpiece
of the 2 de Diciembre was the high-altitude, high-density superblock. Introduced by TABO architects in 1951, in concept the superblocks consisted of
freestanding vertical communities, or *unidades vecinales*, modeled after Swiss-
French architect Le Corbusier's *Unité d'Habitation* in Marseille, France.[56] The
BO inaugurated Venezuela's first superblock in 1954, in southern Caracas.
Designed for middle class residents, the Cerro Grande superblock rose fourteen stories high and held 144 apartments in 3- and 4-bedroom options. It was
equipped with terraced duplex apartments, rooftop walkways and greeneries,
a cross-ventilated design, and community and commercial services at both roof
level and on the first floor, including daycare and laundry facilities.[57]

However, for the 2 de Diciembre, aimed at maximizing residential space
and facilitating reproducible construction, architect Carlos Raúl Villanueva
and his TABO team envisioned a more functional design, to efficiently house
more residents. They drew on the high-altitude, high-density concept of Cerro
Grande, but eliminated various community-building additions. For example,
they cut duplex options and added a floor to bring the total number of apartments per building to 150. By reproducing the superblocks and streamlining
plans, architects designed even-more-massive structures by joining together
individual superblocks into buildings of 300, 450, and even 520 apartments.

The resulting design created the ideal community envisioned by the NIN,
radically transforming physical space while imbuing it with deeply charged
symbolic meaning. The project's colorful master plan was dramatic: over 9,000
apartments distributed among 56 superblocks and 40 four-story blocks in a
space covering three square kilometers, divided into four phases scheduled
for successive inaugurations, on 2 December 1955, 1956, 1957, and 1958 (map 5).
Its initial phase consisted of 13 fifteen-story superblocks—including two
buildings coupled to create a single 300-apartment structure—along with 26
four-story blocks, accommodating a combined total of 16,500 residents. In the
neighborhood's next stage 19,000 residents would occupy 16 superblocks and
9 four-story blocks. Plans for the third stage, the project's largest and most
ambitious, called for the construction of 21 superblocks—including three
triple blocks of 450 apartments, and an experimental 520-apartment building—and 9 four-story blocks, in all able to house 29,000 people. In the fourth

and final stage, scheduled for completion in December 1958, five more super-blocks would house nearly 5,500 residents.[58] Each apartment was fully linked to the electric grid, to the city sewer service, even to television broadcasts—first launched in Venezuela in 1952. Movie theaters, parks, plazas, athletic fields, gymnasiums, churches, schools, clinics, police and fire stations, a civic center, commercial spaces, gas stations, and administrative offices completed the neighborhood.[59] Seventy thousand people housed in Venezuela's largest public housing project embodied Pérez Jiménez's New National Ideal. And at its heart—fittingly represented by a uniquely shaped purple structure in the center of the master plan—would stand a sculpture "whose central figure represents Venezuela, surrounded by three bodies who symbolize the intellectual, the soldier, and the worker."[60]

These figures help capture the scale of the neighborhood itself. But the master plan for 2 de Diciembre reveals a great deal about the project's broader place within the nation. For instance, the Ministry of Defense was symbolically located on a hill overlooking the neighborhood's first phase and the Presidential Palace. Also, a new superhighway connecting Caracas and its airport, thirty miles north behind Cerro El Ávila, was scheduled to be built between two phases of construction. Travelers to Caracas would thus enter the capital through the 2 de Diciembre and its massive superblocks, strategically positioned to face the highway. It was a project seamlessly integrated into a broader vision for an ideal Venezuela, helping transform the capital, as one foreign correspondent wrote in 1955, into "a bursting city overhauling itself so fast that the visitor who returns only once a year can easily get lost. Under clouds of dust, half pulverized rubble and half cement, new super boulevards crash through old slums, and lavender-painted buses soon roll along them."[61]

The image of boulevards crashing through old slums was especially symbolic. Unlike Urdaneta, Pedro Camejo, and other housing projects, construction for the 2 de Diciembre eliminated not only ranchos but well-established neighborhoods such as Tiro al Blanco and La Cañada. This took place despite the formation of a 1954 presidential commission tasked with assessing the impact of the projected neighborhood on the very communities whose lives it aimed to transform.[62] Still, by year's end, work on what became the 2 de Diciembre was under way with the demolition of the areas the study assessed,[63] as crews made no distinction between ranchos and "well-constituted and traditional" barrios.[64] In what became the 2 de Diciembre, Pérez Jiménez consigned ten barrios for demolition, covering roughly three square kilometers,

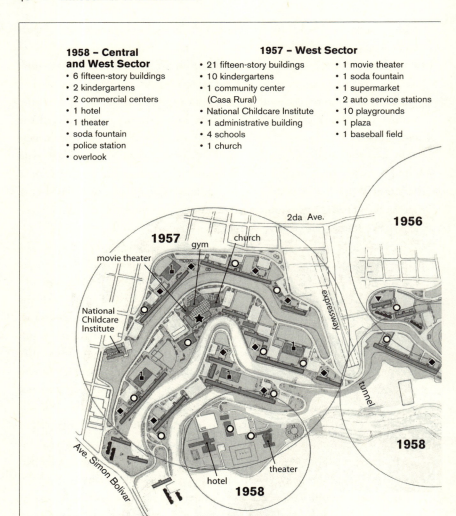

1958 – Central and West Sector
- 6 fifteen-story buildings
- 2 kindergartens
- 2 commercial centers
- 1 hotel
- 1 theater
- soda fountain
- police station
- overlook

1957 – West Sector
- 21 fifteen-story buildings
- 10 kindergartens
- 1 community center (Casa Rural)
- National Childcare Institute
- 1 administrative building
- 4 schools
- 1 church

- 1 movie theater
- 1 soda fountain
- 1 supermarket
- 2 auto service stations
- 10 playgrounds
- 1 plaza
- 1 baseball field

MAP 5. Unidad Residencial 2 de Diciembre (1954 Plan). (Banco Obrero; cartography by Ben Pease)

making use of a 1947 law enabling expropriation "in areas considered essential for the security or defense of the Nation,"[65] further underscoring both the neighborhood's strategic location and its significance for the new Venezuela. Some of those barrios retained their names in the new neighborhood, even if not captured by the project's master plan. Beneath the otherwise nondescript "Sector Este," for instance, lay Monte Piedad, a name that would endure among

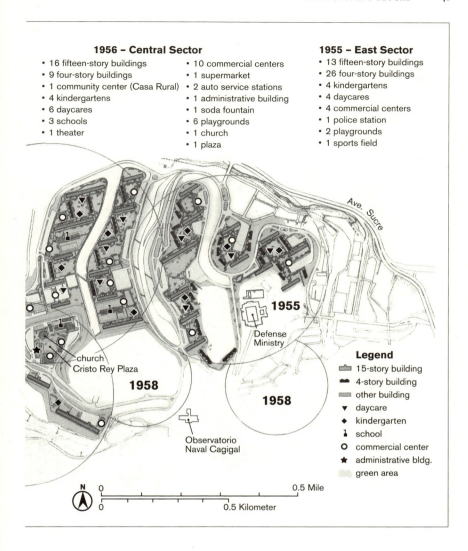

1956 – Central Sector
- 16 fifteen-story buildings
- 9 four-story buildings
- 1 community center (Casa Rural)
- 4 kindergartens
- 6 daycares
- 3 schools
- 1 theater
- 10 commercial centers
- 1 supermarket
- 2 auto service stations
- 1 administrative building
- 1 soda fountain
- 6 playgrounds
- 1 church
- 1 plaza

1955 – East Sector
- 13 fifteen-story buildings
- 26 four-story buildings
- 4 kindergartens
- 4 daycares
- 4 commercial centers
- 1 police station
- 2 playgrounds
- 1 sports field

Ave. Sucre

1955

Defense
Ministry

church
Cristo Rey Plaza

1958

1958

Observatorio
Naval Cagigal

Legend
- 15-story building
- 4-story building
- other building
- ▼ daycare
- ◆ kindergarten
- 🏫 school
- ○ commercial center
- ★ administrative bldg.
- green area

N
0   0.5 Mile
0   0.5 Kilometer

residents of the 2 de Diciembre's first phase, as would La Cañada, razed to make way for the eastern half of the "Sector Central."

Beyond the fray and excitement of the project's inauguration, signs of life remained strikingly absent. The buildings that Pérez Jiménez first inaugurated, the ones shown gleaming against a cloudless sky in government photos taken on 2 December 1955, sat largely completed but vacant, not to be assigned and inhabited for several months. Banco Obrero publications, too, which in promoting previous housing projects had advertised dramatically staged photos of working-class families before and after moving to new facilities, in the case of the 2 de Diciembre were limited to aerial photographs aiming to capture the neighborhood's scale. Before-and-after images looked to highlight the transformation of the landscape as it existed prior to superblocks—laden with ranchos or otherwise haphazardly arranged single-family homes—and following the neighborhood's construction.[66] Meanwhile photo spreads in trade journals and magazines offered striking pictorial arrangements of the new neighborhoods and featured images of the superblocks' polychromatic façades, detailed shots of the areas' commercial facilities and schools, and effusive prose about the project's achievement. The only things missing were people, vehicles, commerce—anything that might evoke life.[67]

LIFE AND PUNISHMENT IN THE EARLY BLOCKS

"That was like lightning, from one day to the next," observes Francisco Suárez. On a Monday around late March 1956, according to Suárez, BO personnel arrived in Tiro al Blanco and by Friday the neighborhood lay razed. At the beginning of the week BO census takers met with each family, determining the number of residents per household, work status, and family income. "Then they assigned you [an apartment]," remembered Priscilla de Carrero, who together with her husband and young daughter had recently moved to an aunt's house in Tiro al Blanco. "They told you how much you needed to pay up front and how much you would pay per month." The choice was stark: either take cash for their house, or move to the superblocks; staying was not an option. For Carrero, the prospect of moving to the new superblocks was a curse: "I used to go by [them] and say, 'Who's going to live in those matchboxes?' because they really looked like matchboxes. Then an aunt told me, 'Watch out, God will punish you.' 'No, God won't punish me because I don't like them.' We even looked for a house, but where we looked there was nothing I liked, so that's why I said [to my husband] José, 'We have no choice but to move.'"[68]

On the day of the move, according to Juan Martínez, "the first thing they did was to tear the roof down from your house, [so] there was nowhere to go." Then, according to Lorenzo Acosta (fig. 7), also of Tiro al Blanco, trucks arrived at 90-minute intervals. "They told you to be ready, because if you're not going [to the 2 de Diciembre] you have to leave, you either go there or it's up to you

FIGURE 7. Lorenzo Acosta in 2004, in the living room of the Monte Piedad apartment where he and his family were relocated in 1956 from Tiro al Blanco. He displays his army enlistment certificate from 1943. (Photo by the author)

to see what you do. . . . So we had to get ready for when that truck arrived; we would have everything all set outside, right outside so we would leave more quickly."[69] As soon as the trucks began to leave, bulldozers razed the remaining walls, leaving behind the wreckage of torn houses and lives sacrificed. Recalled Francisco Suárez: "After they razed the roof of my house . . . I saw my mother sitting on a rock, crying because it had been her life's work. I saw her and turned away, even as a child. In other words, it affected me too."[70] In a week's time, said Juan Martínez, "that was completely cleaned out. There was nothing left. All the debris went into a sort of landfill."[71] Only when they arrived in Monte Piedad did the new residents learn what apartments they were to move into. Meanwhile, BO personnel checked all belongings to ensure everything entering the new apartments, from furniture to clothing to appliances, met proper standards. "You couldn't bring *cachivaches* [worn-out or dilapidated belongings] here," remembered Martínez, "a side table missing a leg, none of that. . . . People and objects going into the place had to be in perfect condition." Once they passed inspection, residents were escorted aboard elevators to their new apartments, handed keys, and ushered into their new lives.

The flood of details that suffuse these testimonies, recalled decades after an event that spanned at most a week in people's lives, illustrates the trauma of relocation, thus suggesting a tension between the abstract ideal and the lived experience of early life in the 2 de Diciembre. While on one hand the nature and pace of the relocation process exposed the authoritarian nature of Pérez Jiménez's power, on the other hand it revealed an unflinching commitment to his national goals, unencumbered by what he had brazenly dismissed as "the necessity of winning demagogic popularity." It was an unflinching process: those not meeting minimum income requirements received enough compensation to return to the interior or had to find housing elsewhere; those who barely qualified were offered rental contracts that gave the BO ultimate control over their housing situation should they prove unfit to continue in the superblocks. Meanwhile those with more-stable employment and income received a purchasing option, a lease arrangement by which residents paying monthly fees could, after 15 years, purchase their apartments outright from the BO.[72]

The totalizing quality that characterized these operations is important to stress because it helps explain why residents, even while benefiting from new, modern housing, still harbored lingering feelings of entrapment that would eventually blossom into outright rebellion. This is especially the case given how regimented life was in the early days of the superblocks. New residents worked to adjust to their new environment, and at times to make the new environment adjust to them. Young people, in particular, struggled to adapt. Prohibited from riding the elevator without their parents, children like Francisco Suárez, who in Tiro al Blanco had charged small fees to ferry water for area families, once in the 2 de Diciembre took to charging families to help them move into their apartments. Meanwhile Suárez and other youths found work taking lunch to the construction workers in other parts of the rapidly rising neighborhood.

New regulations and rules affected adults, too. "If you wanted to have a party," recalled Rafael Gutiérrez, whose family the authorities relocated from La Cañada, "you needed to get a permit at a Banco Obrero office that took care of that for this area. . . . Everything was checked. It wasn't like I'm going to have a party because it's my house, no, no. They took neighbors into account, not bothering your neighbors, whether or not the neighbor wanted it. There were rules." According to Lorenzo Acosta any new appliance residents purchased likewise required special permits from the BO before being allowed into the apartments. The BO "almost had police powers," noted Juan Martínez. "Yes, they had watchmen around here; if by chance you dropped a piece of paper, then they would go and come up [to the apartment] and take you in [to jail]." For some residents, like Priscilla de Carrero, the trouble proved more than it was worth, and they would withdraw into their apartments. At times, three months would pass before she saw her neighbors.[73]

Between 1955 and 1957, experiences like these would happen again and again in areas like La Cañada as construction moved forward on the other phases on the 2 de Diciembre, razing existing neighborhoods to make way for the new Venezuela. Work on the neighborhood took place in six-month cycles. From December to May construction slowed significantly before commencing again at breakneck speed around June.[74] On one hand this peculiar practice made possible, even necessary, expeditious construction rates. "We worked two shifts," said César Acuña, part of a construction team of nearly 700 workers building the neighborhood's largest phase in 1957. "Here we worked from 7 A.M. to 7 P.M.; we worked day and night."[75] Though paid for overtime, "they were a hard twelve hours, *a ritmo caliente* [at a hectic pace]." Francisco Chirinos, too, remembered working "twelve-hour shifts, day and night, even on Saturdays,"[76] which allowed building one 15-story, 150-apartment superblock in as little as 42 days.[77] On the other hand, it also helped to generate bottlenecks in housing distribution, resulting in frustration by those forced from their homes in June only to face months of delay beyond December for their new homes.[78]

But life did thrive, in part because old community networks persisted and at times grew stronger as the same population from a single street in Tiro al Blanco or La Cañada moved en masse, often to the same building, sometimes to the same floor. That was the case with Juan Martínez and his family, who ended up in Block 4 of Monte Piedad, across the way from their old neighbors in Tiro al Blanco.[79] Over time, memories of "the sacrifices we made over years to build our homes," of "the houses one built through the sweat of one's brow, through one's sacrifice," gave way to a sense that "we were getting a good residence, comfortable, dignified, with all the services," said Suárez. "One of the things that bothered people was that discipline, that imposition" of life in a community where residents were being not only relocated, but through more direct forms of social control reeducated to become the lifeblood of a new national ideal. And still, "you start to think about it and in a certain way [Pérez Jiménez] had a sense of national pride" that he looked to impart.

Martínez's conflicted memories are significant because they illustrate a major thread of social and political life in the neighborhood during those early years: though residents grew to appreciate the new space, they also remained disdainful of the authoritarian management experienced in 2 de Diciembre. In this sense, Pérez Jiménez achieved his goal: to create a symbol of his vision for modern

Venezuela. But the underside of this political project remained a palpable sense of social control, felt not in grand ideological terms but in the everyday experiences of residents inhabiting this new national symbol. Both strands were reflected in the 2 de Diciembre, not just in its form but also in the lives of its residents. This tension between modernity and political authoritarianism came to define the Pérez Jiménez government and political culture in Venezuela in subsequent years. At the end of his presidency, the very neighborhood Pérez Jiménez had built would take center stage in his political downfall.

"¡ABAJO EL GOBIERNO!"

When Pérez Jiménez's government fell on 23 January 1958, Inés Oliveira was on the front lines of demonstrations celebrating his ouster. "I didn't know much about politics," she admitted, "but you get carried away in the moment."[80] Oliveira's enthusiasm was in part a release. In the days preceding the coup, residents of the 2 de Diciembre neighborhood found themselves under siege. "My mother forbade us from setting foot outside our apartment," Oliveira recalled, and for good reason. In a final show of force by Pérez Jiménez's government following nearly two months of political unrest, the streets below were "como monte, full of police disguised as military." On 22 January, Oliveira and friend Carlos Germán Rivas were at the plaza behind Block 14 to watch as a group of police assembled. Then a shot rang out: "I'll never forget it . . . my hand was covered in blood." The bullet had hit Carlos in the right eye, knocking him unconscious and leading Oliveira to believe him dead.[81] A crowd of fellow residents gathered around her. "That was a revolution . . . people were going to lynch [the policeman], tear his head off."

But the revolution came on 23 January, when a civilian-military junta took power following Pérez Jiménez's hasty flight from Caracas, on a plane bound for the Dominican Republic, where military strongman Rafael Trujillo awaited. That morning Oliveira, unbeknownst to her parents, boarded a truck, shouted "¡Abajo el gobierno!" and proceeded to the downtown headquarters of Seguridad Nacional, Pérez Jiménez's domestic-security force. "We saw all manner of body parts there, heads, feet, breasts, penises." It was the kind of scene that exposed an ultimately unsustainable relationship between prosperity under Pérez Jiménez and the price his government demanded in return. "With Pérez Jiménez there was no hunger," Oliveira reflected decades later, "but there was pain in many homes."[82]

Pérez Jiménez had received powerful notice of that unsustainable relationship nearly two months before. On 15 December 1957, despite earlier claiming "no intention of trying to become a popular politician," Pérez Jiménez had again tried to win popular legitimacy by holding a plebiscite on his rule. Of course much had changed in the five years since the fraudulent elections that first helped him consolidate power in 1952. Since then, Pérez Jiménez's government had invested enormous sums modernizing Venezuela. Caracas in particular was virtually unrecognizable from the patchwork of colonial homes, hillside slums, and scattered high-rises that marked the city through the 1940s. Now, superblocks peppered the landscape and superhighways snaked through mountains; grand parks, gleaming skyscrapers, and major boulevards abounded. It was the "golden rule" of an oil-financed dictatorship.

But while golden, it was still a "rule," aimed at changing, ordering, and rigidly regulating not just space, but daily life, as accounts from residents of the 2 de Diciembre dramatically illustrated. Now, the contradictions of a modernizing dictatorship—bent on improving the lives of many by force, not consent—brought forth another rebuke at the polls for Pérez Jiménez, who, as in 1952, again declared himself winner. This time, though, he did so without even a pretense of electoral transparency, simply announcing results before all votes were cast. In the days after the plebiscite, Pérez Jiménez's brazen manipulation of a vote he had himself called for sowed discontent even among his strongest base of support—the military. On New Year's Day, an Air Force contingent launched an unsuccessful bid to oust the President, staging a gun battle with government loyalists over the skies of Caracas. Though it failed, the move galvanized political sectors that had organized clandestinely for years to challenge Pérez Jiménez in the open. Public pronouncements from labor, religious, and even business sectors calling for the President's resignation mounted quickly in the first weeks of January. On 21 January, political tensions reached a fever pitch as labor and business sectors joined forces to call for an indefinite general strike, in the process coordinating with dissident military officers in a final push to oust Pérez Jiménez.[83]

As public opposition grew, so did repression, and with special intensity in the showcase neighborhood of the New National Ideal. The 2 de Diciembre's proximity to key institutions of state power—the Presidential Palace and the Defense Ministry chief among them—once thought to symbolize the state's proximity to the nation's working classes, now stood as a potential threat, particularly as authorities quickly lost grip on control. Reports of agitators in the 2 de Diciembre neighborhood in the days leading up to the coup contributed to a climate of confrontation. Ligia Ovalles of Block 31 in the Zona Central, then 25 years old, recalled how in the run up to 23 January "subversive flyers" would appear in the morning, sometimes wet with dew, strewn throughout the neighborhood. "Those flyers would explain to you why this or that was happening. During the general strike [begun on 21 January] they said we had to get rid of the dictator because there was no freedom of expression . . . they told you to get ready, to buy candles, matches, food." She continued: "You had to read them and get rid of them, because if suddenly they raided your house and if they found [flyers], you went to jail." Meanwhile, the neighborhood's broad streets—once a marker of urban modernity—were now a strategic asset for the government, allowing easy movement of troops, which deployed en masse. By 20 January, "you couldn't pick [the flyers] up, because the military took over this place. . . . All those hallways were full of military, armed. They ordered us, with megaphones, not to turn on the lights, or else."[84]

Growing police and military presence also stoked internal tensions in the neighborhood, blurring the lines between what residents had earlier perceived as rigid enforcement of rules for daily life, and outright surveillance. "You had to be careful; you didn't know who was who, who might be watching." One incident in particular continued to amaze Ovalles. "One man here was a reservist. He had a bunch of bullets. And two soldiers ran out of ammunition. So he took bullets to them. Later, when Pérez Jiménez fell, the yelling started. He had to leave at dawn one day, because they were going to lynch him—the people. They said 'We saw you giving them bullets. Watch yourself. You won't leave here alive.'" Reflecting on the story, Ovalles recalled thinking: "That was wrong. . . . How are you going to give bullets to people who were against you? Didn't he think of his children, his family?"[85]

Cornered, Pérez Jiménez had reportedly ordered his security forces to "shoot to kill."[86] In the 2 de Diciembre, the violence proved especially pronounced. Days later, press accounts reported on what they called "a kind of massacre against the defenseless inhabitants" of the 2 de Diciembre, whose residents "from the start," according to *El Universal* newspaper, "demonstrated great strength and unflinching valor in the face of events."[87] News reports likewise made special mention of the neighborhood's dead. Of ninety-three fatalities recorded in Caracas between 11 January and 25 January directly attributable to the events surrounding Pérez Jiménez's overthrow, twenty-one—including nine under the age of eighteen—died in the 2 de Diciembre.[88] Of those, eighteen died on 22 January (see Appendix). They included Aura Figueroa de Ferrer and her one-year-old child, gunned down as she peered out from her apartment in Block 5 of Monte Piedad,[89] and brothers Luis and Douglas Leal, two and six years old, respectively, killed by wounds to the head and lung in Monte Piedad.[90]

Instead of neutralizing political opposition, this type of repressive response had helped to fuel it among residents of the 2 de Diciembre. As Ovalles noted reflecting on the revolution: "There were those who were against the revolutionaries, but most were in favor, because you heard too much about what those people [in the Pérez Jiménez government] did, the tortures. . . . Simply put [*en dos platos*], there was no freedom."[91] Even people like Inés Oliveira acknowledged that Pérez Jiménez's rule, despite significant material benefits, had sacrificed popular support by restricting opportunities for popular participation. This helps explain why, as Pérez Jiménez fled from Caracas at dawn on 23 January 1958, Oliveira and thousands of other residents of the 2 de Diciembre took to the streets to celebrate his ouster. Some of them flocked to Avenida Urdaneta just east of the neighborhood, where tanks controlled by insurgent troops had positioned themselves between the Miraflores Presidential Palace and the Presidential Honor Guard barracks across the way. It was an especially dramatic scene—captured in what became one of the most emblematic images of that day (fig. 8). In the background, several 2 de Diciembre superblocks tower overhead. In the foreground insurgent crowds and tanks converge in front of the Presidential Palace. That the palace remained just out of view marked the promise, after years of dictatorial rule, of a less centralized form of government, where the kind of people filling the streets could openly and more directly participate in the exercise of power.

The image is important because it helps explain how a neighborhood that had occupied a central place in Pérez Jiménez's vision for a new Venezuela—both as a symbol and in the landscape itself—would come to serve a similar function in the new political period about to unfold. It was evidence of the kind of urban support for a change of government that had eluded Pérez Jiménez's own coups, and which would prove a vital political goal for the 23 January coup. The following day, Rear Admiral Wolfgang Larrazábal took to airwaves for the first time as president of the junta that had overthrown Pérez Jiménez the day before, congratulating Venezuelans for condemning "the vices of yesterday," and celebrating their "enthusiasm for the political and moral values" that would shape the new government.[92] On 9 February a crowd of thousands in Caracas greeted Rómulo Betancourt, leader of Acción Democrática, as he returned to

FIGURE 8. On 23 January 1958, tanks and crowds gather between the Miraflores Presidential Palace (out of view to the left) and the Honor Guard barracks (at right). In the background, Blocks 11 through 14 of Monte Piedad. Nestled in the hills on the left, behind the Nuestra Sra. del Perpetuo Socorro Church, the Ministry of Defense. (Archivo Audiovisual de la Nación)

Venezuela after nine years in exile: "The past revolution would not have been possible without a resistance begun [ten years ago], showing Venezuelans, whether in jail or in exile, that the passion for liberty was alive, exploding in magnificent fashion now."[93] Years later, diplomat José Luis Salcedo-Bastardo would write of the events of 23 January 1958: "[They] represented the victory of and for ordinary Venezuelans who rose up in unified rejection of tyranny."[94]

While the dictator fell, his superblocks remained, giving rise to the question of what would become of a place so closely tied to the ousted regime. Within days, the 2 de Diciembre "went from being a symbol of the dictatorship to a symbol of the democratic victory against it."[95] In narrating the events in the ensuing days, the media observed how the "fury unleashed upon residents of that populous neighborhood . . . gave rise to a proposal asking the *Junta de Gobierno* to change [the neighborhood's] name from 2 de Diciembre to 23 de Enero."[96] Later accounts reported the area's new moniker as "21 de Enero," when the national strike had begun.[97] The confusion well reflected the spontaneity surrounding the process by which a revolution took a name, and a symbol. However, in March, a neighborhood delegation presented the Caracas city council with a petition with over a thousand signatures, formally requesting the neighborhood be henceforth known as 23 de Enero, "since Caracas has gotten used to the new name."[98] A year later when the Banco Obrero published its official history celebrating 30 years of public works, the entity that built the superblocks captured the new meaning behind what had by far been its most significant capital investment: the new name was quite simply "a reminder of the date when a heroic popular gesture overthrew Marcos Pérez Jiménez's dictatorial regime."[99]

Upholding popular participation, and in particular the participation of residents of the superblocks, as a primary factor contributing to Pérez Jiménez's fall illustrated the new government's need to harness popular support at the service of an uncertain political project. At best, this was a project that had only tangentially looked to coordinate with the urban populace around its plans for a new regime.[100] Pérez Jiménez had sought to make the 2 de Diciembre and its residents into a symbol of his government's popular foundations. But that symbol had turned into an illusion. Now, as the new 23 de Enero, it would once more honor both popular strength and the promise of a political ideal, only this time at the service of a new democratic order. An emerging narrative now promised an era of "liberty," anchored in the discourse of revolution, and built around the image of an active and mobilized citizenry at its forefront. Constructing the events of 23 January 1958 in these terms would prove prophetic. Endowed with a new opportunity to speak out, to make demands, to participate, residents of the superblocks brought forward needs and grievances both new and longstanding. But just as it had under Pérez Jiménez, a tense interplay between support and opposition would characterize the relationships between the new government (and future governments) and the people living in the neighborhood renamed to honor the founding date of the revolution.

CHAPTER 2

Democracy's Projects

Occupying the Spaces of Revolution

On the surface it seemed little more than a formality. On 28 March 1958, responding to a petition signed by a thousand area residents, the Caracas city council voted officially to change the name of the 2 de Diciembre housing project to 23 de Enero. The vote was unanimous, and hardly surprising.[1] In the previous two months since the overthrow of Marcos Pérez Jiménez, what began as a spontaneous rechristening spread by word of mouth had become a staple in press accounts. The same neighborhood built to embody the ideals of the ousted regime now stood as the emblem of a nation held up by a new spirit of unity. During the coup more people had perished in the 2 de Diciembre than anywhere else in Caracas (see Appendix), sealing in blood what the new name signaled in spirit: here lay the popular foundations of the new democratic Venezuela.

But what seemed like a simple gesture in fact belied a much deeper, and more fraught, transformation. Beyond names and symbols and fancies of unity the 23 de Enero—like post-dictatorship Venezuela more broadly—was a space where the social and physical changes wrought in the days of Pérez Jiménez exploded into open tension. In the span of 48 hours following the coup, nearly thirty thousand people had illegally occupied over 3,000 apartments in the western sectors of the housing project, units that remained vacant despite their formal inauguration weeks earlier. For these newcomers, bypassing the strict screenings and controls that had marked life in and relocation to the 2 de Diciembre set them apart from residents of the eastern sectors of the neighborhood. And in the ensuing weeks and months, many who arrived too late to find even an empty apartment resolved instead to settle in the spaces between the buildings, raising the same ranchos the superblocks had been designed to eradicate, and in the process providing a dramatic coda to Pérez Jiménez's bulldozer years: in the struggle over urban housing represented by the 2 de Diciembre, the ousted dictator may have won the battle, but the ranchos won the war.

For Lourdes Quintero, the scene "was like an invasion." For nearly two years before 23 January 1958, Quintero lived across the way from the 2 de Diciembre, often stopping to gaze at the superblocks under construction, and at the new Venezuela they portended. "What I wouldn't give to get [an apartment] in one of those." Then Pérez Jiménez fell. "Word began to spread that they were handing out keys to the apartments," said Quintero. "Well, everyone started running. I came here, too, with several other women. This was full of people moving, you have no idea." Rumors flew that military personnel from the nearby Defense Ministry were distributing keys. In fact, as Quintero soon discovered, distribution was a far more chaotic affair: "Everywhere we were told 'No, *mamá*, whoever finds an apartment just gets in there,'" she recalled. "So we started climbing the stairs, looking to see where there was an empty apartment." But because elevators remained inoperative, stairs turned into a cluttered mess where "people moving refrigerators, washing machines, everything" collided with those in desperate search of a still-vacant unit.

Finally, Quintero found a two-bedroom apartment on the fourteenth floor of Block 37 in the Zona F, one of the three recently inaugurated, though still unassigned, areas of the housing project: "I got in here, and here I stayed." At dusk, after asking a man next door to safeguard her new unit, Quintero returned home, where her husband had stayed behind with their four children, thinking the whole business too much of a risk: "Who's going to go there? With kids, how will you manage?" he had cautioned Quintero. She replied: "Well, I'm going." Quintero gathered a mattress, some sheets, and her two oldest children, leaving the youngest with their father. "In the morning," she sternly told him, "you take them there." Interviewed nearly fifty years later, Quintero still betrayed surprise at the memory of her deeds that day: "I don't know where I found so much courage. There were so many people."[2]

Quintero's "courage" reflected a common experience from those heady days of transition, as old expectations lay torn asunder in a climate of uncertain opportunity brought about by Pérez Jiménez's ouster. Just two years earlier, official images of the neighborhood had depicted scenes of order, discipline,

FIGURE 9. In February 1958, women and children await distribution of keys to apartments at La Cañada, in the 23 de Enero. (Archivo Audiovisual de la Nación)

and precision. Now the images were of long lines of would-be residents eagerly awaiting keys to the very superblock apartments they had broken into and squatted. Where earlier images scarcely showed the everyday residents who breathed life into the concrete, new images placed those people front and center—women in particular (fig. 9). Much as Quintero had drawn upon reservoirs of "courage" and seized this moment of uncertain opportunity, thousands of other women and their children who stood in line awaiting keys portended the extent to which new actors would come to inform the expectation of popular participation in the neighborhood, and of popular democracy in Venezuela. In ways literal and figurative, "invasion" proved an apt expression of a popular irruption into the public sphere.

This chapter surveys the social landscape of the 23 de Enero as a new collective identity emerged in the wake of Pérez Jiménez's ouster. New residents demarcated the neighborhood's space and its population, creating fault lines between those who had moved into the old 2 de Diciembre and those who had moved into the new 23 de Enero, between those in the eastern sections of the neighborhood and those in its western sectors, between those in apartments and those who came increasingly to inhabit new rancho settlements that rose between the superblocks. In two days' time, a neighborhood otherwise designed to homogenize both space and life for urban popular sectors was transformed into an amalgam where new needs and long-buried grievances uneasily coexisted. The manner in which these disparate groups had come to live in the neighborhood created divergent sets of needs that posed serious challenges to a state whose own shape and direction remained uncertain. As interim Minister of Public Works Víctor Rotondaro said just days after the coup: "A problem that has social complications due to the need for housing that directly concerns the proletariat is that of the superblocks, which though completed, have not been inaugurated with pomp and circumstance because the rebellious population prevented the ousted dictator from doing so." To squatters fearing eviction, Rotondaro stressed the popular character of the superblocks in this new era of democratic revolution: "Those blocks are of the people and for the people. We are looking for a legal formula so those in need can occupy those households."[3]

It was a fine line new authorities had to navigate in the 23 de Enero, between upholding the new residents as emblems of the popular spirit surrounding the January revolution, and contending with the social, legal, and economic ramifications resulting from the spontaneous squatting of thousands of apartments. But the situation also exemplified how, much like the "invasion" of the 23 de Enero, the reality of transition proved a messier affair. The physical and social transformation of the 23 de Enero ensured that the neighborhood's internal dynamics would inform residents' relationship with the new regime, and vice versa. Much as they had done in the "self-inauguration" of the 23 de Enero, residents would shape the community anew, moving from the spontaneous seizure of apartments to the organization of a newly configured community. That they now resided in the same area, and often shared backgrounds of migration to the city and settlement in ranchos, created opportunities for concerted action amid their differences, allowing residents—original renters, new apartment squatters, and rancho settlers alike—to push their collective advantage vis-à-vis a weak state to ensure that newly opened spaces for exerting popular pressure would remain so in the wake of the transition. In this moment between an authoritarian past and a future direction that remained up for grabs, residents of the 23 de Enero would stake a strong claim to the new Venezuela from the process of founding the neighborhood anew, this time from below.

OCCUPYING THE BLOCKS: SQUATTERS AND THE NEW SOCIAL LANDSCAPE OF THE 23 DE ENERO

On the morning of 23 January 1958, Emilia de Pérez and her four children, the youngest merely three days old, were at their home about an hour from the capital when she heard about "the business in Caracas, that Pérez Jiménez had fallen, that Pérez Jiménez had fled." With her husband out of town for work, Pérez's brother arrived from Caracas to pick her up: "He said, 'Let's go, because you never know what may come of this and you're alone here with these kids.'" When they arrived at the city they watched as thousands converged upon the 2 de Diciembre, occupying whatever vacant unit they could find. Alongside her older sister, Pérez took a chance and joined the crowd. Then a Banco Obrero (BO) employee approached the pair: "Look," he told Pérez, "there's an apartment. You and your sister don't have an apartment. Get in there at night with all your kids." So they did. Lacking keys, they forced the door of a vacant unit in a four-story building in La Cañada, where the two sisters, nine children in tow between the two of them, would remain.[4] By nightfall on 24 January, no units remained vacant.[5]

Days later, Pérez received a summons to appear before the local BO office. "The man there told us there was an empty apartment in Block 30 [in the Zona Central], and he needed us to move out of our apartment *urgently*, because it already had an owner. . . . We said okay, and well, we moved." Provided with a truck and laborers, Pérez, her sister, and their children found themselves on the move yet again just days after 23 January. But once they arrived in the promised apartment they found it occupied. Laughing, Pérez recalls: "The same thing we had done, a lady had done. Well, that was beyond words! That woman refused to open the door, she said no and the Banco Obrero people said yes and she said no, no, no, so in the end, the Banco Obrero folks had to push the door open and told us, 'Get in!'" For the next month, Pérez, her husband and four children, her unmarried sister and five children, and the third woman and her children lived in the two-bedroom apartment. "She minded her business, and we minded ours," Pérez recalls, until finally the woman, "who apparently already had a house somewhere," left the unit.[6]

Pérez's predicament shed light on the administrative confusion that beset the Banco Obrero as it attempted to address the mass takeover of still-vacant apartments in the now 23 de Enero neighborhood. At the time of Pérez Jiménez's ouster, almost 3,200 apartments lay vacant in the 2 de Diciembre, distributed primarily across nineteen superblocks in the western sectors of Zona E, Zona F, and Mirador. Most construction on this third and most ambitious phase of the housing project had ended in early December 1957.[7] As before, adjudication of the apartments was slated to begin three months after their formal inauguration on 2 December 1957. Instead, in the wake of the coup, BO officials faced the epic challenge of attending to a sudden influx of squatters like Pérez. Overnight, the population residing in the apartments grew over fifty percent, from approximately 47,000 residents between Monte Piedad, La Cañada, and Zona Central, to over 72,000 across the housing project.[8]

By the numbers, the scale of the problem was staggering. Yet the larger obstacle lay in that, unlike with those that the Banco Obrero had relocated before 1958 and from whom they had gathered some information to guide the selection and adjudication process, BO authorities knew nothing about this new population. Already, Emilia de Pérez's experience hinted at nuances in the social composition of those who had seized apartments. Unlike Lourdes Quintero, who for years had longed for a unit in the superblocks, seeing them as the mark of a better life, Pérez harbored no such relationship to the buildings or to the neighborhood. Instead her testimony spoke more of being swept up in a scene of utter confusion, and then going along with the current. That she had come to the superblocks from outside Caracas, too, made her situation different from those for whom the 2 de Diciembre had been designed. After all, the superblocks aimed to resolve the capital's existing housing shortage, with national ambitions in the long term certainly, but with the immediate goal of attending to Caracas popular sectors first, and to rancho dwellers in particular. And that she came to share an apartment, however briefly, with someone who "already had a house" and who eventually left as a result, suggested that some at least had come to the superblocks out of curiosity more than anything else. In this era of democratic revolution, then, the superblocks may have been "of the people and for the people," in the words of interim Public Works Minister Víctor Rotondaro, but, as an administrative matter, just who "the people" were remained unknown.

In response, one week after the coup the BO unfurled a multipronged campaign to "study the problems of residents of the 23 de Enero." In early February 1958, BO officials coordinated with social workers and some 800 university student volunteers to conduct a census of new residents of the superblocks, aimed at "learning about [their economic conditions], the number of people, and the urgency with which they may need housing."[9] By mid-April the effort had yielded 22,000 surveys.[10] The BO also undertook targeted efforts to determine the social composition and needs of its new would-be tenants. For instance, in late February 1958 Raúl Hernández Silva, newly appointed as BO director, met with a sixteen-person delegation from the neighborhood to learn of their major grievances first-hand.[11] And by year's end, the BO had commissioned an international team of urban-planning experts, sociologists, and architects both to sift through existing data from earlier surveys, and to conduct an even more comprehensive study of the superblocks and their residents.

These various efforts yielded surprising findings. On one hand, they revealed some significant similarities between people in the formally adjudicated east and the squatted west. For instance most neighborhood residents in both locations reported working in similar trades—as bus or taxi drivers, in the retail sector, or as salaried laborers. Most, too, hailed from Caracas, and in both the east and the west "nuclear families" accounted for 60% of apartments. In terms of occupancy, roughly the same number of people lived per apartment in the eastern and western areas of the neighborhood: 7.7 and 8.0, respectively.[12]

On the other hand surveys of new residents in the western sectors of the 23 de Enero told of a more socially complex population than that of the eastern sectors, relocated over the previous two years. While overall most in the neighborhood hailed from the interior, on average squatters in the Zona E, Zona F, and Mirador (in the western sector) had arrived at the capital thirteen years prior—coinciding with the 1945 coup that ushered in Venezuela's first experiment with popular democracy.[13] Most, too, came from the adjoining Catia parish, where established neighborhoods, rather than ranchos, predominated. Both of these facts revealed a population composed of relatively recent migrants to the city, who had not taken up life in ranchos but instead likely lived with relatives, or in the crowded, aging housing of colonial-era neighborhoods, following the pattern (discussed in the previous chapter) of those relocated from areas such as Tiro al Blanco. In contrast, fully 86% of residents of the eastern sector had relocated to the superblocks from ranchos that had since been eradicated. While those in the east had no other housing than their apartments, squatters in the western sector likely had stable housing elsewhere in the city.[14] In fact, some enterprising families had squatted in not one, but in multiple apartments, seeking later to rent the extra unit for income under-the-table.[15]

The case of illegal "subletting" highlighted the most serious issue confronting BO authorities as they tried to develop a social portrait of squatters. That issue was rents: who could afford them, in what amounts, and what to do with those who could not pay. Prior to the coup, and despite efforts to ensure that those who were relocated to the former 2 de Diciembre met minimum income requirements through stable employment, the BO had struggled to secure timely rent payments from residents.[16] Now with an enormous wave of new residents who had not undergone even superficial screening, the problem of rent delinquency threatened to explode. According to income statistics compiled in the wake of the coup, monthly incomes for heads of household averaged 683 bolívares (Bs. 683, equivalent to US$200) among those who had come to the neighborhood before 1958, with a range from Bs. 150 (US$45) to Bs. 2,100 (US$630). Among squatters, average incomes were 5% lower, around Bs. 650 (US$190), a noticeable but not significant amount. Yet the range between low and high income levels was wider, from Bs. 100 (US$30) to Bs. 3,800 (US$1,100) a month, indicating a population more economically diverse than elsewhere in the neighborhood.

Over time, government officials would come to view this gap as a social problem inhibiting collective identity, cohesion, and action. Because of the haphazard way in which these residents settled into the superblocks, residents with divergent income levels may have ended up neighbors, as a matter of chance rather than by design, in the frenzy of occupation.[17] More immediately, though, squatters at the lower end of the income range fell below the threshold that the BO had established for occupancy. This portended serious problems for normalizing rent contracts among those who did not earn enough money to pay for the units they had seized.[18]

For the BO, learning more about the neighborhood's new population was of paramount concern for financial, administrative, and even symbolic reasons. Financially, problems with rent collections even during Pérez Jiménez's rule had generated worrying shortfalls for the BO. But with the post-coup occupation, the problem grew far more acute. Personnel and maintenance costs ran upwards of Bs. 241,000 (US$72,000) a month in the western sectors of the neighborhood, and slightly less elsewhere in the 23 de Enero. Each month that passed without rent revenues forced the BO to write off the entire amount as a loss. By the end of November, the BO reported a massive debt of Bs. 16 million (US$4.8 million) due to unpaid rents.[19] While this figure was not confined to the superblocks' squatters, instead reflecting a wider delinquency problem across BO properties, it was in the squatted areas of the 23 de Enero where the problem centered. According to official BO figures, since January 1958 "nearly 4,580 apartments are occupied by families who ... pay no rent." Of this number, 3,200 apartments were occupied by squatters in the 23 de

Enero, almost 70% of the total of delinquent rents among all superblocks in Venezuela.[20]

Operating losses because of rent shortfalls were problematic enough. But making matters worse, some basic infrastructure and services in the areas occupied on January 1958 remained incomplete, requiring capital investments that only added to the deficit, and more significantly, to problems of everyday life facing squatters. In Block 37, for instance, in addition to inoperative elevators, walls remained unfinished when Lourdes Quintero arrived there on 23 January, the building's bare concrete shell exposed to its spontaneous tenants. By March, electric service in the area likewise faced interruptions, owing to what the company's Director for Public Relations called facilities that were "in terrible condition."[21] More importantly for Quintero and for thousands of others in the newly occupied areas, as early as the evening of 24 January water service began to fail as unprimed pumps quickly overloaded. For several months, Quintero and others in her building walked to a spring in the hills behind Block 37 to wash clothes and collect water for home use.[22] According to one estimate, "less than 30 percent of apartments [in the western sectors] had direct water supply, so that nearly 71 percent of inhabitants found themselves forced to obtain water by other means."[23] By mid-April, residents in Block 41 in the Zona F reported to the press how faulty pipes forced them to purchase "tins of water for 2 or 3 bolívares apiece."[24] All told, reported one analyst, water problems constituted, "without a doubt, the gravest collective sanitary problem faced [by residents]."[25]

These basic problems contradicted the goal of the superblocks—assiduously promoted by the fallen regime—as fully realized beacons of modern urban life and its attendant amenities. They also presented an administrative challenge to BO officials in the struggle to normalize tenancy, since it was difficult to demand rents when access to basic services remained poor. Questions about access to or reliability of water service in the squatted sectors formed part of a larger matrix of uncertainty with negative spillover effects. So long as their future in the apartments remained unclear—feared BO authorities—there was little incentive for residents to care for the space. "Lack of care of the apartment appears to parallel the problem of adjudication," said one report. It went on: "The majority of those who are still not tenants keep their households in poor condition." Resolving their precarious legal standing would, theoretically, provide a formal, permanent stake in the neighborhood and engender a sense of ownership and belonging. Otherwise living conditions would only deteriorate and generate even-more-acute maintenance problems—and costs—for the BO.[26]

But the larger concern lay less in squatters' living conditions than in the impact of their delinquency on the rest of the neighborhood. The same uncertainty that tended to discourage squatters from fully taking ownership of their apartments and common areas also threatened to discourage those elsewhere in the neighborhood from paying rents. "If it was already difficult for delinquent tenants to become current," warned one analysis, "the problem was now all the more serious since they were enabled by the new occupants."[27] As one resident told a survey volunteer: "I won't pay so long as the rent issue is not solved. Most people don't pay. Why should I?"[28] The BO's concerns regarding spillover effects posed by squatters exposed a deeper and more troubling dynamic playing out in the neighborhood in the wake of the coup. Rent collection was not just a financial or administrative matter. More broadly it was an attempt to reassert control following the collapse of institutional legitimacy in the aftermath of Pérez Jiménez's overthrow.

Diógenes Caballero well exemplified the challenges authorities faced trying to reassert control. "He was the leader here, he became famous," remembered César Acuña of Block 45 in Mirador. Like thousands of others on 23 January 1958, Acuña had come to find an apartment of his own after living in a rancho in nearby Catia parish. Once word about the apartments began to spread, Acuña, then 18 years old, immediately headed to the Mirador superblocks, which he had helped build as a construction worker in 1957. Once he arrived, Acuña found that Caballero "had set up a command center here . . . practically an outlaw, like a vigilante [brigada del orden]."[29] Under Pérez Jiménez, Caballero had been a broadcaster and a columnist for the El Heraldo newspaper, aligned with the dictatorship.[30] But in the waning days of Pérez Jiménez's rule, Caballero had tried unsuccessfully to register with Unión Republicana Democrática, one of the parties that in 1957 joined clandestine groups to mount civilian resistance to Pérez Jiménez.[31] Now, in the post-coup turmoil, Caballero reportedly established a "police headquarters" in Mirador with offices, secretaries, and even a jail cell "for those who disobeyed his orders." Recalled Acuña: "It's not that he was a firebrand [alzado], it's just that he had a lot of followers on account of having charisma. But the man spent a lot of time dominating [this area] during the change of government."[32]

By mid-February, in fact, press accounts had branded Caballero "the little dictator of the 23 de Enero." When a local group organized a committee to liaise with the interim government, Caballero responded by forming what he branded a "Representative Junta" in a bid to neutralize criticism about his methods by signaling broad support from area squatters. "We have information," said a member of the local committee, "that [Caballero] currently has under his orders, and spread throughout all the superblocks, more than 3,000 supporters who follow him unconditionally."[33] As his notoriety grew, authorities arrested Caballero on charges of subversion, releasing him days later for lack of evidence.[34]

But while the strange case of "the little dictator" highlighted the extent to which the BO had lost control, and legitimacy, in the neighborhood following Pérez Jiménez's ouster, it was also only one of several ways in which squatters in the 23 de Enero organized to claim a stake in the housing project. Consider the following: while Caballero established a base of operations in Blocks 47, 48, and 49, across the way in Blocks 50 and 51 squatters formed a Junta Cívica Pro-Vivienda (Citizen Group for Housing Matters), a nonelected committee, to liaise with authorities. What brought them together was, as they put it, that "we have our deposits and the irrefutable proof that we were removed from our ranchos with the promise we would be moved to the Blocks." To support their claim, neighbors had begun work on a census of fellow squatters. They had also framed their fight as "the just right to aspire to housing,"[35] navigating a tight space between advancing an aggressive demand and remaining deferential through a frank recognition "that we forced our way into those superblocks." "But," the committee continued, "since they were made for those of us who were removed from the ranchos, we could no longer tolerate living in the streets waiting for Pérez Jiménez to inaugurate them with the usual pomp he used to dazzle the people."[36]

The Junta Cívica's two-pronged strategy to secure apartments—appealing to revolutionary justice on the one hand; organizing to prove their legitimate claims on the other—challenged both Caballero's example and some of the BO's own assumptions about superblock squatters. Even while surveys found that squatters, in a climate of uncertainty, had largely failed to tend for the apartments they had seized, BO analysts also recognized that "a few, in order to secure their rights, keep them in good shape." Yet this "few" turned out to be significant: "Households surveyed found a great number of improvements in the apartments, above all paint and hardware, followed by waxed floors and door, window, and bathroom repairs. This indicates that there is already a favorable attitude toward the new housing." In early March 1958, the BO announced it would reinstate a defunct mortgage program to offer residents the opportunity to buy rather than rent apartments, both as a way to stimulate the housing industry and to "draw from [those sales] stable financial results."[37]

By late March, BO authorities began to "legalize the situation" of superblock squatters, promising there would be no evictions unless tenants showed "that they are people of bad lifestyles and troublemakers who perturb the tranquility and morals of other families."[38] While it would be over a decade before some squatters finally began to pay for their apartments, by late 1958 residents like Emilia de Pérez in Block 30 had begun to sign contracts to buy their apartments outright.

The BO's conflicting assessments of squatters revealed a complex portrait of those who had arrived in the superblocks in January 1958. Caballero and the Junta Cívica reflected two very different approaches by the neighborhood's new population on how best to organize to seek stability. They also pointed to struggles between local groups as each claimed legitimate representation of parts of the housing project. Where "charisma" and intimidation had marked Caballero's efforts to assert control in Mirador, in the case of the Junta Cívica a more collaborative spirit based on claims to rightful housing had prevailed. Yet despite differences and rifts, what residents shared was an enterprising spirit that had brought them to the neighborhood in the first place, despite and in some cases because of the risks that characterized this moment of political and social uncertainty. And in a context of uncertainty, they drew collective strength from the political circumstances that imbued the high-rises with a special meaning. These were new people, inventing themselves in a new urban space, and at the same time inventing that space anew.

PUSHING THEIR ADVANTAGE: SETTLING SCORES IN THE EAST

After the 23 January 1958 coup, squatters and the BO had maneuvered to assert themselves in the newly reconfigured legal and administrative terrain of the 23 de Enero. Doing so had exposed just how fertile a space the transition proved for those able to organize to claim some say in the emerging social and political—and physical—landscape. But for those who had been forcibly relocated to the former 2 de Diciembre, the new landscape provided a different set of opportunities and challenges. Long gestating grievances formerly impossible to articulate under Pérez Jiménez could now take center stage, exposing a side of life in the superblocks that contrasted with the fallen regime's propaganda. Claims of unrealistic rent contracts signed hastily and under pressure, of socially oppressive living conditions aimed at marginalizing or altogether eliminating popular expression—these were just some of the complaints raised by area renters after the coup. But they were more than complaints. They also laid bare the expectations of residents for the future of the neighborhood, for a relationship with authorities that would be fairer, more accountable, and more responsive to their needs than they had experienced previously. Like squatters, these residents were ready to seize the opportunities of transition to mobilize in pursuit of their own just claims.

Above all, existing residents organized around the issue of rents. While squatters in the western sectors had formed committees to seek assurances that they would be able to remain in the apartments they had seized, in the eastern sectors of Monte Piedad, La Cañada, and Zona Central, residents formed their own committees in early February to "coordinate and concentrate as one united front the work of the various civic movements that operate in the parish, and find out and lend dedicated support to the social and educational aspirations that residents of the parish confront and demand, especially those of the 23 de Enero neighborhood."[39] While claiming to represent the interests of the neighborhood as a whole, in fact their aims were more specifically tailored to renters rather than squatters, and drew more widely than just from the 23 de Enero. Three weeks after the coup, tenants from the 23 de Enero and from the Simón Rodríguez housing project—the latter built by the Pérez Jiménez regime as a high-rise solution for urban middle classes—organized a joint delegation of their peers "to undertake the necessary measures" with BO authorities to achieve a fifty-percent rent reduction. "All tenants have the best intention to pay the amounts they have pending," stressed Delcis de Bosca. "They just want the BO to grant them a discount" by taking into consideration their ability to pay and improvements residents had made to their apartments.[40]

The call to consider improvements residents had undertaken—finishing and painting walls, adding windows, fixtures, and plumbing—in reevaluating rent contracts represented more than an economic claim. It was also evidence, indirect but powerful, that residents had already circumvented controls by BO supervisors during Pérez Jiménez's rule and altered their apartments to make them more livable, an implicit critique of the buildings and their rigid, idealized environments. But the call to slash rents by fifty percent was primarily a financial one. According to Bosca, the BO had already agreed to such a reduction prior to the coup, which residents claimed was proof that rent contracts had been established "capriciously."[41] In fact, in assessing the reasons behind delinquency among pre-1958 tenants, a later BO report echoed as much, finding no "indication of a well-defined policy regarding the first tenants, before the events of January 1958."[42] Instead, personal connections between BO personnel and prospective tenants, not technical or financial criteria, had determined how much residents would pay. To be sure, the new authorities had an interest in undermining the fallen regime's technocratic self-image. Testimonies did not suggest that patronage had played a role in assigning apartments, though certainly in a housing project as massive as the super-blocks, petty graft, incompetence, or error could corrupt bureaucratic proce-dures. While it may have seemed haphazard in retrospect, BO policy was precisely to remove rancho dwellers, and any others who stood in the way of Pérez Jiménez's bulldozers, by establishing minimum rather than rigorous relocation criteria. But the larger point remained: problems had plagued the selection and adjudication of apartments—problems now exposed by a popu-lation organized to seek redress.

The BO's response demonstrated just how thinly stretched authorities had become in attending to the multiple pressures besetting their properties. Rather than seeking palliative measures as it did with the population of squatters in March, the BO launched a study of the rents in order to seek a long-term solu-tion.[43] In late April, in a bid to stem collective identity and organizing among superblock tenants, residents in the Simón Rodríguez superblocks won a ten-percent cut in their rents.[44] The move fed hopes among some in the 23 de Enero that they too might enjoy rent reductions. But the BO's decision owed more to the fact that the largely middle-class composition of the Simón Rodríguez population meant that it could more quickly and easily be brought back into the fold of rent collection by way of a smaller reduction than the one demanded by 23 de Enero residents. For them, the struggle over rents would continue. By late May, residents of Monte Piedad, La Cañada, and Zona Central continued to wait for an official response to their rent-reduction demands.

Waiting for answers, the residents pursued a two-pronged strategy. On one hand they drew broad popular support; on the other they drew upon a dis-course of revolutionary agency to legitimize their claims. On 31 March, repre-sentatives from BO housing projects nationwide—an estimated 500,000 people—established the Confederación de Juntas Pro-Mejoras (Confederation of Citizen Groups for Housing Improvements), provisionally headquartered in Block 29 of the Zona Central of the 23 de Enero. In their initial statement to the press and to the BO, the Confederación demanded, in addition to rent reductions, "a reconsideration of the capriciously imposed values of the homes that the BO expropriated or destroyed; forgiveness of the debt we have con-tracted with the BO administration due to rent-payment delays; that the apartments we currently occupy be sold as condominiums; and the removal of reactionary personnel that still works in that institute [the Banco Obrero]." In part the expanded range of demands reflected the breadth of the coalition that tenants of the 23 de Enero had been able to form. But it also registered the long-festering frustrations of those relocated during the height of the bulldozer years. Demanding representation on any commission set up to study tenants' problems well illustrated how prominently participation and inclusion featured in the expectations tenants had about their relationship with the BO going forward.[45] Strength in numbers and the publicity it helped muster also brought tenants the support of otherwise unlikely bedfellows, as Catholic priests and the Communist daily *Tribuna Popular* lent their voices and pages to the plight of the 23 de Enero residents.[46]

In building coalitions, residents of the 23 de Enero emphasized their par-ticular place in the post-dictatorial landscape as a way of turning their emerg-ing image as heroes of the democratic revolution into strategic gain. For instance, a delegation claiming to represent 2,000 heads of households in the neighborhood's eastern sectors petitioned to meet with BO officials to nego-tiate a more gradual rather than wholesale rent-reduction plan, one that matched tenants' ability to pay with their monthly rates.[47] In May, they once again asked to meet with the BO director. They directly appealed to the memory of the January revolution, asking for "exoneration of rents from 23 January to 31 May in honor of the people who fought for liberty."[48] The bid worked. On 30 May 1958, BO director Raúl Hernández Silva traveled to the 23 de Enero, where a crowd of 2,000 residents assembled to lay out their griev-ances, chief among them rent reductions.

However, residents also placed special emphasis on schools for their chil-dren (fig. 10). Roughly 49% of the neighborhood's population—some 30,000 people—were under fifteen years old. In the western, squatted, areas of the neighborhood, primary schools had yet to open, forcing children and youths to attend now-crowded facilities elsewhere in the 23 de Enero. Meanwhile the neighborhood's sole high school was not slated to open until 1959.[49] More broadly, residents wanted "inspections of water piping, the creation of schools, and the reorganization of trash-collection services," thus highlighting infra-structure problems and needs resulting from the sudden ballooning of the neighborhood's population.

FIGURE 10. In June 1958, children plant a tree near Escuela Luis Enrique Mármol, in the La Cañada area of the 23 de Enero. In the background is Block 5 of Monte Piedad. Also visible are newly built ranchos in what would become Barrio Sucre. (Archivo Audiovisual de la Nación)

A week later, Hernández Silva announced a resounding victory for residents: the BO had agreed to reduce rents for residents unable to pay, to freeze evictions on account of rent default, and to allow partial payment without penalty.[50] It would also begin work clearing and widening drainage pipes in La Cañada to prevent flooding; to prevent mudslides, it would reinforce retaining walls in the surrounding hillsides.[51] Both measures also offered an indirect benefit to authorities, since they revealed engineering errors in the neighborhood's design now corrected by the revolutionary government.

Residents' success owed only in part to their clever use of the January revolution. More importantly, it resulted from a temporary collaboration among far-ranging organizations in the neighborhood, which the BO had unwittingly helped foment. By announcing as it did in March that squatters in the western sectors of the 23 de Enero would not face eviction, and by starting as it did in April the process of securing rent contracts, the BO had in essence begun to transform these residents into tenants. In doing so, the BO linked the surging movement for lower rents with this new crop of now increasingly formal tenants, who would go on to draw from the organizing strategies tenants had used to good effect in order to seek solutions to a similar problem of high rents. In signing contracts with squatters, the BO had established a price range from Bs. 133 to 207 (US$40 to $60) depending on residents' income levels, in turn ascertained through the efforts of university students who had surveyed these families months earlier. Yet the rates remained out of reach for many, including some whose monthly incomes were as low as Bs. 100 (US$30).[52]

In response, and borrowing a page from tenants' own efforts to seek rent reductions, in July 1958 former squatters in the western sectors of the 23 de Enero joined efforts and formed a single *Comité Único* or "Unitary Committee" that included sixteen Juntas Pro-Mejoras in order to negotiate with the BO.[53] By August 1958, with the BO appearing to delay on the rent reductions it had promised, the Comité "urgently convoked" Juntas from "all BO neighborhoods in the Federal District" for a summit, to be held in the 23 de Enero, in order to demand compliance,[54] eventually securing further assurances that they would remain in the apartments under favorable contract terms.

Collaboration among BO tenants, whether former squatters or long-standing residents, marked an unprecedented organizing effort that cut across class and geographic differences to reveal instead a supracollective identity based on their common experience as superblock residents. At the same time, it underscored the emerging centrality of the 23 de Enero as a nodal site for articulating and organizing popular demands, based both on the neighborhood's concentration of BO residents and, no less important, on the symbolic link between the neighborhood and the January revolution. This sense of collective identity based on place, both physical and symbolic, signaled an important innovation in the way residents organized and mobilized to secure demands, in the process shaping patterns that would repeat themselves in the decades to come. In those early struggles for rent reductions lay another indication, incipient but powerful, of the ways urban popular sectors would understand their relationship with state authorities, and their opportunities for expression: while they would seek first to organize through formal means such as citizen groups or by cultivating allies in the press, if those proved insufficient they would mobilize in the streets in pursuit of their just demands.

OCCUPYING THE LAND: THE REEMERGENCE OF RANCHOS

While apartment squatters were coming into their own as superblock residents, reflecting needs and, over time, sensibilities akin to those living in the older, eastern sectors of the 23 de Enero, incorporating another group of new residents into the fold of the neighborhood would prove more challenging. After the thousands who flocked to the superblocks on hearing of Pérez Jiménez's ouster laid claim to all vacant units in the area, between 20,000 and 25,000 more people undertook another kind of squatting in the neighborhood. Press reports one week after the January 1958 revolution noted with alarm how "ranchos are being built in green spaces," the same spaces that the just-ousted regime had designed to offer walking and recreation solutions for superblock residents.[55] As with the occupation of vacant units days earlier, confusion and improvisation marked the construction of new ranchos in the 23 de Enero, taking place in stages during 1958 and further adding to the neighborhood's increasingly complex social ecology.

The first ranchos belonged to those unable to find an apartment in the days immediately following the 23 January 1958 revolution. Frequently, those living in these ranchos were relatives of people who had found apartments; by settling next to the superblocks, they reasoned, their chances of eventually securing apartments would improve. They imagined that these constructions would be temporary and built them accordingly, consisting of little more than scrap wood and cardboard.[56] By mid-year, however, the dynamic changed. As the BO delayed on reconciling the issue of high rents for both squatters and longtime superblock residents, ranchos began to emerge less as temporary solutions and more as semipermanent housing. Angelina Ruiz, a single mother of three who had occupied a vacant unit in Block 45 (Mirador) after Pérez Jiménez fell, found it impossible to handle the monthly rent the BO eventually required to formalize her living status, even at the lowest rate of Bs. 113 (US$34). In June 1958, she took to the hills behind the same superblock she had lived in since 23 January, where over 500 ranchos built from zinc, stone, and plywood had gone up in a matter of days.

Even longtime tenants of the superblocks found themselves leaving their apartments and taking to ranchos in the green areas in between. Carmen Manzanilla, for instance, who lived in Block 23 of the Zona Central before 1958, reported to the press how though she "lived better" in her apartment, "with what my husband earns it is very difficult to care for ten children, clothe them, send them to school, feed them, and pay Bs. 173 [US$52] to rent an apartment. My husband's salary is Bs. 500 [US$150]." The rent alone would have swallowed more than a third of their monthly income. Like Ruiz, Manzanilla and her family built a rancho in Mirador, joining thousands of others in the creation of a new rancho community. At times these new constructions used the foundations of the same houses the Pérez Jiménez regime had razed to make way for both superblocks and green spaces, adding to the sense of permanence and, increasingly, irony, of new rancho communities in the 23 de Enero.[57]

The irony of improvised housing resurrected in areas once seen as the front line in a "battle against ranchos" was lost on no one, least of all those whom Pérez Jiménez had forcibly moved to make way for the superblocks. "That was the saddest thing," recalled Ligia Ovalles of Block 31 half a century later. "They moved us supposedly to build green spaces, but it turns out that now there are houses and buildings and everything. . . . Now, there's a building in the same place where our house stood. No green spaces at all." Ovalles's case was somewhat unique. Her family had lived in Catia parish for nearly three years before the BO designated her home for demolition. "My mother," she recalls, "was one of the ones who cried and cursed" as bulldozers razed the house they had spent years building.[58] Yet Ovalles's lingering frustration at ranchos in the 23 de Enero shed light on widespread tension between superblock residents, especially those who had lived in the area since Pérez Jiménez, and rancho dwellers.

Consider the case of Barrio Sucre (fig. 11). In the space between Monte Piedad and La Cañada, Barrio Sucre emerged as a community of squatters in the months after the January 1958 revolution, slowly consolidating in the ensuing decade. Overlooking Barrio Sucre in Block 1 of Monte Piedad, Mireya Maldonado recalled how, on first seeing ranchos, residents organized to prevent further construction because "they were a . . . bad reflection [on the neighborhood]. . . . We would go confront them, go out there or look out our windows and tell them they couldn't do that, how could they think they were going to put up a shantytown [rancherío] there, that that's going to be a den of thieves."[59] On the other side of Barrio Sucre, in La Cañada, Eloy Deslances of Block 17 recalls how "there was a time when we were at war, there were confrontations. We wouldn't accept that they come here, to do as they pleased. So we'd put a stop to them. They would come, to use our [athletic] courts, but that's it."[60] At root lay a very distinct sense of superiority, as Gustavo Parabón of Block 3 in Monte Piedad admitted: "We went about stigmatizing them, how they used to be, starting out with very humble homes, so we would label them rancheros. . . . One always had in mind that we lived better because we were in big apartments, we had our roads, our public services, not like them. They had to draw water from a public well."[61]

In part, strained local attitudes toward the new ranchos and their inhabitants were the product of pressures they wrought upon the neighborhood's infrastructure and services. Already area tenants had reported how streets

FIGURE 11. Before-and-after images of Barrio Sucre (above, 1960; below, 2014), seen from the Block 7 rotary in Monte Piedad. (Top photo: Archivo Audiovisual de la Nación; bottom photo by the author)

and even some ground-floor apartments were prone to flooding during heavy downpours. The problem owed in part to poor drainage of the hills that bordered superblocks in sectors like La Cañada, Zona Central, and Zona F, which BO officials planned to remedy by "reforesting" the affected areas.[62] But these were precisely the areas where those who did not find empty apartments raised their ranchos, further contributing to an already problematic erosion that had helped to exacerbate drainage problems for superblock residents.[63]

Beyond helping to change the physical landscape, squatters left out of the rush for apartments also had an impact on services for the neighborhood as a whole. For instance, after all apartments were occupied, squatters turned both to the surrounding areas and also to vacant commercial spaces not only in the western part of the 23 de Enero but also in the central and eastern sectors of the neighborhood. As late as 1960, BO officials reported that many "still do not operate,"[64] forcing residents to call on authorities to allow an open market to satisfy their needs.[65]

But neighborhood schools bore the brunt of the impact. As with superblocks and commercial spaces, squatters in the western sectors of the 23 de Enero also occupied area schools in the days following Pérez Jiménez's ouster.[66] With the exception of daycare facilities, most schools would open by mid-1959 as the BO successfully relocated squatters. But the new influx of residents pushed the area's school-age youth to numbers—twenty-five thousand by some estimates—that well exceeded the neighborhood's original projections. In response, the BO began construction on three new elementary schools in the 23 de Enero by June 1958, helping assuage educational pressures for students but also unwittingly fostering labor problems as fiscal pressures delayed payment to the newly expanded workforce of educators.[67] Even with the new facilities at the primary level, at the secondary level the 23 de Enero still only housed one high school for the entire population. In the years to come, that one high school brought together students from throughout the neighborhood. It would go on to have a significant impact in the evolution of collective identity and political activism among area youths. More immediately, however, the school helped contribute to the sense by superblock residents that squatters who exceeded the projected number of tenants for the neighborhood were exerting undue pressures on the community.[68]

Beyond pressures upon infrastructure and services, the derision directed at ranchos and their residents by superblock tenants revealed more than a spatial divide in the 23 de Enero. It also reflected a lasting legacy of the Pérez

Jiménez regime, and the way its "battle against the rancho" had buried itself deep in the collective subconscious. Much as the resurgence of ranchos in the 23 de Enero complicated the idea of victory over informal, improvised housing in Caracas (which superblocks presumably represented), prejudicial comments by those who as little as one year earlier had lived in ranchos themselves complicated the notion of a complete defeat. For all the complaints about how relocation took place, at one level residents came to internalize the regime's discourse. Now, as new ranchos rose in their midst, the challenges they had faced in their own former ranchos came into sharp focus. Where many lamented the loss of backyards, lack of restrictions, and other elements of rancho life, few had forgotten the slog of carting water, the stench of open sewers, and the mess of unpaved streets, among other travails. Statements about how ranchos would reflect poorly upon the neighborhood indicated a discursive embrace of the superblocks, and of the broader community. It was the reemergence of ranchos, in other words, that most effectively helped cement a collective identity among tenants of the superblocks.

Still, by reminding superblock residents of their own origins, the new ranchos in the 23 de Enero also helped them to recognize that they were not so very different. Over time, initial animosity eventually gave way to practicality. In Monte Piedad, Mireya Maldonado remembered, the initial conflicts between rancho and superblock residents "didn't last long because once they were all settled, what more could you do?"[69] Asked if her neighbors organized against rancho dwellers, Ramona Velasco in the four-story Block 15 in Monte Piedad echoed Maldonado's sense of resignation. "No. That was that. What could one do?"[70]

Meanwhile, in the squatter communities surfacing throughout the neighborhood, few held any illusions about the disdain residents of the superblocks, especially those in the eastern sectors of the neighborhood, sent their way. Inés Álvarez was only six when her mother, single and with three children, moved from the western state of Trujillo to Caracas. They settled in a squatter community of ranchos near Block 7 in Monte Piedad. "Ever since we arrived," she remembers, "the [people] of the superblocks have never accepted us. They kind of cast us to the side. [They say] 'Those are the hillsiders [cerreros].'" Echoing Eloy Deslances's testimony, Álvarez makes special mention of the strict territorial fault lines that emerged between the two spaces, signaling a split not just spatial but also cultural. "They used to say, 'All this space belongs to us.' . . . There were many disagreements; they didn't want us to have chickens or banana trees because they just didn't like that." The effect on social relations was predictable. "I only had one friend who lived in the superblocks," remembers Álvarez. "We went to school together, to parties. But that was my only friendship."[71] Meanwhile, Deslances paints a similar picture of the situation as seen from the superblocks. "There were very few people who hooked up with them."[72]

If ranchos created tensions among residents of the 23 de Enero, they would generate even greater problems for the BO. While interim authorities had in part conceded the issue of rents for superblock residents, lowering some by as much as 50% in response to popular pressure, in the case of the ranchos they made no such concessions, instead taking a hard line that evoked the days of the just-deposed Pérez Jiménez. In early March 1958 the Ministry of Defense, the Ministry of the Interior, and the Caracas city government convened a joint task force to "study the grave problem created by the construction of new ranchos in the Federal District." Aside from revealing the issue's importance to authorities, the committee's composition—drawing from institutions responsible for the military, police, and city legislature, respectively—also prefigured the kind of response that would mark its approach to ranchos. The first set of "immediate measures against the construction of new ranchos" aimed at prevention, in the short term by deploying "intense police vigilance," and in the long term through a "propaganda and education campaign" aimed at warning of the risks to health and hygiene brought about by living in improvised housing.[73]

But the committee's primary focus was the "destruction of ranchos." On 5 March six contingents of Army and police headquarters personnel began to raze ranchos in six western Caracas neighborhoods, including the 23 de Enero. Captain Pedro Chalbaud Troconis, chief of staff of the police, revealed the institutional interplay between local executive power and the state's repressive apparatus that would lend the operation both a legal and final character: "In accordance with a public announcement published by the Governor of the Federal District, that office will not recognize the claims of ranchos because they were built without permission."[74]

By late March the issue took on added urgency as the national junta convened an emergency meeting of the cabinet and select state governors and city mayors to identify "more efficient actions and . . . impart categorical instructions to completely paralyze the construction of new ranchos." These would include "severe military vigilance" such as "identification checks" of all people entering Caracas in "an effort to contain flow toward the capital."[75] Once again, however, the hallmark of the "special provisions" was rancho eradication. In early April, addressing reporters on their progress, the Director of the National Guard Academy emphasized the protocols National Guardsmen were to use when conducting their mission:

> On arriving at the rancho the patrol captain will ask permission to enter and notify [its occupants] that he will proceed to raze the rancho. He will tell the owner of the rancho to collect his money in order to avoid any subsequent claims; [he will] at all times avoid the destruction of furniture or appliances inside the rancho; if anyone is sick [he will] transport them to wherever family members who live in the rancho indicate . . . ; should the patrol have to detain anyone, they will be handed over to the nearest civilian authority; the patrol will avoid violations or abuses of authority, but they must be firm.[76]

On one hand, publicly detailing procedures around razing ranchos marked a crucial component in the government's long term "education" campaign, serving as a deterrent for would-be rural migrants. In fact the Director was happy to report that in most cases "the people who inhabited the [razed] rancho have come to their senses and have returned to where they used to live." On the other hand, publishing the protocols of rancho eradication offered a transparency that stood in dramatic contrast to the days of Pérez Jiménez. Publishing protocols revealed a defensive posture on the part of the National Guard, an unstated admission of the abuses that had characterized eradication policy in the previous regime. Now, interim authorities tried at the same time to discredit the violence that had marked their previous approach to rancho eradication, and to uphold the language of razing ranchos.

It was a difficult balance to maintain, especially as more and more stories surfaced about the ousted regime's arbitrary use of force to push through its urban housing agenda. For instance, just as the first round of razing was giving way to more "radical"[77] measures in late March, the daily El Nacional published the testimony of Feliciano Carvallo, a popular artist who would go on to win the National Painting Award in 1966. In February 1957, while Carvallo was away, a BO delegation slated his house for demolition to make way for "one of the Blocks of the 'National Ideal,'" alerting Carvallo to move in two days' time. However, "innocent as his paintings, [Carvallo] did not believe such a criminal process was possible," so he made no preparations, and when the time expired, his rancho went up in flames along with 20 works of art. It was, read the article, evidence of "the barbarism of the dictatorship," violent, arbitrary, and evidently different from the far more humane and transparent protocols of democratic revolution in pursuing very similar aims.[78]

Over the next few months, the language of the dictatorship—targeting hygiene, morality, and ultimately, national self-image—resurfaced in press accounts lamenting the "grave national problem" that ranchos posed: "Everyone knows," wrote one editorialist, "that the type of housing designated as rancho is a sign of an absolutely primitive stage . . . where the family lives in promiscuity, [favoring] the destruction of the moral fabric."[79] And while in practice, too, the interim government's approach to ranchos attempted to follow in Pérez Jiménez's footsteps at the service of a "national campaign against the construction of unsanitary ranchos,"[80] figures told of a much different story. In mid-April an executive committee appointed to study the problem of ranchos in post-coup Venezuela issued its first set of reports, focusing on relocation prospects for 1,800 families living in ranchos in Caracas.[81] But data from the BO produced only a week later revealed that the capital housed upwards of 40,000 ranchos, suggesting an enormous gap between eradication efforts and discourse.[82] What these numbers revealed was that though it may have wanted to follow in Pérez Jiménez's footsteps, interim authorities were in no position to undertake the kind of campaign that had marked the former regime's approach to rancho eradication, hamstrung less by claims about democratic aspirations than by the realities of a state in disarray. Instead, the transitional government turned its attention to completing the final phase of the housing project formerly known as the 2 de Diciembre.

On 3 March the BO announced that it would build six additional superblocks in the 23 de Enero, totaling 900 apartments.[83] While the new buildings formed part of the neighborhood's original design, it remained unclear whether the new government would proceed with what, after all, had been the ousted regime's signature project. But the pressures squatters exerted upon the neighborhood, both in terms of ranchos and in occupied schools and commercial areas, left little room to maneuver and required an immediate response—one that, as under Pérez Jiménez, the superblocks represented. The move therefore spoke to those who had tentatively settled in the 23 de Enero hoping precisely for the opportunity to eventually take up residence in apartments.

After a public bidding process aimed at contrasting the new government's transparency with the opacity of the ousted regime,[84] construction on the new superblocks began the second week of April 1958.[85] By October, the first families began to move in, with priority going not to those who had set up ranchos, but rather those who had squatted in auxiliary spaces of the neighborhood, ensuring that even after all the new apartments had been assigned, ranchos would remain.

DEMOCRACY'S PROJECTS ◆ 77

In fact, according to BO estimates, by 1959 over 15,000 people remained in ranchos in the 23 de Enero, and with no plans for additional construction of superblocks on the horizon, their numbers would not just remain steady, but grow over time.

By any measure, the government's end to the superblock project even as ranchos continued to pepper the landscape was an admission of defeat. The saga of the ranchos had exposed a government incapable of delivering on its threats of eradication despite a public posture of maintaining policies initiated under the ousted regime. In short, despite sharing the language of Pérez Jiménez, despite efforts at razing informal settlements, despite building more superblocks, ranchos had won the war, and they would continue to shape the landscape of the 23 de Enero, and of Caracas. Ultimately what was revealed was a dynamic far different from the one that had marked life under Pérez Jiménez: now, who was in control very much remained unclear. And in this space, popular sectors would also have a say, and prove successful. Much like squatters and renters, those who settled in ranchos could also point to this time of transition as one in which they claimed significant popular victories over a state in transition. That same weakness invited reactionary challenges, threatening the opportunities for popular mobilization ushered in by the transition. To maintain these spaces they would need to draw on their shared identity as new urbanites—whether in superblocks or in ranchos—to defend and bolster the promise of democracy.

DEFENDING DEMOCRACY'S PROMISE: STREET PROTEST AND RICHARD NIXON

On 17 June 1958 mass demonstrations broke out in front of the Presidential Palace over the dismissal of Dr. Celso Fortoul as Municipal Engineer. In the previous four months, more and more ranchos had gone up as a result of what some in the press took to calling a "rural exodus" to Caracas following the January revolution.[86] In part, rural migrants came to Caracas because of the *Plan de Obras Extraordinarias*, popularly known as the *Plan de Emergencia* (Emergency Plan), unveiled in March and aimed at responding to the capital city's nearly 60,000 unemployed, among them many who worked in construction or related industries now paralyzed as Pérez Jiménez's once-massive building boom in Caracas drew to a standstill.[87]

As the city's chief urban planner, Fortoul had relied on the Emergency Plan to hire thousands and jumpstart an ambitious construction and reconstruction agenda centered largely in barrios and squatter communities that emerged after

Pérez Jiménez's ouster. Both measures—mass hiring and direct assistance—helped endear Fortoul to urban popular sectors. But for critics, the Emergency Plan reeked of waste and corruption; worse, it encouraged rural migration to the city, exacerbating pressures upon an already strained urban environment.[88] On the morning of Monday, 16 June 1958, Caracas Governor Colonel Vicente Marchelli notified Fortoul that "given the circumstances," he had been replaced, though according to Fortoul those "circumstances" remained unspecified.[89] Later that evening, a government spokesperson reported that Fortoul's dismissal was due to "a minor reorganization" of the city's administrative apparatus.[90]

For those who found work through Fortoul's efforts, losing someone they saw as an ally in government seemed a first step toward the elimination of the Emergency Plan. As news of Fortoul's dismissal spread during the evening, Juntas Pro-Mejoras from throughout Caracas, including the 23 de Enero, began to assemble a response. By 2 P.M. on Tuesday, thousands had gathered in the Plaza Bolívar in front of city hall to demand Fortoul's reinstatement, considering his "dismissal an assault against popular interests and democracy and against the Emergency Plan."[91] When Governor Marchelli asked for 72 hours to "study the case," the multitude proceeded to the nearby Presidential Palace, where members of the Junta de Gobierno promised a delegation of protesters that the Cabinet would immediately take up the matter. Yet protesters refused to budge, prompting the national Junta's President, Wolfgang Larrazábal, to meet personally with representatives. An hour later, Larrazábal had agreed to their demands, promising not only to reinstate Fortoul, but also to replace Marchelli, who resigned that very evening.[92] Wrote the Communist Party daily *Tribuna Popular*: "The popular joy was unbridled after this great victory of the masses, which once again proved that the spirit of January 23 continues to burn and is ever watchful . . . of the enemies of democracy."[93]

In the immediate aftermath of the demonstrations, urban popular sectors moved to give their successful but episodic mobilization organizational form. On Monday 23 June, one week after Fortoul's dismissal, over 200 representatives from neighborhood groups in Caracas assembled to assess the reach of their street actions, and to discuss next steps. Carlos Martínez, president of the recently formed Comité Único of the 23 de Enero, an umbrella group of sixteen citizen groups representing the neighborhood's western sectors, gained unanimous support from the assembly when he stated that the time had come "to create an organization that channels the work of the numerous organizations in the city, and that protects its militants from the attacks of reactionary elements that are still plugged into the government and try to torpedo the just mobilization of the barrios of Caracas." After designating a Steering Committee to determine what shape such a group would take, the assembly issued a statement echoing Martínez's plea: "The time has come to structure a powerful organization capable of centralizing the great popular movement that rose up after January 23."[94] Three weeks later, the 255 delegates to a citywide assembly of barrio organizations voted formally to create a confederation of Juntas Pro-Mejoras, electing a twenty-member directorate, and resolving to "dedicate ourselves to study and solve the most urgent popular problems."[95]

Fortoul's sudden dismissal and reinstatement under popular pressure, and the subsequent organization among popular sectors, brought into sharp focus several features of the Caracas social landscape brewing since Pérez Jiménez's ouster. For one, it highlighted urban popular sectors' ability to respond collectively to real or perceived threats to what they understood as rightfully theirs in a context of democratic revolution. Moreover, this collective response cut across social and geographic lines. While Fortoul drew on the Emergency Plan primarily to address the needs of barrio and rancho residents, a wide range of groups—including superblock residents—mobilized to reject Fortoul's dismissal. This convergence revealed that their concerns extended beyond the immediate goal of reinstatement. More broadly, they aimed to safeguard and deepen their claims to shape the unfolding social and political system. Further, that they quickly took to the streets also helped expose a particular pattern of mobilization characterizing popular sectors in this period. No passive observers, they fully inhabited the image of a people ready to participate, to have a say, and to be answered to, so widely promoted in press and political accounts of 23 January 1958. While they had organized as citizen groups in order to claim a mantle of formal legitimacy vis-à-vis interim authorities and the press, they had also repeatedly used street protest when formal appeals stalled, in order to press their advantage. This dual strategy prefigured patterns that would inform popular politics in the years ahead.

To be sure, institutional weakness both required and enabled popular assertions of power. The government's response to this new mobilizing and organizing fervor by urban popular sectors appeared to reflect a significant change of attitude and approach, informed less by choice and more by the reality of a state in transition, limited by the democracy it now claimed to uphold from reverting to the authoritarianism that had characterized the former regime. Not only did authorities bend to popular sentiment on the streets, but the demonstrations also prompted an immediate popular outreach effort by the ruling junta, which two days later staged a visit to one of the nearby barrios from which Tuesday's demonstrations had originated.[96]

In part, the move revealed a sense by government officials that they were fast growing out of touch with the same urban popular sectors they had upheld as shining examples of the struggle for democracy less than five months before. But there was also a sense that, if left unattended, the gulf between state and urban populace could end in violence, as in fact had happened in mid-May during a short-lived, ill-fated visit to Caracas by U.S. Vice President Richard Nixon. It was the final leg of a goodwill tour of Latin America that had included Colombia, Perú, and Uruguay, with angry crowds converging on Nixon and his wife at each stop. In Venezuela, all along Nixon's twenty-mile route from the airport to the capital, "mobs constantly accused the United States of supporting dictators."[97] Nixon later wrote: "Out of the alleys and the side streets poured a screaming mob of two to three hundred, throwing rocks, brandishing sticks and pieces of steel pipe. . . . Those who had no weapons used their feet and bare fists to beat upon the car."[98] Eventually taking refuge at the U.S. Ambassador's residence, Nixon was greeted by members of the ruling junta, who staged dramatic apologies for the incidents.[99] Come morning, officials deployed "military units, tanks and armored cars . . . stationed at strategic points around the city" to protect Nixon's delegation on its ride back to the airport.[100] By noon on Wednesday 14 May, Nixon departed Venezuela without incident.

The events surrounding Nixon's visit left the interim government dangerously exposed. Institutionally, it had proven itself unable to undertake basic public-safety duties. State Department personnel noted how "the Caracas police force was completely dispersed by the [23 January] Revolution. . . . [I]t did not have a well organized, well trained body of police to deal with the mob."[101] Venezuelan officials shared this assessment, noting how "the inability of the police to safeguard [Nixon's] party was due to the fact that the police force had recently been reorganized, and was composed of teenagers and other untrained and inexperienced persons who were reluctant to take strong action."[102] More broadly, though, the protests and the government's response laid bare a growing gulf between political elites and urban popular sectors. Consular officials in Washington strained to prove "that the demonstrations in no way reflected the sentiments of the Venezuelan people, but of only a small minority."[103]

Yet marginalizing popular discontent was a risky strategy, especially when it was centered in a neighborhood otherwise cast as heroic within a narrative of revolutionary change. The most intense demonstrations against Nixon took place on Avenida Sucre, just below the 23 de Enero. It was there that the tanks and soldiers deployed to safeguard Nixon's departure were positioned.[104] By nightfall, too, police had arrested Diógenes Caballero at his apartment in Mirador, charging him with planning the demonstrations in a bid to kidnap the Vice President and eventually reinstate Marcos Pérez Jiménez. Though released a week later, with no evidence linking him to an alleged transnational conspiracy,[105] Caballero's arrest and the protests that gave rise to it cemented the 23 de Enero's place as a hotbed of popular mobilization, where direct action coexisted with other forms of organization such as rent-reduction committees. The Nixon affair illustrated a tension between popular revolutionary heroism and an emerging reality of independent collective action residing at the margins of the interim authorities' aims, however incipient these remained.

Against this backdrop, on 23 June 1958 Héctor Santaella, who had served as ambassador to the United States during Nixon's visit and subsequently returned to Caracas as Secretary of the ruling junta, offered an insider's account of the Fortoul demonstrations to U.S. Embassy officials. "All that afternoon," Santaella noted, "when [the junta] was attempting to decide what to do," officials lay in fear that "something like the *Bogotazo* of 1948 might develop." In fact Santaella had long been surprised that "despite the high emotional aftermath of the revolution," no significant violence had ensued. "If the government had not retreated from its position," Santaella reflected, "it would have been necessary first to use tear gas, then perhaps machetes and then as a last resort, sub-machine guns. If five or six people had been killed, a real riot would undoubtedly have developed with a most serious problem for the Government and for the country. It was in view of all these considerations that the decision was finally taken to restore Fortoul to his job."[106]

On one level Santaella's account further highlighted the state's continuing fragility, a month after Nixon's visit, when confronted with mass popular mobilization. Faced with the potential of violent instability, officials instead acquiesced to popular pressure. But on another level, in linking the Fortoul protests to the *Bogotazo*, Santaella also dismissed the efforts at popular organization that had begun to surface in the months since Pérez Jiménez's ouster, instead viewing popular collective action through the lens of visceral, spontaneous, and riotous critiques of official legitimacy among urban "mobs," the kind that had scarred neighboring Colombia ten years earlier.[107] Once again, what was exposed was a lingering and growing gap between urban popular sectors and interim authorities.

If by responding to popular demands—whether out of fear or political calculus—the junta had helped close the gap with urban popular sectors, it had also strained relations with other sectors. On 21 July Minister of Defense Jesús María Castro León issued an ultimatum to the ruling junta as prelude to a planned coup he hoped would expel left-wing sectors from the ranks of government.[108] Addressing the recent Fortoul protests, the ultimatum read: "The Junta's conduct and its errant decisions in resolving the case of Col. Marchelli in his post as Governor of the Federal District has erased the inherent authority of the Executive . . . so that the pressure of a group of workers dependent on the government enervates in an embarrassing way the legal attributions of the Executive Power."[109]

Response to Castro León's attempted coup followed in the mold established a month earlier around Fortoul's dismissal. At first only rumors circulated, since according to subsequent press reports, "the government remained absolutely muted." Yet despite and perhaps because of the silence, wrote the Communist Party newspaper *Tribuna Popular* days later, "the capital flocked violently, organized, and resolved to prevent" the coup. Organization had come in the form of coordination between Juntas Pro-Mejoras and political party sectionals throughout the city.[110] That same afternoon, crowds assembled in front of Miraflores to "defend their democracy." Meanwhile in Block 6 of Monte Piedad, the building's newly established Junta Pro-Mejoras announced to the press their "unbreakable purpose to decidedly support the Junta de Gobierno" and to "defend the democratic order" as a fundamental part of their struggles to secure community improvements.[111]

In the streets, reported *Tribuna Popular*, neighbors expressed their support more contentiously. "All night on Tuesday [the neighborhood] was poised for combat," as "Order Brigades" set up barricades throughout and, by Wednesday at noon, had completely sealed off the neighborhood. Women took to "patrolling" their buildings' hallways, while "men were at the barricades and children provided the rocks and steel rods, as well as bottles to make Molotovs." In the meantime, vehicles went from one part of the neighborhood to the other, carrying news and instructions.[112] It was an action mirrored elsewhere in the city's popular sectors, helping give the ruling junta the upper hand. By 4:30 A.M. on 23 July, ruling junta President Larrazábal announced the resignation of Castro León, who fled to exile in Colombia.[113]

Popular response to Castro León's attempted coup reflected in part the ruling junta's success in reaching out and responding to the demands of urban working classes. More broadly, it lay bare that whatever else it meant or would come to mean, democracy for urban popular sectors implied an opportunity to make direct demands of, be heard by, and achieve results from government. Support for that opportunity had helped motivate popular participation in the January revolution; defending it had led neighbors from the 23 de Enero and elsewhere among urban popular sectors in Caracas to take to the streets in July.

On 7 September 1958 they would again mobilize to defend this opportunity, this time in the face of a second, more violent coup against the junta government. Led by dissident mid-level officers, the coup appeared to draw on Santaella's fear, turned to hope by the conspirators, that a rash of civilian deaths would result in a *Bogotazo*-like upheaval, thereby exposing the ruling junta's weakness and, in the ensuing chaos, open the door for its overthrow. U.S. Embassy labor attaché Herbert Baker, on hearing radio reports at 7:00 A.M. "that there had been an attempted coup and that various democratic forces were rallying to the support of the Government Junta," had gone downtown "to observe the crisis." On arriving in the vicinity of Miraflores, Baker reported:

> There was a large group of people assembled in front of the White Palace [Presidential Honor Guard barracks, across from Miraflores]. As usual during a crisis, there was a microphone and loudspeaker mounted on the balcony. Shortly after my arrival, a speaker announced that Admiral Larrazábal . . . was on his way back to Caracas and the crowd cheered. . . . [Then] there was a burst of fire followed by several rounds of submachine gun or automatic rifle gun fire which appeared to me to be directed above the heads and into the crowd. . . . Many of the people attempted to escape down the side streets besides Miraflores Palace and some individuals called for the people running away from the Palace to go back and 'get those killers'. . . . We saw several attempts of the crowd to get into the military police barracks.[114]

Meanwhile, in the nearby 23 de Enero neighborhood, "armed groups . . . installed barricades in key sites" such as the road leading to the Ministry of Defense in La Planicie, between Blocks 7 and 9 of Monte Piedad.[115] When a truck left the Ministry, neighbors, suspecting its occupants of being part of the coup, stopped it and nearly lynched its passengers, "whose lives were practically saved . . . by the timely intervention of the Naval Forces" stationed in the Naval Observatory, just up the street from Block 7. Elsewhere in the neighborhood, in the ranchos that had risen behind the superblocks in Mirador, "nearly a hundred residents, men and women, detained two armed spies after a gunfight and handed them over to authorities, not before getting a sound beating [*paliza*] at the hands of *el pueblo*." By afternoon, a mass rally took place in nearby El Silencio, where residents of the 23 de Enero joined thousands of demonstrators flocking from of other Caracas popular sectors such as San Agustín, Las Adjuntas, San Juan, El Valle, and Pedro Camejo.[116] By nightfall, the coup was quashed. In all, eighteen people had lost their lives; one hundred had been wounded.[117]

The failed coup had once again exposed a state in the throes of transition, uncertain and unstable. But it had also showcased an urban populace increasingly organized in defense of spaces and opportunities they had seized, sometimes literally, in the wake of Pérez Jiménez's ouster. Channeling their grievances through organized but determined street actions, urban popular sectors' success in reinstating Fortoul in June had only confirmed their power, while forcing the ruling junta to move to resolve the balance between institutional and social stability in favor of the latter. But urban popular grievances and their attendant forms of organization, contentious or otherwise, extended only so far. Threatened with a return to the days when it was impossible to make demands of the government, they had shown themselves ready to defend their newfound ability for mobilization.

As they did with lands, apartments, and rent reductions, residents of the 23 de Enero also laid claim to the ideal of popular participation embodied in the revolution that had taken place on the date after which the neighborhood had been renamed—at first through decentralized, spontaneous actions, and over time through more-concerted forms of mobilization. Moreover, they drew from a wide array of groups sharing common origins, most of them—at one time or another—squatters in a new city. All told, whether contending with the Banco Obrero's administrative disarray, or the larger state's frailty, their victories during this time of transition—when the practical and the ideal of revolution continued to run separate paths—were hardly given to them; they were won through struggle. Over the next decade, as Venezuelan politics followed a tortuous road from transition to consolidation, passing through coup attempts, guerrilla war, tense elections, and continued migration to Caracas in the process, residents of the 23 de Enero would draw from their experience in the months following January 1958 to safeguard their right to the city and the country, as central actors in the unfolding plot of democracy.

PART TWO

Paths to Democracy

CHAPTER 3

From Ballots to Bullets

The Rise of Urban Insurgency, 1958–1963

"It was the first time I saw people descend like that. He was going to pass through Avenida Sucre, and people came down from the hillsides, like ants. I was looking on from above, and you could tell the avenue was full. All Avenida Sucre was full of people waiting for Fidel Castro."[1] One year after Pérez Jiménez's ouster ushered in Venezuela's "democratic revolution,"[2] Emilia de Pérez watched from the window of her apartment in Block 30 of the Zona Central as ecstatic crowds greeted the leader of Latin America's newest revolution.

Castro arrived in Caracas on 23 January 1959, his first overseas trip after triumphantly entering Havana two weeks earlier. He had come to thank Venezuelans for the example they had set a year before and, in turn, Venezuelans embraced the "hero of Cuba." At the airport hundreds broke through police barricades to greet his plane. "This is amazing," Castro reflected, "I cannot say if they are Cubans or Venezuelans, but I am certain they are my brothers." City officials declared him one of Caracas's "favored sons."[3] Government authorities held a lunch in his honor. "Intellectuals, political party leaders, and journalists" jockeyed to meet him.[4] At a massive rally downtown he told the crowd that "Cuba and Venezuela are united in the ideals of liberty and democracy,"[5] concluding: "If with a single phrase I could express the emotion I have felt today, I would say it all by affirming that I feel more moved arriving in Caracas than I did entering Havana."[6] The scenes were similar everywhere Castro went during his four-day visit to Caracas.

But his first stop had been the 23 de Enero. It was residents of the neighborhood who on 12 January first invited Castro to headline celebrations planned for the anniversary of Venezuela's revolution on 23 January.[7] For weeks they had readied to commemorate Venezuela's own struggle for liberty and democracy: in Monte Piedad a "National Unity" monument went up; in La Cañada a plaza honoring the dead of the revolution was set to open. On 23 January 1959, early-morning fireworks kicked off celebrations including a memorial Mass, sports events, and a "popular parade" of residents, athletes, and cadets. At day's end in Cristo Rey Plaza in the Zona Central, national political, labor, student, and religious leaders led a rally honoring the revolution.[8] And there was Castro, met by crowds waving Venezuelan and Cuban flags along area streets.[9] Days later, to mark his visit, residents named the area housing the last five superblocks ever built in the 23 de Enero and Venezuela, not by Pérez Jiménez but by the junta that succeeded him, after the mountain range from where Castro's guerrillas staged their revolution: Sierra Maestra.[10] All in all, it was a fitting capstone to a year marked by victories large and small for area residents, over rents, lands, apartments, services, jobs, and of course, democracy itself. Of the whirlwind visit, Emilia de Pérez recalled: "That was such a reception they gave him, the people, *the people.*"[11]

Three years later, from the same window where she watched as Castro toured the neighborhood amid enthusiastic crowds, Emilia de Pérez heard her neighbors yell: "Forgive us, Pérez Jiménez, for we knew not what we were doing!"[12] Below, tanks and troops squared off against communist insurgents posted on the rooftops, inspired by Castro's example and seeking to seize state power.[13] Headlines gave a sense of the violence: "The 23 de Enero . . . Gunned Down"; "1,500 National Guardsmen and Political Police Agents Assault the 23 de Enero"; "Unrest All Day in the 23 de Enero: 6 Dead, 40 Wounded."[14] Testimonies went further: families huddled in bathrooms away from the gunfire, spotlights lighting superblocks against the night sky, security forces raiding apartment after apartment, National Guardsmen harassing youths, guerrillas setting ablaze vehicles and looting stores. Years later one paper reported: "Police patrols were shot at, and they returned fire, almost always killing innocent bystanders. . . . Undoubtedly, there were violations by some authorities."[15] What had gone wrong?

The next two chapters follow residents of the 23 de Enero through the tortured process of consolidating democracy in the 1960s, when the neighborhood was transformed into a hotbed of violence far removed from the heady days of popular anticipation that marked the early transition. After Pérez

Jiménez's ouster, residents new and old had seized opportunities suddenly thrust open, giving rise to a social landscape from a physical landscape originally intended to homogenize social life. Renamed to memorialize the founding date of the new political system, the area had emerged as a center of mobilization sometimes in support, sometimes in opposition to the budding regime, all the while defending what residents understood as the promise of democracy: a system that would be fairer, more accountable, and more responsive to their needs than they had known before. But, before long, residents found themselves abandoned by a state that shifted resources away from Caracas, pushing the 23 de Enero into material disrepair while alienating urban voters. Meanwhile, communist efforts to build grassroots support by filling the gap left by the government, championing residents' needs and demands, gave way to an ill-advised policy of armed struggle, exposing contradictions as the left targeted urban popular sectors strategically while alienating them tactically. And while the urban insurgency's tactics staved support, the state's violent, generalized repression created a distrust of the major parties in power that would never fully recede.

The result was an ambiguous popular relationship both to the insurgency and to the democratic system. Residents largely rejected the insurgency, embracing the rubrics of liberal democracy—in particular the vote and its promise of responsive, accountable government. Yet they remained skeptical of the parties in power, voting for outsider candidates, materially if not ideologically supporting insurgents, and deepening a sense of urgency about day-to-day issues that remained unattended, and growing worse. In short, the same features that marked their social landscape would now be reflected in their politics. By decade's end, residents of the neighborhood Pérez Jiménez built to embody his regime's urban ambitions turned out to vote for the former dictator as he ran for Congress, in a final bid to return to Venezuelan politics. Though largely symbolic, residents' electoral support for Pérez Jiménez nevertheless made for a powerful gesture of their discontent with the nation's leadership in the decade since the coup that their neighborhood's name memorialized, if not with the underlying democratic system they had helped to usher in. All told, the political battles of the 1960s, marked by ideological struggles over control of the state, sidelined local politics in the neighborhood and squandered in the process the promise of 1958, while at the same time leaving an undercurrent of radicalism in the neighborhood that would resurface in due time.

THE ADMIRAL AND THE REDS: POPULIST COMMUNISM
AND URBAN PROTEST IN THE 1958 ELECTIONS

At first glance Castro's January 1959 visit to Caracas showcased a nation united toward consolidating democracy. In December, Venezuelans had successfully staged competitive, multiparty elections, the nation's first in over a decade. By February President-elect Rómulo Betancourt, who as founder of Acción Democrática (AD) had helped lead his party to an overwhelming electoral victory in 1947 largely by mobilizing rural voters, would take office as the nation's new, popularly elected president. Yet Castro's visit exposed a society on edge. During his speech on the evening of 23 January 1959, the crowd jeered at each mention of Betancourt.[16] The next day as Castro spoke to Congress, an unidentified voice cried out from the gallery: "We haven't had a revolution here!" And that evening, students at the Universidad Central de Venezuela again booed every time Castro mentioned Betancourt, prompting political leaders to rebuke the public's "lack of civility" toward the President-elect.[17]

What officials interpreted as public contempt in fact reflected tensions simmering since the coup Castro had come to celebrate: between military and civilian sectors, political parties of the left and center, currents pushing for gradual reform and those clamoring for radical change, and especially, between urban and rural electorates. The 7 December 1958 elections marked more than the nation's first democratic vote since 1947. They were also the first to be held in the new urban Venezuela, a nation remade in the frenzy of Pérez Jiménez's bulldozer years, then remade anew after his ouster.

Few areas reflected this transformation more than the 23 de Enero. By some estimates, when polls opened, nearly 10% of Caracas—around 100,000 people—called the neighborhood home, reflecting a more urban, popular, and densely concentrated electorate than ever before, one that had favored not Betancourt but ruling-junta President Wolfang Larrazábal in the December vote. Betancourt's strong support outside the capital secured his victory. But it was Larrazábal—the young, charismatic military officer who had been the face of the 23 January 1958 coup and went on to preside over the junta entrusted with leading Venezuela to elections in December—who decidedly won in Caracas, beating Betancourt by a whopping 50 points. In the 23 de Enero as a whole, Larrazábal won 70% of the ballots cast, with some areas reporting returns as high as 85% for the former junta president.[18]

The strength of Larrazábal's urban support owed in part to a personal link forged between the junta president and urban popular sectors who had come to view him as their major ally in government in the months after the January coup. When destitute widows of those who died during Pérez Jiménez's ouster met personally with Larrazábal, his promise to offer them aid was enough to ensure that he would do justice by "the victims of the revolution."[19] At one point, key chains with a picture of Larrazábal on one side and the Virgin Mary on the other became a hot commodity in Caracas. A devout Catholic, Larrazábal ordered them confiscated.[20] When rumors began to circulate of a possible Larrazábal candidacy, neighborhood citizen groups in several Caracas barrios began independently to collect signatures to nominate him.[21] "The unclassified masses of Caracas who did not want to fill party ranks, nor carry union cards, found in Larrazábal their leader," wrote historian Ramón J. Velásquez. Larrazábal was someone "who speaks the simple language of simple people, who crosses himself in public and offers blessings and who is understood by the illiterate who surround him when he descends from the offices of the Presidential Palace to dialogue with agitators leading a demonstration."[22]

Yet more than emotional attachment underlay popular support for Larrazábal. Since taking up the interim presidency in February, Larrazábal had directed state policy toward popular sectors in Caracas, resulting in loyalties based on tangible benefits that over time grew into political support. Consider the case of César Acuña (fig. 12), who at eighteen years old had worked in the crews that built the Mirador superblocks in 1957. When Pérez Jiménez fell, like thousands of others Acuña raced to the neighborhood and squatted an apartment in one of the very areas he had helped build. Then he found himself unemployed, as the once-booming Caracas construction industry drew to a standstill leaving an estimated 60,000 out of work. In response, interim authorities implemented the *Plan de Obras Extraordinarias* (Supplemental Public Works Plan) in March 1958. Popularly known as the *Plan de Emergencia* (Emergency Plan), the measure provided regular pay for sporadic, small-scale work—"patching potholes, fixing streets," remembered Acuña. And the Emergency Plan offered new migrants "materials, you know, so that people could build their ranchos again."

When in July 1958 Defense Minister Jesús María Castro León issued an ultimatum to Larrázabal, denouncing among other things Celso Fortoul's reinstatement from popular pressure as an embarrassment to executive power,

FIGURE 12. César Acuña (center) and brothers in December 1957, on
the roof of recently completed Blocks 45–46–47 of the Mirador section
of the then 2 de Diciembre. (Courtesy César Acuña)

Acuña joined a reported 100,000 people to "defend the truth of the Plan de
Emergencia.... It's what was putting food on the table." But more specifically,
Acuña demonstrated to back Larrazábal: "He was the leader . . . he had a lot
of support [tenía mucha gente], and we also had hope in Larrazábal." Of the
moment when his livelihood was at stake, Acuña reflected, "From then on,
that's when we more or less began to have a notion of politics." Acuña would
go on to join the local vanguard of URD, which later formally nominated
Larrazábal for president.[23]

The Emergency Plan consolidated support around Larrazábal among
Caracas popular sectors broadly. But in the 23 de Enero Larrazábal forged an
especially close link with residents, and they with him. In March 1958, as it
launched the Emergency Plan, the transitional government also announced
it would move ahead with construction of six additional superblocks in the 23
de Enero: 900 apartments in all.[24] Though it meant completing what had been
the ousted regime's signature project, the move was also a direct response
to the needs of area squatters.[25] By April, workers broke ground, and in
October the first families began to move in.[26] Dalila Roa had squatted an
apartment in Mirador, and would eventually be among those relocated to one
of the newly built blocks in the area that would come to be known as Sierra
Maestra. Decades later she would observe that in contrast to the buildings
that squatters occupied in the fray of Pérez Jiménez's ouster, the Sierra Mae-

stra blocks "were better done than all the other blocks. Wolfgang Larrazábal built those."[27] Of course, it was precisely the coup that Larrazábal led that prevented those squatted superblocks from being completed under Pérez Jiménez. But that Roa linked the new buildings' completion so directly to the junta president was a powerful reflection of the lasting connection between Larrazábal and area residents.

The new buildings were a direct and highly visible response to the needs of area squatters. But Larrazábal also addressed the rent-reduction issue that primarily affected residents of the eastern 23 de Enero. In late September, Larrazábal personally met with a tense gathering of thousands in the neighborhood clamoring for sizable rent reductions after several half measures; one newspaper called it "one of the most heavily attended rallies of the people to fight for their grievances."[28] In the ensuing weeks and months, the Banco Obrero (BO) restructured contracts to reflect major rent reductions for residents. Ravín Asuase Sánchez of La Cañada recalled the great relief his parents felt at the move: "Even though an apartment cost Bs. 18,000 [US$5400], when Larrazábal came people started paying Bs. 76 [US$23] a month. At home I remember they used to pay Bs. 200 [US$60]. And that was a bunch of money [un realero], 200 was too much."[29] Moreover, in a major departure from previous public-housing policy, the BO expanded its mortgage program to include area residents, allowing many to purchase apartments outright rather than merely rent. "When Pérez Jiménez fell and the government of Larrazábal came in, that's when he put in the policy that whoever wanted could opt to buy," remembers Rosa Amelia de González of La Cañada. "For instance here I paid Bs. 117.35 [US$35], opción a compra . . . 20 years to pay. But at that time it was difficult. . . . To find Bs. 100 [US$30] took a whole lot."[30]

The common thread was how residents personally associated Larrazábal with the interim government's actions. Larrazábal "put a lot of people to work," recalled Rafael Gutiérrez of Block 11, who would take lunch to his older cousin at the Plan de Emergencia's office in Monte Piedad.[31] "Larrazábal gave a lot of cash," observed Lourdes Quintero of Block 37 in the Zona F, who recalled thick crowds forming at another Plan de Emergencia office near the rotary below. "He paid weekly to those without a job, by order of the president."[32] When rumors of an impending coup surfaced in July, neighborhood committees in Mirador issued a statement expressing their support less for the government than for "President Admiral Larrazábal for his patriotic gestures aimed at leading the country to a constitutional regime which is what most Venezuelans demand."[33] Yet Larrazábal's personal appeal was tied to his ability to deliver to urban popular sectors, illustrating a deeper reality about urban politics in this new context: it was specific attention to the pressing needs of a rapidly expanding electorate that made charismatic leadership most effective.[34]

The Communist Party of Venezuela (*Partido Comunista de Venezuela*, or PCV) moved quickly to embrace this reality, dedicating major time and resources to court 23 de Enero residents. In the months after the January 1958 revolution, the party weekly, *Tribuna Popular*, published occasional columns devoted solely to local grievances.[35] It also regularly reported on the conditions of squatters, basing its stories on wide-ranging interviews that amplified residents' voices.[36] The PCV also tried to make inroads in the area's various neighborhood committees, or Juntas Pro-Mejoras. When Monte Piedad residents organized a local neighborhood committee shortly after 23 January 1958, a PCV militant, Carlos Del Vecchio, became its deputy. The party also made of the 23 de Enero its unofficial headquarters, launching both its Caracas "Growth Campaign" in June[37] and its formal electoral campaign in October at the neighborhood.[38] Both events were built on the strength of local organizers and concerns. In one, Del Vecchio outlined the party's platform as it pertained to area residents: rent reductions and "popular housing" for workers earning less than Bs. 200 [US$60] a month.[39] In another, the party announced it would nominate Eloy Torres of La Cañada as one of its three national candidates for the Chamber of Deputies.[40]

The party's strategy in the neighborhood aimed to take advantage of a major gap in the emerging political landscape. Before Pérez Jiménez, Acción Democrática (AD), the nation's largest political party, had developed a strong structure around rural sectors and labor unions. But as it returned to the political fray after the dictatorship, AD leaders chose to develop that base rather than build new constituencies in Caracas. For his part, Larrazábal could and did mobilize state resources toward urban popular needs. But he lacked the apparatus to build sustained grassroots support, relying instead on charisma to develop popular links. The PCV's grassroots campaign in the 23 de Enero drew from elements of both. Without significant resources to distribute, the PCV offered residents solidarity and voice, lending its media and party apparatus to make visible neighbors' grievances while nurturing local leadership in the style of Larrazábal, who had shown how the combination of charisma and attention to immediate concerns could generate enormous popular appeal.

But the move to stress local needs and leadership also came at the cost of downplaying the party's ideological aims: "The Communists," wrote one U.S. Embassy analyst, "had established simple club houses in these areas, offering recreation and a minimum of political doctrine."[41] Likewise Talton Ray, who in the early 1960s conducted a major study of Caracas barrios such as the 23 de Enero, observed: "The Communist maintained support because his neighbors liked the way in which he related to them and what he did for the community. That his beliefs became those of his friends can be attributed more to his charismatic qualities than to their conviction of the validity of his ideology. In his barrio, the Communist made good use of his personal qualities. He became intimately associated with group activities and worked hard for the community's welfare. If anything needed to be done, people learned that he was the man to call on."[42] But the PCV's strategy was not confined to grassroots work alone; it also aimed to achieve demonstrable gains and a measure of state power. Ahead of elections, it threw its support behind Larrazábal, citing his "popular and democratic mentality. In the conflicts that the *Junta de Gobierno* experienced, at the time of decision making, he always did so in favor of the people."[43]

In part the Communists' embrace of Larrazábal was a move born of necessity. In October 1958, AD and two other major political parties—the centrist Unión Republicana Democrática (URD) and the center-right Comité de Organización Política Electoral Independiente (COPEI)—signed a pact to respect the electoral outcome by ensuring that the winner would apportion ministries and political posts between them. AD and COPEI quickly moved to nominate their respective founders, Rómulo Betancourt and Rafael Caldera. However, URD's founder Jóvito Villalba offered the nomination to the youthful Larrazábal, who resigned as junta president to accept the party's candidacy. Three days later, blasting the pact that had excluded them but realizing it could not win on its own, the PCV announced it would back Larrazábal, hoping to receive enough votes to claim six Deputies and two Senators in Congress. Party leaders also stressed that they would not seek any cabinet post in a Larrazábal administration. But they promised to opine "vigorously" on appointments such as Minister of Public Works, responsible for the Banco Obrero and public housing nationwide.[44] It was a strong indication of where the party aimed to make its mark, in a post with most immediate impact to the constituency the PCV was targeting.

The PCV's strategy was successful, especially in the 23 de Enero. On 7 December 1958, Election Day, Communists received 160,000 votes nationwide

FIGURE 13. The caption for this 5 December 1958 cartoon reads: "State of Alert: Yes, my 'weapon' is the vote . . . but conspirators beware, because I also know how to use other 'weapons'!" (*Últimas Noticias*)

in congressional balloting, giving the PCV two Senators and seven Deputies. Of those, nearly half came in Caracas alone.[45] In working-class areas like the 23 de Enero, the PCV emerged as the solid second party of choice, behind Larrazábal's URD but ahead of both the center-left AD and the center-right COPEI. Among the PCV delegates elected to Congress was Eloy Torres. "As the 'outs,'" surmised one analyst assessing the PCV's Caracas showing, "Communists are looked upon by many persons as being outspoken and independent on local issues."[46] That Communists could claim an independent mantle despite supporting Larrazábal reflected a nuanced understanding of the dynamics that informed popular mobilization in the months after January 1958. At Larrazábal's final rally in Caracas three days before the vote, though officially a URD event, PCV leader Guillermo García Ponce told the crowd: "The struggle will not end on December 7. To the contrary, that's when it will begin. Larrazábal must make good with the people, who have a perfect right to demand that promises made to them be kept."[47]

It was a powerful message. On the one hand, García Ponce was stressing Larrazábal's need to remain responsive to those who would support him. On the other hand, he called on those would-be supporters to remain vigilant beyond Election Day. In other words, popular support for legitimately constituted government was not limited to personal appeal. Instead it was tied to concrete actions, and the accountability provided by a vigilant electorate. A cartoon (fig. 13) that ran in *Últimas Noticias*—Venezuela's largest newspaper—two days before the vote well captured this dynamic. With a ballot in one hand, a rock in the other, and a mischievous smile on his face, a man meant to embody the popular "Juan Bimba" character warns: "Yes, my 'weapon' is the vote, but don't let the conspirators be fooled, I also know how to handle other weapons!" Street protests on the one hand, electoral politics on the other: bookends of a spectrum of popular political participation that informed the emerging meaning, and promise, of democracy for urban popular sectors.

The cartoon proved prophetic, but not because of conspiratorial threats. On the evening of 7 December 1958, totals in the 23 de Enero heralded a massive Larrazábal victory.[48] In fact Larrazábal's victory in the capital cut across class lines.[49] Yet, outside the capital, it was Betancourt who scored a decisive victory, winning 49% to Larrazábal's 35% and Caldera's 16%.[50] As officials declared Betancourt President-elect, protests broke out across Caracas. In the 23 de Enero, neighbors discovered twelve stuffed ballot boxes in the surrounding hillside. Suspecting fraud, thousands of area residents flocked to challenge elections officials, who explained that the ballots were simply unused, not stolen. Unsatisfied, neighbors scuffled their way into the polling station, eventually appointing Carlos Del Vecchio to deliver the boxes to the Supreme Electoral Council for review. Their suspicion proved unfounded.[51] But the episode and showed deep distrust in the vote's outcome not just in the 23 de Enero but elsewhere in Caracas, where hundreds more were arrested for protesting Betancourt's win, mainly youth flogged in the press as "antidemocratic" and "immature."[52]

At the height of the protests the interim government had moved to suspend rights of speech and of assembly, an ironic first act following the democratic revolution's first elections.[53] By 10 December 1958, however, demonstrations waned and the process to suspend guarantees stalled.[54] Ultimately, it was Larrazábal's call for "all Venezuelans to accept the outcome . . . and to support the elected President" that eventually quelled passions.[55] Yet Fabricio Ojeda, leader of the civilian wing of the movement that ousted Pérez Jiménez, blasted those who had branded demonstrators "lumpen proletariat, petty criminals [hampones], or prostitutes."[56] Communist journalist Servando García Ponce likewise sprung to protestors' defense. Some "elements of poor standing may have infiltrated the demonstrators," he wrote, but "in the majority they are from La Charneca and the 23 de Enero . . . the same ones I saw ward off the fascist Castro León and secure democracy, generously spilling their blood in front of the [Presidential Palace]."[57] Meanwhile popular sectors expressed concerns about the future. When protests broke out on 8 December, one U.S. Embassy official on the scene reported how some in the crowd "asked how if Betancourt lost in Caracas, he could govern here."[58]

The protests had revealed a contentious split between the nation and its capital. U.S. Embassy officials reported how AD and Betancourt were "frankly surprised at their poor showing in Caracas." They need not have been. Ahead of elections, AD focused most of its time and resources outside Caracas while leaving capital-city efforts to youth militants. In part the move owed to an emerging view by party leaders, and Betancourt especially, that "the city had prospered at the expense of the countryside during the Pérez Jiménez years, and one way to redistribute Venezuelan wealth was to reverse the spending patterns of the 1950s."[59] Yet it had also resulted from mistaken assumptions about the new urban electorate. One long-time Betancourt confidant and AD militant wrote years later: "Ten years in exile . . . were enough to disconnect him deeply from reality,"[60] a reality of a new urban population well embodied by the 23 de Enero. In fact in March 1958, referring to the neighborhood, Betancourt reportedly observed to his biographer, Robert Alexander:

> It is notable that the popular insurrection found its strongest support in the very housing blocks which Pérez Jiménez had built. The workers had no gratitude towards him for putting in these blocks. They had been uprooted by force from their old homes, and had been given no compensation for them when they were torn down by bulldozers. They had to pay Bs. 130 [US$39] a month for these apartments, and in most of them there was no running water, there were no stores located near them, there were no schools in the vicinity, and the elevators usually didn't work, so that women had to climb ten flights of stairs with cans of water on their shoulders. The workers hated Pérez Jiménez for his housing blocks.[61]

Residents' attitudes toward the project and its founder were far more ambiguous than Betancourt allowed. His assessment accurately reflected many of the infrastructure and design problems area residents faced. But, as paraphrased by Alexander, it also appeared to conflate the conditions found by January squatters—without acknowledging the attraction that would drive thousands to flock to unoccupied, unfinished apartments in the first place—with the sentiments of those forcibly and sometimes unwillingly relocated to the superblocks years earlier. And while he recognized the problems they faced, for Betancourt it seemed enough that residents "hated" Pérez Jiménez to take their electoral support for granted. After the vote, Betancourt quickly downplayed the poor showing in the capital, noting that "he did not feel at all hopeless about it. . . . The great majority Larrazábal had received in Caracas represented a pro-Larrazábal vote but not necessarily an anti-AD vote." Still, Betancourt remained "very cognizant of the problems in Caracas, as well as the popular devotion to Larrazábal as a democratic symbol."[62]

But if U.S. Embassy personnel showed public support for Betancourt's optimism, they betrayed it in private correspondence. On 31 December 1958, they bluntly wrote to the State Department: "Caracas may be a problem for Betancourt. . . . AD leaders are aware that one of their primary problems will be to establish party control in Caracas and . . . to assure that the city will be in a mood to accept Betancourt's inauguration publicly and even with enthusiasm."[63] Instead, the gulf between incoming authorities and the Caracas electorate only widened as press outlets aligned with AD and COPEI blamed Larrazábal for stirring the crowds during Fidel's Castro's visit.[64] Though he was eventually cleared of any wrongdoing,[65] that Larrazábal had faced scrutiny at all heightened tensions in Caracas,[66] tensions that boiled over on 28 January 1959 when hundreds of unemployed workers demanding jobs scuffled with soldiers and police outside the Presidential Palace.[67] The protest ended peacefully after government authorities offered job assurances to demonstrators, but four days later 3,000 workers returned to Miraflores to demand that authorities uphold their promise. When they tried reaching Miraflores, clashes broke out with police and Palace guards. For several hours police fired tear gas while workers paralyzed traffic. By late afternoon, interim President Edgar Sanabria released a statement promising 10,000 jobs by 2 February.[68] All told, five people were injured and seven cars set ablaze.[69]

But the episode, just two weeks before Betancourt's inauguration, sent the government into panic. Vowing that "public order will not be altered by coup-plotting groups advancing a subversive campaign," Defense Minister Josué López Henríquez banned unauthorized demonstrations and doubled patrols in Caracas. Political leaders from all sectors quickly backed the move. "[I am] absolutely in agreement with the measures taken to guarantee order," said Betancourt, adding: "the exercise of liberties cannot be confused with *bochinche* [troublemaking]."[70] Yet it was Larrazábal, again, who assuaged the rift between Caracas popular sectors and the new government. After meeting with Betancourt on 6 February 1959, Larrázabal announced his support for the junta's measures: "The more precautions the better so that the people can have the government they elected," a second concession by the candidate who had overwhelmingly carried Caracas.

Days later, just before Betancourt's inauguration, Larrazábal boarded a ship to Chile, where he would remain for years as Ambassador, warning as he left: "Those who invoke my name to foment disturbances are not my friends and I am not with them."[71] By 13 February 1959, Betancourt assumed the presidency of Venezuela. As he did so, difficult questions remained about the extent to which he would be able to govern in Caracas. In particular the 23 de Enero—the "Bastion of Democracy" in the words of the PCV's *Tribuna Popular*—would come to embody the problems of a budding democratic regime faced with an urban electorate very much its antagonist and left to wonder: "Where is the democracy we conquered?"[72]

"CARACAS MAY BE A PROBLEM FOR BETANCOURT": ANTI-URBAN STRATEGY IN THE DEMOCRATIC TRANSITION

The December 1958 elections brought AD and its founder, Rómulo Betancourt, to power. But the vote was contentious: cries of fraud, violent protests, threats to suspend civil liberties. In the 23 de Enero, problems abounded. On the eve of 23 January 1959 residents reported roving gangs bringing mayhem to entire sectors,[73] vandalizing parks and public spaces.[74] Then there were ongoing land occupations between the superblocks. New ranchos rose up citywide, but in the 23 de Enero they dramatized the government's inability to attend to housing shortages and new migrants after the coup.[75] In some areas residents reported paying exorbitant daily water fees as pumps and pipes failed under growing demand.[76] These grievances revealed a deep rift between the neighborhood as a showpiece of democratic revolution and growing discontent over everyday problems facing its residents. Betancourt's administration would widen the gulf. A month after taking office, Betancourt called for reversing Pérez Jiménez's urban focus: "[It] is a mistake," he noted, "to make Caracas and the other capitals macrocephalic entities which absorb the human element with all the problems that such a situation brings, not only from the economic point of view but also in its social ramifications." Instead, according to newly appointed Banco Obrero (BO) President Luis Lander, the government's "view will be directed toward the province."[77]

Betancourt went further still, singling out superblocks as "costly and anti-human,"[78] and prompting the BO to undertake a comprehensive assessment of the housing project.[79] The final, scathing report, delivered in 1961 by an international team of urban planners, found deep problems at every level. In design: "The neighborhood gives an impression of monotony due to the constant repetition of the same element and the lack of human scale." In construction, evaluators found poor and fragile materials used in common areas, requiring constant upkeep and repair. In services, the team found shortages in "education, health, recreation, social aid, and cultural programs in general."[80] Administrative issues were gravest. Unclear channels of communication, poorly articulated systems and procedures, and "excessive centralization of the operational activities of the superblocks" marked the BO.[81] These problems begat financial issues: "Since the electoral campaign of 1958, only a small percentage of families living in the superblocks regularly pay rent," observed the report, concluding: "In effect a state of peaceful civil anarchy prevails. The losses that the country suffers as a result of this situation are serious." Monthly costs per block neared Bs. 1.5 million (US$450K), while rent delinquency approached Bs. 16.5 million (US$5 million) per month, not including squatters.[82] The final analysis was grim: "The BO may have no other alternative but to stop collecting rents or reduce them considerably."[83]

This bleak assessment shed light on a deep paradox. Only by first resolving grave infrastructure and service deficiencies could residents reasonably be expected to claim a stake in the neighborhood.[84] But that would require attention and resources that the report dismissed, urging that "the government must suspend all type of superblock construction" as a failed project with few prospects of ever meeting operating costs.[85] Implored to focus resources elsewhere, and to attend to pressing problems in the neighborhood, the report offered contradictory conclusions.[86]

Cost and quality-of-life issues partly informed Betancourt's policy and rhetoric toward the superblocks. But political considerations were paramount. Further investing in Caracas, even in response to growing need, meant adding to the capital's primacy and marginalizing AD's traditional base of support. But in the case of the 23 de Enero especially, it also meant strengthening opponents, as the report observed:

> If we add the political situation after the revolution of January 1958, the attitude taken towards them as a result of the invasion, and the social grievances being made on a national scale, we can better understand the current position of the people who live in the superblocks. The notion that they are social housing, that they have more rights than obligations, that they constitute a very important political force and that as the most disadvantaged social class they require all

manner of attention and assistance, has been strongly reinforced in their mind. In this attitude, moreover, they have been encouraged by politicians and other interested persons who have led to the current situation of unrest that one notices in these neighborhoods.[87]

Though these "politicians and interested persons" remained unspecified, the PCV had claimed a strong stake in the neighborhood especially after Betancourt excluded Communists from the coalition government in a bid to cement friendly relations with the United States. Through *Tribuna Popular*, the Communist Party daily, they proclaimed representation and spokesmanship of Caracas popular sectors. In June the paper launched "Voice of the Barrios," a regular column printing grievances and complaints by barrio residents.[88] After Betancourt summarily ended the Plan de Emergencia in August 1959, protests broke out and his government suspended rights of assembly and habeas corpus in Caracas, further weakening AD's tenuous position with urban popular sectors.[89] Coalition parties supported the move. But PCV's *Tribuna Popular* blasted it: "The suspension of liberties does not go against the enemies of the people but against the masses."[90] Congressman Fabricio Ojeda, who would later resign and join insurgents, warned that "democracy must be defended democratically."[91]

But *Tribuna Popular* paid special attention to the 23 de Enero, launching a weekly column dedicated exclusively to the neighborhood just as AD undertook its anti-superblocks rhetoric and policy.[92] Local coverage served two purposes. For one it exposed the state's inability to attend to urban popular demands even in this iconic neighborhood; highlighting problems in the 23 de Enero quickly turned into broader critiques of the political system. Showcasing Communist activism in the 23 de Enero also helped project the party's strength, keenly recognized by Betancourt, who as early as March 1958 had warned: "They have made considerable progress. . . . The Communists now have to be dealt with."[93] In October 1959 *Tribuna Popular* detailed a visit to the neighborhood by the PCV's congressional delegation, among them Eloy Torres from La Cañada. As the only area resident from any party to hold a seat in Congress, wrote *Tribuna*, Torres registered the deep links between the 23 de Enero and the PCV.[94]

Yet at the heart of *Tribuna Popular*'s local coverage lay an internal tension that had begun to surface in 1958. While it attempted to cast its coverage of local grievances as an indictment against government failures more broadly, the link remained largely unstated. Instead most coverage focused on microissues of everyday concern, thus primarily serving as a catalog of grievances rather than as an effort to generate ideological support. Throughout 1959 and into 1960 *Tribuna* covered rent-reduction struggles, water problems, rat infestations, calls for fumigation, electricity rate hikes, demands to review power meters, and inflation in area stores, among other issues.[95] In splitting coverage of political activism and microissues, *Tribuna Popular* and the PCV more broadly divided ideological aims and pragmatic concerns. Over time, this split would deepen as insurgents sacrificed the latter in seeking state power through quick victory against Betancourt's government.

Shifting from the local focus that characterized early Communist Party strategy took place slowly. It happened more by circumstance than choice as the governing coalition fractured, opening the door for short-term, tactical strikes to replace long-term, strategic efforts to build mass support. The nature of the shift proved significant; it enabled popular sectors to separate between radical and mainstream sectors of the left. As calls for insurgency gestated, left sectors agreed that Betancourt's brand of social democracy was neither social nor democratic. But doctrinal debates regarding the contours of real democratic socialism generated factions; among these, the PCV was only one tendency among many—despite government efforts to paint all opposition as Communist. In fact, the PCV more often proved critical than supportive of armed conflict.[96]

Instead it was the Revolutionary Left Movement (*Movimiento de Izquierda Revolucionaria*, or MIR) that most agitated for insurgency. Youth sectors of AD had formed the MIR in April 1960 after breaking from Betancourt's party. Most were activists who had sustained AD clandestinely under Pérez Jiménez, and found themselves sidelined by party leaders returning from exile. They had come to view Betancourt's courting of the United States and business interests as a deep betrayal, and drew inspiration instead from Cuba and Castro, from his use of state power to redistribute wealth and critique capitalist imperialism.[97] But they were also responding to what even long-time supporters admitted was Betancourt's self-styled persona as "the maximum leader of AD, the true caudillo of his party." In an otherwise broadly sympathetic biography, a close friend and ally of Betancourt reflected: "Betancourt was born to rule. His confidants and collaborators knew it well."[98] In fact, Betancourt later confided to his biographer that he "did all he could to precipitate the split, since he felt that the MIR were an outside group which had wormed its way into AD."[99] By his own telling, on one occasion responding to students who "were going to start campaigning in factories in the Caracas area, [Betan-court] called together the AD trade union leaders, and discussed the situation with them. They agreed to let the students into the factories, but then to slightly beat them up. This worked, they never returned."[100]

Betancourt's manner and machinations alienated more than just youth sectors. According to Luis Lander, son of Betancourt's first Banco Obrero (BO) President who directed the superblocks evaluation project, Betancourt's "fetish for domination, to have people around him never challenge him, to be recognized as the maximum leader of the thing" also contributed to his father's ouster from the BO. Following MIR's split from AD, Betancourt reportedly ordered the summary dismissal of all public-sector employees who joined MIR. As the younger Lander recalled: "In the BO there was a group of engi-neers who went with MIR. My father didn't fire any of them, so there were rumblings." Within a year, the older Lander had resigned from the BO in protest, after Betancourt maneuvered to appoint a BO vice president without Lander's input or consent.[101] This despite the fact that around the time of Lander's resignation, Betancourt had admitted that "AD is basically a party of workers and peasants, and there are too few trained people. Of the party's engineers, for instance, only one, Luis Lander, has postgraduate training in the United States."[102] Lander had brought that training, and his international contacts among urban planners, to the task of evaluating the superblocks. He had also been among the party's founders, going back to 1936, before it was named AD. Yet on failing to uphold Betancourt's line, Lander found himself out of favor, sidestepped, and out of office.

The MIR split and its underlying power dynamics revealed a Betancourt keen to respond to challenges—direct or indirect—with single-minded deter-mination, even ruthlessness, as part of a grand vision of his leadership and that of his party as the legitimate stewards of Venezuelan politics. On the campaign trail in 1958, Betancourt reportedly proclaimed to AD militants, "We are going to govern again, and this time our party will remain in power for 50 years."[103] Internal challenges from youth and independent voices could be marginalized in the short term, but in the long term Caracas popular sec-tors posed a far greater threat to Betancourt's vision, as they had demonstrated in the December elections. Three years after the vote, in 1961, Betancourt remained wounded by the way the Caracas vote had transpired, despite the earlier lack of concern he had expressed to U.S. officials. "The people of Cara-cas voted for Larrazábal," Betancourt now observed, "because he was very *simpático* [affable], in contrast to the hard faced Pérez Jiménez; because of the Plan de Emergencia dole; because the people in the government housing projects, who amount to 100,000 votes at least, didn't pay a cent of rent under Larrazábal."[104]

Casting urban popular sectors as unsophisticated, superficial freeloaders, and singling out residents of the 23 de Enero for special scorn, exposed a deeply cynical appraisal of a population whose support he had once assumed. Seen in this light, the 23 de Enero became a stand-in for the threat that Caracas popular sectors more broadly posed to Betancourt's project of consolidating power for himself in the short term and for AD in the long term, a threat that would grow more pronounced as the PCV maneuvered to use Betancourt's marginalization of Caracas popular sectors to attack his democratic legitimacy. Over the next three years, residents' isolation grew into political alienation, even as the neighborhood occupied a central place in insurgent and counterinsurgent battles.

MOVING TOWARD INSURGENCY

In late June 1960, agents of dictator Rafael Trujillo, of the Dominican Republic, bombed Betancourt's motorcade in retaliation for his outspoken criticism of the Dominican regime. Betancourt escaped with burns to his hands and face. But his response was unsparing. Fearing a broader plot, he indefinitely suspended civil liberties.[105] Two months later the Communist Party accused AD's Caracas Secretary Hugo Soto Socorro of launching "repressive brigades" of party militants against alleged Communist agitators.[106] In the 23 de Enero, residents reported a siege of police, military, and armed AD militants.[107] *Tribuna Popular* called it "police hysteria"[108]—even if claims of state repression in the 23 de Enero originated from local activist Carlos Del Vecchio. The *popularazo* of late October exposed a pattern of outsized government reaction to public demonstrations. On 19 October authorities detained several MIR leaders after an editorial in the party paper, *Izquierda*, called for "a change of government, the substitution of the current regime by another that responds to the interests of the people," adding: "there is no solution within the current framework."[109] As youths and students gathered outside Congress to protest the measure, police fired tear gas into the crowd, wounding six.[110] Over the next two days, schools and universities across Caracas erupted in violence. In response, Betancourt warned: "The government will energetically repress any attempt to subvert order. . . . The Government has the right and duty to impede that, making ill use of liberties contemplated in our laws, individuals or groups disrespect the President of the Republic and Public Institutions or incite insurrection."[111]

Betancourt's promise of "energetic repression" of urban protest reflected a larger battle over the definition of democracy in this critical juncture of Venezuelan history. By 1960, escalating tensions allowed the Communist Party to undermine Betancourt while upholding the basic apparatus of democracy. In late June, amid mounting opposition from within and outside party ranks, Betancourt reminded critics that "94% of the people voted for and back this government."[112] For Communists, however, legitimacy was less a matter of origins than of practice; said one PCV congressman: "If this regime wants to continue calling itself democratic, it must do something for the people."[113] Unsurprisingly, Communist critiques aimed more at Betancourt's government than at the underlying democratic system. After all, elections had afforded the PCV political clout it now tried to widen. Instead, by linking the meaning of democracy to specific government actions, the PCV could harness expressions of popular discontent as proof not just of AD's inability to govern, but also of Betancourt's growing contempt for the ways urban popular sectors especially had refashioned the social and political landscape since Pérez Jiménez's overthrow.

"The communists," writes Daniel Levine, "argued that 'the streets belong to the people,' and therefore could be used for demonstrations of any kind at any time." Yet Betancourt warned that, "a country cannot live and work, acquire culture and forge riches, if it is always threatened by the surprise explosions of street violence, behind which the ancient enemies of democracy, totalitarians of all names and colors, seek to engineer its discredit." But as Communists understood, Betancourt's electoral victory owed in large part to the spontaneous street protests that had formed part of urban popular sectors' repertoire of mobilization throughout 1958, as they again and again took to the streets against threats—real or rumored—of coups or other disruptions to the fragile promise of democracy. Still, as President Betancourt now warned, "any time uncontrolled groups go into the streets, on whatever pretext, they will be treated with neither softness nor lenience," backing up the threat by "banning all unauthorized street demonstrations."[114]

In practice, urban repression meant deploying security forces with broad discretion to "plan their actions according to their needs."[115] In one account of protests in the 23 de Enero neighborhood, police were met by "strong attacks with firearms, Molotovs, and other means, which stretched until four in the morning."[116] In another, "in the eastern sectors of [the 23 de Enero] . . . several superblocks, from which rocks were thrown against police vehicles, were shot at."[117] In both accounts, sustained violence stretched into the next day, leaving six dead, 40 wounded, and 190 arrested. Meanwhile, the National Guard— Venezuela's militarized police force—dispatched "several buses and trucks full of personnel and in the first hours of the night, [it] posted a greater number with the intent of undertaking an evolving operation [operación evolvente]." From neighboring areas, witnesses recounted how "one of the platoons surrounded a superblock," later searching individual apartments.[118] These examples exposed a pattern in the state's approach to superblocks, less surgical than generalized, in order to "energetically repress" disorder.

Tribuna Popular highlighted the worst allegations of abuse of so-called "Operation Clean Sweep" in the neighborhood. Communists, MIR activists, and other leftist groups denounced "persecution" by police and armed AD militants, who would later operate in the 23 de Enero under the shadowy name *Cobra Negra* [black cobra].[119] "It started as a pretext to fight crime," recalled Ravín Asuase Sánchez, a veteran of the local guerrilla struggles, "but as it developed it aimed for militant revolutionaries."[120] According to Danilo Aray of La Cañada, who would go on to form part of the militant left group *Ruptura* in the 1970s: "The Cobra Negra were *adecos* [adherents of the AD]. . . . Several *compañeros* tell me that they would grab them, they would turn around and some guys with ski masks would jump out and beat your ass. . . . They also went to your home and they would draw a cobra and put something on there, whatever, and you knew you were marked."[121] Whether or not groups like Cobra Negra had formal links to the party in power, their association in the minds of insurgents more broadly, decades later, hinted at the deep distrust that would continue to exist toward AD among some area residents.

Still, it was government forces that deployed most repression. No doubt self-servingly, *Tribuna Popular* estimated 1,500 National Guard and police had mobilized to the area for Operation Clean Sweep,[122] and reported fourteen dead (excluding one National Guard corporal and two police officers) and over 200 wounded throughout Caracas. It also provided what it called an "exact" account of police operations in the 23 de Enero—including the names of officers it accused of leading raids in the superblocks—while noting how neighbors repelled the police's initial assault.[123] Doing so served a purpose.

Most of its coverage had emphasized residents' status as standard-bearers of popular democracy. An editorial titled "Glory to the 23 de Enero" played on this theme; its portrayal of the neighborhood both memorialized the democratic promise of the 1958 coup, and highlighted the betrayal expressed in the state's subsequent repression.[124] In this light, casting residents as passive victims of state violence would have undercut *Tribuna*'s image of the 23 de Enero as a bastion of mobilization.

But it was not just a strategic portrayal. Raids had yielded caches of weapons and plans for urban rebellion, casting the 23 de Enero as a locus of the still-gestating insurgency.[125] Interior Minister Luis Augusto Dubuc warned "extremists [to] desist in their crazy plans to foment popular rebellion . . . or definitely become isolated."[126] Caracas police commander Aníbal Sánchez Gómez blamed 23 de Enero residents, insisting that "it is citizens who with their spontaneous collaboration and obedience to authority determine the subsequent actions of police officers."[127] One officer suggested that the government's response was in fact muted, since police casualties resulted from "condescending" to residents.[128] But residents' experience—violence, deaths, raids—spoke otherwise, and downplaying the budding insurgency turned state response into overreaction. Also, Sánchez Gómez's declaration placed residents in the awkward position of being told to submit to authorities' defense of democracy, order, and property while seeing all three violated in the 23 de Enero. Tensions between a discourse of isolated extremism, and a pattern of more-generalized repression thus marked official approaches to the neighborhood.

Violence crippled life for residents of the 23 de Enero. So did the banning of the MIR and PCV in May 1962 following a failed bid to seize state power through quick, decisive blows, bypassing the work of building mass support.[129] The plot called for coordinated attacks on military garrisons in east and west Venezuela, while clashes in Caracas would spur rebellion among urban popular sectors. In the 23 de Enero, guerrillas reportedly posted on superblock roofs exchanged fire with police and military units below, units that eventually "raided several blocks . . . with the purpose of searching for weapons and capturing sharpshooters."[130] One resident died when a homemade bomb accidentally exploded in his apartment.[131] After again suspending civil liberties,[132] Betancourt warned: "To those who rise up against the legitimately constituted order, to those who bear arms against the legitimately constituted government, the government's answer is the gun."[133] Along with banning MIR and the PCV in 1962, Betancourt also formed a War Council that charged Communist congressman Eloy Torres, of La Cañada, with treason and insurrection, ordering his arrest.[134] "This is not a lax, soft, or weak democracy," Betancourt warned. "If friends of Eloy Torres think they can continue to defy the laws of the Republic, they will end up accompanying him in the same place where he is now."[135] Coupled with the intensity of the violence in the area, Torres's arrest underscored the neighborhood's central place in the armed conflict. Moreover, against the ironic backdrop of the suspension of freedoms to defend democracy, statements about defying laws seemed contradictory at best. They also illustrated a deeper tension, between Betancourt's pursuit of regime consolidation, and the way popular sectors in Caracas had become his major antagonists in that effort.

The major blow for Communists, however, had less to do with banning political parties and more to do with silencing what had been perhaps the most direct and effective tool connecting the left with its urban base. Outlawing MIR and the PCV also meant outlawing *Tribuna Popular*. With no representation in Congress and no media to relay its message, the PCV could not sustain its outreach strategy to urban popular sectors, amplifying local grievances as it had before. And as grievances mounted ahead of full-scale armed conflict, residents of the 23 de Enero found themselves increasingly unheard and unrepresented, both by the government and its opponents. Over time, insurgents' inability to connect with urban popular sectors grew clearer, and absent a Communist counterpoint, triumphalist narratives tended to conflate popular rejection of insurgents' broader aims with support for the government. In January 1963, Communists and other radical-left groups like the MIR again failed to mobilize Caracas popular sectors to overthrow the government during the January 23 celebrations. In response, new Interior Minister Carlos Andrés Pérez confidently proclaimed: "The minority is every day becoming more of a minority."[136] Meanwhile, popular daily *Últimas Noticias* heaped praise on urban popular sectors for refusing to heed insurgents' call: "On January 23 the people won a battle, this time against the reds."[137]

This was the context in which elections to determine Betancourt's successor went ahead in December 1963. Both insurgents and the government cast them as a referendum on Betancourt's brand of democracy. Well aware of Betancourt's unpopularity, especially among urban popular sectors, coalition parties divorced the institutions of democracy from the President who had sworn to defend them. Rafael Caldera, running again as the center-right

COPEI candidate, stressed ahead of the vote that "the elections are of the people, not of Betancourt."[138] But these remarks were offered against the backdrop of insurgent calls for abstention, promoted through a fierce guerrilla campaign centered especially in Caracas. In the 23 de Enero, insurgents opened fire on police patrols and set ablaze four vehicles to hinder reinforcements.[139] The following day there were reports of an "intense firefight in the 23 de Enero"[140] that left five people dead and at least 17 wounded in the neighborhood alone, on top of ten dead and over 100 wounded tallied two days earlier throughout Caracas.[141]

On Election Day voters flocked to the polls. Observers and political elites alike interpreted the defeat of guerrilla calls to boycott the election as a success for their brand of democracy, especially when Raúl Leoni Otero, of Betancourt's AD party, won. But a closer look at the results showed that Caracas especially continued to reject the AD-COPEI coalition.[142] In the 23 de Enero, voters once again supported Wolfgang Larrazábal—whom they had overwhelmingly backed in 1958—although he had spent most of the Betancourt presidency outside the political fray, as Ambassador to Chile.[143] His support in the neighborhood in part reflected local hopes for a return to the promises of the coup that Larrazábal had led on 23 January 1958. But it was also a rejection of the coalition government.[144] All told, the AD-COPEI-URD coalition that had sought to consolidate popular democracy after 1958 could not even muster 30% of the vote in the neighborhood whose name—at least in rhetoric— reflected the popular origins of that democratic project. That this occurred while the government engaged in the most intense period of state repression Venezuela would experience for thirty years—during which Betancourt suspended constitutional liberties for nearly half of his term,[145] during which more people died in Caracas in one year than during the entire Pérez Jiménez dictatorship, during which residents of the 23 de Enero had faced both administrative abandonment and armed siege—only set in sharper relief the distance between the government and its people in the barrios of Caracas, who despite it all continued to flout insurgent calls for abstention. As political alienation begat social stigmatization, residents would continue to inhabit a space of ambiguous loyalties born not of the abstract notion of armed conflict but of their everyday experiences with insurgent and counterinsurgent battles.

CHAPTER 4

"The Fight Was Fierce"

Uncertain Victories in the Streets and the Polls, 1963–1969

"Peace," blared the headline, "has returned to the 23 de Enero." On the seventh anniversary of the founding of Venezuelan democracy, the housing project named after democracy's founding date lay in unfamiliar calm. In the previous five years the neighborhood had come to be known as "one of the most dangerous in Caracas." But by 23 January 1965, when the daily *El Nacional* ran a four-page piece on the neighborhood, residents reported a dramatic shift, a "one hundred percent" improvement, a "spirit of optimism that was not here before." "The fear that reigned," the paper concluded, "has been buried."

In fact, residents' accounts revealed fears that ran deep and conflicted. They told of raids on their homes that came "on several occasions." They told of nightly gunfights and their deadly effects: "police patrols were shot at, and they returned fire, almost always killing innocent bystanders." And, they bared indignation at the stigma that had come to mark a place not long before hailed as the cradle of democracy: "The neighborhood cannot run with all the blame. The 23 de Enero has been greatly slandered." The common thread in their testimonies was a pattern of generalized violence that residents pinned on both the government and insurgents: "Many instances of violence were provoked by outsiders. [But] undoubtedly," the paper admitted, "there were violations by some authorities."[1]

In the space between the stability they welcomed and its steep price was an ambiguous view of the emerging political system that escaped most analyses of the 1963 elections, widely seen as a popular stamp of approval for the government in its fight with insurgents. But testimonies suggest a more complicated relationship where support for the abstract idea of democracy, though cemented at the polls, grew not because, but in spite of, residents' experience during the period, reflecting their understanding of who comprised the insurgency on one hand, and their continuing aspirations for what they imagined the political system should concretely deliver on the other. Beyond the spectacular violence captured in headlines of the period,[2] the contradictions it wrought for the government, and the uses to which Communists put it in appealing to urban popular sectors, most residents experienced those years in terms of the impact of the violence on their everyday lives, which even after four decades remained seared in their memories.

"YEARS OF ANGUISH": VIOLENCE AND IDEOLOGY IN THE EARLY 1960S

"After 1960 and AD came to rule, Betancourt, it was five years of anguish here in the 23 de Enero," recalled Silveria Ríos of Block 37 in the Zona F. She had arrived in the neighborhood in 1960 in time for the worst of the violence, after a friend vacated the ground-floor apartment she had squatted. "That was horrible. *Plomo* [lead, bullets] day and night. [Guerrillas] would come and climb on the hallways, the rooftops, and they weren't from here. And I had [three] small children, five years of anguish. The experience was pretty disastrous." It was enough to keep Ríos from venturing outside: "One didn't go out. I was completely shut in with the kids." But continuing problems with water service two years after the revolution of 1958 meant that "we had to carry the water, but we did have pipes," highlighting the government's contradictory place in the neighborhood—sidelining service needs while staking a strong security presence. These problems would only worsen. In 1963, newspapers reported that the fifth anniversary of the 1958 coup also marked the twentieth day of water shortages in the neighborhood whose name memorialized it.[3] Ríos even considered moving, "but I didn't have the means," so she and her family stayed. Yet the memory of life under AD and Betancourt would inform her political choices—she would go on to vote for the center-right COPEI party.[4]

Lourdes Quintero (fig. 14), on the thirteenth floor of Block 37, had voted for Betancourt in 1958. But like Ríos what she recalled of his term was "the *plomazón* [gunfire], we had to sleep on the *floor*. . . . It was a regular shootout, horrendous." Then in her late thirties, the mother of four had braved uncer-

FIGURE 14. Lourdes Quintero, from Zona F, 23 de Enero. (Photo by the author)

tainty to squat an apartment after Pérez Jiménez's ouster. Now she and her family tried to make sense of the violence that left them dodging bullets in their apartment: "What the fight was about, I don't remember very well. . . . Here in the blocks they threw bottles, that street below had armored things, tanks. That was full of tanks there." Asked if they shot at the buildings, Quintero replied "at the buildings, because from the buildings they threw the Molotov bombs, the students. That was, well, that was up to here with students, horrible."[5]

Luis Correa was among them, a student at the Universidad Central. In January 1961, Communist Youth militants fired at police and military units attempting to search the campus. Students were aided in part by laws barring state security forces from entering university grounds. But after a week, aiming to "'raise the tension, the political temperature of the moment' in order to create the conditions for a civilian and military insurrection," they left the campus and took up the fight in the 23 de Enero, where no autonomy existed. "It was almost fifteen days stuck in the blocks," he recalled. "No one left, no one could leave. That was even tougher than the University because there you had participation of the people. They threw rocks, chairs, made barricades, everything. Something fierce."[6]

Correa's account highlights how insurgent leaders imagined the relationship between the university as the intellectual core of the insurrection, and the 23 de Enero as its heart, the place from where, much as it had on 23 January 1958, popular rebellion would take root and unleash a revolution. But what Correa billed as "participation of the people" was far more fraught. Consider Quintero's testimony, recalling armed clashes in the early days of the insurgency:

> LQ: One time the police were chasing some kids, students, coming up [the stairs] with crates full of bombs. We opened the door [and said], "leave those bombs here and keep on running."
>
> AV: They came in?
>
> LQ: Yes, we opened the door. . . . They were running, yelling "Help us! Help us! Help us!" And we opened the door, and they left a crate here and then we threw it down the chute, all bombs. There were many, *la pelea era brava* [the fight was fierce].

To be sure, it is difficult to glean the extent to which these forms of seemingly spontaneous support reflected broader ideological affinities. In Quintero's case, what emerges is material aid for the insurgency reflecting familial solidarity, where insurgents were more likely to be seen as restless youth than as hardened political partisans. Recalling another instance, Quintero notes:

> AV: But did you sympathize with the students? That is, did you understand them?
>
> LQ: Well, it's not that we understood them, but we helped them.
>
> AV: How did you help them?
>
> LQ: For instance one time a kid burned his back with a bomb, because when he threw it, it fell on his back. Two kids brought him here, we kept him, treated him, well, we helped them, we gave them water, and food, and whatever we could. They were going around hurling . . . and this was full of students, but I don't remember for what purpose, why, how it all started. I know it was during the government of Betancourt, very tough.
>
> AV: Were the students Communists?
>
> LQ: Apparently. They came here because of that. They came from below because of that. Downstairs it was full of tanks.
>
> AV: And were there many soldiers or police?
>
> LQ: Many military, not police, military.
>
> AV: And did you have to help a lot people?
>
> LQ: Yes, of course, everyone around here helped the students.
>
> AV: So the people in the building helped?

LQ: Of course, they were young kids, students.

AV: And were there people who did not want them here?

LQ: No, everyone lent a hand, some didn't because they were afraid, but others did, we helped them a lot, because they were young students.[7]

Quintero could distinguish between material and ideological support because, by their own admission, local youths involved in the struggle did so with little "preparation." Getting involved "was the thing to do," recalled Andrés Vásquez of Monte Piedad, sixteen years old at the time of the most intense clashes in 1963; it was a way to be recognized: "There he goes, that's the *ñángara*,"[8] said Vásquez, adding: "There were many my age, we were in high school, and from high school we got into trouble. We knew that the government was giving away all the country's riches. We fought for that, but many times, many of us didn't even know why we were fighting. What we were interested in was shooting at the police so that they wouldn't shoot at us."[9] Rafael Gutiérrez of Monte Piedad mostly felt "indignation" at the deaths of those "you studied with and were part of your group, you were together all day, you knew their true feelings and idiosyncrasies. . . . They weren't doing it because they were really political. For some it was amusement, even fun, for others it was snobbery, to tell the girls 'I was there.'"[10] Carlos Palma of Mirador was fourteen in 1962 when he first threw rocks at police. Reflecting on the experience, Palma observed "in the great majority of cases, lack of awareness prevailed. Solidarity, yes. They hurt a student, they beat him, they killed him, and we have to be there. In solidarity. But at the end of the day you're in school because you want your degree . . . That's how it is."[11] Even among those like Ravín Asuase Sánchez of La Cañada (fig. 15), who would at fifteen in 1964 formally join a local guerrilla cell, ferrying materials and messages from the city to rural units while also fighting state agents in the neighborhood, the question of popular support was riven between his aims of "taking power" and what he understood as a more muted reaction from his neighbors:

The *pueblo* supports you based on how that same *pueblo* gauges the government. Maybe it didn't translate into militancy, but it did translate into a sentimental support. That might mean you were running from the police through the stairs and suddenly a door opened and you went in there. For instance, you climbed on the 12th floor, as a sharpshooter, and suddenly the police came into the building, and you could only rely on the community. In other words, you need somewhere to hide, be it weapons or people, to escape if you weren't from there. So that was part of the thing, and one way or another there was always some family.[12]

FIGURE 15. Ravín Asuase Sánchez,
from La Cañada, 23 de Enero.
(Photo by the author)

These accounts illustrate a difference between insurgent youths and youths
in the insurgency, where political consciousness and participation reflected
parts of a spectrum rather than any more formal dichotomy. To suggest that
youths who engaged in clashes with the government did so only or even primarily without a larger sense of purpose would be to overstate the case; nor
did all youths form part of the insurgency. Said Carlos Palma of the fluid
dynamic at play:

> It started as rebelliousness. There was a mutiny in the *liceo* [high school] . . . some-
> one started throwing rocks. What happens? Maybe you start throwing rocks
> because you are restless, because they killed so-and-so student. But from that
> experience, you begin to talk about things. And there are many people who are
> more advanced than you, are conscious of things. And they start—words some-
> times sound too harsh—but to indoctrinate. Today it's ideology? Instruction?
> Recruitment? In the end it's all the same. You needed indoctrination.[13]

In particular, Palma recalled "a little book, of comics, called 'Cuba for Begin-
ners.' It told you the history of Cuba in a humorous way. . . . You started there.
They had contacts. Many contacts. 'I want to go the guerrillas,' some said.
And some did. But there were bridges, little bridges, to see what you could
do, if at some point you could do something, some task." At the heart of the
conflict, then, lay a loose structure that allowed local youths to travel different

FIGURE 16. Schoolchildren in Plaza Cristo Rey, Zona Central, in January 1965. On the walls in the background are allusions to the guerrilla conflict. At left may be read: "Navidad sin sangre" [Christmas without bloodshed]. (Archivo *El Nacional*)

paths within a wider insurgency, forming stronger or weaker attachments to reflect increasingly intense experiences of life under siege.

More broadly, the various accounts of local youth involvement in the conflicts of the early and mid 1960s exposed a feature of the insurgency's evolution in the 23 de Enero tied especially to the neighborhood's built environment. Beyond questions of ideology, participation, or indoctrination, what linked local youth was the Liceo Manuel Palacio Fajardo. Originally located at the geographic center of the neighborhood in the Cristo Rey (fig. 16) cultural, commercial, and entertainment complex, the Liceo Fajardo was a space unique in the neighborhood, the only site where all sectors of the 23 de Enero—eastern and western, squatters and renters, blocks and ranchos—converged. It was here that area youths between 12 and 18 years of age were formed, against the backdrop not only of a raging political conflict, but more immediately of facilities reflecting many of the administrative and physical pressures facing the neighborhood as a whole. By the time the school opened in October 1959, almost two years after the overthrow of Pérez Jiménez, its spaces were already ill suited to attend to the growing number of area youths. In 1961 the Banco Obrero's scathing report on the area's services had made special and repeated emphasis on the need for an additional *liceo*. In 1963, as more and more migrants settled in ranchos in the neighborhood, residents again called for the immediate construction of a second high school in the area.[14] But expansion and relocation would not come until the mid-1970s. Instead, throughout the 1960s the school's deficiencies gave students the opportunity to make their first forays in collective action; at times, they overlapped into the wider insurgency, as protests over immediate needs exposed systemic problems that helped shape understandings about democracy's weaknesses and opportunities.

For example, in the midst of the insurgency, Carlos Palma remembered peers setting ablaze tires on the street to protest inadequate laboratory facilities at the Liceo Fajardo. Several days later, "they started building new labs. Maybe it wasn't because of [the protest]," he acknowledged, "maybe it was already budgeted, I don't know. But the lesson stayed, that if you don't start shit, you get nothing. So that was always there as a referent: remember that thing with the lab, we had to burn some tires. So for anything, that was the formula, maybe unconsciously, and that has continued, that has stayed. And maybe for many things people throw rocks before they even say anything."[15]

Palma's account of the Liceo Fajardo labs sets in sharp relief the relationship between physical space, street protest, and incipient political consciousness in the neighborhood during this period, especially as grievances over the area's infrastructure mounted in the face of twin pressures—a growing population, and dwindling state resources. Local insurgents were certainly attuned to this reality. Said Ravín Asuase Sánchez: "Small struggles are where leadership is created . . . it's the ones who find the things that the community needs, well, they create leadership from below. Based on basic needs, understand?" Sánchez went on: "I feel that at that time, the war, the political issues, we went toward that and left working with the masses. . . . And as we abandon[ed] working with the masses, we were more and more isolated, we lost more and more touch with the people and we were defeated."[16] But while they abandoned the strategic work of building mass support by mobilizing around the neighborhood's growing material needs, insurgents nevertheless continued to view the 23 de Enero in terms of the tactical advantages its physical space provided in their military and political struggle to seize state power.

THE SPACES OF INSURGENCY

Once insurgents' view of the neighborhood shifted, when it seemed no longer a place from where a popular rebellion might emanate, local rebels turned to their knowledge of the 23 de Enero's built environment to mount an increasingly effective urban guerrilla campaign through the creation of Tactical Combat Units (*Unidades Tácticas de Combate*, or UTCs) beginning in 1961—highly mobile cells that operated independently with only sporadic instruction.[17] "Stairs were the safest," recalled Ravín Asuase Sánchez, out of view and therefore out of gun range of the National Guard troops posted below. Each 150-apartment superblock held five stairwells, set in from the outdoors and invisible to the exterior. They opened to hallways that spanned the length of the building and looked out below on floors four, eight, and twelve, which allowed insurgents "to be in the stairs and have someone in the hallways keeping watch, or even sharpshooting, depending on the action you were doing." The same stairs allowed for access to rooftops, where insurgents discovered that besides providing an elevated firing position, the altitude and valley winds helped to scatter leaflets throughout the neighborhood and much of the surrounding areas. In Monte Piedad, for instance, "those blocks, the first one, since it was at the head of a peninsula of sorts, well they climbed there on the roof, and threw flyers, and the wind grabbed them, and those flyers ended up in Chacao [east Caracas]. . . . They spread all over."[18]

But the area's roads offered the greatest tactical benefit for insurgents, according to Asuase Sánchez. "If you started a mess in Block 7 [in Monte Piedad], that meant you could paralyze the entire intersection, and that intersection is where everyone went to El Silencio [downtown], or Mirador, or Zona F, understand? So they were strategic sites. . . . Anytime there was some action that meant paralyzing the neighborhood, that was one site you needed to take."[19] Especially since that intersection also led to the Ministry of Defense, nestled between Blocks 7 and 9 of Monte Piedad and overlooking the Miraflores Presidential Palace below. Rosa Amelia de González of La Cañada remembered giving "a hell of a fight" in 1963 to disrupt traffic to and from the Ministry. A long time AD militant then in her early forties, González had left the party ahead of the 1963 elections because of "all the things Betancourt had done," joining the short-lived splinter AD-Opposition party in its bid to defeat Betancourt's successor, Raúl Leoni. But she also linked with local guerrillas. "The *muchachos* would put bags of caltrops [on the road] so when the ministers drove by, their tires would blow." Laughing, she recalled, "I was the one who bought the bags of caltrops," a risky proposition, since buying them in bulk raised suspicions about their use in the insurgency. "'No, that's for the political types and *guerrilleros*, not me. I'm building a house!'" she would tell vendors. "Those caltrops would appear in the morning, I don't know what time they put them out, and when the cars came to the Ministry of Defense you could hear the tires, you know, it was a tactic, a protest."[20]

If the neighborhood's physical features helped shape insurgent tactics, they also forced counterinsurgency innovations by the state. In October 1960, "Operation Clean Sweep" had brought an unprecedented show of force to the neighborhood, aimed at overwhelming the still-budding insurgency in accordance with Betancourt's order to "energetically repress" suspected subversives. In its wake, Tactical Combat Units (UTCs) emerged in March 1961 to meet blunt force with small, nimble, independent cells capable of inflicting quick strikes whenever opportunities arose. Beyond their tactical advantages, UTCs proved successful by exploiting weaknesses in the security apparatus, in particular poor coordination among several different police forces attached to individual ministries, government offices, and city jurisdictions. By early 1962, Betancourt resolved to break the back of the insurgency, entrusting the task to his former personal secretary and protégé Carlos Andrés Pérez and appointing him Coordinator of Public Order in late January. On his appointment, U.S. *chargé d'affaires* C. Allan Stewart wrote to State Department officials: "When Carlos Andrés took over things began to happen, with the military getting a free rein to move in and with the police forces working more closely together."[21] By March Betancourt had promoted Pérez to Minister of Interior; in that capacity Pérez personally oversaw the purge of Revolutionary Left Movement (*Movimiento de Izquierda Revolucionaria*, or MIR, made up mainly of disenchanted AD youth who broke off from Betancourt's party) and Communist militants from government offices beginning in June 1962.[22]

But Pérez's primary mission remained the security situation, especially in Caracas as rumors spread in 1963 of a Cuba-backed insurgent plan to disrupt the December elections, and as insurgents staged spectacular assaults that put the government on the defensive. Consider the following U.S. Embassy report: "More serious was a gunfight between government forces and machine-gun armed dissidents in the famous 23 of January District, which livened the night of April 17. This began when two municipal policemen standing guard near a gasoline station were brutally machine gunned to death by unknown assailants. In the ensuing fracas . . . an estimated 400 municipal policemen converged on the area and recovered the bodies under fire."[23] On 1 May, insurgents killed another policeman on patrol in the 23 de Enero.

In the wake of these incidents, Pérez came to recognize that stemming a highly mobile urban guerrilla force would require more than the blunt instrument of an oversized security presence. Instead, he revised the plans that had given rise to "Operation Clean Sweep." On the advice of U.S. counterinsurgency personnel and in consultation with Betancourt, a new counterinsurgency plan for Caracas took shape in the summer of 1963. Later identified as Plan Ávila—in reference to the mountain range shielding the capital from the Caribbean Sea—it drew on Clean Sweep's division of Caracas into eight "neuralgic points," among them the 23 de Enero district,[24] each one assigned a unit empowered to "plan their actions according to their needs."[25] Behind these units, a unified police command would assess developments and deploy escalating levels of force: police, National Guard, and eventually the Army, which would take final command.[26]

Decentralized commands with the support of repressive forces gave authorities maximum agility in rapidly changing urban environments.[27] But it also meant that individual operatives had discretion over violence, enabling widely divergent responses within a plan otherwise imagined to progressively escalate violence. The net effect was a cauldron of fear and indignation among residents young and old, whether militant or, as Rafael Gutiérrez of Monte Piedad put it, "alien to all that type of activity." In Block 1, overlooking the Presidential Palace, Andrés Vásquez remembered that "they had to bring the tanks, and set them up there, one pointing this way, the other that way." The show of force made searching apartments more efficient, and because of it, more traumatic. "To search a block," Rafael Gutiérrez of Monte Piedad vividly recalled, "they would first come quietly, then make a racket, so everyone was caught off guard, because while they entered it was a refuge. They entered and then they started, apartment by apartment . . . looking for hotheads, for weapons, for explosives, flyers." At the height of the insurgency in 1963, "it was constant, it was common, the *allanamientos* [searches]," says Gutiérrez. "They would search your apartment, search the block. I remember for me it was sort of traumatic. I remember once for instance, we were all sleeping and suddenly boom boom boom boom boom, a war. So everyone woke up, 'Shit, what happened? What's going on?' . . . I could have died. Some guy tearing down your door with a rifle, a machine gun, some crap in his hand, threatening you. The most dangerous thing I had was a slingshot."[28]

The experience made for a level of violence so seemingly disproportional that it lent itself to lasting conspiracy theories, even forty years after the fact.

In Monte Piedad, then thirteen-year-old Gustavo Parabón understood what appeared like everyday searches as "state violence. Even being very young, you watched as men, armed, would come and shoot against the building because according to what I heard, the government assumed that there were guerrillas in the apartments, and by whatever means they sought to terrorize the population, a community that I would dare say was innocent of all that was going on." Searching for an explanation, he offered: "Of course, because this neighborhood was built by the dictatorship, they tried whatever they could to dissuade families who identified with the dictatorship, but through terror." In other words, everyday repression emerged for him as blanket retaliation less for insurgent activities than for the neighborhood's origins in the ousted regime.

For Parabón, however, the collective experience of state violence brought with it a "principle of solidarity that when a neighbor's apartment was searched, well, because he was an activist and belonged to the Socialists, well it made you sad how they terrorized a whole family, tore up his apartment, ruined his stuff. So that motivated you, you had to be in solidarity with your neighbors."[29] It was the same across the neighborhood in Block 44 of Zona F. When National Guardsmen stopped and began to beat and harass Alexis Alzolay, also thirteen at the time and well known by neighbors as an avid athlete, as he returned from school, "people screamed at them to stop, but that just made [the Guard] more angry. They had no problem attacking youth, it didn't matter if they were guilty of something or not. . . . It was so common," said Alzolay, "that I didn't even question why it was happening." For Alzolay, the experience sparked resentment that over time gave way to a consciousness of the strained relationship between the government and its people in the neighborhood.[30]

Yet not everyone proved so ready to dismiss the actions of insurgents as a source of the government repression. "There were many people, not just me" said Rafael Gutiérrez of Monte Piedad, "who were disgusted by the police for the way they behaved, and were disgusted by the situation [we] were living in. . . . In a building like this one maybe there were just four Communists. So because of those four Communists, every fifteen or twenty days my house would be searched, and I'm not political." The effect was unsurprising: "There wasn't the harvest of conscience for those people who saw the situation poorly."[31] Raids, troop deployments, and firefights with insurgents were deadly and terrifying. But so were the burning of public-transportation vehicles and the looting of area stores, in particular the Central Madeirense in Zona Central, sacked repeatedly during the most intense period of fighting.[32] "That was an expropriation," said Ravín Asuase Sánchez, who added with a laugh: "At times it was a robbery, a holdup, but for us it was an expropriation."

The burning of public-transportation vehicles would become part of the standard tactical repertoire of insurgents, who used charred remains as barricades against police and military assaults. But the looting of major grocery stores came across as a problem of petty crime. "The truth is that it was very uncomfortable, because food became scarce," said Elaya de Delgado of La Cañada. "You had to jump around to find food. That had a big impact on me. . . . I remember they would wake my brother and me up at dawn to stand in line to buy milk and meat."[33] And when UTCs raided payroll registers to raise quick cash for the insurgency, it was the very popular sectors it aimed to represent who felt the brunt of the impact.[34] Whether tactical or criminal, the cumulative impact of "expropriations" was to seriously erode the quality of life of residents of the neighborhood as a whole and popular sectors more broadly, limiting their access to resources and transportation. "There was a time," area residents later recalled, "when the 23 de Enero was practically isolated from the rest of the city."[35]

That residents of this centrally located neighborhood considered themselves isolated was certainly remarkable, and helps illustrate the all-encompassing scope of the conflict for the men, women, and children of the 23 de Enero. It also marked the climax of the armed struggle in the area. Following the 1963 elections, guerrilla strategy shifted more and more to the countryside, from where insurgents hoped to regroup. Yet despite occasional outbreaks in urban guerrilla activity, over the next three years the broader guerrilla movement fizzled both as rural counterinsurgency efforts grew more sophisticated, and as internal rifts about the wisdom of armed struggle fractured the forces of insurgency.[36] When PCV leaders formally renounced armed struggle in April 1967, it was the culmination of a long-gestating process seeking "Democratic Peace" and reentry to the political system ahead of elections in 1968 under the slogan "Neither continuity nor Caldera: Change!" in reference to the center-right COPEI party's founder and once-again presidential candidate, Rafael Caldera.[37]

In the 23 de Enero, too, residents had begun the process of seeking social reintegration after years of conflict-ridden isolation. Neighborhood associations flourished anew, focusing their work especially on youth outreach and

FIGURE 17. In August 1967, children at play in front of Block 37, Zona F. In the background, graffiti signed JVC (*Juventud Comunista de Venezuela*, Communist Youth of Venezuela) demands the release of Gustavo Machado, leader of the Communist Party of Venezuela, at the time jailed for his role in the insurgency. (Gustavo Beltrán / Archivo *El Nacional*)

staging athletic events (fig. 17).[38] The neighborhood's administrator, the Banco Obrero (BO), also built a new gym in the Zona F in late 1963.[39] And in 1965, following years of organizing by rancho residents who had been left out of the Sierra Maestra superblocks, the BO began construction on the "La Libertad" residential complex, comprising sixteen four-story apartment blocks nestled at the intersection of La Cañada, Sierra Maestra, and Monte Piedad, near the rotary of Block 7, in the eastern 23 de Enero.[40] It was part of a general increase in both public and private investment in Caracas following the lows of the Betancourt years.[41] Meanwhile, after registering the lowest level of rent compliance in 1963, the BO reported steady increases in rent payments, and attendant decreases in rent delinquency, beginning in 1964.[42] The ebbing conflict also gave the government an opening to reposition tanks from area buildings to the Central Madeirense to ward against looting, generating a measure of goodwill from residents.[43] And in 1966, city government officials formally declared the 23 de Enero a parish [*parroquia*], entitled to its own mayorally appointed administrator, clerk, and registrar of records. The 23 de Enero was no longer only a neighborhood; it was now a separate jurisdiction in Caracas.[44]

The neighborhood's designation as an independent parish streamlined basic administrative functions in an area whose population had ballooned since its inauguration ten years prior. It also recognized the neighborhood's distinctive physical and demographic features and attendant needs. Prior to its constitution as an independent parish, the 23 de Enero neighborhood was split between Sucre and Catedral parishes, both consisting primarily of long-established colonial-era neighborhoods that the original housing project had replaced. Now as its own parish, all areas of the original housing project—and the ranchos that had emerged since 1958—fell under the same jurisdiction. But the new designation held an underside—enabling generalizations about an area now formally set apart as its own entity. As the armed conflict abated, so too did the sense of isolation that residents had experienced. Yet just as residents began to overcome their neighborhood's physical isolation, a more lasting alienation of the neighborhood took root. Residents referred to it as "slander"—the headlines and commentary that broad-brushed the neighborhood and its inhabitants as insurgents or troublemakers, responsible if not by action then by omission for failing to contain the guerrillas among them.[45] To be sure, they did not object to characterizations of the neighborhood as a hotbed of the insurgency—that much was unquestionable. It was the incomplete narratives that failed to account for the complex, uneasily generalized web of contradictory support and opposition that shaped residents' relationship both to insurgents and the government.

These narratives would continue to inform not only press accounts and popular culture after the most intense of the fighting eased. They would also shape period analyses of the neighborhood, resulting in lasting characterizations that projected from headlines while downplaying the 23 de Enero's recent history. Consider the following. In contrast to hope—"the prevailing mood in the barrios" where "freedom for improvement and expansion" among rancho settlers created a spirit of opportunity and self-achievement—Talton Ray's 1969 study of urban popular sectors identified the 23 de Enero as a "slum of despair," similar to the "ghetto-like areas in more industrialized countries." It was a place where "working class families live in buildings which belong to absentee landlords and pay high rent for shabby quarters; where physical improvements have to wait for the landlord's initiative; and where tenants are evicted at his discretion. . . . Something approximating this industrialized urban mentality appeared in the *superbloques* . . . until very recently Venezuela's most authentic example of real slums."[46]

Of course, residents had not waited for the BO. Especially in 1958 they had actively mobilized to secure everything from material improvements to rent reductions to additional area housing. Insofar as that activism abated after 1958, it owed largely to the violence that came to grip the neighborhood. Neither were experiences—and attendant needs—similar across the neighborhood, as residents of the eastern and western sectors had laid bare. Yet folding an imagined experience of squatters into that of the neighborhood as a whole gave rise to problematic causal explanations. "They soon created an atmosphere of destitution unknown in most barrios," Ray continued, a "degrading experience [that] was certainly one reason the parties of the extreme left were able to gain complete dominance over life in the *superbloques*." But to suggest that insurgents had dominance in the 23 de Enero was to overstate the case dramatically. At best, residents' support was contingent, and tempered by overwhelming backing for the electoral process if not the leading parties in power. Taken together, these portrayals of the neighborhood exposed a legacy of the period less direct but more durable. Long gone were portrayals of area residents as bulwarks of democracy; the neighborhood had instead become a "red zone" synonymous with unrest and irresponsibility.[47]

EARTHQUAKES PHYSICAL AND POLITICAL: THE (BRIEF) RETURN OF PÉREZ JIMÉNEZ AND THE "CONSOLIDATION" OF DEMOCRACY

The ground shook for nearly a minute. At 8:02 P.M. on 29 July 1967 an earthquake measuring 6.7 on the Richter scale struck 20 kilometers north of Caracas, sending ripples throughout the capital. "That was ugly, ugly," remembers Andrés Vásquez of Monte Piedad. "I was behind Block 2 and that just started to move." In Block 1 Mireya Maldonado was relaxing with friends "when we felt like a movement. . . . 'A quake, a quake,' I said. So we opened the door and that was an avalanche of people, screaming. That was something very big." In Block 37 in Zona F, Lino Álvarez knew immediately it was an earthquake; he had lived through one before rushing to the superblocks in January 1958. "I was in the apartment and held on to a column while it passed," he says. Elaya Delgado of La Cañada was in the middle of dinner "and we had the glasses and dishes and they started *tiquitiquitiqui*. So we got up and my husband says, 'It's shaking!' And really, the table moved, everything moved. We tried to open the door to go downstairs but it was stuck. I think we were among the last to make it downstairs." In the fray a neighbor had even left her daughter on the stairs, and Maldonado grabbed her on her way out. Fearing aftershocks, many refused to reenter the superblocks for days afterward. "That was like a festival, tents from here to there," says Vásquez, "everyone sleeping outside with music and games." But slowly they returned. Eloy Deslances of La Cañada remembered that people "would sleep outside at night, and in the morning they would go up, bathe, do whatever, and then they came back down." Though not Deslances: "Why would I sleep poorly [outside] with my bed upstairs?" Asked if he felt safe, he replied: "I was fine, relaxed. No big deal . . . that's sturdy construction, like all the buildings Pérez Jiménez did. It's just that people got scared and all those people went outside."[48]

In fact, once fears subsided and the toll of the strongest earthquake to hit Caracas in over 150 years began to emerge, what residents of the 23 de Enero drew from the experience was the contrast between their neighborhood and the more affluent sections of Caracas. There, several buildings collapsed, leaving 236 dead and nearly 2,000 wounded. But in the 23 de Enero "nothing really happened," said Vásquez, adding: "It was out in the east of Caracas where two or three buildings fell. But here in the 23 de Enero, this didn't move, it didn't even crack, absolutely nothing happened." Delgado too, asked if there was any damage to her building, recalled: "No, nothing. I tell you, [the earthquake] was strong. But no. Over there [in the east], a building caught fire and there were aftershocks. But I went back upstairs." Stressed Deslances: "It was violent. I didn't suffer anything. Nothing to tell, as they say, and there were buildings that split, that cracked. [But] the blocks stayed intact, just as you see them."

Nearly ten years after the overthrow of Pérez Jiménez, the 1967 earthquake had dramatically illustrated the durability of the dictator's superblocks. Against the backdrop of the derision in which Betancourt and his administration held the housing project on taking office, and the subsequent years of violence, isolation, and alienation that befell their neighborhood under a popularly elected government, the earthquake had unwittingly served to call up images of Pérez Jiménez and his project for popular housing. In the span of a minute, the criticisms about exorbitant costs, grandiose designs, even misplaced ambitions that had enveloped the 23 de Enero after 1958 lay buried in the rubble. Observed Luis Lander—whose father ran the Banco Obrero early in the Betancourt administration—reflecting on the durability of Pérez Jiménez's construction projects, especially in the wake of the 1967 earthquake: "That [was] something absolutely ostentatious, [but] it was a clear demonstration of how talent and resources produce imposing works. Of course without talent many resources do not produce the same, but that is something that would not have been remotely possible if there had not been an unlimited use of resources."[49]

If the 1967 earthquake called up memories of Pérez Jiménez, its political aftershocks would extend well into the elections of 1968. On the surface, COPEI's Rafael Caldera won a stunning electoral victory over AD. After consecutive victories in 1958 and 1963, AD had emerged as Venezuela's major political party. But those victories had come at a cost. Its reversal of Pérez Jiménez's urban policies had bled support from popular sectors in Caracas,[50] which its battles against insurgents had then decimated. Meanwhile Betancourt's rule over AD had resulted in party splits and high-profile defections that further shrank the party base. In fact, much as he had engineered the MIR's split in 1960 in order to consolidate his leadership over the party, and as he had moved to secure Raúl Leoni's nomination in 1963, ahead of elections in 1968 Betancourt again maneuvered to place his chosen candidate, Gonzalo Barrios Bustillos, as AD's candidate for president.[51] In doing so Betancourt circumvented the AD primary process that had nominated Luis Beltrán Prieto Figueroa, who had made of reaching out to urban popular sectors—among them the 23 de Enero—a centerpiece of his campaign for the nomination.[52]

In response, Prieto left AD and formed a splinter party—the People's Electoral Movement (Movimiento Electoral del Pueblo, or MEP)—to vie for the presidency. Yet in the wake of the AD-MEP split, it was COPEI's Caldera who won the vote with a plurality of 30%, to become the third president in the post-1958 era.[53] Caldera's victory marked the first peaceful transfer of power from a dominant party to its opposition in Venezuelan history. It also a signaled Venezuela's consolidation as a stable multiparty democracy, undergirded by inter-elite pacts crafted precisely for this pivotal moment.[54] That Caldera had won with a plurality of the vote, edging AD by mere tenths of a percent, seemed only to confirm the resiliency of Venezuela's political system and its broad popular support. That he had made pacification with guerrillas and legalization of the Communist Party bedrocks of his campaign seemed, especially coming from a candidate of Christian Democracy, final proof that Venezuela had turned the corner from transition to consolidation. In short, a decade after the fall of military dictatorship, analysts and observers alike agreed, Venezuelans had shown their political maturity, accepting the primacy of electoral democracy, the alternation in power that it invariably promised, and the two main parties that had surfaced from the fray of political options to lead their country in a new decade.[55]

But while Caldera's victory spoke of a turning point, a political drama unfolding at the margins planted doubts about the direction that turn might take. Marcos Pérez Jiménez had also scored a stunning electoral victory as the leader in exile of the Nationalist Civic Crusade (*Cruzada Cívica Nacionalista*, or CCN), claiming a seat in the Senate.[56] To win, Pérez Jiménez had relied on electoral support in Caracas, where CCN beat both AD and COPEI in the concurrent congressional ballot.[57] In response, Attorney General Antonio José Lozada filed a brief on 7 February 1969 in the Supreme Court seeking to invalidate Pérez Jiménez's victory.[58] Two months later, on 9 April, the Court ruled in favor of Lozada and annulled Pérez Jiménez's win on grounds that he had failed to register to vote—compulsory in Venezuela—and thus had forfeited his right to vie for elected office.[59] Over the next several days Pérez Jiménez supporters staged protests outside the Court and in public squares proclaiming that the decision slighted the "votes of the people" who voted for CCN.[60]

Among political elites opinions split. AD hailed the decision for having defined the right to vote, while COPEI called it "absurd" because the Court had encroached upon Congress's prerogative to determine its membership. Meanwhile the PCV warned that AD had "turned [Pérez Jiménez] into a martyr, a persecuted man, a good man."[61] And from Lima, Pérez Jiménez himself blasted the decision as a "political maneuver" by his political adversaries in the Court, namely those judges identified with AD which he branded as "my irreconcilable enemy."[62] He concluded: "Three or four [judges] have invalidated the will of 160,000 voters who cast ballots for me in Caracas."[63] It was a remarkable statement for someone who had once consolidated power by invalidating the votes of millions. But it also spoke to how powerful the vote had become as the pillar of Venezuela's political process.

Caldera's victory notwithstanding, the disjointed response to Pérez Jiménez's election to the Senate set in relief the still-tenuous nature Venezuela's democracy ten years into its founding. For analysts, Pérez Jiménez's strong showing in Caracas reeked of misguided wistfulness. Wrote political scientists John Martz and Peter Harkins: "One can only speculate that lower-class recollections of the mid-50s boom led some to a nostalgic if seriously flawed memory of 'the good old days' economically."[64] Fears of turning Pérez Jiménez into a martyr, added to discontent by some about institutional overreach, revealed a latent insecurity about how solid the foundations of Venezuelan democracy in fact remained. But what Pérez Jiménez's electoral victory unquestionably reflected was a deep contradiction facing Venezuelan democracy as it consolidated, namely, a lingering split between the Caracas and the national electorates.

Even as Caldera won the presidency, he lost in Caracas to Miguel Ángel Burelli Rivas of the URD.[65] In congressional voting, COPEI's loss in Caracas was more significant still, sliding to third behind both URD and Pérez Jiménez's CCN.[66] That Caldera had failed to win in Caracas reflected a pattern begun in 1958, when AD, too, had lost in Caracas while nevertheless claiming the presidency, a feat it repeated in 1963. Together, AD and COPEI's inability to secure constituencies in Caracas—the seat of power and comprising nearly 20% of the national vote—well exposed how the two parties emerging as Venezuela's main political brokers had failed to respond to an increasingly urban electorate during the years of democratic transition. According to later studies of COPEI, as late as 1968 the party remained identified with "rural and small-town middle classes."[67] Meanwhile AD's base had long since been solidified among labor unions and a rapidly dwindling peasantry.[68] Ten years after its founding, then, Venezuelan democracy remained riven by an uneasy relationship between the government and its primary concentration of voters, the urban electorate in Caracas.

It was a fact underscored in the 23 de Enero, where the 1968 elections well reflected this peculiar relationship between support for the electoral system expressed in voting, but continuing rejection of the parties then emerging as Venezuela's most powerful. Ten years after his overthrow, residents flocked to Pérez Jiménez's CCN, relegating the eventual winner COPEI to fourth in the polls in congressional voting.[69] To be sure, "nostalgia" for a period when they figured prominently in the state's plans for Venezuela partly accounted for their embrace of Pérez Jiménez. But such romanticism was forged against the backdrop of what had emerged as a contentious relationship with the democratic regime in the intervening ten years. Though renamed to reflect the founding date of the new democracy, the neighborhood nevertheless had grown into a hotbed of opposition to the budding regime. Most expressed this opposition at the ballot box, again and again rejecting AD and COPEI. Others voiced their rejection more violently, through armed conflict seeking to oust the nascent political system. As they entered a new decade, residents of the 23 de Enero would continue to exercise a fraught relationship with the government even as they came to accept the primacy of the AD-COPEI regime in the 1970s.

PART THREE

Streets of Protest

CHAPTER 5

Water, Women, and Protest

The Return of Local Activism, 1969–1977

For all the enthusiasm of political elites, in the 23 de Enero the change of government to COPEI seemed to begin much like the AD governments that it replaced had left off: mired in violence. On the morning of 4 May 1969—less than two months after Rafael Caldera took office—cars and buses making their way through the strategic Block 7 intersection in Monte Piedad were met by barricades of "barrels, tires, tree trunks, rocks of great size, broken bottles, and even the remains of an abandoned car."[1] For over six hours traffic was blocked, "practically isolating the whole sector." At the barricades people "burned tires [and] improvised bonfires on public streets, keeping a state of open rebellion."[2] In short, it bore all the hallmarks of the kind of insurgent violence that had characterized the previous decade.

Rather than militants seeking to topple the government, however, the people on the streets were "men, women, and children, [who] in joint action, took turns to guard the blockades." Their demand was as simple as it was dire: "We've spent 72 hours without water and we don't want any more promises," said one resident, who joined hundreds of others reportedly from various sectors of the 23 de Enero, all of whom had previously resolved to take to the streets.[3] At the water service, president Gustavo Maggi Calcaño recognized that residents "are correct" about the lack of water. But he chastised them all the same: "I don't think there's any need to resort to violence to demand a service," he said. "Rather, use dialogue, coordination."[4] Residents agreed, to a point. They had long tried dialogue and coordination. "On numerous occasions," said Juan Maita, Arturo García, and Pilar Córdova of La Cañada, "we have complained to the Banco Obrero how they have abandoned the neighbor-hood, and they haven't paid attention to us." It was enough to make them think that this latest water crisis was retaliation for neighbors' repeated com-plaints. Others had stopped paying bills for service that was faulty at best. Still others, in desperation, had tapped into water pipes after 22 days of irregular service, causing thousands of bolívares in damage.[5] Maita added, with a hint of regret: "We have also talked with the water service [*Instituto Nacional de Obras Sanitarias*, or INOS] about the shortages, and they finally heard us when we took a somewhat violent action."[6] By the afternoon on 4 May, "the problem was provisionally solved" as several trucks arrived to "pro-vide the precious liquid to families."[7] Within 24 hours, neighbors reported, service had returned to normal.[8] "If in fact this situation continues," they cautioned, "we won't have any more issues with the water service."[9]

The much-publicized May protest in the 23 de Enero came two months after what analysts hailed as the final act in the consolidation of Venezuelan democracy by political elites—marking as it did the third consecutive hando-ver of power from one president to the next.[10] Caldera had quickly moved to make good on his campaign promise to seek "pacification" with guerrillas, which his newly appointed Defense Minister called "a political, not a military, problem."[11] A Christian Democrat, Caldera tapped church leaders to spear-head negotiations with insurgents that would culminate in executive pardons and, eventually, the creation of several new political parties, such as Movement Toward Socialism (*Movimiento al Socialismo*, or MAS) made up of former guerrillas who renounced the armed struggle and now entered the political system in earnest.[12] Caldera had also reinstated the *Movimiento de Izquierda Revolucionaria* (MIR), and the *Partido Comunista de Venezuela* (PCV), over the loud objections of their erstwhile AD adversary Rómulo Betancourt.[13]

These moves pointed to significant national-level shifts as Caldera and insurgents moved formally to turn the page on the armed conflict. But these shifts reverberated strongly at the local level, too, especially in Caracas, where pacification brought a new emphasis on policing rather than militarization.[14] Eight days after taking office, Caldera ordered a restructuring of police services in the capital, formerly dispersed through various ministries and jurisdictions. "In order to ensure public order," his decree stated, "an adjustment of the Police Forces is necessary, providing them with proper plans of action, training, and technical direction."[15] The result was the Metropolitan Police (*Policía Metro-politana*, or PM). According to newly appointed Caracas Governor Carlos

Guinand Baldó, the new PM aimed "to achieve a better and more discriminate application of the repressive administrative justice that we are obligated to execute."[16] A new police academy followed shortly, and by mid-April Caldera appointed National Guard Colonel Hernán Delgado Sánchez as commander to "organize, professionalize, and coordinate" the new force.[17]

Two weeks later, hundreds of residents took to the streets of the 23 de Enero to protest 22 days without water. At first, police launched tear gas and arrested several youths. Then military police from the nearby Defense Ministry arrived, firing shots into the air and generating a "state of alarm" among the gathered crowd.[18] It was a familiar story of rapid escalation and militarization such as had marked much of the urban guerrilla struggle. But then, as tempers flared at the barricades, neighbors used megaphones to "call on the population to act peacefully, to avoid provoking bigger alterations or disturbances."[19] Later, Delgado Sánchez arrived on the scene "to learn of the nature of the protest and avoid bloodshed."[20] City councilman Héctor Marcano Coello also made his way to the neighborhood, "to take notes on residents' demands and assure them that he would take the necessary steps so that this problem does not persist," two days later bringing water service president Maggi Calcaño to the council for a public hearing.[21] Residents, meanwhile, stressed that "their actions had only one goal: to obtain free-flowing water." As water trucks arrived and neighbors received assurances that service would be restored, they began to disperse. The next morning, Governor Guinand Baldó met privately with parents of the detained youths, who won their release and took the opportunity to detail a long list of grievances afflicting their community.[22]

Much as Caldera's inauguration marked a turning point for Venezuelan democracy's institutional stability after a decade of conflict, the May 1969 protest also signaled a shift in residents' approach to mobilization. In particular, it inaugurated a decade of street protest spearheaded by neighbors at large, rather than by partisan insurgents, with aims that centered decidedly and explicitly on local concerns and community grievances, rather than on seizing state power. Stressing that their protest had as its "only goal" to secure water service was not just a way to underscore a particular demand. Coming as it did at the end of a decade when street actions were linked to political insurgency, residents instead distanced themselves from the ideological battles of a previous era. In turn, police de-escalation also marked a new approach to engaging with street protest, one characterized—at least at first—by outreach and negotiation efforts rather than outright repression of the sort that had marked the 1960s. The result was a period of intense mobilization throughout the 1970s as the accumulated grievances of a decade spent largely under siege thrust residents of the 23 de Enero anew into the streets, in a frenzy of activity not seen in the neighborhood since the earliest days of political transition in 1958, before Betancourt, MIR, armed struggle, and a decade of squandered opportunity.

In the ensuing years, however, victories proved few and far between as the scale of area problems mounted alongside the growing pressures of an urban explosion that had not abated since it began in the 1930s. And this against the backdrop of skyrocketing oil prices that left the state flush with petrodollars, and urban popular sectors grappling with the paradox of life under an oil boom while local conditions deteriorated. Meanwhile the early promise of a new, professional police force eroded as crime soared and repression returned in earnest, directed especially toward youth, whose disaffection grew with time and was more and more expressed in violent, and increasingly deadly, clashes with security forces. It was this youth to whom demobilized militants, largely muted in the wake of pacification but still present if one knew where to look, would eventually turn to help guide, and train, a new generation of radical political leaders. Still, for most residents, it was the vaunted party system and its major players that had proven victorious in the battles of the 1960s, and they resolved to abandon their support for small parties and instead embrace AD and COPEI in earnest, even if they grew increasingly skeptical of the vote's ability to achieve concrete goals. By decade's end, even mainstream political sectors would join a growing chorus to demand major reforms of the political system, critiquing the democracy that they helped institutionalize after 1958 as too rigid, while proposing its reinvention to accommodate the evident clamor of popular sectors for greater participation and accountability. Whether, and how, these various forces for change would come together would remain the decade's lingering question.

"A NEW DIRECTION IN POPULAR EXPRESSION": THE RETURN OF POPULAR PROTEST

"It had been a long time," read the *Últimas Noticias* editorial on 11 May 1969, "since Venezuelans took to the streets, to protest, in demonstrations." The piece came in direct response to the actions of 23 de Enero residents a week earlier that had captured headlines as well as the attention of authorities, who quickly mobilized to attend to neighbors' grievances. In fact, the paper added, "the first popular demonstrations of this type happened on the days before and after January 23 [1958]. At first it was an effort to overthrow the order of things. Then, to support a new order of things." In the intervening decade, however, the scale and tenor of popular protest had shrunk and shifted as mass demonstrations gave way to state repression, guerrilla insurgency, and repeated suspensions of constitutional rights. Now, as the actions of the 23 de Enero residents portended, a new era was afoot, or at least a return to an era of promise and opportunity, of mass protest and mobilization, that had marked the early transition to democracy. And it was the outgoing regime, even as it celebrated democracy's consolidation, that could take dubious credit for the shift. "Before leaving the government," the paper wrote, "AD can bask in the luxury of having given birth to a new direction in popular expression, not of protests against rights denied, or against repression, or even against democracy itself, but against negligence, government malfeasance, incubators of an anemic collective state akin to desperation." From that desperation would emerge this new direction, marked as it was by people in the streets, setting aside ideological arguments and instead expressing specific grievances over issues affecting their daily lives, "violently demanding solutions to problems after having petitioned, peacefully, again and again."[23] In fact, in the days that followed the protest in the 23 de Enero, residents of other popular sectors in Caracas, and even as far as the State of Bolívar, in southeastern Venezuela, would also take to the streets to express grievances ranging from water shortages to sewage leaks.[24]

The May protest revealed a manner and content to popular mobilization that seemed novel primarily because so long had passed since the last such demonstrations in Venezuela, and in Caracas in particular. But if the protest signaled a new era of mobilization, over the days and weeks that followed what also lay exposed was the scale of issues and grievances that would motivate them in the years ahead, grievances previously suppressed in the context of armed conflict and as urbanization in Caracas reached new levels of haste. Between 1961 and 1973, as planning policy shifted away from Caracas, the capital's population jumped from 1.6 million to 2.6 million, bringing new housing, sanitation, and transportation demands to an increasingly saturated city whose poverty rates now hovered around 50%.[25] In the 23 de Enero, protests over access to housing and sewer services by those who had squatted during the 1960s, and over improvements to basic infrastructure by superblock residents, marked the tenor of mobilization throughout the 1970s.

In fact, the day after the May 1969 protest, residents began to report on a host of area problems that had gone unattended, and grown worse, in the preceding years. Water shortages, of course, had plagued residents of the 23 de Enero almost immediately after the fall of Pérez Jiménez, as the occupation of apartments in the neighborhood's western sectors strained pumps and pipes. And while city officials observed that the problem was widespread throughout Caracas, water service officials reported that the exponential growth of western Caracas, and the 23 de Enero in particular, would require new infrastructure to offer a "long-term" solution to residents.[26]

But water was just one among many issues. "One of the main and most serious problems is the lack of educational facilities for our children," neighbors in the La Libertad sector reported, while Magdalena Arcia and Juana Paiva of Sierra Maestra added: "For a population as large as the 23 de Enero's the few existing schools are insufficient. . . . there are at least ten thousand children without a school, since the ones that are here can't fit them all."[27] Precise numbers were difficult to confirm, but the broader problem of inadequate schools proved telling; as early as 1959, residents and authorities had already identified it as a major area problem, and a decade later it remained so.

This was also true of drainage problems, in particular in the low-lying La Cañada sector, which in 1961 a Banco Obrero report on the superblocks had identified as a significant design flaw. As construction of ranchos in the surrounding hills after 1958 continued, those flaws became more severe: open sewers flowed toward the buildings below, generating standing pools of trash and waste that became breeding grounds for rats, flies, and mosquitoes and raised alarms among parents and public health officials about an impending epidemic.[28] In Block 45 in Mirador, heavy rains occasionally led to mudslides that came increasingly close to the building, causing lingering fears among residents that would surface again and again whenever the rainy season came to areas where hillsides, poor drainage, and squatter settlements combined (fig. 18).[29]

Demanding solutions to these and other long-standing grievances had taken residents to the streets to exert direct pressure upon authorities, much as they had in 1958 during the early transition to a system billed as democratic and therefore responsive to popular needs. But much as they had also done in 1958 through citizen groups or *juntas cívicas*, residents coupled their street actions with more-concerted organizing efforts. In the course of the 1960s, the citizen groups figured among the casualties of the armed conflict, as

FIGURE 18. Collapsed ranchos behind Blocks 20–21, La Cañada, in June 1970. Just above, the recently completed La Libertad complex: a low-altitude, low-density public-housing project inaugurated in 1969. (Archivo Audiovisual de la Nación)

popular mobilization abated amid the violence. As protest and mobilization resurged, residents would again begin to organize both formal and informal associations in order to sustain and coordinate their activism.

Youth and women, in particular, would spearhead most organizing innovations around community needs. In the Zona Central, *Juventud en Marcha* (Youth in Motion) brought together a reported 3,000 youths from throughout the neighborhood around "cultural, athletic, social, and recreational activities, in order to bring about the work of community development." When financial support from the Banco Obrero, with whom they had formally registered, unexpectedly stopped, the youths successfully courted area businesses to fund their activities.[30] Elsewhere, in Sierra Maestra, neighbors recall groups like the Social, Cultural, and Artistic Movement (*Movimiento Social, Cultural, y Artístico*, or MOSCA) forming around this time to stage musical and theatrical events, hold arts and crafts workshops, and promote health- and drug-awareness campaigns, all in an effort to court local youths and encourage greater community participation. (The acronym MOSCA had a double meaning: a fly

FIGURE 19. Pastora de Guevara (center) in 1975, with a youth soccer team from Blocks 52–53 of Sierra Maestra. (Courtesy Pastora de Guevara)

that travels about, but also a colloquial expression meaning to "be alert.")[31] Meanwhile the Zona Cultural Cristo Rey complex near Zona Central experienced something of a renaissance after a decade of neglect. Its movie house, theater, meeting rooms, and "Liberty Park" with its outdoor concert venue all began to draw more and more use.[32] By 1974, the National Library Institute made plans for and eventually built a branch in La Cañada.[33] Other organizing efforts for youth outreach proved more limited in scope, but no less significant. In Sierra Maestra, Pastora de Guevara, following divorce and a period of depression, organized and directed a boys' soccer team, and later a girls' volleyball team, for youth in her superblock, as a way to provide for them after-school structure and recreation (fig. 19).[34]

Guevara's story sheds light on two important developments in neighborhood life in the 1970s. One was the rise of drug-related crime in the neighborhood. Although in the early and mid-1960s reports had circulated of drug trafficking and even of cultivation in the area (namely marijuana, especially in the western sectors of the 23 de Enero),[35] violent crime and narcotics-related arrests had remained even and unexceptional throughout most of the preceding decade. For instance, of sixteen parishes in the Libertador district, of which the 23 de Enero formed part, and after 1967, as an official designated parish of its own, the neighborhood always ranked among the bottom half of areas in incidents of violent crime.[36] And while no neighborhood-level statistics are available for drug-related crimes in the 1960s, in the capital overall—after a peak of 511 drug arrests in 1965—the number steadily decreased to 209 arrests by 1969. But 1969 witnessed a slew of high-profile drug busts in the neighborhood, including one at an apartment where police found "a gang of youths" operating a marijuana growing and trafficking ring.[37] Crime statistics also bore out this sudden rise in drug-related activity, especially involving youth. In 1970, drug arrests in Caracas almost doubled, from 209 the year before to 409, before exploding to nearly 1,200 in 1971. Of those detained, over 80% were between the ages of 15 and 29. In the 23 de Enero, though violent crime remained low compared to other district parishes, 43 drug arrests in 1974 was the sixth highest number reported in Libertador district that year.[38]

But Pastora de Guevara's experience also revealed how women stood at the forefront of local activism during this period, rekindling traditions and experiences of organizing set aside during the era of armed struggle in the 1960s in the pursuit, especially, of addressing new challenges like the influx of drugs and the rise of crime. On 11 May 1969—International Women's Day—neighbors in La Cañada inaugurated the "Rosita de Ratto-Ciarlo Mothers' Center" in Block 18, named after a recently deceased city councilwoman who "concerned herself a lot with the problems of the barrios and especially the 23 de Enero and its surroundings," according to Ana Aparicio, Carmen de Paz, and René Colina of the Center's steering committee. It was the culmination of a local organizing and fundraising effort led by 120 area women that included "raffles, bake sales, and other social activities that generate revenue." In part the Center sought to offer a support space for local mothers—free day care, medicine, food.[39] But the group also had larger aims: to draw on the collective actions of its members to make direct demands on the city government. For instance, to coincide with the Center's inauguration, the women designated a commission to deliver to Caracas Governor Guinand Baldó a document "expos[ing] the area's problems . . . among them the painting of the Blocks, a solution to the sewage that flows from the surrounding barrios, the creation of a school cafeteria, a kindergarten, and other needs."[40]

Over the next fourteen months, the group would organize into a *comité de oficio* (working committee) to expand their range of activities beyond La Cañada and bring more area women into the fold of local activism. In particular they would focus their efforts around securing direct gas and telephone lines for each apartment.[41] "When we formed the *comité de oficio*," recalls Dalila Roa of Block 17, "we walked the entire parish; we didn't just walk one Block, because we had to involve everyone; everyone had to fight. And we created that *comité* to teach people that we needed a service, direct gas." It was that work of organizing, of "teaching" her neighbors, that Roa especially remembered thirty-five years later. "Many of them maybe hadn't realized, and we taught them why we were doing it, the danger of having a propane tank in your kitchen, with children around, that most mothers work outside the home and have to leave them alone, without phones because we had no phones."[42]

Roa's testimony sheds light on the interlacing grievances leading them to identify specific areas on which to focus their mobilizing efforts. It also helps capture the broader aims underlying their organizing, not just narrowly defined around specific demands, but rather seeking to promote and encourage greater community involvement. Here in particular, pacification—Caldera's term for bringing to a formal conclusion the period of guerrilla war—would bring new opportunities, for both local organizers and newly legalized parties like the PCV, to frame local demands in a larger political context, drawing on the resources that each brought to the table. Organizers such as Roa and the *comité* brought the drive and credibility of local residents able to mobilize neighbors around specific concerns. Political parties such as the *Partido Comunista de Venezuela* (PCV), and later the *Movimiento al Socialismo* (MAS), provided opportunities to give those grievances greater visibility and exert institutional pressure upon state entities through the political process. It was, in short, an opportunity to reclaim the dynamic that had informed the relationship between parties of the left and area residents as early as 1958.

In fact, almost immediately after Caldera lifted the ban on the PCV, the party relaunched its *Tribuna Popular* paper—now as a weekly. As it had in 1958, *Tribuna* quickly restarted its column highlighting problems afflicting the 23 de Enero, this time under the title "Tribuna del 23."[43] Over the next several years, *Tribuna Popular* would continue to use its pages to spotlight community grievances on the one hand,[44] and on the other to highlight efforts by party activists to reclaim spaces of political organization in the neighborhood: the 1970 launch of a local PCV cell under the name "Ho Chi Minh," the inauguration of a PCV meeting house in April 1971, and in October of that year, a mass rally in support of the party,[45] featuring erstwhile local Communist leader Eloy Torres before he left the PCV to help found MAS as a more viable electoral vehicle.

But it was Carmen Torres, Eloy's wife, who had the most impact locally in this new era of mobilizing in the neighborhood. "That was at Carmen Torres's [apartment]" in Block 18, remembered Dalila Roa of the meeting where the *comité de oficio* first took shape. Through Torres's political contacts and experience, the *comité* began "to do social work," according to Elka Larío Roa of Block 17, "but mixed with politics, because there were already elements within it"[46] like Torres and Argelia Laya of Block 15, also of the PCV and a former guerrilla but who would later, like both Torreses, go on to help found MAS. Through this association, the "Rosita de Ratto-Ciarlo Mothers' Center" expanded in 1970 to include a free clinic, staffed by volunteer doctors and nurses with ties to the Communist Party, such as Antonio García Ponce, and named after the recently deceased President of the Caracas College of Physicians, Jesús Yerena. Torres told *Tribuna Popular* that the name was meant to honor Yerena as a person with "great regard and concern for political prisoners and their fate . . . [and] as someone who was always linked to popular sectors."[47] It also signaled a subtle but recognizable shift: whereas in the inauguration of the Mothers' Center residents had made no mention of underlying political motives, the clinic's name aimed decidedly to draw a tie to a recent past of political struggle.

But while parties of the left worked to gain or regain footholds in the neighborhood, seeking to tap into local organizing efforts, AD and COPEI also attempted to make inroads in an area that had as recently as 1968 continued to shun the two major national parties. Unlike small parties like the PCV or upstart parties like MAS, what AD and COPEI could do as the major parties in power was to provide direct access to the very resources—material and institutional—that informed residents' mobilization in this postinsurgency era. In particular, the relationship between residents and AD and COPEI would play out in the *comités sociales* (social committees). The *comités sociales* had emerged in the mid-1960s following the erosion of the *juntas cívicas*, as part of a Banco Obrero (BO) measure to promote "community development" by organizing representative bodies of neighbors in each Block. Unlike the ad hoc *juntas cívicas*, the *comités sociales* held legal status as neighbor associations under the BO, which regulated their procedures, registered their actions, and recognized their representatives as legitimate interlocutors with the agency.[48]

At first the groups aimed primarily to foster morale among residents, and especially to forge institutional trust, after the most intense period of armed conflict in the early 1960s. Local BO officials organized "beautification" competitions, awarding plaques to buildings deemed best kept from year to year, for instance. But as pacification unleashed long-pent-up grievances, the *comités* became sites *par excellence* for the distribution of resources through the development of partisan clientelist networks. In Block 31 in Zona E, for instance, the person who "organized" the Block, as some residents recall, was a ranking AD militant who skillfully exercised his clout to forge patronage ties with residents and cement control over the local *comité*.[49] Over time, the building developed a reputation as a "white elephant,"[50] in reference to the perception that residents stood staunchly behind AD and its party color. As *comités* grew into a partisan apparatus, controlling them became a more intense, even violent affair. Francisco Suárez, from his apartment on the fifteenth floor of a Monte Piedad superblock, could see threats against his life painted on the walls of the building directly in front. His participation in the AD-controlled *comité* prompted this attack. Eventually, the *comité*'s president moved to Guarenas, thirty minutes east of Caracas, after someone detonated a pipe bomb on her doorstep.[51]

In part, *comités* became the site of partisan struggle because by 1973 neighbors had at long last resolved to back AD and COPEI electorally as the two parties cemented their dominance over Venezuela's political system. In December 1973, Venezuelans elected as President AD's Carlos Andrés Pérez, Betancourt's former Interior Minister during the most intense period of urban guerrilla conflict in 1962–1963. His victory had followed a breathless campaign effort in which Pérez traveled the nation extensively, making deft use of media and especially television to amplify his image as a youthful man of action capable of connecting with, and bringing together, all sectors of Venezuela. His image contrasted with the more staid presence of Betancourt, Leoni, or Caldera before him, and also of COPEI's candidate Lorenzo Fernández, 22 years his senior, and all of them associated with a generation that came of age during the dictatorship of Juan Vicente Gómez. On election night, Pérez had scored a decisive victory nationally, winning by 12 percentage points.[52] The real story, however, was the combined 85% vote for AD-COPEI, which marked an almost 30% jump relative to 1968.

In the 23 de Enero, the difference from 1968 was even more pronounced. Residents had cast their ballots overwhelmingly for AD and COPEI—which together took 73% of the local vote, compared with 41% for the two parties in 1968. Yet they also split their vote evenly between AD and COPEI, backing each party's congressional slate at roughly 36%. All told, at the national level the vote revealed the consolidation of the AD-COPEI supremacy over the political system. Locally in the 23 de Enero, it meant that residents as a whole would no longer dabble with small or upstart parties, resolving instead to support the major national political parties in order to have a greater claim to the rewards of the political system. That they split their vote between AD and COPEI also signaled an electorate whose loyalties remained very much contested, not clearly identified with either major party.[53]

Pérez's election and the calculations it reflected among area residents would shape local mobilizing efforts in contradictory ways during his administration. On one hand, expectations for solutions to local problems grew both as the neighborhood had finally backed a winning presidential candidate, even if only by a slim plurality, and as oil revenues skyrocketed beginning in 1974 following crisis in the Middle East. On the other hand, the same economic boom that helped to generate expectations about long-standing grievances also exerted greater pressures upon the very services that residents clamored for, especially as Caracas's population—and that of the neighborhood, as reflected in more and more ranchos (fig. 20)—continued to grow.[54] In the comités, despite the strong partisan tensions within them, debates more often reflected quotidian concerns about conditions of life in a nation of growing contradictions, and about how these contradictions played out in a state-owned and administered neighborhood, Venezuela's largest urban housing project.

Much as the 1969 protests had marked the onset of a new era of mobilizing, water would prove a major mobilizing factor. Aging pipes and equipment at the city water service, coupled with recurrent droughts and rapidly increasing demand, contrived to create cyclical water shortages in Caracas generally, but in working-class sectors in particular.[55] As these tensions became more acute, protests grew increasingly contentious. In September 1976, lightning damaged Caracas's main water-supply station. After three weeks without water, neighbors in the same sectors that had set the stage for the 1969 protests took to the streets, shutting down main access roads. When police arrived, gunfire erupted, leading to one dead and one wounded.[56] A year later, similar protests over water shortages resulted in the deaths of two minors.[57] And in October 1978, two more people died when another demonstration demanding water service turned violent, including a ten-year-old shot by a stray bullet from the events below while he played at home.[58] Commenting on the violence, Interior

FIGURE 20. New ranchos in the Zona Central of the 23 de Enero in June 1970. (Archivo Audiovisual de la Nación)

Minister Manuel Mantilla labeled "maniacs of disorder" those "who try to find problems where none exist."[59] Meanwhile, President Carlos Andrés Pérez went further, noting that "events like those of the 23 de Enero make existing public-service deficiencies more acute."[60] Pérez's comment laid bare a paradox of collective action in the 23 de Enero toward the end of the 1970s: though characterized by an explosion of mobilization, and more directly identified with the party system that had come to define democracy in Venezuela, it was a time when organization of the kind that had helped set the tone in the early decade nevertheless increasingly gave way to more contentious, less successful protest.

YOUTH REPRESSION, RADICAL UNDERCURRENTS

Ahead of the elections of 1973, Ravín Asuase Sánchez watched bewildered as "an Acción Democrática rally came down this road [in La Cañada], openly identified as *adecos*." As a teen in the 1960s Sánchez had joined the urban guerrilla campaigns in the neighborhood. He had quit school, found work at a local bottling plant, been fired when supervisors discovered he had stolen property—to use in the insurgency—and continued to harbor hopes for a violent revolution even after the Communist Party formally abandoned the armed struggle. But watching that AD rally, he remembered over 30 years later, "I felt that, well, that we were screwed. When I saw that march come by here with people carrying Acción Democrática flags, for me that was the final proof that we were screwed . . . we, in that era, were defeated by the *adecos.*"[61] For Asuase Sánchez, admitting defeat proved as painful as his attempt to reenter society. After Pérez's victory, Asuase Sánchez resolved to leave Caracas, settling in a plot of land in the Andean state of Mérida, a world away from the 23 de Enero. In need of money, he put his insurgent skill set to use and robbed a bank, but was caught, tried, and spent eight years in prison.

While most insurgent leaders had rejoined or would go on to rejoin the party system, or in the case of MAS, create new vehicles to newly enter that system, Asuase Sánchez's postinsurgency saga revealed one of many paths that rank-and-file guerrillas took in the wake of pacification. For some, the process translated into at-times very active—and paradoxical—cooperation with the state, as was the case with those from the 23 de Enero who went on to fill the ranks of the military, the urban or political police services, or intelligence agencies—in short, the same repressive apparatus against which they had squared off as insurgents.[62] For others, however, pacification—and recognizing defeat in the 1960s armed struggle—created opportunities to develop a social vocation over and above partisan political activism. In the early 1970s Gustavo Rodríguez of Monte Piedad, like Asuase Sánchez a veteran of the urban guerrilla struggle in the neighborhood, dropped out of college to work alongside a friend who had recently returned from studying theater in the United States, and who had been influenced by the Black Power movement. By that time, in Block 3, where he had lived since the days of Pérez Jiménez, "there was a group of youths who were very restless, very animated, who were in need of an organization, needing to have someone shape them." So they took over an abandoned local church in Monte Piedad and established a *Casa de la Cultura del Pueblo* (House of the People's Culture), where they held workshops about "politics, sex, abortion," and where they showed Cuban, Mexican, and Chilean revolutionary cinema.

When Rodríguez's friend and his family were "kicked out [of the 23 de Enero] at gunpoint," as he remembered, the work turned clandestine and covert. For instance, they organized puppet shows with explicitly revolutionary content, performing throughout the parish for local youth. Like Rodríguez, Gustavo Parabón in Monte Piedad also placed his energies into "cultural work" in order to reach a new generation of potential militants. Though he had not been part of the guerrillas, several raids on his apartment when he was a teenager had left a deep impression on him. By the 1970s, he remembers, "you wanted to insert yourself in a different political project than what was going on, and that was one of the ways. Through cultural work, you could do political work, but very carefully, because militants of the old parties would see that as something very dangerous. And that's when a series of persecutions began against all of us who did cultural work. Because they saw us as dangerous."[63]

While harassment and persecution drove their efforts underground, they had a growing and increasingly receptive audience in area youths. What Rodríguez recalled as "restlessness" in fact belied a severe and deadly pattern of repression directed toward youths throughout the decade in the neighborhood. As early as 1969, long-haired young men, at the time pejoratively referred to as *melenudos*, reported having their heads shaved on their way to or from school.[64] Andrés Vásquez, then a teenager, recalled other forms of harassment, as well as the consequences of resistance:

> They used to make you sweep that whole thing—that was good—you ventured outside and then you had to sweep half the block before going to work or going to school. To talk back [*ponerse rebelde*], there were many rebellious youths who resisted, well they beat them, they shot at them, in fact there was, Cheo is still around, Cheo had his leg blown off, he's still around. And that's how they killed many people, they killed so many people here.[65]

Periodical sources support Mr. Vásquez's testimony. Between 1972 and 1979, local high school and middle school students in the 23 de Enero staged on average five major protests a year resulting in clashes with police and garnering national press coverage. Reasons varied widely, from demanding the reinstatement of dismissed teachers, to calling for improving school resources, to opposing the military draft.[66] For some, protesting reflected mere curiosity, an opportunity to engage in youthful adventuring and rebelliousness. At times, even the threat of protest yielded positive results. In June 1974 authorities at the Banco Obrero transferred control over a local youth center, used to promote cultural and drug-prevention activities, to police. In response students at the nearby Manuel Palacio Fajardo high school mounted a public challenge, contacting media and promising to take to the streets should the measure move forward.[67] Two weeks later, in an appearance in the 23 de Enero, the Caracas mayor personally overturned the measure, while also promising new resources to revitalize the youth center.[68]

Over time, however, the tenor of student protests grew increasingly contentious, even lethal, while aims and outcomes grew less clear and effective. Earlier in the decade, staging barricades, hurling rocks, and firing Molotov cocktails against police had marked the limit of violent collective action by students. Yet by decade's end the violence routinely extended to setting ablaze local stores and public-transportation vehicles and exchanging gunfire with police and national guardsmen, leaving in its wake scores of injured police and several dead students. Between 1977 and 1979, seven youths were shot dead during protests in the 23 de Enero. The result was a cyclical pattern of mobilization and repression, where ill-defined protests led to violent clashes resulting in student deaths, in turn generating more protests and violence. A team conducting research in the 23 de Enero in the 1980s concluded: "The youth's effervescence was so brutally repressed [in the 70s], by different means, that to be young actually constituted a crime."[69]

By decade's end signs of an emerging unity between 1960s-era militants skilled at tactical organization and 1970s youth simmering with mounting frustrations had begun to surface. Police reports of protests in the neighborhood in October 1978 that left two people dead, for instance, noted that "*encapuchados* [hooded protesters] with high-caliber rifles" took part in the events, reflecting a level of violence seldom seen since the days of urban guerrilla war.[70] In this context, political activism did not disappear entirely, though its reach had grown much more limited, and its constituency had passed to new generations of activists who had cut their teeth in local struggles over community demands. Ongoing state violence throughout the 1970s provided a space for groups of 1960s militants to continue their work leading informal political-education groups with a rising generation of activists in the 23 de Enero. Other 1960s militants remained politically active in the neighborhood but through "subliminal" rather than clandestine means, shifting their energies to what one veteran of the urban guerrilla referred to as "cultural work," such as organizing street theater troupes, musical ensembles, and athletic events.[71] In this context, where in general terms the pendulum swung between political and social activism during the 1960s and 1970s, respectively, the 1980s would witness a synthesis of the two overarching trends.

FROM THE STREETS TO THE BALLOT BOX:
TOWARD THE ELECTIONS OF 1978

In December 1978 Venezuelans swept Luis Herrera Campíns into office, cap-ping a stunning electoral feat for the Christian Democrat COPEI party. After years of rapid economic growth, massive oil-derived revenues, and rising per-capita income under the administration of AD's Carlos Andrés Pérez, Ven-ezuelans opted for an opposition candidate campaigning on a reformist platform, and a dramatic one at that.[72] Since early in the decade, Herrera Campíns had sounded increasingly forceful calls to "reinvent democracy" in Venezuela, which since its founding in 1958 had relied on power-sharing pacts among political, business, labor, and clerical elites to ensure stability and alternation in power by parties of different political stripes. Still more remark-able was that Herrera Campíns's victory came with the majority support of urban popular sectors in Caracas, who had long shunned COPEI as a party identified with "rural and small-town middle classes."[73] In fact, voters in Caracas had only recently come to accept the primacy of a two-party system in Venezuela, again and again favoring smaller parties over not just COPEI, but even the nominally center-left AD associated with trade unionism and working classes more broadly.

As one of the more populous working-class neighborhoods in Caracas, the 23 de Enero well reflected this peculiar pattern. Since 1958, most residents had continued to support the new democracy by flocking to the polls every five years. To be sure, compulsory voting proved a strong motivator. But even so, in the 23 de Enero, which had experienced some of the most intense violence of the urban guerrilla conflict in the 1960s, residents consistently returned some of the lowest abstention rates in Caracas, while flouting insurgent calls to shun the electoral system altogether. And yet area residents' participation in the electoral system belied a pattern of rejection of AD and COPEI, the two parties that emerged as the main political brokers of the era. In the first decade of democratic rule between 1958 and 1968, even as AD and COPEI traded the presidency, the two parties combined never received more than 29% of the vote in the 23 de Enero. Instead residents had backed a wide spectrum of third-party candidates. In 1958 they voted overwhelmingly for Wolfgang Larrazábal, the young officer who commanded the 23 January coup, and his supporters in the Communist Party of Venezuela (PCV). Larrazábal again secured the most votes among residents of the 23 de Enero in 1963, this time coming in fourth nationally. In 1968, the 23 de Enero again bucked the national trend and instead supported candidates of the CCN, a party created by Pérez Jiménez as he attempted to return to political life. Meanwhile COPEI, which narrowly won the presidency, came in fourth in the 23 de Enero. By 1973, AD and COPEI had broken through, securing 62% of the vote. COPEI in particular more than doubled its support in the neighborhood, from 12% in 1968 to 28% in 1973. Yet it still trailed AD, the eventual winner, by six percentage points. It would be up to Herrera Campíns to close the gap, which he did in 1978, when COPEI received 31% of the vote to AD's stagnant 34%.[74]

Against this backdrop, that Herrera Campíns's message of sweeping change resonated among urban popular sectors like the 23 de Enero owed to three key developments shaping Venezuela's political landscape in the late 1970s, and to his campaign's ability to recognize them and respond effectively: the consolidation of a new electorate, the growing gulf between oil-fueled growth and deteriorating everyday matters like public services, and popular craving for greater participation in the political process. Throughout the 1970s, migration to urban areas in the northern industrial corridor stretching from Caracas to the western, oil-rich state of Zulia continued upward trends it had begun in the 1950s.[75] In Caracas alone, internal migration helped double the population from 1.3 million in 1960 to 2.6 million by 1973.[76] A more startling figure lay in the unevenness that characterized this growth. In 1959 just 17% of Caracas residents lived below the poverty line; by contrast, in 1978 that figure had ballooned to 48.5%.[77] The result was a far more urban and working-class electorate than ever before, concentrated especially in Caracas, which by 1970 accounted for one fifth of Venezuela's total population. As one analyst reflecting on the 1978 elections noted, "a successful campaign for the presidency must respond to the demands of city people."[78]

Generational shifts had also reshaped the electorate. After 1958 Venezuela experienced something of a baby boom. Between 1960 and 1965 the proportion of Venezuelans under the age of 19 rose from 55% to 57% of the population, boosted by a three-percentage-point increase in the rate of growth of the population under 4 years old. These children would come of age in the mid- and late 1970s, as reflected in census data. Between 1970 and 1980, the number of Venezuelans under the age of 19 dropped steadily, matched by a corresponding rise in the number of Venezuelans between the ages of 20 and 39. Between 1970 and 1975 alone, the population of Venezuelans aged 20 to 39 grew by 10 percentage points faster than it had five years earlier. Politically these figures would translate into an electorate whose formative years had passed under the democratic regime installed in 1958. In polling conducted ahead of elections in 1973, for instance, nearly 22% of respondents indicated they were first-time voters, up four percentage points from 1968, and eleven percentage points from 1963.[79] And among first-time voters, interest in politics ran high: in polling conducted ahead of the 1978 elections, 85% of respondents born between 1956 and 1960 reported having either "passive" or "very active" participation in politics, compared to 15% who reported being "not very active" in politics.[80] Young voters also tended to support center-left candidates and parties more than did the general population. Ahead of the 1978 elections, for instance, youth voter preferences for the center-left MAS, MEP, and MIR parties ran 17%, compared to 11% among the population as a whole.[81]

Changes in the electorate required Herrera Campíns to target urban, youth, and working-class sectors formerly not identified with Christian Democracy, sectors like the 23 de Enero, where COPEI had long fared poorly.[82] To do so he deployed a three-pronged strategy. To court urban working classes, he moved away from the "songs and jingles" that had marked previous electoral efforts and, following the advice of campaign consultants, moved instead to "speak out honestly and not try to paint a pretty picture" about everyday hardships such as cost-of-living increases under Carlos Andrés Pérez.[83] In practice this meant sidelining mass rallies in favor of reaching out directly and personally to urban barrio populations. In the 23 de Enero, for example, Herrera Campíns made repeated visits to the neighborhood, dining with residents at their homes while in the process hoping to foment an image of an accessible candidate in touch with urban masses.

Consider the case of Lino Álvarez and Silveria Ríos, of Block 37 in Zona F. Álvarez had lived in the 23 de Enero since the 1958 coup, when he had been one of the thousands who flocked to the vacant superblocks to secure an apartment. He had never much cared for politics, even if politics seemed to care much about him. Born in 1919, he came of age at the height of the dictatorship of Juan Vicente Gómez, whom he met and came to admire for paying off Venezuela's foreign debt. A year after Gómez's death in 1935, Álvarez arrived in Caracas, eventually driving a taxi in the burgeoning city. His union belonged to AD, yet Álvarez stressed, "I had my own way of thinking" even as peers insisted AD spoke for those like him, the working class. Under Pérez Jiménez's dictatorship, Álvarez kept to his own even when intelligence agents disguised as taxi riders recorded his conversations for hints of dissent. Álvarez's mother was a lifelong *adeca* [supporter of the center-left AD]; his wife, a committed *copeyana* [supporter of the center-right COPEI]. On her account he joined the party of Rafael Caldera, stressing nevertheless: "I was never a card-carrying militant."[84]

In April 1978, Álvarez and his wife hosted COPEI's presidential candidate for breakfast. Álvarez remembered Luis Herrera Campíns as a large, jovial person with an appetite to match his size. After eating, the candidate napped in his children's bed. They did not much talk politics, although Herrera Campíns did briefly inquire about problems afflicting Álvarez's family and measures Herrera Campíns might take, as president, to help resolve them.[85] Afterward, Herrera Campíns visited with other residents of Block 37, people like Silveria Ríos. Like Álvarez, Ríos had been among those who had found an apartment in the superblocks after the overthrow of Pérez Jiménez. Also as with Álvarez, politics had surrounded Ríos even if personally she took it all in stride, admitting: "I talked to anyone who wanted my vote, but I never went to rallies." Her father had been a lifelong *copeyano*, so much so that "you couldn't even mention AD in his presence." And while she was not one to rally, Ríos did join the *damas de COPEI* [ladies of COPEI] in her building. So when Herrera Campíns went to her building, he paid her a visit. "There were so many of them . . . reporters and such" she recalled, "all cramped in my small apartment." A quiet woman, Ríos remembered asking the candidate if he would help her two daughters if elected. "And he did," sending Ríos a telegram upon taking office giving "work to one, and a scholarship to the other."[86]

This form of direct outreach to sectors like the 23 de Enero was especially important as it signaled a key departure from the prevailing presidential image, nurtured especially by Carlos Andrés Pérez, of grand and enlightened leadership. Herrera Campíns would also court urban sectors by relying heavily on television; in the late 1970s Caracas alone harbored 25% of the nationwide viewing public.[87] And to reach out to younger, left-leaning voters, he would seek out alliances with left-wing sectors, condemning AD's "anti-Communist attitude" and eventually earning the support of PCV leaders.[88] By 1977, polls revealed that, of the three leading candidates, 40% of Venezuelans viewed Herrera Campíns as the most "progressive," compared to 31% for Luis Piñerúa Ordaz of AD, and 29% for José Vicente Rangel of MAS.[89]

REINVENTING DEMOCRACY: PUBLIC-SERVICE COLLAPSE
AND THE RISE OF *HERRERISMO*

Herrera Campíns would make most inroads by focusing his campaign on the issue where urban and working-class concerns converged: the deteriorating state of public services.[90] A glaring disjuncture had marked Pérez's presidency: where oil-industry-derived revenues had fueled tremendous economic growth, even spurring major investments in water and electric services,[91] the administration of public services had steadily deteriorated during his government, much as it had during every previous government. Even AD's candidate had to contend with this reality, stressing throughout the campaign that he "would be the candidate of public services and housing" after recognizing that Pérez's government had sacrificed "certain needs of the people" in order to focus on macroeconomic growth.[92]

Few areas had experienced this problem more sharply and for longer than the 23 de Enero. Just days after the overthrow of Pérez Jiménez on 23 January 1958, residents of the newly renamed 23 de Enero neighborhood warned that a "lack of water and trash collection" in their community threatened the health of children and adults alike.[93] By the mid-1960s, even as the leftist insurgency raged in the neighborhood, political figures of the hard right had joined residents in decrying the physical and symbolic effects of irregular trash collection in the community named after democracy's date of birth, especially as AD governments scaled back the operations of the Banco Obrero, the entity charged with administering the 23 de Enero.[94] Meanwhile, the proliferation of squatter settlements throughout the neighborhood as rural migrants flocked to Caracas further contrived to spoil efforts at normalizing trash collection in the area.[95] By the 1970s, waste management in the 23 de Enero had reached crisis proportions. Longer and longer interruptions in trash collection helped create ever larger, and more hazardous, "mountains of trash" in areas where children once played.[96] Meanwhile contacting media had proven increasingly ineffective, emboldening more and more residents to take to the streets to seek any manner of resolution to their problem with trash (fig. 21).[97]

During Carlos Andrés Pérez's presidency, the Caracas government attempted to rein in the garbage crisis in the 23 de Enero as well as in other popular sectors by implementing trash buy-back programs, encouraging residents of areas where access by compactors proved difficult to take their

FIGURE 21. In January 1974, children play behind Blocks 54–55–56, of the Sierra Maestra sector of the 23 de Enero. On the buildings behind them may be seen broken trash chutes. (Pedro Garrido / Archivo *El Nacional*).

refuse directly to central processing stations. In the 23 de Enero, seven barrios formed part of the pilot program, servicing over 23,000 residents in over 4,000 households.[98] The following year, the city government began regular trash collection service in two areas previously covered by the buy-back program.[99] But as the city's population grew, so did waste. By late 1976, aiming to "optimize" waste management in Caracas, Pérez created the Municipal Urban Waste Institute (*Instituto Municipal de Aseo Urbano*, or IMAU) to centralize trash collection and disposal. Yet the IMAU was soon overwhelmed by a 47% rise in trash collection, resulting in part from a system of "transfer stations" implemented to streamline delivery of garbage from Caracas to outlying landfills. In fact, owing to the 23 de Enero's strategic location at the center of Caracas, as well as its wide roads, IMAU located its pilot way station at a busy intersection in the neighborhood.[100] Though designed as a community-improvement measure, the transfer system and its location soon proved a curse, as disruptions in transferring trash to the landfills meant a dangerous back-logging of waste in the transfer station.

In this context, and in a move that would resonate in the 23 de Enero, Herrera Campíns would turn public services into a key campaign issue. As early as 1977, COPEI had made of the "efficient functioning of public services" one of six major policy aims of a future administration.[101] A year later, in a 400-page publication detailing plans for an eventual Herrera Campíns administration and titled *Mi compromiso con Venezuela* (My Commitment to Venezuela), public services had jumped to second among his priorities,[102] behind education, which polls indicated ranked third in voters' list of concerns.[103] What accounted for the shift was a sense by Herrera Campíns that public services, though ranked 10th among 18 issues of concern to voters, often represented the state's most direct and everyday contact with citizens at large. As he noted in *Mi compromiso*: "It is through public services and state enterprises that the people measure the efficacy and efficiency of government. . . . Public services operate as an immediate gauge for the people to see the state's capacity to make the resources that the state invests socially reproducible and humanely useful."[104] Herrera Campíns's plans to improve public services rested on a program to reverse the trend under Pérez of centralizing services, and move instead to "stimulate and facilitate . . . the creation of public, mixed, and private enterprises for urban and residential waste management, and to promote the active participation of users, through their organizations."[105]

Decentralization, privatization, and direct citizen participation especially were more than just timely campaign issues for Herrera Campíns. They reflected the core of an ideology of *herrerismo* years in the making, and which contrasted sharply with the hyper-presidentialism that had marked Pérez's government. In particular, *herrerismo* held the promise of a broad-based reform program resting on the premise that Venezuela had successfully transitioned into a period of political stability under representative government. The democratic system therefore should begin to set aside the inter-elite pacts once required to make the transition possible, and move toward a "participatory democracy where people and communities are present, in solidarity, and creatively, in decision making; [where they] responsibly develop their initiatives, provide their opinions, and receive a fair share of the benefits of their effort."[106]

Here in particular residents of the 23 de Enero would find a more lasting connection with Herrera Campíns than even the promise of better public services. Their periodic protests over public-service deficiencies in the previous years had only scratched the surface of deep grievances about the evolution of

Venezuelan politics since 1958. That they had again and again shunned AD and COPEI at the polls, even supporting Pérez Jiménez's failed electoral bid in 1968, reflected significant ambivalence about what many considered the false promises of the "revolution of '58."[107] But their disenchantment with the political system ran only so far. Most had also rejected guerrilla violence in the 1960s as counterproductive. By 1973 most had also accepted the primacy of a two-party system. Yet their continued recourse to street protests reflected a desire for greater accountability, and for greater voice, than the quinquennial elections provided by pacted democracy.

In these three areas—rejection of violence, respect for electoral democracy, and calls for more-direct forms of participation and accountability—residents of the 23 de Enero well reflected nationwide trends. In a poll conducted ahead of the 1973 elections, 64% of Venezuelans had reported that the vote was the only way to influence government; an even higher number, 93%, reported that the vote was "a very important factor in politics," and 88% responded that elections were necessary in order to have democracy. But when asked if they felt they had influence over politics, 66%, about the same number who said voting was the only way to influence government, reported feeling that they in fact had little influence, suggesting that most saw the vote as a rather weak form of participation. Asked if they would still vote if it were not compulsory, 48% said they would do so, while 49% reported they would abstain.[108] In 1978, among youth voters, that number was higher—51%—compared to 46% who said they would still vote if it were not compulsory.[109]

Nationally, support for democracy ran high: asked in 1977 "What do you think about democracy, that is, about Venezuela's political system?" 77% of those polled reported being either "very happy" (27%) or "more or less happy" (50%), compared to 13% who thought democracy should be replaced and 10% who did not know.[110] Among youth in 1978, the number who felt "another type of system" should replace the existing one was higher than that of the general population, 26%, while 58% thought the existing system was either working well (8%) or should be "fixed somewhat" (50%).[111] All told, what these seemingly contradictory figures suggested was that disenchantment with the pacted system was actually growing, but support for democracy itself remained strong. What most sought was greater influence through a fine-tuning of the existing system.

For years, this was precisely the message Herrera Campíns had championed, even against mainstream currents within his own party. As a lifelong

Christian Democrat, Herrera Campíns adhered to what analysts identified as one of the major premises of Latin American Christian Democracy, namely the "belief (derived directly from Catholic social doctrine) in subsidiarity and, as a result, in the need to control state intervention and respect the primacy of civil society."[112] This stood in contrast, at least nominally, to the kind of Social Democracy AD espoused, which sought to marshal state resources—especially oil wealth—to fund social programs and push public investment toward development. But Herrera Campíns's own brand of Social Christianity, which some even labeled COPEI's "radical current,"[113] went further.

Beginning in 1969, just as COPEI made history by becoming the first opposition party in Venezuela to take the reins of government through elections, Herrera Campíns had begun to decry the system of inter-elite pacts that prevailed after 1958 as exclusionary, tending to prevent a sense of popular ownership in the political process: "It is not enough to vote every five years. New and truly participatory forms are what citizens long for. . . . Real participation must replace the current formal representation."[114] Even with his party at the helm over the next five years, then-senator Herrera Campíns continued to sound off on the limits of representative democracy. In September 1972, as he battled unsuccessfully for the presidential candidacy as part of the so-called *Avanzado* wing of COPEI,[115] Herrera Campíns assembled Christian Democratic figures from throughout the Americas for a seminar on participatory democracy. His own keynote address, to burnish his credentials as a mainstream politician nevertheless attuned to popular demands for greater influence, argued for the need to "reinvent democracy" by moving from a "representative to a participatory" form of government.[116]

Ironically, COPEI's 1973 loss to AD allowed Herrera Campíns to coalesce the party around him, as it meant, according to historian Donald Herman, that "the party would now be ready to support a candidate of the left."[117] His message of reform received another boost once Pérez's administration came to be marked by greater, not less centralization. In this context, Herrera Campíns set out to give final shape to *herrerismo*. In January 1977 he organized a public seminar aimed at lending specificity to "participatory democracy," the preliminary results of which informed COPEI's platform at its August convention.[118] Though short on details, it promised to "promote people's consciousness [*toma de conciencia*] about matters that affect them," especially at the local level "where [they] encounter democracy's efficiency or lack thereof every day."[119] Reflecting polling data, COPEI's platform also upheld the primacy of democracy while making forceful calls for citizens to seize its promise of accountability: "No other system provides the resources democracy offers to punish corruption . . . and denounce and correct bad mechanisms and practices of government." By the time in 1978 when he published *Mi compromiso*, Herrera Campíns formalized participation as "the central axis of my government," further stressing that the government would use "all its resources to stimulate the personal and social actions" of citizens through what he called "state advocacy."[120]

All told, a state acting as the advocate of a citizenry encouraged to participate more actively in their local, everyday political life was a powerful formula for sectors like those in the 23 de Enero: urban, working-class, and long eager for precisely this kind of message from a mainstream candidate with a legitimate chance to win. Come election night, Herrera Campíns won handily, with 47% of the vote to AD's 43% nationally. In Caracas, too, Herrera Campíns won a plurality of 46% of the vote, a first for a COPEI candidate. And in the 23 de Enero neighborhood, Herrera Campíns scored a narrow victory, edging AD's Piñerúa Ordaz by one percentage point, 39% to 38%.[121] Many in the 23 de Enero had taken a chance on a candidate calling on citizens to seize a greater stake in government by demanding accountability. As *herrerismo* faltered, and the political system with it, they would do precisely that.

CHAPTER 6

"A Weapon as Powerful as the Vote"

Seizing the Promise of Participation, 1979–1988

Days before Christmas in 1981, Earles Gutiérrez, his brother, and two friends stood waiting at the busy Block 7 rotary in the Monte Piedad sector the 23 de Enero. When they spotted a city trash truck approaching, the four youths set up a roadblock and stopped the unwary driver. Earles then forced his way onto the cabin and drove the truck to the garbage depot behind Block 7. It was the first time since the partial privatization of municipal waste management five weeks before that any manner of trash service had come this way. And, as President Luis Herrera Campíns himself had indicated while campaigning for office, "it is through public services and state enterprises that the people measure the efficacy and efficiency of government."[1] Evidently, Earles and his group had measured the government's efficiency, and judged it poor. Earles then instructed the driver to catch a bus at a nearby stop, take it a mile up the road to the local police station, and notify the duty officers that they had taken the truck, and where to come and find it.[2]

Direct action was a fact of life in Monte Piedad, as in other areas of the 23 de Enero. On 23 January 1958, the date the neighborhood's name memorialized, residents took to the streets to support the overthrow of a ten-year dictatorship and the start of a new democratic era. In the 1960s leftist guerrillas engaged in pitched battles against state agents, turning the sector into a hotbed of political violence. And for most of the 1970s groups of residents had set ablaze tires, refuse, and whatever car or bus passed by, as a way to denounce problems from irregular water service to police abuse. Yet even against this backdrop, what came of this mobilization in December 1981 was quite extraordinary. That they did not mask their faces or set the vehicle ablaze was uncommon for activist youth in the 23 de Enero, especially those like Earles who fashioned themselves keepers of the old anti-establishment guerrilla tradition, more concerned with toppling the state than with parochial community problems. That they called for police response to their illegal seizure of a city vehicle was decidedly rare. The *Diario de Caracas*, first to cover the story, called it "a very *special* way for [the 23 de Enero] to get the attention of the trash collection service."[3]

In the time it took police to respond, Earles and the others had gone door to door to seek support for their deeds. They sounded a general "invitation" to participate, but they especially targeted "workers of the home, those who most feel the problem."[4] When police arrived, the crowd of mostly women they found gathered around the truck was the result of this effort. Some of these women were veterans of a different tradition of mobilization, one that had long shunned the likes of Earles and their anti-establishment agitation, even as they understood the role of, and had themselves engaged in, contentious protest to draw attention to their neighborhood's aging infrastructure. Like most in the neighborhood, they had supported the promise of accountable government provided by the democratic system begun in 1958, again and again taking to the polls even as their candidates lost one election after another. Then there were those "who never participated and were always accused of being *sapos* [collaborators of the ruling parties]."[5] Hours later, Caracas waste management authorities promised to dispatch a crew of 35 in order to "fully satisfy the neighbors." In turn, neighbors also made a promise: to return the truck undamaged only after they had seen "the last ounce of trash removed from the area."[6]

Over the next few days and weeks this group of radical youth and the women who answered their calls to mobilize, a coalition as unprecedented as it was unlikely, would seize more and more public service vehicles, in the process throwing the bulk of the state apparatus for a spin. On the second day President Herrera Campíns, whose government had clashed violently with youth in the 23 de Enero for nearly a year, "furiously" chastised heads of public institutions and ordered an immediate "cleanup" of the neighborhood.[7] National media, which had earlier dismissed the 23 de Enero as a "red zone," picked up on the story and sympathetically reported on its progress.[8] Later, city council members split on the merits of neighbors' tactics even as they moved to penalize municipal waste management service officials.[9]

Meanwhile other popular sectors in Caracas, even while lamenting becoming associated with the neighborhood, threatened to protest "in the style of the 23 de Enero" in a bid to draw attention to long-standing problems besetting their own communities.[10]

The hijacking reached its climax on the morning of 19 January 1982, a month after it began. Hundreds of firebrand youths, stay-at-home women, guerrilla veterans, and lifelong mainstream party militants—reflecting the protest's remarkable breadth—crammed into a local elementary school to meet with high-level representatives from various public service institutions. By meeting's end neighbors had secured signed affidavits from each official committing his or her agency's resources to revamping the community. Within days work crews began the monumental task of removing tons of waste, refitting long-stalled elevators, installing phone service, rewiring power lines, and repaving local roads, among other projects. It was the most extensive overhaul of the area in over a decade. And, as neighbors had vowed all along, once repairs were underway they began to release the seized trucks that made it all possible.

In the wake of the hijackings, or *secuestros*, one editorialist encouraged residents to look beyond street protest and ahead to 1983, when they could use "a weapon as powerful as the vote" to channel their grievances more directly. In fact, it was the vote that had framed their actions. In 1978, for the first time, residents had awarded COPEI an electoral plurality in the neighborhood. By 1981, Herrera Campíns had abandoned the calls to "reinvent democracy" that informed his presidential bid. Yet the vision of a "participatory" politics proved a lasting stimulus for popular mobilization. In particular, it legitimized bold, even extra-institutional demands of the government, in the process giving residents powerful leverage. These demands focused less on goods and services, such as had largely shaped their mobilizations in the 1970s, and more explicitly on better governance. Residents drew on a contradictory legacy of support for democracy at the ballot box, on one hand, and radical agitation in the streets, on the other, bringing together once-conflicting currents while taking advantage of their electoral support of Herrera Campíns to claim a mantle of legitimacy for actions that otherwise stood outside the formal bounds of the law and of democratic governance.

Events like the *secuestros* affirmed residents' democratic values as they combined long-standing support for representative democracy with tactics forged in the fray of contentious protest to pursue a basic principle of liberal citizenship: accountability. But these innovations held an underside. Just as their demands for accountability grew more sophisticated—embracing a discourse of participatory democracy while imbuing it with contentious muscle drawn from local traditions of organizing and mobilization— economic crisis hamstrung the state's ability to respond, forcing authorities into innovations of their own. Facing a crushing debt crisis as oil prices plummeted, authorities began to reverse the centralizing frenzy of the Carlos Andrés Pérez administration, experimenting with privatization of public services and utilities. But it was in the 23 de Enero where the government made its most ambitious move, establishing condominium arrangements in one building after another in order to pass ownership of the buildings—and responsibility for their upkeep—to residents themselves. At long last, authorities had rid themselves of the economic albatross that was the massive public-housing project they had inherited from Pérez Jiménez.

For some residents, the transition from public housing was much welcome, an opportunity to take control over their lived environment and build reputations for leadership. Activist youths in La Cañada, some of whom had participated in the hijackings, ran in and won local condominium elections, providing a first experience in organizing through formal channels, engaging in local electoral politics, fostering working relationships with political antagonists, and becoming known to neighbors in a new light, less as impulsive youths than as pragmatic stewards of collective will. But as local leaders discovered, holding the state accountable was one thing; holding fellow neighbors accountable was quite another. Personal rifts, budget battles, allegations of corruption, all contrived to make the task of self-administration at times a bane rather than a boon to community building. Others saw in the transfer of ownership the shrewd cost-cutting move of a state abdicating its responsibilities. So they continued to mobilize to ensure that even as authorities ceded formal control of spaces to residents, they would do so by holding up their legal responsibility to leave the buildings in perfect condition before formally passing title to the new condominiums. As economic crisis deepened, conflict and negotiation continued to mark the relationship between state and populace as each struggled to adapt to a changing landscape, the people turning as they long had to the polls to express their frustrations with—and aspirations for—the political system.

"STRAIGHT FOR THE ABYSS": THE FALL OF *HERRERISMO*

In late February 1981 Rómulo Betancourt took the floor of his party's annual convention and dropped a bombshell. Addressing attendees, Betancourt cited an "ultra-confidential" report allegedly produced by members of President Herrera Campíns's cabinet. The report assailed Herrera Campíns's government, describing a picture of growing dependence on oil revenues, rising unemployment, "failed" schools, and stagnant investment, all compounded by a bloated state bureaucracy. In this climate, he warned, basic democratic principles proved insufficient to sustain social stability. "We enjoy civil liberties, freedom of assembly, of verbal and written speech," noted Betancourt, but "a lack of faith has spread across the country, a lack of confidence in the democratic regime."[11] Elsewhere in the political spectrum others had similar warnings. In early February, José Vicente Rangel of Movement toward Socialism (*Movimiento al Socialismo*, or MAS) had told the press: "if the national leadership does not reflect on . . . their continued irresponsible behavior, [then] Venezuelan democracy is headed straight for the abyss."[12]

More than partisan alarmism underlay their remarks. Since his taking office in March 1979, Herrera Campíns's popularity swayed wildly and initial admiration turned to contempt. At first he took several significant steps to address the calls for reform that had informed his campaign. Responding to civil society groups, he established a cabinet-level position on women's affairs, demonstrating how the axes of "participation" and "state advocacy" that inspired his vision of democratic society might successfully converge.[13] Through a program of weekly roundtables with citizens at large, Herrera Campíns fashioned a direct channel of communication with popular sectors outside the realm of organized civil and political society, in the process demystifying the image of the "almighty state" that had risen up during Carlos Andrés Pérez's presidency. And he attempted to obtain a more accurate measure of the needs of urban popular sectors by having the Foundation for Municipal and Community Development (*Fundación para el desarrollo de la comunidad y fomento municipal*, known as Fundacomun)—a once-touted USAID-funded urban-renewal agency that had long since fallen into bureaucratic stupor—conduct the first nationwide census of urban barrios in 1979, followed by a second census in 1980.[14]

In the beginning of Herrera Campíns's term, the 23 de Enero also witnessed changes for the better. While violent student protests had greeted Herrera

Campíns just days after his inauguration, these were more signs of youth disaffection with the outgoing government, under whom twelve students had died in clashes with police,[15] than with the new administration. In fact, youth and leftist sectors in the 23 de Enero quickly warmed to Josefina Delgado, Herrera Campíns's appointee to *jefa civil* (the neighborhood's highest civilian authority). According to Manuel Mir from the Observatorio sector of the 23 de Enero, who would later work with Delgado during her tenure, Herrera Campíns had personally named Delgado to the position during a visit to the neighborhood following his election.[16] Though capricious, Delgado's appointment cemented Herrera Campíns's ties to a neighborhood where he had just scored a historic victory after making it a centerpiece of his presidential campaign.

Once in office, Delgado moved quickly to establish ties with leftist sectors of the population, in turn reflecting Herrera Campíns's own overtures to parties like the PCV. When a Mirador day school run by a Communist Party militant burned down in late 1981 under mysterious circumstances, the director recalls being "surprised" at the sympathy and support Delgado offered her.[17] Others who were youths at the time recall how she interceded on their behalf when police detained them for political activism in the 23 de Enero.[18] When police at the time arrested several youths, including seventeen-year-old Juan Contreras of La Cañada, for participating in student protests at the Manuel Palacio Fajardo high school in the Zona Central, Delgado personally interceded on their behalf and had them released.[19] Delgado would remain *jefa civil* for nearly all of Herrera Campíns's term, a dramatic departure for a post long marked by pomp and rapid turnover, and a move well reflecting Herrera Campíns's efforts to bolster local government.

By 1980, most contentious collective action of the kind that had characterized the 1970s had given way to cooperation between government and civil society sectors in the parish. Women's groups in the 23 de Enero and surrounding communities had found new support for their grievances, while once-skeptical neighbors had begun to work alongside police to fight crime.[20] Resources for education and athletics had increased, to the point that Bernardo Piñango, a local youth trained in a local gym, won Olympic silver in 1980.[21] Plans to install a parish council to interface with city officials on matters of public services and order—long a linchpin of Herrera Campíns's thoughts on generating popular political consciousness—had begun in earnest after a presidential decree mandating "community participation in regional development" took effect. In part these measures helped COPEI in mid-1979 to sweep municipal elections the first time they were held separately from presidential and congressional elections.[22] By early 1980, pundits openly speculated on whether a new era in Venezuelan politics was afoot, marked by the rise of the so-called "Christian left" and its champion, Luis Herrera Campíns. Wrote one analyst: "Never has the future been brighter for Venezuela's Social Christians."[23]

But by the time Betancourt and Rangel had warned about an impending abyss in February 1981, little of that early optimism remained. During 1980 a quick succession of crises struck at the core elements of *herrerismo*—fiscal stability, state advocacy, participation, efficiency in public services—effectively ending efforts at state-led reform. In 1979 the administration had tried to stem the tide of debt and spending that had marked Pérez's presidency. Government expenditures shrank by 22%, the current account balance closed at a surplus, and the rate of foreign borrowing declined by half of its 1978 level.[24] But the administration's most controversial austerity measure, eliminating Pérez-era price controls and subsidies, quickly spiraled out of control. Inflation spiked 74% from the previous year, closing at 12.4% in 1979. To mitigate the day-to-day impact of rising costs, Herrera Campíns had decreed a wage hike of 30% in his 1980 New Year's address. But the measure proved a stopgap at best, creating a temporary sense of prosperity that quickly vanished as the flood of cash in the economy was not matched by greater production, generating even greater inflation.[25] By the first quarter of 1980, 44% of Venezuelans considered the elimination of price controls the Herrera Campíns government's worst policy decision.[26] Finance Minister Luis Ugueto Arismendi had called it a "painful necessity." Schoolteacher Yazmira Rodríguez laid bare the public's reply: "When you push a cart through a supermarket here you should hear what the housewives say. . . . There are no kind words for the government."[27] A foreign diplomat summarized the collective lament: "[Herrera Campíns is] a good man, he raised high hopes, but he implements things badly and can get no support for them."[28]

Even voices within the administration acknowledged the gulf between its once-lofty rhetoric of promoting participation and their difficulty in bringing it to fruition. In an early-December 1981 "Seminar on the Needs of the Population" sponsored by the World Bank, Alba Illaramendi of Fundacomun took up the matter directly: "We are aware that it is not enough to speak about popular participation to show that we have a democratic system; it is more important to create the mechanisms and facilitate the conditions so that participation is made real." Still, she reaffirmed the administration's basic commitment to a more participatory model of democratic governance as both viable and necessary in order to encourage popular ownership of the political system, especially among urban popular sectors: "The [Herrera Campíns government] is emphatic in stating that participation is the form by which the people take an active presence and don't delegate their abilities to think, to act, and to create."[29]

But where *herrerismo* most suffered was in the area Herrera Campíns had again and again indicated was the everyday "gauge" of democratic performance: public services. Already in 1980 deteriorating services in Caracas had helped sink the President's poll numbers. In March, Herrera Campíns's planning minister, exasperated, remarked to the *New York Times*: "Things have gotten so bad that it is almost impossible to improve the efficiency of public services."[30] Waste management in particular reflected the worst of the state's failure. Where Carlos Andrés Pérez's had consolidated waste management services around a newly created IMAU, Herrera Campíns's response, in keeping with his decentralization efforts, instead tried to transform IMAU into an administrative entity.[31] Rather than collecting trash it would lease routes to private contractors selected by a bidding process, reflecting Herrera Campíns's call to find "public, mixed or private" enterprise solutions wherever needed. It would be the first effort toward privatizing public services in Venezuela.

But in January 1981 the effort exploded in scandal when Alí Buniak, an operations manager, was arrested for soliciting over USD$20,000 in exchange for lucrative trash-route contracts.[32] In response IMAU's director, Edmundo Arias, termed the allegations "a vendetta by those who have been hurt by the end of a business plagued by irregularities, and who wished to stop the process that will turn IMAU into a private company." He also announced that he would seek the approval of Herrera Campíns himself for all winning bids, thereby involving the president directly in the trash issue.[33] By month's end, what began with the arrest of a "lowly operator" had ensnared not just Arias but six more high-level IMAU officials called to give grand-jury testimony.[34]

What the press dubbed the IMAU *affaire* presented Herrera Campíns with problems on several fronts. Ongoing public service deficiencies in Caracas struck at the heart of what had been a bedrock issue in his campaign. Likewise Herrera Campíns had staked his campaign on a promise of more-efficient government, but the IMAU scandal instead spoke more of the administrative clumsiness that had marked much of his reform efforts in 1980. And while the scandal did not implicate Herrera Campíns directly, corruption in the IMAU nevertheless constituted an affront to the President's widely recognized "reputation for honesty."[35] But where the IMAU scandal proved most fateful was in the way Herrera Campíns would henceforth become associated with the waste management problem.

By 1981, then, a bruised and battered administration had fallen into the same patterns of corruption and mismanagement that had plagued his predecessor and which Herrera Campíns had vowed to end. Worse, despite scattered signs of greater citizen participation in decision making, Herrera Campíns had decidedly abandoned the calls to "reinvent democracy" that informed his presidential bid. Yet the vision of a "participatory" politics, rising from a "conscious and organized" citizenry to forge a "truly democratic society" remained a powerful call to arms.[36] In this light the fall of *herrerismo* at the level of the state would serve to provide an opportunity for residents of the 23 de Enero to reinvent democracy, but from below, and in their own terms.

"CLEAN BY CHRISTMAS": RESURGENT RADICALISM AND PUBLIC SERVICE COLLAPSE

In late November 1981, officials at IMAU announced that after over a year of bidding, negotiations, and scandal, they had leased trash collection services in Caracas to four independent firms.[37] It was an unprecedented move toward privatization in Venezuela, promising to bring efficiency to an area of everyday life that had come to symbolize the state's administrative incompetence. But much as confusion had marked most of the process, it would also eclipse this final stage. Just days after the announcement, the Caracas city council convened to discuss ongoing trash problems afflicting the city. According to press reports, an otherwise "lukewarm debate" was "revolutionized" when Lino Álvarez, councilman for MIR (Revolutionary Left Movement), read IMAU's charter. According to Álvarez, the charter gave the council oversight of the institute even though they had long since "relinquished" that role, assuming IMAU to be autonomous.[38] Embarrassed, the council quickly summoned both IMAU's director and private company chiefs. In the ensuing days each would add drama to what was already, by one reporter's account, an "enthralling" circumstance. For instance, after his meeting with the council, an exasperated IMAU director all but begged to be rid of his post, saying "they would be doing me a favor" by asking for his resignation.[39] Meanwhile seeking to bring some measure of calm and optimism, owners of the newly hired companies vowed to have Caracas "clean by Christmas."[40]

Two weeks later, a group of Monte Piedad residents in the 23 de Enero reported that fifteen days had passed since the last time trash was collected in the area—a stunning lapse in a neighborhood of over 100,000 residents. "Right now most of the chutes are totally full and the trash has rotted, bringing as a result the proliferation of rats and a strong stench" said Ednio Rosales of Block 13. They had repeatedly called the company newly charged with waste management in the area, to no avail. "It seems," he said, "that we will spend Christmas surrounded by trash."[41] Meanwhile elsewhere in the 23 de Enero other residents reported water shortages even as a broken pipe, and a botched effort to repair it, spewed tons of water daily.[42]

Twenty-five years after the founding of the 23 de Enero, these were just the latest examples in a long list of grievances that had been accumulating throughout 1981. In August, for instance, a sewer-pipe leak months earlier in Monte Piedad had unleashed a "river" of waste, and despite repeated pleas to the agency charged with administering the blocks, no repairs had come.[43] At the same time residents in Blocks 42–43–44, in the neighborhood's western edge, alerted media that besides perennial water shortages, only one of six elevators servicing 450 apartments was in working order, some having broken down seven years earlier.[44] In September, mud slides in Monte Piedad claimed several of the neighborhood's main access roads, again with no repairs in sight despite repeated efforts to contact authorities.[45] By early December, just as contractors promised to clean Caracas, a major report in the national daily *El Universal* reported on living conditions in the 23 de Enero, concluding that the neighborhood was in a "terrible state of abandon."[46]

That residents would respond violently to this crisis, and that authorities would react in kind, seemed a foregone conclusion. Failing services were just part of the problem affecting the 23 de Enero throughout 1981. As the city council debated the trash situation in late November, violent clashes between local youth in the 23 de Enero and Metropolitan Police had resulted in the "takeover" of 18 blocks in Monte Piedad, Sierra Maestra, and Zona Central by police.[47] In part, the clashes were sparked by the death a sixteen-year-old girl, which neighbors blamed on authorities' negligence after she was wounded during a shootout in Monte Piedad.[48] As the clashes intensified in early

December, one fourteen-year-old died, reportedly after falling from the roof of a local high school.[49] However, days later an investigation revealed he had died from a shotgun blast fired from a police helicopter hovering above.[50] By mid-December the violence between the government and secondary-school students in the 23 de Enero showed few signs of ebbing; in fact it had expanded to surrounding areas. A new round of clashes on 9 December resulted in one burned bus, set ablaze by students outside their middle school in the Zona Central.[51] Days later, teachers at the school reported that students had burned nearly a dozen of their vehicles, since they had refused to cancel classes to honor their fallen peer.[52] In the ensuing days students released their frustration on area streets, looting several distribution trucks and setting other vehicles ablaze.[53]

All told, as Christmas neared, the 23 de Enero was a cauldron of pent-up grievances, violent agitation, and police presence, a far cry from the first two years of Herrera Campíns's government. In fact as *herrerismo* faded in early 1981, radicalism in the 23 de Enero had seen a steady resurgence. In late January police had opened fire on students demonstrating outside the Manuel Palacio Fajardo high school, killing fifteen-year-old Miguel Ríos and seriously wounding a second student.[54] Students had responded by blocking major roads throughout the parish, setting ablaze tires, and hurling bottles at passing vehicles.[55] As democracy celebrated its 23rd anniversary on Friday 23 January 1981, the Metropolitan Police resorted to a tactic they had previously employed: dispatching several hundred officers to take up posts in the super-blocks.[56] As it had in the past, the measure backfired. Rather than easing tensions, the show of force led to more clashes, leaving one sixteen-year-old shot and a rash of protests that would not abate for nearly two months.[57]

What was particular about this resurgence of youth activism in 1981 was that throughout the protests, reports had surfaced that holdovers from the years of guerrilla war in the 1960s, sensing an opportunity to make inroads with a new generation of disaffected youth, had turned the protest into larger political movement. According to one account, "a group of *zagaletones* [vagabonds] arrived in front of the Luis Razzetti school [in the Zona Central], yelling chants against the police and the government."[58] Later, members of the Workers' Revolutionary Movement (*Movimiento Revolucionario de Trabajadores*, or MRT), a short-lived radical-left splinter group with an active youth wing in the 23 de Enero, informed the press that police stationed in the blocks had begun to stage arbitrary beatings and detentions. A few days later, flyers surfaced throughout the neighborhood railing against AD and COPEI for failing to bring about "the revolution," while at the same time tapping into popular disenchantment by critiquing public service failings and the high cost of living. In addition they accused police of using the superblocks as "target practice," meeting rocks with gunshots in a display of excessive force.[59]

But if the political undertones of this type of radicalism rang familiar, so too did the response from the community at large. Residents representing public transportation and small businesses in the parish mounted a public rebuke of what they referred to as "criminal actions . . . with no justified bearing in the political stage, and which resort to throwing rocks and targeting the private property of popular sectors who when they move about the parish it isn't exactly to go to the Country Club." The problem lay in the ancillary effects of the protests both for the daily life and for the future of a community that media had—in a throwback to the bitterest days of urban conflict at the height of the 1960s—again taken to referring to as a "red zone." "These *ultrosos* [extremists]" they noted, "prevent local youth from work and study . . . and constitute a permanent threat for everyone." And, recognizing that police repression fueled rather than quelled tensions, they turned to parents, urging them to take the necessary precautions in order to prevent their children from participating in the protests. The accumulated grievances were enough for one reporter covering events in the 23 de Enero to opine: "ultraleft groups . . . confused their tactics and strategy by burning private cars and buses that either belong to the poor or are used by them, and who under such circumstances can never ally themselves with these *encapuchados*."[60]

These remarks well captured the underlying gulf between youth militants and the wider community in the 23 de Enero. To be sure, practical concerns regarding the impact of protests and attendant repression on daily life remained a major factor tending to keep the two separate. But what most ensured their continued split was the lack of attention to local issues that was the hallmark of radical political mobilization in the neighborhood. In this respect, the seemingly resurgent political activism among students in 1981 most clearly resembled the 1960s era of guerrilla conflict to which it traced its ideological and tactical roots. As youth militants like Lisandro Pérez of the militant-left Bandera Roja group conceded in hindsight, seizing state power primarily through destabilizing actions and more generally by holding aloft the possibility of a revolutionary alternative to liberal democracy had "marginalized" questions of local outreach.[61] Protests, then, marked more than a nuisance; for residents at large, they reflected the youths' selfishness and lack of seriousness, winning them dismissal rather than support.

Read against the grain, however, the words and deeds of both militants and residents at large laid bare areas where radical political activism and local interests might converge. In condemning youth protests, neighbors had stressed the kind of "rock throwing and targeting [of] private property" that long characterized students' contentious repertoire. At root, it was disruption of public life that stoked popular scorn, and the destruction of property that residents repudiated about militant tactics. These were specific rather than wholesale critiques of contentious mobilization that suggested spaces for acceptance if not outright collaboration. Also, in condemning student protests as having no bearing in politics, residents were asserting their belief in the democratic system, affirming rather than attacking its ability to respond to demands when pressured nonviolently. But it was far from a rejection of political protest in general. Taken together, these were primers for a different kind of collective action, contentious within limits, political but not antisystemic. And militants had shown signs of beginning to understand. While still not localizing their message, their flyers had nevertheless addressed issues of specific social concern—continuing public services deficiencies, rising inflation—thus marking a significant departure from the broad anti-statist message they had long conveyed.

Meanwhile, the Herrera Campíns administration tried to reclaim the mantle of reform. On 5 December 1981 the Caracas city council announced plans to "remodel" the 23 de Enero, by adding phone lines and repairing elevators.[62] On 17 December, just days before the first hijackings, the Caracas governor, alongside the city council, installed the first "parish council" in the 23 de Enero. Said one councilman: "We want [to end] the *manguareo* [paper shuffling] of some public servants who don't do their duty, and offer an image of effective services in this parish, the image of a respectable community that wishes to participate in and become integrated to solving the problems it faces."[63] But it was too little too late. The resurgence of radicalism in the 23 de Enero in December 1981, coupled with mounting grievances among the population at large and renewed calls for greater popular participation in democracy, set the stage for an unlikely collaboration, and for the beginning of a new era of popular mobilization that would challenge all levels of the state. In retrospect, the opening lines of an article by some of democracy's elder statesmen seemed prescient: "Among the most celebrated attributes of political leaders was always their ability to detect when an era has ended and determine the signs of the era that is beginning. . . . But woe to the nation whose political elite fails to understand its times."[64]

"WE HAVE TO FIND ANOTHER WAY": THE *SECUESTROS* BEGIN

By the time on 19 December 1981 when Earles Gutiérrez, his brother, and two friends set out to hijack a trash truck, "public services had disappeared" in the 23 de Enero. Only the "well connected"—literally—had home phones; electrical wiring had corroded and been replaced by dangerous "spiderwebs" of cables hanging outside windows; water service remained at best inconsistent, at worst absent; working elevators were rare. And of course, trash lay everywhere, uncollected now for over three weeks. Some ducts were backed up to the fourteenth floor. Recalled one resident: "The worms had started to eat the blocks."[65] In response, the four young men undertook to "do something." They slowed traffic in the rotary in front of Block 7, waiting until a trash truck en route to the local way station passed by. When it did, they blocked the road and Earles, holding a metal tube under his shirt, boarded the truck, telling its frightened driver, as he remembered: "Unfortunately, you will pay the consequences for what we are suffering. You will be fired, and we will have our trash picked up." When police arrived, they stood their ground: "All we want in exchange for the truck is that you commit to send someone to pick up this trash." Some argued that they should not give up the truck, but Earles recalled: "In a hijacking, you have to negotiate." So they gave up the truck, in exchange for a promise that cleanup personnel would arrive by Monday 21 January 1982. As the *Diario de Caracas* said when it picked up the story, it was a "very special way" to protest. "The police authorities initially treated the news as an act of violence, the kind that frequently occurs in the west [of Caracas]. But," the article went on to remark, "when they went to the site they were met with a *civic* claim."[66]

The decision not to burn the truck, but rather to seize it, was born of a long-running struggle among militant youths in the 23 de Enero, who by 1981 were reeling from a dual dejection. On one hand, internecine struggles among clandestine political factions in the neighborhood had resulted in a "fading" of militancy, as some who had partaken in student protests throughout the 1970s had fallen into drugs and crime.[67] On the other hand, their reputation among the community at large had suffered throughout 1981: "They called us *malandros* [petty criminals] for our political work." The trajectory of Earles and his brother reflected some of these conflicts. At as young as eight, Earles had formed part of a group of "Revolutionary Pioneers," which tried to attach itself to veterans of the guerrilla struggle. Among them was Gustavo Rodríguez, a former guerrilla who in the 1970s had started cultural associations that doubled as clandestine revolutionary groups, and who would go on to mentor Earles and help coordinate the *secuestros*.[68] By contrast Earles's brother, several years older, was part of a generation that shunned guerrilla veterans for having given up the armed struggle. The result was a conflicting approach about how best to move forward a message of revolutionary change.

Consider the following example. During a massive demonstration to protest water shortages in the neighborhood in 1978, Earles recalled fighting with his brother about whether they should run out an AD militant, and therefore someone whom Earles's brother derisively called a *sapo* (toad, informant). As Earles recalled, he told his brother:

> It's not that they're *sapos*, it's that we create terror when we climb onto the rooftops [and throw stones at the police], and when they're terrified, people need to find an escape, and that escape may be to reject us; it will never be to support us because they don't identify with that. So it's not that they're *sapos*, it's that we haven't had the methods to incorporate people into the process. And that woman is fighting because she feels affected by the problem of water and repression. And she's also affected by the terrorism that ensues when we climb on the rooftops.

This kind of talk earned Earles a reputation as a "liberal" among his brother's circle. Yet he continued to argue that the way to generate support was by finding common ground: "The only people who mobilized in the 23 de Enero were women, and the only men were militant youth. All the others were busy playing the ponies."[69]

Still, when the matter of hijackings came up in December 1981, according to Earles some among this group feared it as "extremely radical, terrible, we're going to end up in jail." Some proposed instead that they take the piled up trash and burn it on the streets, but as Earles recalls saying: "we've tried that crap forever and it's always the same, we're the ones who end up picking up the trash, people from the community ended up picking up our mess." Others proposed other tried mechanisms, like climbing up on the rooftops to throw rocks and yell chants. After a while, they agreed: "We have to find another way." Reflecting some of the political breadth he claimed characterized his outlook, Earles asked a friend who was an AD militant to join him, his brother, and a third friend in staging a hijacking. After going door-to-door alerting neighbors of their deed, and their intentions not to burn the truck but rather to use it as leverage, they successfully assembled the crowd of mostly women that greeted police on their arrival.

On Monday 21 December, however, no signs of the promised cleanup had materialized. Neighbors then reportedly staged an emergency assembly, and agreed to hijack "everywhere and anyone who had anything to do with" the problems in the 23 de Enero. Meanwhile their tactics became more militant, using weapons and taking to major roads, not just in the 23 de Enero, in search of passing trucks from the electric, telephone, and water companies, and the press. Still, their support increased, especially among those with little record of participation. "Blocks 1 and 2 were the most reactionary. Later they participated the most. That shows that we had had a wrong political approach to things." According to Earles, even an AD militant who had collaborated with an underground antiguerrilla movement in the 1960s joined in. The reasons were clear: "It was a matter of services," said Earles. "Everyone was affected." But that did not mean that the kind of revolutionary politics they had espoused were out of the picture: "We took advantage of that situation, yes. We went in deep into every building, [and it was] excellent. We achieved a knockout punch [tubazo]. . . . From twelve organizers in Blocks 1 through 7, we went to nearly 200 overnight. . . . Even in Block 1, where we never had anything, we ended up controlling thirty apartments."

By the next day, all major national dailies picked up the news of the secuestros. The popular Últimas Noticias gave the protest a full-page spread, sympathetically reporting on their demands while stressing the difference between the violence that had characterized previous mobilizations, even as recently as a week earlier.[70] El Nacional devoted several pictures and a headline of "Tons of Trash in el 23" to the protest,[71] while El Universal, which had a truck hijacked, wrote of "a disaster of trash" in the 23 de Enero as residents had yet to receive the "Christmas bonus . . . promised by the IMAU director."[72] Asked why they had taken to hijacking the trucks, neighbors replied: "[Our] action is an opportune contribution to help contractors fulfill their promise to 'clean Caracas in December.'"[73]

In the discourse of the hijackers, the "radical" character of neighbors' methods seemed not to defy but rather to rely on their loyalty to the institutional structure of representative government; it derived its power not by challenging the legitimacy of the state but rather by appropriating its own claims of popular involvement in the pursuit of a democratic government accountable to its people. From the viewpoint of the state this approach marked a significant enough departure from prior narratives of violent protest to limit severely the repressive response that had characterized its approach to the 23 de Enero throughout the year.

On 23 December, Herrera Campíns made a dramatic intervention. Caracas's major daily blared on its front page: "[Herrera Campíns], 'furious,' gave public services 48 hours." The announcement followed a "stormy" emergency meeting called by Herrera Campíns between the Caracas governor and the heads of public service institutions. According to the President's chief of staff, Asdrúbal Aguiar, "Herrera Campíns understood that the protests that happened in the 23 de Enero and other areas of the capital were not to 'alter public order.'" Instead, they were the "natural reaction of a community that feels unattended in its basic needs." Aguiar went further, noting that by "express orders" from the President, there was to be "no retaliation against protesters." Instead, he ordered the agencies to sign "an affidavit of commitment" so that in 48 hours' time they would attend to the public services of the 23 de Enero in particular, but also of other areas of Caracas, in order "to detect irregularities before they reach critical levels, as they did in the 23 de Enero."[74] Over the next two days, IMAU authorities reportedly deployed nearly 200 trucks and two dozen bulldozers to the neighborhood (fig. 22).[75] In addition, the water service dispatched crews to fix leaks in both sewer and water mains in Monte Piedad.[76] Asked by reporters how they viewed the measure that had forced their presence, public service authorities on the scene coincided in stating that "residents are perfectly justified in staging their protest."[77]

Comments like these helped to galvanize other popular sectors around Caracas, who pointed to the 23 de Enero as they contemplated seeking solutions to long-standing grievances of their own. In Caricuao, for example, another high-rise, government-built community dating to the early 1960s and located in southwestern Caracas, residents reported to the press that "maybe the forms of pressure of the 23 de Enero are more convincing." But a sense of cultural disdain tempered an otherwise veiled admiration for what residents of the 23 de Enero had undertaken, and the attention they had managed to receive. According to one local woman: "One day I told the people at INOS [the water service] that if they didn't send water, we were going to do the same thing as in the 23 de Enero. Of course it's not that

FIGURE 22. Emergency trash-collection operation in Monte Piedad, in December 1981. (Archivo *El Nacional*)

we want to act like them in the 23 de Enero because . . . well we are a more cultured area than the 23 de Enero, but it looks like things in this country can only be fixed *a la mala* [by force]."[78] And in fact, as the *secuestros* raged, authorities rekindled talk of participatory democracy. Addressing urban popular sectors in the southern state of Guarico, Alba Illaramendi of Fundacomun once more urged communities to seize the mantle of participation: "It is indispensable that [communities themselves] promote, participate, and protect the work that is developed to resolve the needs that you yourselves have pointed out."[79]

Meanwhile in the 23 de Enero the cleanup measures begun before Christmas had proven to be stopgaps at best. By 26 December 1981 all equipment and personnel had cleared out while much trash remained uncollected. Public service entities took to accusing one another of ongoing problems in the 23 de Enero, with IMAU officials blaming the superblocks administrator, the *Instituto Nacional de la Vivienda* (INAVI), of negligence.[80] The media captured neighbors' frustrations. Said one neighbor: "We were taken for saps;"[81] others seemed to lose hope they would ever resolve their "eternal calamities."[82] In this light, beginning on 3 January 1982, residents hijacked another batch of official trucks, vans, and cars.

To sustain the protest over time, neighbors relied on an intricate system of task sharing drawn from the 23 de Enero's multiple organizing traditions. Erstwhile guerrillas and militant youths formed the core of those who staged the roadblocks, seized the vehicles, and guarded them overnight, drawing from their tactical experience forged in the fray of anti-establishment conflict—for instance by deflating tires so that the only way to move the trucks was to tow them out. According to Earles, all trucks seized were "assigned" to a building, whose residents then assumed responsibility for the truck. Meanwhile *amas de casa* [housewives] gave the protest its public face, speaking to reporters about the nature of their specific grievances and following up to ensure the coverage was *fidedigno* [fair]. During daily assemblies at the various buildings in Monte Piedad where vehicles were being detained, the community at large discussed their options as days turned to weeks, also setting up guard shifts to ensure the vehicles' safekeeping. When it seemed like attention to the protest was waning, and the state was ready to wait them out, neighbors organized mass rallies to which other sectors of the 23 de Enero contributed "representatives" to assist with logistics and stand in solidarity.

But sustaining the protest took its toll. William Rangel, who alongside Earles had helped organize the *secuestros*, recalled that during nightly meetings with neighbors disputes routinely erupted as long-standing personality conflicts flared up. Some even used the assemblies to vent marital problems, hinting at the level of intimacy that developed over time. In another instance, a National Guard general confronted some of the youth militants over the release of one of the trucks—specifically, one owned by the *El Universal* newspaper. As tempers flared, guns were brandished; several minutes passed before tensions eased. The general, meanwhile, left without the truck.[83] Later, *jefa civil* Josefina Delgado arrived to make a personal appeal to the youths spearheading the *secuestros*, including Juan Contreras, for whom Delgado had earlier advocated when police detained him for participating in student protests at the Palacio Fajardo high school. But as Contreras recalled the encounter, feeling emboldened, he and the others rebuffed Delgado.[84] And when mid-level public service officials showed up at an assembly where neighbors had expected directors, one neighbor yelled "then you are also *secuestrado* [kidnapped]!" before the rest of the assembly talked him down.[85]

The major source of dispute remained what to do about the trucks. One faction, led by youths, advocated burning them. Another faction, led by adults, forbade it. At root lay a careful balancing act between pressure and violence, one that threatened to spill over at any moment. For instance, on 9 January 1982, neighbors staged a demonstration aimed at keeping up the pressure on authorities, and securing the media's attention. But when unidentified gunmen shot at the crowd, leaving one woman wounded, some among the militant youths argued that the time had come to fight violence with violence. Some even began burning tires, blocking the streets for several hours, before other neighbors reminded them of the fragility of their alliance.[86] By 17 January, to show they continued undeterred, residents seized another three public service trucks.[87]

Their resolve paid off. In an assembly on 19 January at a local elementary school, 400 residents filled the dining hall to watch as the directors of IMAU, INOS, and the electric service signed affidavits guaranteeing that they would commit enough resources to conduct a complete, long-term overhaul of the neighborhood.[88] Four days later, 24 years since the overthrow of Pérez Jiménez had set Venezuela on a path toward democracy, residents celebrated as the first of the crews began work, and the last of the hijacked trucks rolled out.[89] Asked if they had lost an opportunity to build a political movement, Frank León, one of the young militants, admitted they had, to an extent. "There were frustrations," he said, but "it was politicized in that people identified you as revolutionary, they respected you." Above all, said León, "we had the satisfaction that we achieved what we set out to do."

THE AFTERMATH OF THE SECUESTROS

In the immediate aftermath of the *secuestros*, the Caracas city council debated the merits of residents' tactics. Its president denounced the practice as "beyond all established order; it is lamentable that this should take place for the simple reason that it has negative consequences . . . especially when there are perfectly acceptable mechanisms to reach an understanding." A councilman from the ruling COPEI party concurred, criticizing residents for presumably acting against their own interests by letting themselves be manipulated: "By no means do I think violence is the solution. . . . If the community allows itself to be taken by activists who don't want solutions to problems because they live off of that cauldron, they will never be able to live decently." A councilman for the MAS party offered lackluster empathy while counseling dialogue:

"I understand that what took place in the 23 de Enero is a reflection of the dramatic neglect that affects the people of that area, forced to use extreme measures, even though I think that the correct approach would be to attack the root of the matter and the most convenient initiative to that end is dialogue."

But Gladys Gavazut, an independent, broke ranks and issued a blanket condemnation of the council while lending full support to residents' measures:

> The council has ceased to be a popular instrument, to become a museum instead, and the participation offered by [the government] was nothing more than a ploy that was discarded when they realized that it might be useful for the people to hold accountable, at a given time, those who direct the fortunes of the nation. . . . I justify [the *secuestros*] and even more in the case of a neighborhood that has been so beaten. The time comes when a community tires and takes actions that are the externalization of a *pueblo* that cannot find solutions to the problems it faces.[90]

In the press, columnists reflected on the underlying implications of the *secuestros*. Artist Mateo Manaure, who years earlier had collaborated in the design of the superblocks, offered a scathing rebuke of public officials who would fail to see the larger problems of representation exposed by residents' protest, opting instead to focus on the legal aspects of the hijackings: "They are the symbols of a *pueblo* . . . that continues to hang on to the hope that Venezuela will go down the path of authentic legality. . . . The very fact that there exists a popular sector like the 23 de Enero, which keeps alight the torch of just claims, is living proof that the light of hope has not died out." For Manaure the implication was a clear portent of things to come: "This community will have within a short time the opportunity, once more, to use efficiently and wisely a weapon as powerful as the vote is in a democracy. We are certain they will use it in the next elections with reflective criteria, as a crushing protest in the face of the cruel injustices they have endured."[91]

Manaure's exhortation to view the *secuestros* as a larger commentary on the broken pacts between the government and its citizens, and to view the illegality of the hijackings as a plea for "authentic legality," laid bare a deeper reality about the 23 de Enero: that residents could mobilize political sectors on behalf of a democratic claim even while engaging in extralegal tactics reflected their paradoxically privileged position vis-à-vis a state by which they felt ignored. In this space, between the "civic" attributes of their claims and the uncivil character of their means, neighbors experimented with how to respond to the effects of a coming economic crisis.

FIGURE 23. June 21, 1989. Antidrug mural in the Block 7 rotary of Monte Piedad. This mural was one of many by the *Grupo Cultural Hombre Nuevo* and other muralist collectives of the period. (José Grillo / Archivo *El Nacional*)

Over the next few years, this dynamic would find expression in debates among the more militant wing of activists in the 23 de Enero: how—if at all—to combine social and political organizing in their community. The debate reflected a synthesis in the dialectic between political and community work that had marked the previous decades of activism. Consider the case of the *Grupo de Trabajo "La Piedrita."* This group emerged from one of the oldest squatter settlements in the 23 de Enero, Arbolitos. The settlement of Arbolitos sits strategically at the crossroads of four sectors of the neighborhood—Sierra Maestra, Monte Piedad, La Cañada, and La Libertad—which rendered it a favored spot for criminal, and especially narcotics, activity during the late 1970s and early 1980s.[92] By the mid-80s neighbors had formed a "working group" to seek collective solutions to a scourge threatening to unravel their once close-knit community, a phenomenon playing out throughout the 23 de Enero. Their response was twofold: on one hand, renew a sense of pride and solidarity in their community through the organization of festivals for local youth, the formation of a muralist brigade to propagate messages of solidarity (fig. 23), and the construction of a commons where strict rules of conduct were observed and imparted to all members; on the other hand, exercise para-police action against criminal elements, regardless of where they came.

On the face of it, then, *La Piedrita* arose as primarily a social response to crime and its consequences for community life. In fact, politics underlay nearly every facet of *La Piedrita's* trajectory, from its inception to its strategies to its goals. For the founders of *La Piedrita*, the presence of crime and drugs in the 23 de Enero was but another, if effective, face of state repression. In this they coincided with a widely held perception in the neighborhood that government policy to neutralize dissidence in the 23 de Enero helped explain the rise of violent delinquency starting in the mid-70s.[93] In their cultural work, the *La Piedrita* group likewise incorporated music and images reflecting demands for social justice, rebukes of representative democracy, rejection of state violence, and the memorialization of activists gunned down either by thugs or police. Especially in their police actions *La Piedrita* drew directly from a tactical repertoire picked up from the associations that some members forged in the 1970s with veterans of the so-called *Unidades Tácticas de Combate* (UTCs) living in or near their community, while other members of the group drew their military training from time spent as conscripts.

As its name implied, the political aims of the group were decidedly more modest than those that had informed the 1960s insurgency. "We thought of ourselves as a *piedrita* [pebble] in the boot of the government," recalls Valentín Santana of the title they gave to the local circular that eventually identified the group.[94] It was far from a claim to state power. They aimed instead to irritate and perturb, to serve as a nagging reminder, as Mateo Manaure had written in the context of the *secuestros*, "of a people that is beaten but not yet defeated."[95]

Elsewhere in the 23 de Enero, residents engaged in similar forms of organizing, politically informed but community-oriented. In Block 37 of the Zona F, for instance, neighbors organized into self-defense brigades to curb the impact of drug trafficking in their area (fig. 24). As with *La Piedrita*, the surface actions of residents organizing to defend their communities spoke of an effort with few overt signs of political content. But as Alirio Moreno—one of the organizers of the self-defense brigades who later went on to preside over the building's neighbors' association—recalled, the building's self-defense brigades were primarily made up of residents disenchanted with what they viewed as neighborhood associations rendered ineffective by squabbles between AD and COPEI partisans. Taking measures into their own hands while still collaborating with police was in this context aimed both at safeguarding their community and at critiquing the government's inability to

FIGURE 24. December 7, 1984. Members of a self-defense brigade in Block 37, Zona F. (Luis Aguilera / Archivo *El Nacional*)

undertake even the most basic functions of governance, such as security.[96] Their actions would lead those involved in the brigades to overhaul the discredited residents' associations, and through elections claim the leadership of the revitalized groups.

It was a pattern repeated in Blocks 42–43–44 of the Zona F, as residents there engaged in similar forms of antidrug campaigns in the mid 1980s.[97] In La Cañada, Juan Contreras, once a youth radical and among the leaders of the *secuestros*, would by the late 1980s join with friends in Block 19 to vie for the leadership of his building's neighborhood association. They developed a platform and canvassed their building, apartment by apartment. The group won, and Contreras claimed the presidency of the association, edging out tickets aligned with AD and COPEI. During their tenure, the youth block worked alongside former association members to implement youth outreach programs, organize weekend cleanup brigades, and lobby the *jefatura civil* for resources to effect structural improvements to the building. "We were very cognizant," said Contreras, "that we were setting an example as an alternative to the major parties." Over time, they shed their image as youthful troublemakers, garnering the support of broad sectors of the community and eventually securing reelection.[98] The vote had proven a powerful weapon indeed.

The success of the *secuestros* transformed more than the physical face of the 23 de Enero. In their wake a new era of popular mobilization ensued, one where community struggles were imbued with political content as usually mainstream sectors embraced a leadership and tactical repertoire fashioned around radical ideological goals. But these sectors also placed limits upon insurgent leaders and tactics, forcing once anti-establishment groups into negotiating with Venezuela's state. As community activists gained a radical political edge, one-time insurgents came to recognize the legitimacy of the representative system. The result was a hybrid political consciousness that held direct-action tactics and loyalty to the founding premises—and promises—of liberal democracy as complementary rather than antithetical. By hijacking the property of the state while adopting its logic of accountability, residents of the 23 de Enero were marking not just a new form of protest but also the emergence of a new consciousness of participatory politics in Venezuela.

THE CHALLENGES OF POPULAR VICTORY: PUBLIC-HOUSING REFORM AFTER THE *SECUESTROS*

Residents' increasing efforts to take matters into their own hands—whether policing, area improvements, or even building administration—owed in large part to the organizing and mobilizing innovations of the *secuestros*. But they were also born of necessity, reflecting new spaces and opportunities for participation as authorities responded to the ongoing economic crisis, and to residents' new demands in the 23 de Enero. On 17 December 1984 officials from Venezuela's *Instituto Nacional de la Vivienda* (National Institute of Housing)—known as INAVI and founded in 1976 to replace the erstwhile Banco Obrero that built the superblocks—gathered in the 23 de Enero to usher in a new era in the country's public-housing history.[99] For the first time since the agency's founding as the Banco Obrero in the 1920s, INAVI was set to transfer ownership of one of its public-housing units to residents themselves, providing favorable terms of sale to anyone meeting a few basic criteria, while making a newly elected condominium association responsible for collecting rents from those unable to purchase.[100]

At first glance the mood was celebratory. INAVI's press release noted that "great jubilation" marked the event, and it upheld the move as a model for others to follow in the path to self-governance and housing independence. In fact already four other buildings in the neighborhood were scheduled to pass into condominiums.[101] A closer look, however, suggested less a celebration of a historic moment than a hasty affair undertaken in a climate of lingering misgivings, especially among residents. The same congratulatory press release revealed that residents learned "the good news" about their new status at the same time as they were told to vote on their governance. Somewhat belatedly, residents were also "given orientation about the benefits of cooperative ownership" while officials "responded to many of them regarding several concerns about which they had doubts, while promising to cooperate with them in various requests such as [installing] direct gas service, better water service, and others."[102]

Interviewed two days later, INAVI's chief collections officer, Iván Beirutti, spoke frankly about the underlying reasons for the move from public to private ownership: "With this plan . . . INAVI will be able to unload all the costs of maintaining those properties [in the 23 de Enero], approximately [USD$1.25 million] annually, which means a significant discharge of the Institute's limited funds." He added that, "once these blocks pass into cooperative ownership, the Institute will have the financial breathing room to allow it to invest in new urban projects and to continue works that have begun but are currently paralyzed due to lack of funds." Evidently, the neighborhood had become a financial albatross undercutting new urban-planning efforts, making the move to pass ownership of the buildings to residents "the most viable solution"[103] to a funding crisis that two years earlier had forced INAVI to restructure USD$500 million in accumulated debts.[104] And besides, noted Beirutti, "it will allow people to take care of what they have, because they themselves will be the owners and administrators."[105]

As Beirutti revealed, the move primarily owed to a spiraling economic crisis at the heart of the government. Though alarms about political and economic weaknesses in Venezuela's democratic system had long sounded, by the early 1980s they had become mainstream. Severe contractions in the global price of oil had begun to lay bare major systemic inequities hidden during years of oil-fueled exponential growth. In a country that had long enjoyed Latin America's highest per-capita income, by some estimates one sixth of its people now lived in extreme poverty.[106] Wild fluctuations in world crude-oil prices exposed Venezuela's dependency on oil—in 1982 accounting for 70% of government revenues—while finance ministers traveled abroad in search of loans to cover basic expenditures. Quickly faltering confidence in the economy generated both bank runs and capital flight, leading eventually to the devaluation of a long-established fixed exchange rate on a day now remembered as "Black Friday."[107] Academics debated the causes of the crisis. Sociologists pointed to flawed development models based on political patronage that tended to de-incentivize initiative.[108] Political scientists faulted clientelism for "ruining" the nation.[109] Economists tried to jolt the social subconscious, warning that "Venezuelans must awaken from the lethargy of false abundance,"[110] a curious claim in a context where over half of the population lived in poverty.

Meanwhile political challenges added to the mounting economic and social critiques. In part, the partisan fray of presidential campaigning ahead of elections in December 1983 stoked the fires of uncertainty and anxiety. Opposition politicians decried as "painful and shameful to have to recognize that Venezuela is broke,"[111] while Acción Democrática (AD) called on COPEI's Luis Herrera Campíns to declare a national emergency and convene a national unity government.[112] Former president Carlos Andrés Pérez, of AD, who had presided over boom years in the 1970s, sounded a more conciliatory if somber tone in affirming that "the time has come" for self-reflection [autocrítica] by Venezuela's political leadership writ large.[113] Wolfgang Larrazábal, who had presided over the transition to democratic elections after helping lead the 1958 coup, proposed barring former presidents from traveling abroad until a special tribunal cleared them of any wrongdoing during their term in office, exposing concerns about corruption and accountability at the highest levels.[114] Meanwhile a guerrilla movement presumed defunct since the pacification of armed struggle in the late 1960s showed new signs of life, as clashes between insurgents and military forces left scores dead in rural regions of the country.[115] For the first time in a long time Venezuelans openly speculated about the possibility of a military coup.[116]

To be sure, the heat of looming elections tended to inflame passions and generate posturing. But the fact that 1983 marked the 25th anniversary of a now broadly critiqued political system undergoing deep structural crisis served to sharpen contrasts between the promises and the realities of a democracy ostensibly being celebrated as Latin America's "most enduring."[117] Preparations for a "day of jubilee"[118] to commemorate democracy's founding on 23 January 1958 aimed to connect the populace anew with the roots of a system now in crisis. In Caracas the city government planned a "popular program of reencountering [reencuentro] January 23rd," marked by fireworks and floral parades in barrio sectors of the capital to celebrate the madrugonazo [predawn strike] that had ushered in representative democracy in Venezuela.[119] Left-wing youth of the *Movimiento Electoral del Pueblo* (MEP) called for "rescuing what was positive from January 23rd" while acknowledging the shortcomings of the system that ensued, in the process hinting at the generational gap between those who had witnessed the birth of democracy and those born in its wake.[120] A full-page spread in the popular daily *Últimas Noticias* offered snapshots of interviews with everyday Venezuelans as they reflected on the contradictions implied in celebrating democracy in a climate of crisis and uncertainty. Among the range of responses: "those who long for, those who complain about, and those who praise democracy."[121] All told, while government officials warned that there was "no truth in cataclysmic versions of the national situation,"[122] a *New York Times* piece seemed best to capture the sense of anxiety suffusing the public discourse: "Among Venezuelans, from cab drivers to men of letters, field hands to presidential candidates, this saying, 'The party's over,' is [now] the most repeated."[123]

At the 23 de Enero, anniversary celebrations for Venezuelan democracy proved at once especially pronounced and especially problematic. On one hand, and in a very concrete way, the neighborhood refracted through residents' accumulated grievances the growing gap between representative democracy's promises and its shortcomings. On the other hand, it continued to be held as the representative of national popular will by political players seeking the mantle of popular legitimacy. Candidates aspiring to the presidency followed a now-familiar pattern of launching their campaigns in the neighborhood.[124] As the 25th anniversary neared, another familiar pattern of flooding the neighborhood with resources to satisfy immediate infrastructure needs also surfaced, if accentuated. INAVI officials committed over USD$11 million in capital investments for the neighborhood.[125] City government officials announced plans to build a market and remodel the central Cristo Rey plaza in the neighborhood.[126] State media reported on the start of weeklong festivities including sporting events, fireworks displays, youth programs, community leadership award ceremonies, and the staging of a specially commissioned play titled "Requiem for the Dictatorship" in the neighborhood's theater.[127]

Most accounts proved far less celebratory, as national-level economic pressures intersected with very local community grievances to spoil festivities. In one sector of the neighborhood, residents learned from INAVI that they would need to wait until the national budget was finalized in order for problems ranging from broken elevators to rotten garbage chutes in their buildings even to be entertained, much less resolved.[128] Two weeks prior to the anniversary, media reported on the "abandonment into which [the neighborhood's] installations have fallen,"[129] while offering residents' skeptical take on the flood of improvements planned in anticipation of the commemoration.[130] Facing concerns that the work was but a "scrubbing" due to the upcoming celebrations,[131] *jefa civil* Josefina Delgado issued a declaration ensuring that plans for neighborhood improvements represented a longer-term investment and were "not just because of the 25th anniversary."[132] Still, on 25 January tense protests including the looting and burning of a food truck erupted in the neighborhood, well exposing the state of disaffection among certain groups of residents and laying bare general tension in the community.[133] Reflecting on these contradictions, one journalist put it simply: "the 23 de Enero still waits to be repaid for the debt it is owed by democracy."[134]

Continuing infrastructure problems proved particularly trying for residents of the 23 de Enero, where lingering service problems like the ones that led to the *secuestros* had resulted from a botched effort, the first of its kind, to privatize a public entity, in this case the IMAU.[135] The *secuestros* had only exacerbated these issues. Two months after a privatization meant to defray costs and bring efficiency to the waste management service, IMAU continued to report staggering losses in the order of USD$7 million per week.[136] Just days after residents of the 23 de Enero let up their protest, five thousand workers laid off in IMAU's privatization process staged a sit-in at the agency's headquarters to seek fair compensation.[137] Throughout the year and into 1983 both labor and operational problems continued to plague the newly private service as one emergency cleanup measure after another failed to yield results,[138] while in October 1982 workers threatened "legally or illegally" to halt trash collection altogether.[139] By October 1983, the same city council that had green-lighted the privatization of waste management services in Caracas was forced to provide IMAU a USD$10 million bailout to continue operations.[140]

It was in this context of early and unsuccessful privatization efforts in urban public services that reform of INAVI went ahead beginning in 1982, marking the unceremonious demise of a once flagship institution. Since its founding in the 1920s as the Banco Obrero (BO) this institution had undergone several significant transformations that placed it more and more at the center of cementing national progress in a rapidly urbanizing Venezuela.[141] Under Pérez Jiménez the BO had lived its heyday, with massive projects like the superblocks transforming the Caracas landscape.[142] Throughout, though, even as construction priorities changed after the transition to democracy in 1958, the BO's basic formula of charging rents, rather than selling properties outright, in housing designed for working-class sectors remained unchanged.[143]

When in 1976 the BO became INAVI, the move was designed to centralize affordable public-housing policy and execution nationwide during an era of nationalization and centralization of state services and industries that marked the oil-boom years of the 1970s.[144] Able to acquire money easily in a climate flush with petrodollars, INAVI undertook a significant building campaign financed mainly through cheap debt that by 1982 had reached USD$500 million.[145] To the price of new housing were also added the costs of maintenance of existing housing, to the tune of USD$5 million a month. Meanwhile tenant rents in those existing properties, including the 23 de Enero, were both heavily subsidized and notoriously unreliable as a revenue source, further complicating the financial picture for INAVI as petrodollars dried up by 1981.[146]

As the largest single group of properties owned and operated by INAVI, the 23 de Enero was at once the costliest, among the oldest, and, given the dimensions of the buildings themselves, the most difficult to maintain of the Institute's holdings. The hijackings of 1981–1982 had set in sharp relief many of these complications. While garbage collection problems had sparked the protest, and would persist, as the protest grew neighbors had expanded their range of demands to include major repairs and area improvements. Among these were 56 new elevators, one for each of the fifteen-story superblocks in the neighborhood. Delivery and installation of the units became mired in bureaucratic wrangling between INAVI and elevator manufacturers,[147] to the point that following over a month of delays and flaring tempers among neighborhood residents, the Caracas city council called for criminal charges to be filed against the companies for breach of contract.[148] Still, a year after the hijackings, INAVI had invested USD$11 million in building repairs and general upkeep, a considerable sum in the context of shrinking budgets and looming austerity.[149]

It was precisely the combination of a protest rooted in claims to citizen empowerment, and the attendant state investments in response to residents' demands, that helped create the conditions for neoliberal reform of public-housing policy as seen through the lens of a cash-strapped bureaucracy looking to "unload" a sizable financial burden. At the heart of INAVI's policy shift lay the pressure of austerity on one hand and the appeal to self-reliance to the neighborhood residents on the other. However, to comply with recently passed revisions to the Law of Horizontal Property—which governed cooperative ownership of housing in Venezuela—INAVI was required to ensure that any building it transferred to residents' control must have no pending repairs.[150] Residents had proven themselves resilient and well organized in seeking accountability from state institutions; in turn, state institutions and notably INAVI had been compelled to bring into working order buildings it had long struggled to maintain. In short, the very factors that made the protest successful laid the groundwork for the eventual transfer under the terms laid out by INAVI.

And in fact, in the wake of the transition from public to private housing, signs of what INAVI officials had called upon regarding citizen autonomy, initiative, and responsibility certainly surfaced in some quarters of the 23 de Enero (fig. 25). A year after the initial transfer of ownership of buildings, media reported on the donation of vehicles to local police by residents of several of the buildings that passed into cooperative housing, a community effort aimed at bolstering public safety in the neighborhood.[151] Another story, headlined "The 23 de Enero Sets the Example: When You Resolve to Live a Better Life," detailed how in the months after they gained ownership of their building, no longer constrained by restrictions imposed by INAVI, residents of Block 13 had refurbished common areas, put up lighting with "better finish," installed a fence around their building and parking areas, and "incessantly promoted athletic activities" for youth. It represented, the story noted, "a radical change in the attitude of its inhabitants, now residents."[152]

Each of these accounts, however, also laid bare a less glowing underbelly. That residents undertook to provide police with vehicles spoke to deepening community ties between citizens and the security apparatus. But it also spoke to funding and operational shortcomings in the police, shortcomings that would now fall upon the neighbors themselves to meet. In the same Block 13 where a "radical change" had transpired, the deeper story of transformation—as told by residents—in fact had begun years earlier as residents undertook to organize self-defense brigades to "make war against antisocials, whether from inside or outside the community," in light of police deficiencies.[153] The same had been true of communities throughout the 23 de Enero, which facing the scourge of drugs, crime, and the twin perils of police corruption and inattention, had in 1984 created armed groups to fend off criminals, and where "children played under the armed vigilance of their parents."[154]

By January 1986, thirty years after Pérez Jiménez inaugurated the first superblocks, the narrative of glorious self-reliance that seemed to pervade early interpretations of public-housing reform in the 23 de Enero had begun to shift,

FIGURE 25. In October 1984, children participate in a trash-collection drive in the Monte Piedad sector of the 23 de Enero. (Juan Quijano / Archivo *El Nacional*)

if slightly. "Despite having been abandoned," reported one neighbor ahead of the 23 January festivities, "the community is looking to solve its problems." In particular, he pointed to recent successful demonstrations aimed at shuttering a major trash compactor facility located in the heart of the neighborhood. He also held up the recent change of several new buildings to condominium status.[155] In other words, while formal autonomy coupled with continuing pressure through direct action had brought changes for the better, this was a reflection less of democratization won than of the abandonment to which the neighborhood named after democracy's founding date had to contend.

Over the next five years, almost 70% of the 23 de Enero would be converted from public housing into condominiums, increasingly under conditions not of residents' choosing but rather as the imperative of fast-plummeting eco-nomic conditions afflicting INAVI and most other state entities. As the economic crisis that started earlier in the decade matured by the late 1980s, the neighborhood again became a symbolic flashpoint for assessing the gulf between expectations and realities, with ever-increasing sharpness. "The 23 de Enero has become a dictatorship of problems," wrote one journalist in 1986,[156] adding that "millions of cockroaches and guns [were] hidden in the 'Wild West' of the 23 de Enero."[157] Another reported that life in the neighbor-hood had become a "debate between rats and delinquents."[158] Even the ephemeral satisfactions of periodic investments had begun to give way to exasperated frustration. One neighbor lamented that "a mere 'touchup' to commemorate its anniversary is what the 23 de Enero gets every year."[159] These investments continued to showcase the real links between the neighborhood and the political system whose founding date the neighborhood's name memo-rialized. In 1986, President Jaime Lusinchi, for instance, personally intervened to "order a full cleanup of the 23 de Enero."[160] Later that year he would inau-gurate a computing center, among the first of its kind, in the neighborhood, again demonstrating how political and symbolic centrality interfaced in the 23 de Enero.[161]

But the link between the concrete failings reflected in the neighborhood and the larger crisis of the political system grew stronger as both worsened.[162] One resident lamented: "The abuses we're subjected to are not proper to a 28-year-old democracy,"[163] while the neighborhood's *jefe civil* noted in reflect-ing on the state of his charge: "The 23 de Enero superblocks are feeling the weight of time,"[164] a comment easily extended to the very political system to which it had long been bound. Ultimately, the politics of public-housing reform in 1980s Caracas, while couched in a language of self-empowerment, in fact heralded an era of severe structural adjustment whose result was less deepen-ing participatory practice than deepening disaffection with a key state institu-tion at a time of general erosion of public trust in government.

The lessons of early privatization efforts and the response to them by residents of the 23 de Enero, including the hijackings of 1981, thus appeared misread. Their underlying message had not been one of self-reliance, but rather of institutional responsibility. By holding the state directly accountable for its responsibilities to citizens, through methods both legal and extralegal, resi-dents of the 23 de Enero had demanded not autonomy—certainly not under the auspices of economic exigency that marked the transition from public to private housing in the neighborhood. Instead, they had demanded effective governance. Public-housing reform offered neither.

Transferring ownership of buildings in the 23 de Enero was no mere administrative matter, nor simply a local affair. That the 23 de Enero became the first neighborhood in Venezuela to experience the transition from public to private ownership—twenty five years after Marcos Pérez Jiménez's grand effort to modernize Caracas, and by extension Venezuela, through mass construction of high-altitude, high-density public housing for urban working classes—held potentially contradictory meanings at levels both symbolic and bureaucratic. On one hand it seemed to reflect not just the transfer of administrative control from a state entity to a community of residents, but a larger transfer of power from state to populace, an expression of democratic maturity through popular empowerment. For residents, self-management should have proven welcome. Almost as soon as the neighborhood was founded they had begun to protest deficiencies in the government's management of the area; more recently they had adopted a language of participatory democracy to exert more-direct and more-effective forms of pressure and accountability upon INAVI and other state institutions.

On the other hand, against the backdrop of economic crisis, and specifically its manifestations in the 23 de Enero, the same shift seemed less a sign of institutional maturity and democratic coming-of-age than of a fissuring of the social pact between a state no longer able to meet its responsibilities and popular sectors suddenly forced to fend for themselves. Whether the former or the latter interpretation took precedence would set the tone for subsequent and more wide-ranging efforts at structural reform by the state, and their attendant popular responses.

CHAPTER 7

Killing Democracy's Promise

A Massacre of People and Expectations

By the time it was over, nearly 300 people lay massacred. Unmarked graves found months later added hundreds more to the toll—men, women, and children hurriedly wrapped in plastic trash bags and left to a humiliating fate. It was the butcher's bill for a week of fire and rage that gripped Venezuela beginning on 27 February 1989.

Days earlier, facing a mountain of debt and dwindling revenues, the newly sworn-in President of Venezuela, Carlos Andrés Pérez, went back on a campaign promise and signed a financing agreement with the International Monetary Fund.[1] In exchange for sorely needed cash, the once oil-rich nation would undertake a dramatic austerity program that included selling public industries, cutting social spending, and raising the price of gasoline, long valued as the cheapest in the world. To allay concerns from public transit, authorities approved an across-the-board 30% increase in bus fares. But word circulated poorly, and on the morning of Monday 27 February, when the new plan went into effect, some drivers capitalized on the confusion and charged prices that went well beyond the new legal limit.

Carlos Quintana of Block 13 was there to witness what came next. Five years earlier, Quintana's superblock became the first public-housing building in Venezuelan history to pass into private ownership. At dawn on 27 February, he again stood at the center of a historic event, one that would transform not just his neighborhood but the entire nation. While visiting family in the bedroom community of Guarenas about thirty minutes east of Caracas, Quintana watched as students and workers en route to the capital began to set buses ablaze to protest fare hikes. "A mess [*lío*] started," he recalled, "with a guy saying, 'No that can't be, how are you going to charge so much for the fares?' this and that. And the people rose up [*se amotinó*] and the problems started with the bus drivers and that it is where it was unleashed, right there, what later happened in all Venezuela."[2]

By mid-morning, as news of events traveled by telephone, television, and motorcycle to Caracas, scattered protests began in the Parque Central business and residential complex near the terminal for buses coming from Guarenas.[3] By noon a truck carrying groceries lay looted, while demonstrators stopped traffic in the nearby Francisco Fajardo highway connecting east and west Caracas. Around 1 P.M. police opened fire on the increasingly large and agitated crowd in Parque Central, killing 22-year-old university student Yulimar Reyes. Meanwhile Freddy Parra, a 23 de Enero resident and a student at *Universidad Central de Venezuela* (UCV), was shot in the leg while he protested fare hikes in the nearby Plaza Venezuela (see map 2).[4] By 6 P.M. sixty-five people were dead, none among them police.[5]

As violence escalated, public transportation in Caracas stopped, forcing people like Juan Contreras of La Cañada into epic journeys back to the 23 de Enero. It would take Contreras and a friend—both in their twenties at the time—hours by car, bus, and foot to travel from La Urbina in east Caracas to La Cañada. Along the way, they "saw all the scenes. Burned cars, chaos, people looting . . . we were desperate to get home." Once there, the pair found "all the streets blocked." In La Cañada, a trash truck was on fire outside the Agua Salud metro station, which had earlier shut its doors as protests grew.[6] Ramón Molines was also there, coming from Block 1 in Monte Piedad on hearing of the burning truck. Betraying stunned observation, he remembered: "All we did was watch, we were there as spectators."[7] By evening, a tense calm reigned in Monte Piedad. "When I arrived here . . . things were peaceful," recalled William Rangel, who years earlier had helped organize the *secuestros*. "But you could smell in the air, in the environment, that something was happening."[8]

The contours of what "was happening" took shape over the next five days as Caracas was gripped by the deadliest wave of protest, violence, and repression in the nation's twentieth-century history. By nightfall on 27 February 1989, newly inaugurated President Carlos Andrés Pérez ordered Army troops from Venezuela's interior to "restore order" in the capital; within hours nearly 9,000 soldiers had taken positions in "strategic" areas of Caracas, the 23 de Enero among them.[9] And they did restore order, following a plan to seek and destroy urban guerrillas first hatched in the 1960s to quash what was then a raging left-wing insurgency.[10] With Army troops and tanks in the streets of the capital, Congress imposed a curfew from 6 P.M. to 6 A.M. and suspended constitutional rights for the first time since the 1960s era of guerrilla war, when Venezuelan democracy was in its infancy.[11] As night settled on 28 February Caracas was militarized. Mass killings followed. At city hospitals, bodies pierced by military-grade high-caliber bullets began to collect. Overwhelmed city morgue officials hurriedly placed unclaimed bodies in mass graves.[12] It would take five days for what one newspaper editorial called a "precarious normalcy" to return to Caracas.[13] By the time authorities restored most constitutional provisions on 11 March, officials reported 276 deaths, while later discoveries of mass graves led some to estimate between 750 and 1,000 fatalities. Of these, just two came from the military, plus one police captain, the latter gunned down amid clashes in the 23 de Enero.[14]

What began as a protest against fare hikes became, said one human-rights activist, "an act of historic proportions, unique and unrepeatable." One political leader flatly admitted, "we were taken by surprise," while days later a stunned Pérez concluded: "It is dangerous to defy poverty."[15] The Inter-American Court of Human Rights (IACHR) later found that "the Armed Forces opened fire against crowds and against homes, which caused the death of many children and innocent people who were not taking part in criminal acts. . . . There was a common pattern of behavior characterized by the disproportionate use of the Armed Forces in poorer residential districts."[16]

This chapter examines the lived experience of residents of the 23 de Enero during what has come to be known as the *Caracazo*. Widely held as a turning point in Venezuelan history, the 1989 protest and its aftermath exposed a deep fissure in the social pact between political elites and the electorate established in the wake of the 1958 democratic revolution that ousted Pérez Jiménez. In the years after 1989, failed coups, presidential impeachments, and financial meltdowns exposed the institutional frailty of Venezuelan democracy, overtaking the *Caracazo*'s significance as an independent indicator of systemic strain. Yet its basic transcendental quality continued to hold sway.[17] Thus identified, the *Caracazo* became an abstraction, a stand-in for the accumulated problems of the democratic system as a whole and emblematic of the broken pacts between state and citizenry that would eventually bring about the collapse of a once-vaunted political system. Rendered and deployed as a device, the *Caracazo* lost its specificity. But that specificity is where clues about why the *Caracazo* proved a turning point emerge. To focus more closely on the week-long event is to see the full dimensions of that fissure and to rethink the inevitability that came to be associated with the *Caracazo*. It did not immediately follow either that the *Caracazo* would transpire, or that it would lead to the collapse of the political order established after 1958. Only by considering the precise breakdown of preexisting norms of what was and was not expected, from both state and populace, do the full implications of the *Caracazo* emerge.

Set against the backdrop of the 23 de Enero's history with Venezuela's government—marked as it was by the strategic interplay of protest and electoral politics—this chapter offers a reading of the *Caracazo* that highlights the contingent rather than totalizing aspects of the events. What emerges is a picture of not one but many *Caracazos*. The routinization of conflict in the preceding three decades had rendered elastic the boundaries both of the possible and the predictable in the 23 de Enero's relationship with the state. If anything, events like the *secuestros* in the preceding decade—where majority participation in the two-party electoral system had expanded the range of legitimate expressions of grievance that fell outside institutional channels—seemed to forestall the possibility of the kind of violence that would grip the neighborhood.

But in a context of generalized upheaval, old patterns quickly lost currency. A trash truck on fire was hardly novel, but against the backdrop of a city in flames it gained greater significance. Deadly clashes between students and police had marked much of the 1970s, but police had rarely been among the dead. Military occupation, too, had precedents in the early 1960s, but images of three floor segments punctured by bullets fired indiscriminately had no parallel. Even the violent death of local youth was not uncommon, including ones like that of eight-year-old Francisco Moncada of Atlántico Norte, shot on the afternoon of 28 February. But bodies strewn on the streets for hours as a result of intense gunfire indicated a different order of brutality. Ultimately the vast gulf separating the state's response from resident's expectations—in turn founded on decades of experience—exposed how the remarkable elasticity established during the thirty-year relationship between the government and residents of the neighborhood lay shattered. This dynamic also had a parallel, but not one that authorities likely cared to admit. It was the violence that thirty years earlier Pérez Jiménez had unleashed as the last gasp of a dying regime, leading to its ouster and "democratic revolution."

VOTING FOR HOPE: THE 1988 ELECTIONS AND CARLOS ANDRÉS PÉREZ'S RETURN

Reflecting on the violence weeks later, 23 de Enero AD leader Trina Quevedo noted: "I don't understand why the Army unleashed on us in this way, because we've always had disturbances and agitators here, and the police come and seize the blocks and control them in an hour."[18] Quevedo's disbelief at the state's response revealed a dramatic transition from hopeful anticipation, to fast-escalating protest, to repression on a scale unknown and, in fact, unimagined. It was a sense of utter surprise that befell all levels of Venezuelan society during the last two days of February 1989. On the evening of 27 February, well after the outbreak of protest in Caracas, President Carlos Andrés Pérez had flown to the plains city of Barquisimeto to address a meeting of the Venezuelan Executives Association. He had done so despite knowing of the growing signs of unrest, according to Pérez's executive secretary, Ignacio Betancourt, who had received calls throughout the day from ministers and other officials alerting Pérez to what was taking place. But "the President didn't believe it." Once shown footage of looters and demonstrators in Caracas, Pérez again dismissed the events as old news: "That was at noon . . . by this time everything has calmed down."[19] Later, addressing the executives' meeting, Pérez once more downplayed what was taking place. "There is nothing to be alarmed about," he told them. "We are going to take advantage of the crisis to generate well-being."[20]

That Pérez's initial response was to minimize events while sounding a call to generate "well-being" spoke of the unanticipated nature of the events and of Pérez's continuing sense of confidence and optimism just days after taking office. Three months earlier, on 4 December 1988, Venezuelans had swept the AD candidate into the presidency, capping his return to executive office after presiding over Venezuela during a period of rapid growth in the mid-1970s. His election marked the seventh time since 1958 that Venezuelans had taken to the polls to pick their president, cementing the country's image as "the region's showcase democracy."[21] It also reflected a collective desire for a return to days remembered as prosperous, albeit against the backdrop of nearly a decade of deep economic recession unleashed after the devaluation of Venezuela's currency in 1983, late in the administration of Luis Herrera Campíns. And, in fact, Pérez's inauguration on 2 February 1989 had sought to signal Venezuela's reentry onto the world stage, drawing 22 heads of state and dozens of dignitaries from around the world. Among them was Fidel Castro, whose fleeting one-day visit marked a departure from the euphoric scenes that had accompanied his arrival in Caracas thirty years earlier. Asked by reporters about his thoughts on Pérez, Castro responded: "He is aware of the problems he has to face. . . . He was very optimistic and enthused with the work he wants to accomplish."[22] In short, it was a time of optimism as Venezuelans readied to turn the page on a difficult decade.

Two weeks later, on 17 February, Pérez announced a series of economic reforms designed to reduce the country's massive debt, contracted largely during his first term in office between 1973 and 1979, when high oil prices had created an illusion of unlimited wealth among political elites, leading to large public spending. But plummeting oil prices in the 1980s had left Venezuela with little income to meet its staggering debt obligations, forcing cuts in social spending and measures such as the devaluation of the currency in 1983 in order to steer resources into servicing the foreign debt. By 1988, inflation rates of 35% and poverty rates of 70% reflected the effects of economic crisis. In addition, Pérez's predecessor had decimated Venezuela's foreign reserves, which at USD$300 million were dwarfed by the country's USD$34 billion debt. Facing national bankruptcy, Pérez negotiated a USD$4.5 billion loan package with the International Monetary Fund, agreeing to austerity measures that included raising gasoline prices and lifting price controls on all but the most basic goods. Anticipating the effects of higher gasoline prices, Pérez also authorized a 30% increase in public transportation fares, which he offset with a 30% increase in the minimum wage. Somber but hopeful, his speech betrayed no lack of confidence or certainty about the need to carry out these measures, concluding with the same fiery phrase that had been his campaign slogan: ¡Manos a la obra! [Let's get to work!]. It did, however, break with campaign promises not to negotiate with the IMF, which he had reportedly called "the bomb that only kills people."[23]

At the 23 de Enero, Trina Quevedo had much to feel hopeful about in Venezuela's new president. As a local AD leader in Block 1 of Monte Piedad, she had helped Pérez win in the 23 de Enero, consolidating its shift from a sector whose relationship with AD had been openly hostile under the presidency of Betancourt, to one where the party was now dominant. This was no small feat. In 1983, the overwhelming victory of AD's Jaime Lusinchi in the neighborhood, as in the rest of Venezuela, had resulted from a large-scale repudiation of Herrera Campíns's administration across all national sectors, one which irreparably tarnished COPEI's image despite the party's efforts to distance itself from the President.[24] This dynamic helped account for Lusinchi's 22-percentage-point drubbing of Rafael Caldera, who was running for a second term in office promising a return to better times, a promise similar to the one Carlos Andrés Pérez would make in 1988. In the 23 de Enero, Lusinchi's margin of victory had been greater still: 24 percentage points.[25]

But during Lusinchi's administration the problems that had plagued Herrera Campíns—rising inflation, poverty, and unemployment—only worsened. Under those conditions, warding off another protest vote in 1988, similar to the one that had decimated COPEI in 1983, seemed like a tall order. And, in fact, COPEI recovered across the board in the 23 de Enero in 1988: its candidate, Eduardo Fernández, received 37% of the vote to Caldera's 29% in 1983, and the party as a whole did better by two percentage points compared to 1983. Still, Pérez and AD staged a decisive victory nonetheless. On election night 1988, Pérez came away with 52% of the vote in the 23 de Enero. It marked the second time that an AD candidate had won a majority in the neighborhood, and only the third time in the neighborhood's experience with elections that a majority of its residents had supported one candidate (the other, besides Lusinchi, was Larrazábal in 1958).[26]

At the national level, Pérez's victory despite his predecessor's performance was a testament to his success in transcending party labels and creating a message of optimism that harked back to a time in the 1970s when high oil prices had propelled Venezuela to the center of the world stage, led by a hyperpresidential administration.[27] In the 23 de Enero, it also attested to local party activists' ability to mobilize a now well-oiled machine around a candidate whose earlier presidency had been far from propitious. Pérez's presidency from 1974 to 1979 was a time of deadly student protests and worsening infrastructure in the 23 de Enero, in the context of their first-ever mass embrace of the two major political parties of the post-1958 era—AD and COPEI. When set against the backdrop of a narrative of national greatness, the 23 de Enero's experience under Pérez in the mid-1970s had created a deep fissure between discourse and reality. Over time, this fissure manifested itself in the turn toward COPEI's Luis Herrera Campíns that marked the elections of 1978. Herrera Campíns promised greater participation, to break from Pérez's concentration of executive power, which he again invoked as the way to rein in Venezuela's many problems. In this sense, Pérez's 1988 victory in the 23 de

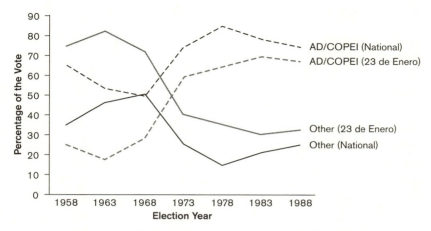

FIGURE 26. Electoral trends in congressional balloting in the 23 de Enero and nationally, from 1958 to 1988. Compiled from *Las cuatro primeras fuerzas políticas en Venezuela a nivel municipal, 1958–1978* (Caracas: Consejo Supremo Electoral, Dirección de Estadística, 1990); *Elecciones del 4 de Diciembre de 1983* (Caracas: Consejo Supremo Electoral, División de Estadística, 1984). (Graphic by Ben Pease)

Enero was a remarkable turn that suggested that residents in the neighborhood were willing to take a chance with Pérez not because of but despite their prior experience.

Beyond Pérez's successful electoral run, signs of growing doubt both about AD and about the political system within which AD and COPEI had traded power since 1958 also revealed themselves in the 1988 elections. Voting trends nationally and in the 23 de Enero belied the electoral domination suggested by Pérez's 52% win in the neighborhood and 55% win in Venezuela. Congressional vote figures for the 23 de Enero highlighted an electoral pattern marked by three stages. In the first, between 1958 and 1973, AD and COPEI remained marginal parties in the 23 de Enero, again and again losing decisively to parties that fared poorly nationally.[28] A second stage, between 1973 and 1983, brought the rapid rise of AD and COPEI as the neighborhood's major parties, combining to receive between 60% and 70% of the vote. But the 1988 elections, heralding a third stage, exposed a dip in preferences for AD/COPEI vis-à-vis other parties, marking the first time since 1963, following Betancourt's presidency, that the two parties had posted lower returns than in the previous electoral cycle (fig. 26).[29]

All told, results of the 1988 elections held indications of concern, but the overarching sentiment remained one of resignation about the reforms needed to correct, at once and as a whole, Venezuela's "profound accumulated dis-equilibriums," according to Pérez. In the days following his 17 February announcement, few signs of popular unrest emerged, though a slew of alarms sounded to anyone willing to listen. Politicians of the left warned that despite the absence of protest "popular sectors are terrified with the government's economic announcements."[30] Academics such as Héctor Silva Michelena, who in the early 1970's had called Venezuela's democracy an "illusion" based on an unsustainable dependency, noted that the conditions were ripe for a "grave social explosion."[31] Meanwhile more-concrete signs of alarm also revealed themselves, as doctors in the capital warned that the economic "package" was curtailing their ability to budget, leaving hospitals "paralyzed."[32] By 21 Febru-ary 1989, the medical workers' guild announced an imminent closure of medical facilities in the capital since "most Caracas hospitals cannot guaran-tee the health or life of their patients because they lack the necessary resources."[33]

Still, plans to enact the first wave of reforms on 27 February went ahead. On the morning protests broke out, Planning Minister Miguel Rodríguez was at the International Monetary Fund in Washington, to sign a letter of intent formally committing Venezuela to the loan regime Pérez had announced ten days earlier.[34] In a page-long interview published the same day in a local paper, Rodríguez sounded an optimistic note, stressing that by "1990 the economic plan will mature."[35] All told, perhaps the clearest marker of the sentiment on the days before 27 February came weeks later, as officials and others struggled to make sense of what had transpired and how they had responded. Addressing a congressional committee convened to investigate the events, Minister of Defense Italo del Valle Alliegro summarized the sense of collective surprise, and resulting cognitive dissonance, linking a successful electoral event with the largest urban protest in Venezuela's history: "Nothing suggested, just three months after elections which took place in complete normalcy, that events like these could happen."[36]

"THIS HERE WAS VERY TOUGH": CONFUSION AND DIFFUSION IN THE EARLY PROTEST

On the morning of 27 February, Manuel Mir was at work at the *jefatura civil* in the Mirador sector of the 23 de Enero when he first heard about the protests unfolding in Guarenas, and later Caracas. Mir had interned, staffed, and worked at the *jefatura civil* since the early 1980s. Still in college at the time, he was inspired by Luis Herrera Campíns's call for participatory democracy to become involved in local affairs at the 23 de Enero, eventually serving as aide to the President's handpicked *jefa civil* in the neighborhood, Josefina Delgado. Working alongside Delgado, whose tenure was marked by outreach and collaboration with a wide range of local groups and activists during protests like the *secuestros*, imbued Mir with a sense that anyone hoping to administer the neighborhood required calm under pressure. So it proved surprising when around 3 P.M. on 27 February 1989, "desperate because they had put up barricades in the rotary of Block 37 [in Zona F]," the then *jefa civil*, Teresita de Cortes, "abandoned" and fled the neighborhood.[37] Cortes was not a resident of the 23 de Enero, and had only taken up the *jefatura* three weeks earlier. That she was unfamiliar with the tenor of conflict that marked local mobilization patterns likely contributed to her decision. But it left the neighborhood with no local authority and, in view of the *jefa civil*'s role as liaison with the local Metropolitan Police contingent, with no one to help coordinate and mediate between civilian and police factions.

With Cortes gone, Mir returned to his home in the hill overlooking Blocks 47–48–49 of Mirador, next to the *jefatura civil*. Mir's parents had been among those who settled in ranchos around the superblocks in the days after Pérez Jiménez's overthrow; like most such once-squatter communities, the Barrio Mirador had long since become integrated into the local infrastructure. Once home, Mir saw the first signs of looting. "Some acquaintances came with a truck full of all manner of things, and what they gave me was a bottle of rum, which of course I took." They had found their wares in the nearby La Silsa area, suggesting that the looting was limited to neighboring areas rather than within the 23 de Enero itself. But around 6 P.M. Mir returned to Blocks 47–48–49 and found that "all the grocery stores in Mirador were looted."[38] These included the burned stand of a local resident, indicating that community membership had not protected area businesses from becoming targets of the early popular upheaval, and that in the Mirador sector of the 23 de Enero opportunity guided the first lootings. The dramatic escalation of events in three hours' time prompted Mir and several others to walk to other sectors of the neighborhood in order to "feel the reality of the situation." Together they walked to Block 7, taking the route from Mirador, through Sierra Maestra, and finally to the Block 7 rotary linking La Cañada and Monte Piedad. Along the way they passed through makeshift barricades of burning tires in the Block 37 rotary, but what Mir most recalled was how "many walking around were armed, in other words, this around here was very tough [*esto aquí fue muy fuerte*]."[39]

Lisandro Pérez of the Barrio La Redoma, just above the Block 37 rotary, was among those who had armed themselves, as he remembered, "preparing for combat." His action and language had roots in a radical politics with which he had become engaged as a teen in the late 1970s and early 1980s, eventually becoming a cadre in underground political groups like Bandera Roja (Red Flag), and organizing cells in the 23 de Enero and other working-class sectors of Caracas. Yet in the early 1980s, under the tutelage of 1960s urban-guerrilla veteran Paquita Giuliani, Pérez had also learned to integrate his radical politics with community-oriented direct action. For instance, in the fray of the *secuestros* in January 1982 Giuliani, Pérez and two other youths had approached newspapers to denounce problems in the Mirador and Zona F sectors of the 23 de Enero, a first for people otherwise committed to armed struggle.[40]

On the morning of 27 February 1989, Pérez was at work delivering notices throughout the city for an accounting firm. By the time he arrived in La Redoma around 5 P.M., he had already seen the looting unfolding in several parts of Caracas, and especially Avenida Sucre. In La Redoma, members of Pérez's activist core had set up the barricades in the rotary of Block 37 that had prompted Cortes to flee. One of them greeted Pérez while wearing a bulletproof vest, saying: "The moment has come, the moment that had to happen." Pérez, however, saw it differently. As he recalled, when neighbors conferred with him about what actions to take, Pérez froze: "I was still dumbfounded by the events." Eventually, they organized to go to nearby Catia to loot stores, at first for groceries and later for home appliances. In his political training Pérez had come to see activities like bank robberies and theft as legitimate forms of "expropriation," but when asked if he considered the looting of grocery and appliance stores in Catia that evening part of the framework of legitimate "expropriations," Pérez stated firmly: "No. That was a popular looting [*saqueo popular*]."[41]

Pérez's testimony sets in relief how once-radical activists in this part of the neighborhood were surprised by the sudden popular upheaval—a key point, since claims about the role of these sectors in planning and staging the *Caracazo* would later emerge as an explanation for the intensity of repression that followed. But while they had no forewarning, people like Pérez also quickly adapted to the evolving panorama once they came to acknowledge, especially after setting out on that first night of looting, what Pérez referred to as a sense that "everything had changed." That they drew upon their tactical repertoire to partake in the looting was meant less to direct than to assist in the aspirations of their neighbors. On that first day, activists in Barrio La Redoma provided both organization and defense, but did not take for granted what experience had taught them would likely emerge as a consequence. That is, they well expected "combat" and framed their actions—like setting up barricades—in anticipation of confrontations with police, which actually did not materialize in La Redoma on the evening of 27 February. Instead, by the time Pérez returned from Catia around 5 A.M. on 28 February, "there were some engagements, but there was more order," so much so that Pérez and a friend instead left the 23 de Enero to see how events were unfolding elsewhere.[42]

In Monte Piedad—ground zero for the *secuestros* of 1981–1982—once-radical activists in the area put their organizing skills to other uses on 27 February. Andrés Vásquez had been among the first residents of Block 1, moving as a young child with his parents to the neighborhood while Pérez Jiménez was in power. Over the years, Vásquez had developed into a self-described *ñángara*, widely known in Monte Piedad for his activism with the Communist Party while it was illegal in the 1960s. In the 1970s, disenchanted with the electoral route the party had taken, he worked clandestinely with organizations farther to the left, such as the *Liga Socialista*. In the 1980s, Vásquez was among those who drew on a tactical repertoire forged around radical political activism to combat local criminals. He recalled, perhaps self-servingly, that "when people around here wanted to deal with a *malandro* [petty thief] they wouldn't call the police, they would call us!" But on 27 February, Vásquez and another activist from Monte Piedad watched as their fellow residents attempted to break into the *bodega* [grocery store] on the first floor of Block 2, whose owner "always sold at high prices." As Vásquez recalls the incident, the pair at first attempted to intercede with their neighbors: "I told them, 'Look, brother, you are looting this and it is going to harm us . . . shit, just leave this as is.'" Apparently unmoved, neighbors continued in their attempt to loot the store, leading to escalation: "We stood there, with pistols in our hands and in the store in Block 2. 'You are not going to loot these stores [in Monte Piedad], no, you will not loot them.' And we didn't let them."[43]

This incident in Monte Piedad highlights the multiple layers of internal friction unleashed as patterns of the possible began to collapse on 27 February

1989. That neighbors would target a local store in part because the owner "sold at high prices" spoke less about the opportunity of proximity and more about underlying grievances among neighbors. At the same time, the incident also reveals that, in the face of these events, otherwise politically minded sectors turned toward pragmatism, echoing Lisandro Pérez's experience in La Redoma. Looting a local store would, in the short run, force residents to leave to find groceries elsewhere, and in the long run, risk that the stores would remain permanently closed. This was not an opportunity to create consciousness or engage in political critique. At the same time this brief standoff among neighbors shed light on local power dynamics in Monte Piedad in the prelude to 27 February. That Andrés Vásquez had attempted to impose authority on the basis of what he perceived as an argument about the pragmatism of short-term gain versus medium- and long-term losses, only to be rebuffed, underscored the limits of his self-proclaimed role as a community enforcer. Residents only responded when he spoke with the weight of a weapon behind him, the realm within which his standing in the neighborhood had been cemented in the preceding years. They left the stores untouched on the basis of mutual understanding about what had been established as permissible in the area, even in a context of rapidly changing norms. In this context, then, it was unsurprising that when William Rangel returned to Monte Piedad on the evening of 27 February, he found "things were peaceful," because the peace was enforced on the basis of the same coercive tactics and that had brought them legitimacy in the years before 1989.

"WHAT'S COMING WILL BE FIERCE": FROM CONFUSION TO ESCALATION IN LA CAÑADA

While local organizers laid down the law in Monte Piedad, in the adjoining La Cañada sector the night of 27 February held a much different experience. Juan Contreras had first sensed trouble as soon as he returned to the sector around 7 P.M., following his peripatetic trip from La Urbina in the eastern edges of Caracas. After running past burnt-out stores in Avenida Sucre, Contreras and three others made their way over to the Agua Salud metro station and arrived in front of Block 15 of La Cañada. "When we end up here . . . we see a trash truck burned, a bus burned, the streets blocked, and so forth, and the people looting businesses."[44] For Contreras these were far from uncommon sights. During the 1970s, still in his teens, Contreras had become active in the politics—and armed tactics—of radical-left groups with a strong underground presence in the 23 de Enero, in particular the Marxist-Leninist wing of Bandera Roja. As a young, self-described "extremist," Contreras had participated in many of the confrontations typical for activist youth of the day: scuffles with police, student barricades, an occasional shootout. Early in the decade, he had helped stage an armed assault against a newly opened Metropolitan Police substation located just below Block 19, where Contreras's family had lived since 1962.[45] By the mid-1980s, Contreras had undergone a similar evolution as other one-time radicals in the neighborhood, slowly incorporating a language and practice of community work into a repertoire of direct action that would see him participate in the *secuestros*, and eventually land him in the presidency of the local neighbors' association, a dramatic shift for a once self-described "abstentionist."[46]

In this context, what made the scenes unfolding stand apart for Contreras was the looting, but in particular, its composition. Years later, his recollections of those early moments in the *Caracazo* at La Cañada still lay bare a struggle to reconcile his contentious past in the neighborhood with what he was witnessing below: "We were standing on the fourth floor [of Block 19]. . . . 'But look, the same people who are always criticizing us are the people who are looting, there's so-and-so, and look.' And we were the ones who ended up as the troublemakers [*revoltosos*]." From his apartment in Block 19 he watched as his neighbors sacked the corner store in Block 20. But "instead of getting involved . . . we stayed put."[47] Yet, as night progressed, standing by became increasingly untenable for Contreras and his fellow activists, especially after the first signs of a state response emerged. As the looting went on in Block 20, according to Contreras a police jeep sped by and "let off a few rounds." Though brief, this encounter portended a rapid escalation of an already explosive situation in La Cañada. The police's eventual appearance between 7 p.m. and 8 p.m., several hours after barricades had emerged in the Block 37 rotary and after stores in Mirador had been burned and looted, reflected what journalist Fabricio Ojeda identified as the moment in "the high afternoon [when] apparently the Metropolitan Police received instructions to repress with force."[48]

Here, understanding the Metropolitan Police strike that preceded 27 February 1989 proves critical. Two major grievances motivated subaltern sectors of the Policía Metropolitana (PM): the demand for higher wages and benefits, and the demand for changes in the institutional structure of the force.[49] The nonresolution of the first grievance resulted in the active participation of some police personnel in the looting that took place on 27 and 28 February.[50] But the second grievance held more-significant implications for understanding the rapid escalation of repression. Since its founding in 1969 the PM had been a two-tiered institution: while its rank and file comprised officers specifically trained to work with civilians, its leadership drew from the National Guard. Two conflicting professional cultures coexisted in the institution, one based on a civilian code of conduct, the other based on military training.

Two weeks before 27 February, middle-class neighborhood associations had expressed their solidarity with police subalterns' grievances, especially their institutional dimensions, by pointing out the operational differences between a civilian-based police force and one based on military codes: "The criteria of the National Guard are 'lightning operations' [*operativos relámpago*], and therein lies the repression and effect-seeking."[51] On 18 February, following a high-level meeting between President Pérez, the Minister of the Interior, and the Minister of Defense, the government announced a "general review" of the nation's police forces in the interest of having "all members of the police be careful in their actions, very even, and not commit any type of excesses."[52] As part of this review, the government announced that some career officers would indeed be promoted to command roles, with the first two scheduled to take command just four days before the *Caracazo* took place.[53]

Juan Contreras's account supports this analysis of the rapid escalation of events in La Cañada, which highlights a type of confrontation marked by immediate—though as yet indirect—use of weapons against civilians in the context of general upheaval, well exceeding what President Pérez himself would later describe as the major difference between police and military personnel: "The police officer," he would note, "is the one who goes in with persuasion and only at the last minute takes out his weapon to defend himself."[54] But for Contreras, the police's delay also reflected a larger reality about the way in which the *Caracazos* in the 23 de Enero were unfolding. "We said, well, things must be so bad" elsewhere in Caracas, as in fact his earlier cross-city travel had laid bare, that by comparison what was taking place in the 23 de Enero seemed far less pressing to a police force already stretched thin, and already well acquainted with the potential response of organized sectors of the population.[55]

This point is central. In La Cañada police delay proved crucial for two main reasons. The first was the way in which it forced a rapid amplification of rules of engagement. Authorized to "repress with force," police transitioned from absence to live fire with little gradual escalation. The second was that it allowed local activists like Contreras to process, and begin to prepare, a response to what their own histories with armed conflict in the neighborhood suggested was to unfold. Said Contreras, "At night when the police was going to come in here we said: well, let's pick up all the bottles we can, let's take from the store all those bottles, all those crates. And that's what we did. We started bringing up bottles, crates and crates." Yet, he clarifies, "we did not get involved in any looting . . . we saw looting as almost ugly. I mean, how can it be, where are we going to buy things tomorrow? But you have to remember, the masses overflowed all of that, so we decided well, we have to prepare, because the repression is coming, huge."[56]

Contreras's interpretation of seizing property as preparation for anticipated engagement with police highlighted how the interval between the first popular actions and the first police actions allowed local activists to structure responses by drawing on repertoires of action anchored in local histories of violent activism. At the same time, it also again showcased how, in order to understand their eventual participation in activities they otherwise dismissed as apolitical (such as looting), seasoned political activists well steeped in the traditions of violent conflict in three different areas of the 23 de Enero— Lisandro Pérez in Mirador, Andrés Vásquez in Monte Piedad, and Juan Contreras in La Cañada—had to resort to new structuring mechanisms, namely pragmatism.

It was in this context that the first armed confrontations in the 23 de Enero took place in La Cañada on the night of 27 February. Manuel Mir, still conducting rounds and, as member of the civilian authority of the neighborhood in the absence of *jefa civil* Cortes, receiving periodic reports from the Metropolitan Police contingent in the area about the situation in the neighborhood, recalled how police tried to regroup at the module in La Cañada on the evening of 27 February to organize a response to the looting, including raiding apartments in search of stolen goods. As the police did so, residents of the neighboring Blocks 18 and 19 began to "throw Molotovs . . . and a series of things. They were prisoners, many of the police personnel could not get out."[57] From the twelfth floor of Block 19, where Contreras and several others had retreated with whatever bottles they had been able to recover from the store in Block 20, they were able to watch "all the police movement": "The police arrived, the *jaulas* [cages; police detention vehicles] arrived, shooting and so forth, and there was a strong attack [*arremetida*] by the police. There was also a strong attack, guns blazing, from the buildings toward the police, and the company captain goes down, dead. He falls dead, the police retreat, it was impossible for them to enter the Block, and from all over people yelled at them, from everywhere there are shots, and he falls dead."[58] According to Mir, at the time coordinating with police, the captain had "gone to the rescue" of his men, who were trapped in the module, when he "perished."[59]

Eduardo Meza Istúriz, thirty-four years old and a father of two, became the first casualty of the *Caracazo* in the 23 de Enero.[60] His death certificate recorded a "gunshot to the thorax" as the cause of death.[61] Contreras remembered the moment he saw Istúriz hit, from above in Block 19: "We saw that they were dragging him and right around then they took him away." But it was not until the following morning that Contreras learned Istúriz had died, not from press accounts, which did not report it until 1 March,[62] but from neighbors who warned Contreras and his friends to "get out of here, go on get out . . . what's coming will be fierce." But for Contreras the episode was embedded in a much broader context of fast-changing boundaries of the possible, an interregnum between what had been and what was to be. Reflecting on the warnings from neighbors directed at him and his friends, Contreras notes: "We had gone out, doing the rounds, watching everything that was happening, [so] we said, how can it be, it will have to be a massive repression, they will have to arrest everybody, and in our case we weren't involved with the looting."[63]

Istúriz's death marked the most dramatic in a series of early events that lay bare, in the words of Lisandro Pérez, how "everything had changed." Placed in the context of recent history, at first glance little seemed novel about a group of area residents violently engaging police in the 23 de Enero. Yet even at the height of battles between police and area youth in the 1970s, police had rarely figured among the casualties. Contreras's own reflection of what transpired that evening well suggested that in the fray of attempting to make sense of Istúriz's death, local militants nevertheless struggled to draw upon past experience, coming up empty. In the context of generalized violation of the law, generalized repression of the same scale seemed implausible. At the same time, selective repression seemed futile. In this space between knowing that a response was to follow, but being unable to imagine its scale, militants like Contreras hoped to render otherwise unrecognizable events in terms that they could historically locate within a lived experience of engagement with police. But in the fray of what in fact was a situation of chaos, these attempts proved useless. History and hysteria clashed, and the former lost. As Manuel Mir, reflecting on the events of La Cañada on the evening of 27 February 1989, later summarized: "It was very rough here in the neighborhood. Here, we had it tense, the people."[64]

THE RETURN OF THE 1960S

The tension Manuel Mir referenced primarily revolved around expectations of what would follow after a night when, in La Cañada as elsewhere in the 23 de Enero, expectations had lost referents. As Tuesday 28 February dawned on the neighborhood, the previous day and night's events seemed to hold few clues about what would transpire in the hours ahead. In Monte Piedad, the same sectors that had on 27 February prevented their neighbors from sacking local stores helped to organize lootings elsewhere in a bid to respond to local pressure. William Rangel recalled that on 28 February, "a group of us stayed here, protecting the stores, and another group went out to loot."[65] Andrés Vásquez, who had helped prevent the sacking of a local store by a crowd of his neighbors the night before, was among those heading to nearby San Bernardino the next day, including some of the very neighbors he had warded off earlier:

> We were there, I was in the Barrio Los Erazos, then I saw a bunch of people; there was a Central Madeirense [supermarket] and I started the looting. In that multitude all that's needed is for someone to say something. So we were in the Central Madeirense and there, I didn't know if I did right or wrong, but I started [chanting]: 'the people are hungry, the people are hungry!' And there, when they came, they went into that Central.

Vásquez's experience revealed the continuing confusion gripping Caracas twenty-four hours after the first protests began, as well as the underlying motivations informing people's decision to partake in the events. Yet it also revealed the tenuousness of organization in a context of flux. For instance, still in the supermarket, Vásquez remembered how "the most wily [los más vivos], instead of going into the Central Madeirense went into Super Volumen [an electronics store] which was next door and brought back everything, everything."[66]

Then a 25-year-old Army lieutenant, Jesús Manuel Zambrano, was ordered on the afternoon of 28 February to take a contingent of troops to the same area in San Bernardino. "The order was: 'Go and neutralize that looting, how you do it is not my problem, but neutralize it.'" While another lieutenant on scene fired a round into the air, Zambrano took a different approach: "We organized the looting," distinguishing between need and opportunity. "We organized it because they were taking things like the cash registers, which really didn't correspond to their needs. 'If you really rose up because there are problems, needs, and you want to take the food, then go ahead and take it: form a line one-by-one for meat; a soldier over there to control things.' And the people went in, took, and carted off their things."[67]

The Army's presence in San Bernardino responded to their deployment late the previous evening, following an executive order that President Pérez issued to Minister of Defense Italo del Valle Alliegro at 11 P.M. on 27 February after Pérez returned to Caracas from Barquisimeto to find the streets near the Presidential Palace strewn with debris.[68] According to Del Valle Alliegro, the Army's mission was to "restore the legal order which has been subverted," although one eyewitness recalled that Pérez, after issuing the order, had second thoughts after speaking to Gonzalo Barrios, one of the founders of AD: "When the Army goes out into the streets," warned Barrios, "it's to kill people."[69]

In the space between reestablishing order and mass repression lay the Plan Ávila. Designed in the 1960s, the plan was intended to respond to a contingency in which urban guerrillas might overwhelm local police and National Guard, requiring the deployment of regular Army troops obeying a battle plan with a loose command structure. Unencumbered by rigid chains of command, acting as cells with wide-ranging operational discretion, individual units would be able to mobilize quickly and effectively in response to equally nimble guerrilla forces. As General Manuel Antonio Heinz Azpurua, commander of the Caracas garrison and of the capital Strategic Command during February and March 1989, later conveyed to an investigating tribunal in 1996: "All of us are responsible for implementing the Plan [Ávila]."[70]

Zambrano's testimony above tends to support this interpretation of the tactical range of the Plan Ávila, giving field officers broad discretion to "restore the legal order" within their prescribed theater of operations. The broader implications, of course, concerned the effects of this kind of tactical discretion in a situation of mass public unrest. As Francisco Espinoza Guyón, a lieutenant during the *Caracazo*, recalled to Marta Harnecker in 2003:

> No one gave me a direct order to shoot to kill, but they did tell us that constitutional rights were suspended and that, if we needed to use our weapons to repress a looting, we were authorized to do so because nothing was going to happen to us. In

other words, maybe they didn't explicitly order us to kill, but they did insinuate that if we needed to, it was within the rules of engagement to do so.[71]

In fact, at noon on 28 February 1989, President Pérez and his full cabinet signed Decree No. 49, suspending freedoms of speech and assembly as well as habeas corpus, in addition to declaring an indefinite curfew to begin at 6 P.M. and to last until 6 A.M.

The deployment of troops in accordance to Plan Ávila, the suspension of constitutional rights, and the imposition of a twelve-hour curfew marked a confluence of proscriptive measures never before seen in Venezuela's democratic history, especially when aimed at suppressing what even President Pérez recognized was an expression of popular discontent, not an "antigovernmental action."[72] Even the nominal precedent for regimes of exception in democratic Venezuela—the early 1960s period of guerrilla war—had been aimed at combating political movements seeking state power, and never revised accordingly. As Defense Minister Del Valle Alliegro pointed out to a congressional commission, Plan Ávila had been "in place since the 1960s . . . [and] was carried out despite a long period without putting it into practice."[73]

In the main, the practical effect of drawing on an unrevised military plan aimed at combating political subversives was twofold. The first was to focus the bulk of the military presence on areas deemed a strategic threat in the context of a threat to the government, whether or not they represented an immediate center of the public unrest actually gripping Caracas. In this sense, as a focal point of the 1960s-era guerrilla insurgency, as well as because of its strategic location overlooking the Presidential Palace, the 23 de Enero was one of three areas to which the Army deployed.[74] The second effect was to draw upon a logic, and language, of insurrection that, much as was the case for militants in the 23 de Enero, prompted military personnel to view events through the prism of a history long since past. For instance where some in the government saw *gatillos alegres*, trigger-happy shooters firing at random from buildings in the 23 de Enero, among the military far more menacing "sharpshooters" emerged as the enemy.[75]

More than semantics separated the two terms. In the early afternoon of Tuesday 28 February, a contingent of Army troops arrived in the same La Silsa sector of Caracas where Manuel Mir's neighbors from Barrio Observatorio had taken to loot the day before. Using a local factory as a staging area, the troops prepared to deploy to the 23 de Enero, in particular the Atlántico

Norte sector, in the western edge of the neighborhood. Just above, in Block 1 of Atlántico Norte, Francisco Moncada, his wife Alicia, her deaf sister Milvia, and two neighbors took in the troop movement below, while Moncada's children—twelve-year-old Katiuska and eight-year-old Francisco—played in the apartment. According to testimony subsequently submitted to the Inter-American Court of Human Rights, at around 4 P.M. Moncada was jolted out of the shower by his wife's screams. While he was in the bathroom, Moncada's son, Francisco, and his sister-in-law, Milvia, had peered out the terrace, when the troops below opened fire, after allegedly alerting them to step back.[76] A bullet grazed Milvia in the neck. Young Francisco fared far worse. Another bullet shattered his frontal lobe, rendering him blind and unable to speak.[77] Over the next three hours, as his son bled out, Moncada raced to various hospitals seeking help, only to be rejected in the first two due to the same lack of resources that had led city health care workers to contemplate a strike the week before. "He couldn't talk or see after they shot him," testified Moncada, "but he could hear me. . . . I asked him questions and he squeezed my hand, he squeezed my hand to tell me that it hurt. And so on until I left him [at the Lídice hospital], later they notified me he was dead."[78]

As eight-year-old Franscico fell mortally wounded in Atlántico Norte, on the other side of the 23 de Enero the Army's deployment would serve a different purpose, nevertheless resulting in similar bloodshed. In La Cañada, troops had taken positions outside the Agua Salud metro station in front of Block 15, where on the previous night residents had a set a bus on fire. However, several hundred yards away, between Blocks 18 and 19, the engagements between local militants and Metropolitan Police that had left Captain Mesa Istúriz dead the previous night continued, though with less intensity, limited primarily to the stoning of the La Cañada police module by residents in Barrio Sucre. Yet, emboldened by the Army's presence, police responded with force. Late in the afternoon, twenty-nine-year-old Carlos Antonio Dorantes Torres, then in his first semester at the Universidad Central de Venezuela, was among those stoning the module when police opened fire, shooting Carlos in the chest.[79]

The successive deaths of the boy Francisco Moncada and of Carlos Dorantes on the afternoon of 28 February heralded the manner and scale of violence that would grip the neighborhood in the ensuing days. That the two deaths took place on opposite ends of the 23 de Enero suggested a comprehensive response that would not discriminate against specific areas of the neighborhood.

Francisco Moncada's death in Atlántico Norte shed light on the kind of "indiscriminate firing by agents of the Venezuelan state" that the Inter-American Court of Human Rights would later identify caused most deaths.[80] Meanwhile, the police's response to rock throwing in La Cañada, coming as it did on the heels of the death of one of their own the night before, indicated a far more determined and aggressive approach than had marked their earlier actions. Undergirding both responses was the Plan Ávila in both its tactical and strategic dimensions, the former providing security forces with the necessary latitude to deploy force arbitrarily, while the latter helped to reconfigure all residents as potential threats to the state. In this sense, the deaths of Moncada and Dorantes marked a watershed, as the eyes of the state subsumed into a single entity the multiplicity of *Caracazos* that had developed in the neighborhood the night before. The specter of the 1960s had now fully materialized.

Testimonies about the events of the evening of 28 February bore out this dynamic. María Betilde Hernández, for thirty-one years a resident of Block 25 of the Zona Central, reported how she had planned a birthday party for her granddaughter that night, but the quickly worsening situation had led her to cancel the event.[81] As afternoon turned to night and the curfew set in, "gunfire erupted [*empezó la plomazón*]. . . . After the first shots I jumped on the floor, grabbed my six children and we crawled to our neighbor's apartment after spending several hours in the bathroom." During that time, she recalled, "they fired at twenty-minute intervals for half an hour [each time]." Then troops raided her apartment: "The military came up and with such cruelty [*con tantas sañas*] burst in shooting, managing to make a *piñata* of Donald Duck bleed out its candy and toys. They confused the duck with a sharpshooter." In the process they had also managed to wound Hernández's daughter, and to destroy her apartment.[82] Illustrating the tactical problems facing a military operating under loose rules of engagement in a context of high tension, María later told reporters: "Thank goodness that after a while a lieutenant came up and when he saw the destruction he was amazed at what his troops had done. After that they left."[83] And while her family had found shelter at the home of a neighbor who had barricaded his apartment, the shooting continued all through the night and into the following dawn. One newspaper's headline summarized the violence: "Pure Lead [*plomo cerrado*] This Morning in the 23 de Enero."[84]

The night of 28 February also brought a different modality of repression. Around midnight police began to raid the apartments of known militants in La

Cañada, among them Juan Contreras in Block 19. Police had identified Contreras as a possible leader in what they referred to as "this mess," immediately transferring him to the DISIP (*Dirección de los Servicios de Inteligencia y Prevención*), Venezuela's intelligence service responsible for investigating political threats to the state. In fact, as Contreras recalls, "that was a line full of yellow patrol cars [DISIP] from Block 20 all the way to Block 7." For the next ten days, as they unsuccessfully sought evidence pointing to his culpability in the assassination of Captain Meza Istúriz, DISIP officials held Contreras incommunicado at their headquarters, alongside dozens of other suspected militants from all over Caracas.[85] Searching for and detaining militants had also formed part of the military's actions in Zona Central. Noraima Hernández reported how, as they burst through her apartment door, officers "showed me a list, threatening me and pointing out an ambulance that was downstairs, telling me, 'You see, *vieja*, that's where we're going to put the dead, all dead, if you don't help us.'"[86] Against the backdrop of the military's presence in the Zona Central and the Metropolitan Police's counteroffensive in La Cañada, Contreras's experience with the DISIP set in relief the close interinstitutional collaboration among the agencies of the state's security apparatus in the 23 de Enero by 28 February.

"NO-MAN'S-LAND": THE WAR IN ZONA CENTRAL

The night's events were but a prelude for what transpired over the next twenty-four hours. As Lisandro Pérez recalls, "the third day was the toughest." In particular for this long-time militant, the day was framed in the context of direct engagement with the Army after what they had come to view as a disproportionate state action in the neighborhood requiring a response from armed and organized sectors. During the day, groups of militants took up positions in the "showcase" blocks facing Avenida Sucre, activating networks of underground cells to communicate and provide resources for what they well acknowledged was a disparate engagement requiring new tactics. Asked how they prepared to confront a military opponent, Pérez replied: "It meant we had to adjust, we had to be much more cautious in our approach," meaning in particular the disciplined use of limited firepower and ammunition. "We had pistols; they had FALs [a type of semiautomatic rifle], 50-caliber machine guns, tanks."[87] Pérez's testimony illustrated how area militants had come to interpret the state's actions in the neighborhood as a political act requiring a political response in the realm of armed confrontation. In this sense, the state's

FIGURE 27. Army tank stationed on Avenida Sucre, outside the Agua Salud metro station, in March 1989. In the background, Block 15 of La Cañada. (José Grillo / Archivo *El Nacional*)

response to an imagined political threat had helped call that threat into being in the 23 de Enero.

By the afternoon of 1 March 1989, clashes between militants and state security forces had begun to yield casualties, turning parts of the neighborhood into a battlefield (fig. 27). In particular, the area between La Cañada and Zona Central emerged as a "no-man's-land" where military posted in front of the Agua Salud metro station exchanged gunfire with militants in Blocks 22–23.[88] A recent migrant to Caracas from the western state of Zulia, twenty-year-old Alirio José Cañizales fell dead from a gunshot wound as he left the Agua Salud metro station on his way to his cousin's home in the Zona Central. As the shooting continued, Cañizales's blood-soaked body remained on the street overnight before friends and relatives could claim it the following morning.[89] The drama of Cañizales's body lying for hours in public view as gunfire raged caught journalist Régulo Párraga by surprise. Then living in Blocks 22–23, Párraga recounted in the press what he termed his "night of terror" between 1 and 2 March 1989, highlighting the experience of dodging bullets coming both from the buildings above and from the troops below, and racing past what was likely Cañizales's body. In the early hours of curfew, according to Párraga, the clashes that had gripped the area in the afternoon seemed to abate, although by 9 P.M. they resumed, as chants like "The people united will never be defeated [*El pueblo unido jamás sera vencido*]" and "People, listen, join the struggle [*Pueblo, escucha, únete a la lucha*]" began to echo.

Over the next seven hours three waves of gunfire, the most intense at midnight, terrorized residents of the building—roughly 1,500 men, women, and children in all, in 300 apartments. Lending credence to the levels of organization by militants that Lisandro Pérez's testimony had already prefigured, Párraga noted how "two times the military [intensified] their attack and on both occasions [*sendas ocasiones*] the opposing side [held] their positions firmly." Meanwhile military personnel struggled to keep pace with militants "because they are constantly moving, they go from one floor to the next through the trash chutes." For Army officers planning operations in the area they had codenamed "Zulu," militants' mobility presented problems both tactical and strategic. "It's not a matter of firepower," one officer on the scene later told reporters. "We don't want to massify our actions; we are trying to obtain information to specify in which building and in which apartment they are [located]." But that was only part of it. "We are also facing a dilemma: there are soldiers who live in critical sectors, who might have to fire upon the same Block where their own family lives."[90] Yet the fighting continued until 4 A.M., when "only sporadic shots [could] be heard, indicating that the worst of the battle [had] passed and the nearness of day heralded the end of hostilities."[91]

Still, Thursday morning dawned with evidence of the previous night's battle scattered throughout the neighborhood's streets. From the El Valle sector of Caracas, one of three major areas of military presence in the capital and where similar forms of violence had gripped residents the previous night, photographer José Grillo made his way to the 23 de Enero.[92] There he captured the scene as friends and family collected Alirio Cañizales's body. In another shot a different set of residents laid a sheet over an unidentified corpse that had also remained overnight in the parking lot behind Blocks 22–23 (fig. 28). With some rhetorical flair nevertheless anchored in scenes unfolding throughout, journalist Fabricio Ojeda wrote how "In the morning, following the second night of curfew, those who descended from the barrios to go to work tripped over bodies shot up during the curfew."[93]

While morning on 2 March brought a respite, it was short-lived. By early afternoon the fighting that had characterized the previous day flared anew. Around 2 P.M. fifty-four-year-old José Calixto Blanco, a messenger for the Ministry of Justice, was shot in the face as he stepped out of the Agua Salud metro station.[94] Subsequent investigations by the Inter-American Commission on Human Rights determined that military personnel were responsible

FIGURE 28. At the parking lot of Block 22 in the Zona Central of the 23 de Enero, on 1 March 1989. (José Grillo / Archivo *El Nacional*)

for his death.[95] Blanco's death, taking place well before curfew, exposed how a logic of war continued to grip armed forces deployed to the neighborhood, especially as they faced very real hostile fire, as Párraga wryly put it in his account of the previous day, "bullets that really kill [*disparos que matan de verdad*]."[96] As Lisandro Pérez remembered the events from within the ranks of the militants, "we were determined not to the let them enter the blocks."[97] And as reporters covering the continuing violence in the 23 de Enero noted from interviews of area residents, militants were in fact proving successful in this objective. "There the Army still has not penetrated; there are groups who resist laying down their weapons." But their tactical successes were proving strategically costly. "The agitators [*revoltosos*] don't want to enter into reason at a time when all sectors of national life are asking for it."[98]

But for militants like Lisandro Pérez, the issue was less about when to lay down their weapons than how to confront the moment when their ammunition finally ran out. Lisandro's earlier tactical assessment ahead of the first engagements had already acknowledged their position of weakness vis-à-vis an adversary they had never confronted: the Venezuelan military. Embedded in his testimony was a sense that fighting in this context was more a matter of political principle than of strategic success. Accordingly, for a second day on 2 March, militants in the Zona Central clashed with military personnel stationed below, resolving to continue their stand until their ammunition ran out and in this sense playing into the strategy of attrition that military planners had settled into after the first clashes on Tuesday night, establishing "a defensive perimeter as a siege until the sharpshooters run out of rounds."[99]

In fact, that the continuing clashes took place so close to the Miraflores presidential palace presented the Pérez administration with more than a military problem. It also posed a public relations problem as the government sought to impose a narrative of normalcy that nevertheless ran against a narrative of ongoing skirmishes just outside. For instance, on Thursday at noon Pérez boarded a helicopter—shadowed by an armored attack helicopter—to assess the situation in Caracas from above. After returning to Miraflores he declared: "There's normalcy in the city. I return very satisfied with the flyover I have made. All of the city, all the barrios are in complete normalcy . . . everything is normal." Yet, as reporters noted, Pérez offered his views "despite the fact that while he gave his statements ceaseless gunfire in the 23 de Enero could be heard."[100] Still, Pérez's assertions of normalcy found some expression in deed as he ordered a scaling back of the curfew, from 8 P.M. to 5 A.M.

Contending with ongoing clashes was not the only problem facing the Pérez government as it tried to reassert control. On Friday 3 March, in his first remarks to foreign correspondents since 27 February, Pérez offered initial assessments of the events that had gripped Venezuela now for nearly a week. "There was no civil war here," he asserted. Neither had the protests been politically motivated, antigovernment or antiparty. "One didn't see a single party office looted or burned," he noted. Instead, the protest had been "against the rich," a product of festering inequality coupled with the sudden impact of higher gas and transportation costs. And while he did not dismiss the possibility that 1960s-era "revolutionary" groups had "as a result of these events reactivated their actions," for Pérez the underlying issue remained the structural problems of an oil-dependent economic system that had created an illusion of wealth only to find that "we did not have the bases that an economy should have to face difficult situations."[101] For Pérez, explaining unprecedented mass protest in the context of structural inequality helped to lend a seamless narrative to otherwise ineffable events. But it failed to capture the reality of state efforts to reassert control that had been imagined, and deployed, precisely to deal with political threats against the state.

This reality continued to play out in the 23 de Enero. Just hours after Pérez offered his statements to foreign correspondents, forty-three-year-old Carlos H. Cuñar of Block 1 in Monte Piedad took advantage of the extended curfew hours to purchase groceries for his mother, also in Block 1, and to do maintenance work on his car. Around 3 P.M., according to the testimony of Cuñar's mother, soldiers aboard an armored personnel carrier stationed nearby shot him three times. Gravely wounded, Cuñar nevertheless managed to drive himself to an area hospital, where by 6 P.M. he died. Cuñar's death illustrated the extent to which the government's response in the neighborhood had come to cast the 23 de Enero writ large as a combat zone, its residents constituting legitimate targets in a context of continuing collective anxiety. As reporters covering his death later noted, Cuñar "had become popular in the Block for battling against the guerrillas in the 1960s; he was an unconditional supporter of the military and even chauffeured a general for years." As an Army reservist, Cuñar had also served overseas. In this sense, his death underscored how, in casting a wide repressive net while drawing on a tactical repertoire targeting insurgents, the Pérez government had blurred differences in the 23 de Enero and in the process alienated sectors otherwise disposed to support a robust military presence in the neighborhood.[102]

Cuñar's death also exposed the ongoing violence in the 23 de Enero despite claims to citywide "normalcy" by government officials. As the evening's curfew began at 8 P.M. on Friday 3 March, militants in the Zona Central mounted a last stand against Army troops below.[103] As Lisandro Pérez recalled, "on Friday night we ran out of ammunition and retreated. Then we waited to be detained. But we had the satisfaction that [the military] never took the buildings."[104] In fact, not all stayed behind. William Rangel, who had partaken in armed engagements with the military at Monte Piedad, fled to Guarenas to evade the anticipated wave of retribution, which began on Saturday morning as troops set out to conduct house-to-house searches, nominally to recover looted property,[105] but additionally to seek out area militants suspected of battling the military and police the week before.

Even in this context, as the week ended and confrontations abated, residents of the 23 de Enero remained under siege. In Blocks 45–46–47 of the Mirador sector, Rosario Rojas heard the gunshot that killed her twenty-six-year-old son José Alejandro López around 8 P.M. on Saturday 4 March. Ironically, José Alejandro had spent the day at a local hospital at the bedside of a friend, shot on Thursday night. At that time José Alejandro and several others had reportedly defied the curfew and orders of police to "leave him in the stairs because we'll pick him up tomorrow," and instead had taken their injured friend to get medical care. But on returning from the hospital as curfew set in on Saturday, according to Rojas, police opened fire on her son. His brother later told reporters: "The shot was to the back and came out of nowhere [*a la espalda y en seco*]. He died instantly."[106] Hours later, as night turned to morning, twenty-five-year-old Enrique Napoleón Soto Vilera became the last recorded casualty of the *Caracazo* in the 23 de Enero when a shot fired from the Naval Observatory on the hills above shattered his skull as he walked out of his home in the ranchos behind Sierra Maestra. The cause of death: "Cranial wound with loss of brain matter."[107]

CAPTURING DIFFERENCE IN AN IMAGE

"That was very sad. I will tell you why." Emilia de Pérez had lived in the 23 de Enero since 1958. From her window on the eighth floor of Block 31 in Zona Central she had witnessed history many times over. In January 1959 she watched as Fidel Castro triumphantly made his way into Caracas through the Avenida Sucre below. In the 1960s she peeked out her window as tanks and troops stationed below waged war against urban guerrillas, and overheard those who screamed "Pérez Jiménez, forgive us for we knew not what we were doing!" In the 1970s she could see below as students in the Manuel Palacio Fajardo high school, located next to her building, clashed with police. And in the 1980s she watched as neighbors organized into self-defense brigades tied alleged criminals to trees and beat them in a bid to stem the tide of drug dealing in the building. All told, it was a life lived in the fray of conflict. And none of it prepared her for what took place between 27 February and 3 March 1989.

"I was horrified by the number of dead people in the streets. It would dawn and people would be lying dead in the streets." By week's end, when the worst had passed and she made her way to work in the Cementerio sector of southwestern Caracas, Emilia vividly recalls how, "as I was walking in the morning, I would see the corpses lying about in the corners, barely covered, in the alleys, lying about." From her window, she could see as military troops dispatched to the 23 de Enero relentlessly fired on Blocks 22–23 just down the road from her building. "Those Blocks were pure fire [*candela*]. Those Blocks had their walls full of holes . . . from the shots, because those people were very combative over there." Asked what she thought of the scenes, Emilia flatly stated: "What was I going to think? That was something that had no logic. People, with stones, with bottles, and them with bullets? That's unfair."[108]

Later images would capture the scale of that violence (fig. 29), offering a sense of the kind of horror it must have been "to live among bullets," as one

FIGURE 29. Above, bullet holes riddle the walls of Blocks 22–23 in the Zona Central in June 1989. Below, the same building in June 2014. Behind a makeshift paint job, the original bullet pattern remains visible. (Top photo: José Grillo / Archivo *El Nacional*; bottom photo by the author)

journalist who later interviewed area residents described it.[109] Between 28 February and 1 March 1989, Army troops nominally deployed to prevent looting in Avenida Sucre claimed to have come under fire from sharpshooters positioned in the superblocks above. Clashes continued into the following day and night, finally abating by Friday 3 March. In later accounts, these images contributed to the *Caracazo*'s construction as a massacre of defenseless people by a state that had sacrificed its legitimacy and now rationalized its actions by pointing to sharpshooters. Douglas Blanco, who covered the events as a photojournalist, later discussed his experience. "I was in the parts of El Valle and the 23 de Enero where supposedly there were sharpshooters, but that business sounds strange to me. You can't justify the shape in which those buildings in the 23 de Enero were left with the machine gunning by military and police. Do you have to destroy a building to eliminate a supposed sharpshooter? That's too much cruelty [*ensañamiento*]."[110] Said one resident: "What I can't understand is why they took it out on the whole Block. The police know very well who those people [doing the shooting] are, where they live and what they do, because they usually commit their crimes in the community."[111]

Yet testimonies in which residents well known to both police and neighbors engaged security forces subvert this narrative. Years later, people like Emilia de Pérez could not dismiss the possibility of confrontation, noting that "those people were very combative." These words did not justify the government's response; they acknowledged what, in her view, transpired. But these counternarratives only partially draw on a sense of historical accuracy. Built on a broader sense of local history, these statements stressed that confrontations between the military and area residents did take place. To deny the possibility of engagement would mean denying the history that made the 23 de Enero a symbol of popular struggle and political activism. Likewise, framing a confrontation between stones and bullets as unjust did not signal victimization seen against the backdrop of local histories of conflict in the 23 de Enero. To the contrary, it laid bare the possibility and parameters of a fair engagement, something implicitly understood by residents. In this sense, Emilia de Pérez's testimony, much like the testimony of residents of Blocks 22–23, emphasized acceptable levels of violence and repression. These accounts presented the scale of the violence as the breakdown of historical patterns of acceptability, rooted in their lived experience as residents of the 23 de Enero. Residents used this same register to make sense of what transpired as a massacre less of people than of expectations.

"A MANY-HEADED HYDRA": FROM ONE TO MANY CARACAZOS

Reflecting on her travels through Caracas on the night of Saturday 4 March, alongside an Army convoy during curfew, journalist Cristina Marcano Salcedo remarked: "The 23 de Enero is a many-headed hydra, it has exactly 45 [sic] heads, the number of Blocks in the neighborhood."[112] Drawing on a reference that evokes both monstrosity and multiplicity, Marcano's observation set in relief the ways in which the government viewed—and responded to—the 23 de Enero in a climate devoid of precedents. What was threatening was a visualization of the 23 de Enero as a multitude, many parts acting in concert but independently from one another, nevertheless linked by a common identity.[113] Responding to this monstrous hydra required subsuming differences in the neighborhood, historical differences that in the earliest moments of the *Caracazo* manifested themselves throughout the 23 de Enero in multiple responses rooted in the individual trajectories of the neighborhood's various areas. To attack the hydra meant to attack its constituent parts simultaneously, to imagine the neighborhood as one single, monstrous being.

The testimony of AD partisans in the neighborhood well captured this process of subsuming differences, but more importantly, the effects of dispensing with history and difference in order to mount a collective response to an imagined wholesale threat. "Look, sir," said one Monte Piedad resident to reporters in the weeks after the events, "I work in the government and have two small daughters. How do you think I would play pretend guerrilla? See how they left my apartment. There was no fucking sharpshooter here and they shot up my house like a strainer. . . . It is true that there were people shooting at the soldiers, but this should never have been the reaction."[114] This comment displayed a way of understanding the violence to which they had been subject along lines of plausibility, reason, and historical precedent. Said another Monte Piedad resident when asked about sharpshooters in the area: "No, c'mon. Around here very few people got involved in that mess. How are you going to keep fighting with a 9-millimeter [small-caliber weapon] against an Army that uses FALs and tanks? Plus, if there had been as many sharpshooters as they say, the casualties on the other side would have been fairly high. And where are the dead soldiers?"[115] In fact the military reported no casualties in the 23 de Enero.

Residents drew upon history to highlight what seemed most apparent from their experience: the staggering disproportionality of the government's response. "With all the firepower they had they could well have taken the blocks at a moment's notice and stop whoever was shooting at them," said a Monte Piedad resident to reporters. "It's not as if it was a great logistical feat. Even the Metropolitan Police with fewer resources and means has already done it many times." In the end, the repression was a response of imagined fear. "They unleashed on us. They thought us a subversive threat. They had to terrorize the 23 de Enero. They treated us like an executioner who is morbidly delighted with his victim. There's no other explanation."[116] Taken together, these testimonies reveal that residents at large were trying to understand the violence in the context of what was normal through a historical lens. Unable to discern patterns, they could only dismiss the government's response as hysterical, out of all normal bounds, even downplaying the role of local militants in the engagements. "Next to this," said a longtime worker at the national daily *El Nacional*, "the fall of Pérez Jiménez was kid's play."[117] In this sense, the gulf between state and urban populace that had characterized the postrevolutionary fray following 23 January 1958 had now resurfaced, this time as a potentially pre-revolutionary moment, in turn leading one analyst to ponder: "Who will close the gap?"[118]

Revolutionary Projects

From the rooftop of Block 7, the Museo Militar rises up so close due west that a strong arm might reach it with a stone. It is an imposing structure in its own right—an early twentieth-century Renaissance-revival castle where an elaborate network of turrets, bastions, and parapets punctuate staked walls enclosing a spacious courtyard at its center. Set against the backdrop of the modernist high-rises that overlook it and the webs of barrios that surround it, the Museo stands out all the more. And much like the neighborhood where it is located, the castle is a site deeply bound up with the modern history of Venezuela.

Built in 1906 to house the country's first military academy, it stood as an early effort to bring administrative cohesion to Venezuela by professionalizing the country's military. It sits strategically on a hilltop overlooking the Caracas valley, in particular, the Presidential Palace just below, and the Capitol just beyond. Over the years several future presidents and dictators were trained here; eventually and for decades it housed the powerful Defense Ministry. In the 1960s it became a favorite target of armed insurgents seeking to overthrow the upstart democratic regime installed after 23 January 1958, turning the castle and its environs into a hotbed of violence. By the 1980s that threat was ended and the castle was made into a museum. But a much graver threat to the political system loomed as a widening breach between leaders and populace grew untenable. By 1998, a Bolivarian Revolution promising to found the nation anew had swept aside forty years of two-party rule.[1] Today, in the bowels of the Museo Militar, just a stone's throw away from Block 7, lie the mortal remains of the leader of that revolution: Hugo Chávez.

That Chávez's body should have come to rest in this place, in this neighborhood, was unsurprising. At dawn on 4 February 1992, then-Lieutenant Colonel Chávez and a cadre of fellow mid-level officers launched a coup nominally aimed at ousting President Carlos Andrés Pérez, but more broadly seeking to overturn a political system they felt had grown impassive to popular demands. And there had been no more dramatic expression of that disconnect between the government and its people than the *Caracazo*. In Caracas, Chávez had taken control of the Museo Militar headquarters in the 23 de Enero, from where he planned to coordinate operations and capture President Carlos Andrés Pérez and the Miraflores Presidential Palace below. But by 4 A.M. the attempted coup had failed. As jets readied to bomb the Museo, Chávez surrendered. Later that morning, in a live televised address, Chávez called on insurgent troops nationwide to lay down their weapons. "The country definitely has to head toward a better future," he said, in the process becoming the public face of a coup, and a movement, that seemed to echo the frustrations and aspirations of Venezuela's poor in the wake of the *Caracazo*, and as such captured their imagination.[2]

What came next stunned the many in Venezuela and abroad who had for decades upheld the country as a haven of social and political stability built on enlightened statesmanship and strong institutions, eliding in the process the contentious underbelly of popular democracy so alive in places like the 23 de Enero. Jailed, then pardoned, then turned presidential candidate, and eventually elected in a landslide in 1998 on a promise to found a political system with popular sectors at its heart, Chávez came to preside over a period of intense political polarization pitting those among the elite and middle classes—long at the center of the nation—against those among the poor and working classes long at its margins. Until his death, while still in office, in March 2013, Chávez stoked deep passions at home and abroad. To some he stood as a redeemer of not just Venezuela's but Latin America's long-suffering poor, concentrating power to push through constitutional reforms, while channeling oil wealth into social programs domestically and aid to regional allies internationally, all aimed at breaking from decades of U.S.- and IMF-championed austerity and free-trade policies.[3] To others, Chávez was a populist authoritarian intent on ending the region's longest uninterrupted democracy by eliminating checks and balances, curtailing civil liberties, and attacking private capital. That he used oil money to promote similar policies elsewhere in the region made him, to the U.S. and regional elites, not just a nuisance but a threat.[4]

Throughout his presidency, as political tensions intensified, Chávez often returned to the site from where he had launched his coup, and to the neighborhood that for so long had embodied popular aspirations for precisely the more-inclusive and participatory democracy his Bolivarian Revolution promised to install. Over the years Chávez forged a close relationship with residents of the 23 de Enero, and they with him, becoming one of the staunchest bases of his urban popular support.[5] In April 2002 thousands of area residents braved uncertainty and a media blackout to walk the short way to Miraflores and demand Chávez's reinstatement following his brief ouster in a coup promoted, with U.S. support, by organized business groups, trade unions, and a largely middle-class civil society. In a dramatic turn of events, Chávez returned to office 48 hours later, even though the bitter polarization that had brought about the coup grew in the ensuing years. As polarization increased, the links between Chávez and the 23 de Enero deepened. In 2005 a mural outside the *jefatura civil* in Mirador read "23 de Enero, Bastion of the Revolution." It was here that amid enthusiastic crowds Chávez came to cast his ballot in the almost yearly elections that marked his plebiscitary style of politics. Election returns from nationwide contests consistently located the neighborhood as one of the three major areas of electoral support in Caracas for Chávez and progovernment candidates.[6] Several of the programs that would become highly popular *misiones*—social welfare programs—were piloted in the 23 de Enero.[7] And in 2012, a monument to honor victims of the *Caracazo* formally opened in Zona F (fig. 30). In this sense, the affinities and experiences linking Chávez and the 23 de Enero spoke to a close, even unique relationship that made unsurprising the site of his final repose.

But behind the packed crowds that lined Chávez's funeral procession all along the 23 de Enero, and beyond the hundreds of residents who took to the rooftops of nearby superblocks to catch a glimpse of the departed President, there was also evidence of a much more fraught, tense relationship. Throughout Chávez's presidency, along with expressions of support there also arose in this neighborhood, otherwise seen as a revolutionary "bastion," challenges to the hegemony of *chavismo*. Consider the following. On 2 April 2005 voters in the 23 de Enero took to the polls to participate in a historic election (fig. 31). Over two dozen candidates, representing a wide variety of local groups but linked by their shared support of President Chávez, sought to consolidate a single slate

FIGURE 30. This photo from 2012 shows a monument in honor of the victims of the *Caracazo*, part of a newly completed Bulevar 27 de Febrero, in the Zona F of the 23 de Enero. (Photo by the author)

FIGURE 31. In 2005, a hand-lettered sign in La Cañada identifies a polling place for independently organized, local-level primary elections. Among the offices up for election: city council and parish-level council. (Photo by the author)

of progovernment forces ahead of nationwide neighborhood elections scheduled for August. At first glance these local-level primaries, unique in Venezuela,[8] highlighted the gains of grassroots activism under Chávez. Since first taking office in 1999, his calls to consolidate *poder popular*—popular power—by promoting grassroots participation in the democratic process had been central to his political project. But beyond a dynamic electoral agenda including six nationwide referendums in six years, concrete signs of how "participatory democracy" might in fact be consolidated on the ground remained scarce. In this context, promoting organic community leadership through local-level primary elections lent credibility to what had largely remained a whim.

Yet a closer look revealed more about the limits than the possibilities of popular power under Chávez. Primaries in the 23 de Enero reflected long-simmering tensions between national *chavista* parties and "Electoral Battle Units" (*Unidades de Batalla Electoral*, or UBEs), which emerged in June 2004 after anti-*chavistas* mounted a successful signature drive demanding a recall referendum against the President.[9] That the referendum took place at all reflected the failure of mainstream *chavista* parties to convince voters against calling for the vote. Ironically, Chávez himself contributed to the defeat of *chavista* parties; by constantly railing against bureaucracy and elitism in political parties of old, he had succeeded in undermining the credibility of political parties in general, including his own. By contrast, UBEs functioned as five- to ten-person committees designed to mobilize voters at the most local level by bypassing party bureaucracy.[10] By August, UBEs and their grassroots get-out-the-vote campaign helped score a referendum victory for Chávez. In October, they would secure another victory, helping Chávez-backed candidates sweep regional elections.

These various successes pitted locally-based UBEs against national *chavista* parties as the legitimate interlocutors of popular power. Unsurprisingly, that contest came to a head in the run up to local elections in 2005. Along the way UBE members were barred from state media, denied electoral resources, and prohibited from running as official *chavista* candidates. In response, UBEs and other neighborhood groups in the 23 de Enero formed "electoral committees" to conduct independent primaries.[11] Once held, the winning candidates created FUP23 (United Popular Front 23 de Enero) as an electoral vehicle to run in the August elections, eventually coming in third in the neighborhood behind the officially sanctioned *chavista* party and the Communist Party, both with national reach. Days later, FUP23 candidates staged a protest at the doors of the National Electoral Council to denounce the pressures to which they had been subjected throughout the campaign process, revealing the strength of traditions of struggle well expressed in a local placard: with or without revolution, it said, "*Seguimos siendo rebeldes*" [we are still rebels].

Seen even more closely, the development of local primaries exposed a sharper contest, this one internal to the very social and political organization that lends the 23 de Enero its iconoclastic image. Weeks prior, when mounting discontent over upcoming local elections first turned into proposals for autonomous primaries, community activists representing *juntas de condominio* (condo associations), armed *colectivos* (fig. 32), athletic and cultural coopera-

FIGURE 32. In 2005, a member of the armed Colectivo Alexis Vive masks his face as he stands on the roof of Blocks 22–23 in the Zona Central of the 23 de Enero. (Photo by the author)

tives, and *chavista* parties assembled to discuss logistics. Among these groups were some that earlier, disenchanted with what they regarded as the government's inability to confront the political opposition in Caracas, had coordinated an assault against city police, forcing Chávez to distance his government from what he referred to as "anarchic groups" in the 23 de Enero.[12] Despite their differences they hoped to reach consensus on the basis of a successful and also unprecedented collective effort to self-designate the *jefe civil*, an open challenge to the recently elected *chavista* mayor.

Instead of collaboration, however, the assemblies provided a space for infighting. Long-standing personal feuds fed claims that some sought elected office merely out of personal ambition. Others confronted charges of blind partisanship to Chávez rather than to "participatory democracy" and its best implementation in the parish. Still others faced reproach as opportunists, on grounds that they lacked a track record of involvement in the conflicts that had shaped the 23 de Enero's history. Advocates of a completely independent primary squared off against those arguing for at least some measure of institutional oversight, as represented by the proposed participation of the local electoral board to lend legal legitimacy to the process. In turn, concerns regarding possible co-optation either by the state or by particular strands of activism in the 23 de Enero limited the support of groups that had long combined institutional and extrainstitutional, legal and extralegal forms of pressure in their repertoire of collective action.

In the end only a handful of community groups moved forward with the primaries. These drew mainly from legally chartered organizations such as the *Asociación Civil Antonio José de Sucre*—a self-identified "civil society" group that congregates over fifty condo and barrio associations in the 23 de Enero, securing public investment in the parish through close ties with state institutions. The underlying tensions behind local primaries well illustrate what one local leader calls the "paradox" of community activism in the 23 de Enero: "For many of us who are in this social, cultural, and political struggle, 23 de Enero means that we are parish that doesn't keep quiet; that we always have a voice of protest, a voice of struggle, a voice of organization. We are . . . the most political parish; the most organized of all parishes. But at the same time—and here you feel the paradox—within our organization, we are the most disorganized."[13]

How do we make sense of these wide-ranging expressions of local autonomy, from primary elections to armed conflict? What influences shape popular understandings of the limits and possibilities of revolutionary change in Venezuela? What are the contours of what Sujatha Fernandes has called "critical social movements," neither independent from nor beholden to Chávez?[14] Since Chávez's election, analysts have noted his link to urban popular sectors—from where *chavismo* consistently draws its "strongest base of electoral support"[15]—and the influence of that link on his rhetoric and style and on the government's social spending largesse. At various moments, *chavismo* has emerged as: (1) an example of a cross-class, nonideological, antipolitical movement where *votos castigo* (retribution voting) usher out entire political systems without calling for alternative institutional arrangements;[16] (2) an example of a new kind of institutional arrangement—by some called participatory democracy—yearned for by the electorate and enshrined in new political systems that privilege referendums, constitutional mandates, and bureaucratic innovations aimed at promoting citizen engagement;[17] (3) vulgar authoritarianism, running roughshod over civil rights and liberties while entrenching militaristic rule;[18] (4) classic populism redux, cast in either redistributive, personalist, or discursive terms, but in any event marked by the erosion of institutions in favor of privileging direct links between leaders and masses;[19] (5) a historical consequence of the exhaustion of the previous regime, as a result lacking any particular ideology of its own other than the demonization of earlier political models;[20] (6) a spendthrift bureaucratic black hole, marked by corruption and inefficiency in the absence of institutional mechanisms for state accountability;[21] (7) an example of classic class struggle, propelled by a largely schematic ideological conflict between labor and capital for control of the state;[22] and, more recently, (8) a neoliberal regime, operating at the behest of global capital interests, while willingly in rhetoric but ever more reluctantly in practice ceding spaces to local groups to experiment with alternative forms of governance as long as they do not interfere with the larger economic aims of the state.[23]

What is curious is that the clearest explanation for what characterizes the nature of Venezuelan politics since Chávez is not often advanced: rather than static, or even evolving, Venezuelan politics in the Chávez era may more aptly be understood as spectral, where policy, action, and ideology move in and out of the terrain of classically understood liberal democracy. *Chavismo* in Venezuela at times builds on participatory institutions and frameworks and at other times sidelines them. At times it embraces referendums and at other times flouts electoral outcomes. At times it nationalizes industries and at other times courts foreign capital. At times it relies on classic redistributive politics of the petro-state and at other times advances well-articulated ideological agendas around socialism. Changes over time in the rhetoric and practice of *chavismo*—whether identified as radical, reformist, authoritarian, participatory, populist, neoliberal, etc.—reflect legacies embedded in Venezuelan political history, but they also leave traces of themselves in the present, to be incorporated, rejected, or reformulated by the populace in a dynamic loop. Seen more as a spectrum that resists categorization, indefinability and attendant forms of political practice that chafe against formal institutionalization emerge as key features of Venezuelan politics. And in fact, some of the most recent approaches to Venezuela, from seemingly disparate angles, have begun to tinker with formulas that stress dynamic combinations of political forms rather than ideological evolution or rigid classification.[24] Perhaps the only consensus is that Venezuelan politics—whatever its qualifier—cannot in the Chávez era be referred to in conventional, liberal democratic terms, but must instead be seen as part of a larger continental struggle over the very definition and mode of democracy. As Fernando Coronil writes: "These struggles [during Latin America's 'left turn'] have expanded the agents, agendas, and conceptions of democracy. They draw strength from many local experiences. Just as no single social actor can now be represented as the agent of History without meeting significant resistance from other actors, no one conception of democracy can establish its hegemony without debate. The struggle *for* democracy now entails a struggle *about* democracy."[25]

The trajectory of organizing and mobilization in the 23 de Enero highlights one strand of this new struggle *about* democracy. As the Bolivarian project sought to consolidate what Chávez characterized as a "new historical phase in Venezuela,"[26] it came to rely on a historical genealogy that rests on the rise of Hugo Chávez as the redeemer of the long-suffering poor, whose political awakening can be traced, at best, to the mid- and late 1980s. The long history of popular mobilization in the 23 de Enero, however, suggests otherwise. It shows that early on, struggles by popular sectors to consolidate the promises of effective government unleashed a contest over competing visions of democracy and revolution. The 23 de Enero's symbolism and location fueled intense co-optation efforts; over time, partisan networks emerged throughout the neighborhood on the basis of access to and allocation of state resources. Similar organizing trends informed by partisan political motivations also developed elsewhere in the 23 de Enero. Yet when these networks failed to reap community benefits, residents deployed the same symbolic and spatial qualities to mobilize media attention around forms of collective action that moved in and out of the terrain of legal and extralegal protest. These tactics gave rise to alternative local networks of resistance that arose in parallel to clientelist webs in the 23 de Enero. For instance, in the 1960s antiestablishment groups waged urban guerrilla struggle, while in the 1970s community groups emphasizing local needs took to the streets to protest public-service deficiencies. Their convergence in the early 1980s would signal the rise of a distinctly popular political culture able to navigate both liberal and radical tendencies.

Today these currents remain vibrant. They powerfully call to recast urban popular sectors as fraught constituencies imbued with their own ideological contradictions, which changed over time as residents' engagement with national politics ebbed and flowed, incorporating patterns of representative democracy while also crafting more-radical strategies and interpretations of democratic change out of their experiences with the failures of the political system. The shifting loyalties, contradictory tactics, and internal divisions that underlay these political traditions—seemingly at odds with one another—ensured that visions of a democratic society would vary as widely as the strategies used to wage protest against governments' shortcomings. For some, it would involve expressing political dissent through local primaries. For others, it would involve more-radical means, such as taking up arms to defend against reformist currents in government. Yet the common thread remained as it does today: popular politics as shaped by a sense of community that is neither fully independent from nor fully beholden to the state. As such, it is a relationship marked by conflict and negotiation, drawn in turn from an experience of activism dating to well before the rise of either Hugo Chávez or economic crisis in Venezuela.[27] It is, in short, the essence of democracy in Venezuela—alive, dynamic, enduring—as it has long been in *el veintitrés*.

APPENDIX

VIOLENT DEATHS REPORTED IN THE 2 DE DICIEMBRE: JANUARY 1958

	Name	Age	Location	Date
1	Juan Francisco Oliveros	43	La Cañada–Monte Piedad	22 January
2	Héctor Guillén	1	La Cañada–Monte Piedad	22 January
3	Columba de Ortega	40	La Cañada–Monte Piedad	22 January
4	Enriqueta de Pérez	21	La Cañada–Monte Piedad	22 January
5	Unidentified	—	La Cañada–Monte Piedad	22 January
6	Juana Castro	30	La Cañada–Monte Piedad	22 January
7	Hernán López González	16	La Cañada–Monte Piedad	22 January
8	Luis Rafael Blanco	23	La Cañada–Monte Piedad	22 January
9	Jesús Augusto Olivares	15	Catedral	22 January
10	Domingo Plaza	37	Catedral	22 January
11	Carmen de Ovalles	13	Catedral	22 January
12	Aura Figueroa de Ferrer	26	Monte Piedad	22 January
13	Francisco Manuel Ferrer	1	Monte Piedad	22 January
14	Luis Leal	2	Monte Piedad	22 January
15	Douglas Leal	6	Monte Piedad	22 January
16	José Rafael González	14	Zona Central	22 January
17	Mauricio José Delgado	—	Zona Central	22 January
18	Carmelo Hernández	—	Zona Central	22 January
19	Raúl José Correa Arismendi	30	—	23 January
20	Manuel Tabariz	16	—	24 January
21	Carlos Alberto Garrido Ovalles	37	La Cañada–Monte Piedad	25 January

SOURCE: List compiled from "161 muertos y 477 heridos es el balance trágico de la lucha por la libertad," *El Universal*, 24 January 1958, 20; "Balance trágico de la Revolución," *El Nacional*, 26 January 1958, 8; "Cinco nuevas víctimas enterraron ayer," *El Nacional*, 27 January 1958, 17; "Murieron trágicamente 93 personas en Caracas," *El Nacional*, 26 January 1958, 14.

VIOLENT DEATHS REPORTED IN THE 23 DE ENERO: FEBRUARY/MARCH 1989

	Name	Age	Location	Date
1	Eduardo Meza Istúriz	34	La Cañada	28 February
2	Carlos Antonio Dorantes Torres	29	La Cañada	28 February
3	Francisco Antonio Moncada Gutiérrez	8	Atlántico Norte (Silsa)	28 February
4	Alirio José Núñez Cañizales	23	La Cañada	1 March
5	Jesús Calixto Blanco	54	La Cañada	2 March
6	Unidentified	—	Zona Central	2 March
7	Carlos H. Cuñar	42	Monte Piedad	3 March
8	José Alejandro López Rojas	26	Mirador	4 March
9	Enrique Napoleón Soto Vilera	25	Sierra Maestra	5 March

SOURCE: List compiled from Registro Civil de Defunción, Jefatura Civil, Parroquia 23 de Enero; Elizabeth Araujo, "23 de Enero: Vivir entre balas," in *Cuando la muerte tomó las calles* (Caracas: El Nacional, 1989); "23 de Enero: ¿Francotiradores o víctimas?" *Revista SIC* 52, no. 513 (1989); Germán Mundaraín, *A 18 años del caracazo: Sed de justicia* (Caracas: Defensoría del Pueblo, 2007).

NOTES

PREFACE

1. Boris Muñoz, "Emptying the Tower of David, the World's Tallest Ghetto," *Vocativ* (2014), accessed December 10, 2014, www.vocativ.com/world/venezuela-world/tower-of-david-evictions/.

2. United Nations Global Urban Observatory's Research and Technical Team, *Streets as Public Spaces and Drivers of Urban Prosperity* (Nairobi: United Nations Human Settlements Programme, 2013), 84.

3. Mike Davis, *Planet of Slums* (London: Verso, 2006), 98; 104–108.

4. Andrew Cawthorne, "Venezuela Moves Squatters from 'Tower of David' Slum," *Reuters* (2014), accessed July 22, 2014, www.reuters.com/article/2014/07/22/us-venezuela-tower-idUSKBN0FR19320140722; Hannah Dreier, "End Comes for Notorious Venezuelan Vertical Slum," *Associated Press* (2014), accessed July 22, 2014, http://bigstory.ap.org/article/end-comes-notorious-venezuelan-vertical-slum.

5. Camila Domonoske, "Fall of the Tower of David: Squatters Leave Venezuela's Vertical Slum," in *The Two Way* (Washington, DC: National Public Radio, 2014); Andrew Rosati, "Caracas Is Finally Ending the 'World's Tallest Squat,'" in *The World* (Public Radio International, 2014); Jon Lee Anderson, "Emptying Out the Tower of David," *New Yorker* (2014), accessed July 24, 2014, www.newyorker.com/news/news-desk/emptying-out-the-tower-of-david-2.

6. Wyre Davies, "Venezuela Tower of David Squatters Evicted," (2014), accessed July 22, 2014, www.bbc.com/news/world-latin-america-28426529; Virginia López, "Caracas's Tower of David Squatters Finally Face Relocation after Eight Years," *The Guardian*, 23 July 2014; Julian Robinson, "Slum Which Starred in Homeland Is Cleared," *The Daily Mail* (2014), accessed July 22, 2014, www.dailymail.co.uk/news/article-2701952/Slum-starred-Homeland-cleared-Worlds-tallest-squat-emptied-soldiers-notorious-world.html.

7. "Gobierno comienza desalojo de la simbólica Torre de David en Caracas," *El Tiempo* (Bogotá), 22 July 2014; "Venezuela remove moradores da maior gavela vertical do mundo," *O Globo* (Rio de Janeiro), 22 July 2014; Néstor Rojas Mavares, "El incierto futuro de la Torre de David," *Clarín* (Buenos Aires), 14 August 2014.

8. "Squatters Move out of Venezuela's 'Tower of David' Super Slum in Caracas," (2014), accessed July 24, 2014, www.abc.net.au/news/2014–07–24/venezuela-caracas-super-slum-tower-of-david/5620814; Liu Yang, "Venezuela Military Police Sweep Landmark Slum, Hundreds of Poor 'Move to New Homes,'" *Guoji Zaixian* [China Radio International] (2014), accessed July 23, 2014, http://gb.cri.cn/42071/2014/07/23/6992s4626136.htm. I am grateful to Weiwei Luo for her translation.

9. Michael Silverberg, "The World's Tallest Slum—'A Pirate Utopia'—Is Being Cleared by the Venezuelan Government," *Quartz* (2014), accessed July 23, 2014, http://qz.com/239103/the-worlds-tallest-slum-a-pirate-utopia-is-being-cleared-by-the-venezuelan-government/.

10. Jon Lee Anderson, "Slumlord: What Has Hugo Chávez Wrought in Venezuela?," *New Yorker*, 28 January 2013.

11. Simón Romero and María Eugenia Díaz, "A 45-Story Walkup Beckons the Desperate," *New York Times*, 28 February 2011.

12. Anderson, "Slumlord."

13. Alasdair Baverstock, "Caracas Squatters in Real Tower of David Might Not Welcome Homeland's Nicholas Brody," *Telegraph* (London), 25 October 2013.

14. Nathan Frandino, "'Skyscraper Slum' Gives Venezuelans Escape from Poverty, Crime," *New York Times* (2014), accessed April 7, 2014, www.nytimes.com/video/multimedia/100000002811831/skyscaper-slum-gives-venezuelans-escape-from-poverty-crime.html.

15. Jesús Fuenmayor, "The Tower of David," *domus* (2011), accessed April 28, 2014, www.domusweb.it/en/architecture/2011/04/28/the-tower-of-david.html.

16. Alfredo Brillembourg, Hubert Klumpner, and Iwan Baan, eds., *Torre David: Informal Vertical Communities* (Zürich: Lars Müller, 2013); Markus Kneer and Daniel Schwartz, "Torre David," (U-TT Films; ETH Zurich, 2013); Justin Davidson, "Emergency Architecture: Occupy Caracas," *New York*, 9 October 2011.

17. Gastón R. Gordillo, *Rubble: The Afterlife of Destruction* (Durham, NC: Duke University Press, 2014), 264–266.

18. Fernando Coronil, *The Magical State: Nature, Money, and Modernity in Venezuela* (Chicago: University of Chicago Press, 1997), 3, 5.

19. Federico Vegas, *Falke* (Caracas: Mondadori, 2005), 450: "Dice un historiador que la histeria es como una plataforma donde rebota todo lo que nos acontece, impidiendo que lo vivido pueda transformarse en experiencia. Esto hace que nos quedemos continuamente en la superficie, sin llegar jamás a profundizar, sin llegar a tener una visión interior, sin unir nuestro pasado a la historia del hombre sobre la Tierra. Tenemos pues que Venezuela es un país histérico sometido a una repetición infernal."

INTRODUCTION

1. Marisol Decarli R., "En El 23 la vida es más sabrosa: La barriada emblema de la democracia," *El Universal*, 21 November 2002.

2. Though formally the "23 de Enero," it is as *el veintitrés* ("the twenty-three," pronounced *el-vain-tee-TRESS*) that the neighborhood is broadly known in Caracas and Venezuela.

3. For a classic formulation of the tension between protest and institutions in modern democratic theory, see Robert A. Dahl, *Polyarchy: Participation and Opposition* (New Haven, CT: Yale University Press, 1971). For a useful recent overview of liberal democracy's underlying premises, see Adam Przeworski, *Democracy and the Limits of Self-Government* (Cambridge: Cambridge University Press, 2010). For helpful counterexamples that view social protest and democratization as mutually constitutive, see Charles Tilly, *The Contentious French: Four Centuries of Popular Struggle* (Cambridge, MA: Belknap, 1986); Robert Putnam, *Making Democracy Work: Civic Traditions in Modern Italy* (Princeton, NJ: Princeton University Press, 1993); Sydney Tarrow, *Power in Movement: Social Movements, Collective Action, and Politics* (Cambridge: Cambridge University Press, 1994).

4. See for instance: Robert Jackson Alexander, *The Venezuelan Democratic Revolution: A Profile of the Regime of Rómulo Betancourt* (New Brunswick, NJ: Rutgers University Press, 1964); John D. Martz, "Venezuela's 'Generation of '28': The Genesis of Political Democracy," *Journal of Interamerican Studies* 6, no. 1 (1964); John D. Martz, *Acción Democrática: Evolution of a Modern Political Party in Venezuela* (Princeton, NJ: Princeton University Press, 1966); Ramón J. Velásquez, "Aspectos de la evolución política de Venezuela en el último medio siglo," in *Venezuela moderna: Medio siglo de historia, 1926–1976*, ed. Ramón J. Velásquez (Caracas: Fundación Eugenio Mendoza, 1979).

5. Institutional analyses fell along four axes of investigation. Studies of Venezuela's party system (1) emphasized the effective and seasoned exercise of consensus politics by party leaders, successful in "isolating and containing conflict" from within the state structure through well-oiled clientelist networks, or through political innovation of leftist parties following the 1960s era of armed conflict. Daniel H. Levine, *Conflict and Political Change in Venezuela* (Princeton, NJ: Princeton University Press, 1973); Steve Ellner, *Venezuela's Movimiento al Socialismo: From Guerrilla Defeat to Innovative Politics* (Durham, NC: Duke University Press, 1988). The electoral infrastructure (2) was the subject of quantitative studies that traced the health of the democratic system by way of examinations of voter turnout and preferences at each presidential election. John D. Martz and Enrique A. Baloyra, *Electoral Mobilization and Public Opinion: The Venezuelan Campaign of 1973* (Chapel Hill: University of North Carolina Press, 1976); José Agustín Silva Michelena and Heinz Rudolf Sonntag, *El proceso electoral de 1978: Su perspectiva histórico-estructural* (Caracas: Editorial Ateneo, 1979). The study of labor unions (3)—primarily oil worker, industrial, and peasant unions—centered on recovering the processes by which

organized labor came to be increasingly linked to the state during the 1960s and 1970s as centralization was consolidated. John Duncan Powell, *Political Mobilization of the Venezuelan Peasant* (Cambridge, MA: Harvard University Press, 1971); Paul Nehru Tennassee, *Venezuela: Los obreros petroleros y la lucha por la democracia* (Madrid: Editorial Popular, 1979); Steve Ellner, *Organized Labor in Venezuela, 1958–1991: Behavior and Concerns in a Democratic Setting* (Wilmington, DE: SR Books, 1993). Finally, research on economic policy (4) focused on efforts at economic diversification, industrial decentralization, and oil nationalization. Laura Randall, *The Political Economy of Venezuelan Oil* (New York: Praeger, 1987); Juan Carlos Boué, *Venezuela: The Political Economy of Oil* (Oxford: Oxford University Press, 1994).

6. Brian F. Crisp, *Democratic Institutional Design: The Powers and Incentives of Venezuelan Politicians and Interest Groups* (Stanford, CA: Stanford University Press, 2000), 18. See also: Margarita López Maya and Luis Gómez Calcaño, *De punto fijo al pacto social: Desarrollo y hegemonía en Venezuela 1958–1985* (Caracas: Fondo Editorial Acta Científica Venezolana, 1989); Ramón Piñango, *El Caso Venezuela: Una ilusión de armonía* (Caracas: Ediciones IESA, 1984). Aside from directing new critical attention to the structure of Venezuela's democracy, 1980s scholarship also demonstrated appreciation of the rise of urban protest movements and growing militancy among neighborhood associations, an analytic trend that would move into the mainstream in the mid- to late 1990s. See, for instance, Rafael de la Cruz, "Nuevos movimientos sociales en Venezuela," in *Los movimientos populares en América Latina*, eds. Daniel Camacho and Rafael Menjívar (Mexico City: Universidad de las Naciones Unidas, 1989).

7. Héctor Valecillos T., *El reajuste neoliberal en Venezuela: Ensayos de interpretación crítica* (Caracas: Monte Ávila Editores, 1992).

8. Michael Coppedge, *Strong Parties and Lame Ducks: Presidential Partyarchy and Factionalism in Venezuela* (Stanford, CA: Stanford University Press, 1994); Louis Wolf Goodman, ed. *Lessons of the Venezuelan Experience* (Washington, DC: Woodrow Wilson Center Press, 1995); Daniel Hellinger, *Venezuela: Tarnished Democracy* (Boulder, CO: Westview Press, 1991); Richard S. Hillman, *Democracy for the Privileged: Crisis and Transition in Venezuela* (Boulder, CO: L. Rienner Publishers, 1994); Margarita López Maya, "Venezuela después del *Caracazo*: Formas de protesta en un contexto desinstitucionalizado" (working paper, Helen Kellog Institute, South Bend, IN, 1999); María Luisa Ramos Rollón, *De las protestas a las propuestas: Identidad, acción y relevancia del movimiento vecinal en Venezuela* (Caracas: Editorial Nueva Sociedad, 1995).

9. Moisés Naím, *Paper Tigers and Minotaurs: The Politics of Venezuela's Economic Reforms* (Washington, DC: Carnegie Endowment for International Peace, 1993); Moisés Naím, "High Anxiety in the Andes: The Real Story Behind Venezuela's Woes," *Journal of Democracy* 12, no. 2 (2001).

10. Fernando Coronil, *The Magical State: Nature, Money, and Modernity in Venezuela* (Chicago: University of Chicago Press, 1997), 376.

11. Drawing on dozens of interviews with former leftist guerrillas, rank-and-file militants, and long-time community activists in both urban and rural Venezuela, George Ciccariello-Maher has documented how radical revolutionary currents ran far deeper

and proved much more resilient in Venezuelan society than conventional accounts of the 1958–1998 period once held, presuming them defeated, defunct, or long since incorporated into the mainstream political system. Many of these activists went on to form part of Hugo Chávez's Bolivarian Revolution, directly as members of the government, or indirectly as incubators of local-level revolutionary groups, accounting—Ciccariello-Maher argues—for *chavismo*'s most radical socialist impulses. George Ciccariello-Maher, *We Created Chávez: A People's History of the Venezuelan Revolution* (Durham, NC: Duke University Press, 2013). By focusing not on revolutionaries, whether recent or long-standing, but on a neighborhood where a variety of political identies congregated, *Barrio Rising* further widens the spectrum of popular histories, experiences, and political imaginaries in post-1958 Venezuela, arriving at a more expansive sense of the meanings and future of popular democracy.

12. Michael Conniff, introduction to *Populism in Latin America*, edited by Michael Conniff (Tuscaloosa: University of Alabama Press, 1999), 9. As Anton Rosenthal argues, the "contestatory nature of public space" in urban Latin America cemented a link between politics and spectacle, often accentuated in contexts of electoral conflict. Anton Rosenthal, "Spectacle, Fear, and Protest: A Guide to the History of Urban Public Space in Latin America," *Social Science History* 24, no. 1 (2000): 47–51. Further, historians have linked violence—state or popular—in city spaces to "symbols of public power" for the urban poor. For example, Daniel James's account of 17 and 18 October 1945 in Buenos Aires revealed how an "implicit contest over . . . spatial hierarchy and territorial proprieties" turned the spectacle of thousands of workers from peripheral areas crowding the city center in support of Juan Perón into a form of constituent power that would eventually translate victory at the polls into a mandate for radical reform. Likewise, Herbert Braun observed how the *Bogotazo* riots following Jorge Eliécer Gaitán's 1948 assassination resulted from the frustrated expectations of an increasingly urban electorate, which turned Gaitán's public appeals for increased political inclusion of popular sectors into a public display of violence against erstwhile exclusionary "symbols of public power" in the city. Daniel James, "October 17th and 18th, 1945: Mass Protest, Peronism, and the Argentine Working Class," *Journal of Social History* 21 (1988); Herbert Braun, *The Assassination of Gaitán: Public Life and Urban Violence in Colombia* (Madison: University of Wisconsin Press, 1985).

13. Thus Manuel Castells's study of urban squatters identified relationships of dependency tying urban popular sectors to populist leaders, as Latin American urban movements "exchanged political allegiance and cultural heteronomy for urban services and the right to settle in the appendages of the world economic system." Though exceptions existed, they did not disrupt the trend among urban movements in Latin America toward "subordination to the existing political order" rather than the pursuit of social change. Manuel Castells, *The City and the Grassroots: A Cross-Cultural Theory of Urban Social Movements* (Berkeley: University of California Press, 1983).

14. Andrew Wood and James Baer, examining renter strikes in early twentieth-century Latin America, have noted how "a shift toward more broad-based democratic governance and a corresponding discourse of citizens' rights provided renters, once

excluded from the political process, with a powerful new framework from which to articulate their grievances." Andrew Wood and James Baer, "Strength in Numbers: Urban Rent Strikes and Political Transformation in the Americas, 1904–1925," *Journal of Urban History* 32, no. 6 (2006). For an interpretation of clientelism that does not reduce it to a "realm of submission, a cluster of bonds of domination in opposition to a realm of mutual recognition, of equality and cooperation," but instead undertands it as "the way in which some poor people solve their everyday survival needs through *personalized political mediation*," in turn anchored "in the abiding ties [and] enduring webs of relationships that brokers establish with their clients, and in the—sometimes shared (although seldom cooperatively constructed)—array of cultural representations," that created informal, structured expectations governing both brokers *and* clients, see Javier Auyero, *Poor People's Politics: Peronist Survival Networks and the Legacy of Evita* (Durham, NC: Duke University Press, 2001), 22, 26.

15. Brodwyn Fischer, *A Poverty of Rights: Citizenship and Inequality in Twentieth-Century Rio de Janeiro* (Stanford, CA: Stanford University Press, 2008), 266–268.

16. James Holston, *Insurgent Citizenship: Disjunctions of Democracy and Modernity in Brazil* (Princeton, NJ: Princeton University Press, 2007), 198, 14, 313.

17. Discussing informality as a "new" way of life in the Global South, Nezar AlSayyad writes: "In contrast to such notions of formal social interaction, informality should not be read as social disorganization or anarchy. . . . Thus, the current era of liberalization and globalization should be seen as giving rise to a new form of informality—one with several key attributes. To begin, it has created a situation in which individuals may belong, at one and the same time, to both the informal and the formal sector, often with more than one job in the informal sector. Next, it has allowed informal processes to spread not only among the urban poor and rural migrants, but among what were once seen as the formal lower and middle classes, including such privileged segments of the population as state employees and professionals. Finally, informality is now manifest in new forms and new geographies, both at the rural-urban interface and in terms of developments that may serve as a principal avenue to property ownership." Nezar AlSayyad, "Urban Informality as a 'New' Way of Life," in Ananya Roy and Nezar AlSayyad, eds. *Urban Informality: Transnational Perspectives from the Middle East, Latin America, and South Asia* (Lanham, MD: Lexington Books, 2004): 25–26.

18. Enrique Peruzzotti and Catalina Smulovitz, "Social Accountability: An Introduction," in *Enforcing the Rule of Law: Social Accountability in the New Latin American Democracies*, eds. Enrique Peruzzotti and Catalina Smulovitz (Pittsburgh: University of Pittsburgh Press, 2006), 7–10.

19. Brodwyn Fischer, introduction to Brodwyn Fischer, Bryan McCann, and Javier Auyero, eds. *Cities from Scratch: Poverty and Informality in Urban Latin America* (Durham, NC: Duke University Press, 2014), 7.

20. Historicizing popular understandings of democracy in Latin America is a pressing task. Hugo Chávez's election in 1998 marked the first in a series of electoral victories for left-of-center governments in Latin America. Following nearly two decades of neoliberal governance, these new governments were seen by many to mark a "left turn"

in the region's politics, one cast as a victory for long-struggling popular movements that sought alternatives to austerity-driven regimes and also the violence represented by traditional left-wing groups. Yet recent studies are beginning to examine tensions between governments comprising this "left turn" and the social movements initially thought to anchor their popular support and legitimacy, pointing instead to a resurgence in popular protest in places like Argentina and Brazil as states otherwise identified with progressive reform move to consolidate power at the expense of local histories of activism. Marina Sitrin, *Everyday Revolutions: Horizontalism and Autonomy in Argentina* (London: Zed Books, 2012); Wendy Wolford, *This Land Is Ours Now: Social Mobilization and the Meanings of Land in Brazil* (Durham, NC: Duke University Press, 2010). In Bolivia, for instance, anthropologist Sian Lazar has observed how residents of the satellite city of El Alto, outside La Paz, have long crafted very particular understandings of citizenship based on local histories of collective organizing and mobilization. Sian Lazar, *El Alto, Rebel City: Self and Citizenship in Andean Bolivia* (Durham, NC: Duke University Press, 2008). Meanwhile Jeffrey Webber's critical assessment of Evo Morales's first term in office (2006–2010) captures the tension between progressive social movements and indigenous activists on one side, and on the other the Morales government's promotion of private investment in the country's gas, oil, and other natural-resource sectors, suggesting powerful continuities with basic capitalist and neoliberal policies that belie Morales's socialist rhetoric and promises. Jeffrey R. Webber, *From Rebellion to Reform in Bolivia: Class Struggle, Indigenous Liberation, and the Politics of Evo Morales* (Chicago: Haymarket, 2011).

21. This book neither argues nor claims that the 23 de Enero neighborhood is representative of the experience of Venezuelan popular sectors writ large. Recent work on Venezuelan social movements, spurred by questions similar to the ones raised here but focusing on other areas of Caracas, suggest that while important overlaps exist in the way popular sectors negotiated their participation in the political system that followed in the wake of democratic revolution in 1958, other elements remain particular to the spatial, demographic, and symbolic dimensions of the 23 de Enero. For instance, studying organizing traditions since 1958 in the La Vega and San Agustín barrios of Caracas, Sujatha Fernandes has found that the periodization outlined in Chapters 3 and 4 of this book—namely a 1960s era of political but unpopular radical organizing, and a 1970s era of popular but nominally apolitical organizing around community grievances—similarly played out in these areas. However, far stronger cultural agency rooted around Afro-Venezuelan identity and liberation theology shaped organizing traditions in these sectors. Sujatha Fernandes, *Who Can Stop the Drums? Urban Social Movements in Chávez's Venezuela* (Durham, NC: Duke University Press, 2010).

22. Over the years, the *Caracazo* has again and again surfaced as a turning point in Venezuelan history, marking an obligatory reference highlighting the inability of elites to anticipate and then adequately to respond to mounting crises of their own making. And yet, while the *Caracazo* remains a recurrent theme in much revisionist history, it is also true that it has been only infrequently studied independently, rather than using the massacre to make broader claims about Venezuelan elites. Fernando Coronil and

Julie Skurski, "Dismembering and Remembering the Nation: The Semantics of Political Violence in Venezuela," *Comparative Studies in Society and History* 33, no. 2 (1991).

23. New scholarship on Venezuela has in recent years paid increasing attention to what Sujatha Fernandes has referred to as "critical social movements [that] seek to build spaces of autonomy for themselves," moving away from an earlier view of "Chávez as an independent figure pontificating from above, or [of] popular movements as originating in autonomous spaces from below." Elided in this binary formulation are the "interdependencies" linking both state and social movements, interdependencies that are far more fluid, contentious, and bidirectional than conventional assessments of verticalist leadership or of horizontalist social movements allow. Sujatha Fernandes, "A View from the Barrios: Hugo Chávez as an Expression of Urban Popular Movements," *Latin American Studies Association Forum* 38, no. 1 (2006). Naomi Schiller, for instance, has examined the challenges of community media outlets as they seek to craft autonomous spaces while retaining government financial support. "Catia Sees You: Community Television, Clientelism, and the State in the Chávez Era," in David Smilde and Daniel Hellinger, eds., *Venezuela's Bolivarian Democracy: Participation, Politics, and Culture under Chávez* (Durham, NC: Duke University Press, 2011), 104–130. Rosángel Álvarez and María Pilar García-Guadilla, based on fieldwork among communal councils (promoted by the Chávez government as a grassroots-level mechanism for communities to independently organize, assess local needs, and solicit and administer resources to the government), have found that both citizen-led initiatives and clientelist networks operate simultaneously in these spaces. "Contraloría social y clientelismo: La praxis de los consejos comunales en Venezuela," *Politeia* 34, no. 46 (2012). Gabriel Hetland offers evidence of how, despite originating in the state and designed as verticalist projects, populist regimes can unleash currents of local-level organizing that quickly transcend government designs and generate democratic, participatory initiatives. "The Crooked Line: From Populist Mobilization to Participatory Democracy in Chávez Era Venezuela," *Qualitative Sociology* 37, no. 4 (2014): 373–401. And Rebecca Hanson, in extraordinary ethnographic work with police officers and citizen-security groups, has found that state-led efforts at combating police violence and corruption by ceding more security tasks to communities themselves often produce surprising backlashes among citizens demanding greater state presence, not less. "States Controlling Citizens Controlling the Police: Negotiating Citizen Participation and its Institutionalization within Venezuela's Police Reform," paper presented at the annual meeting of the Latin American Studies Association, Chicago, May 2014. For additional examples, see Sujatha Fernandes, "Informal Cities and Community-Based Organizing: The Case of the Teatro Alameda," in Fischer, McCann, and Auyero, *Cities from Scratch*, 185–207.

I. DICTATORSHIP'S BLOCKS

1. Marcos Pérez Jiménez, "Copia textual del discurso pronunciado por el Presidente de la República, General Marcos Pérez Jiménez a la Nación," *El Nacional*, 3 December 1955.

2. Ocarina Castillo d'Imperio, *Los años del buldozer: Ideología y política, 1948–1958* (Caracas: Fondo Editorial Trópykos, 1990).

3. Manuel A. López Villa, "La arquitectura del '2 de Diciembre,'" *Boletín del Centro de Investigaciones Históricas y Estéticas* 27 (1986): 172.

4. Inés Oliveira, interview with the author, La Cañada, 2005.

5. In Venezuelan vernacular, *saltamonte* (literally, grasshopper) refers to an overactive, carefree young person who escapes parental control.

6. Lorenzo Acosta and Juan Martínez, interview with the author, Monte Piedad, 2005.

7. John V. Lombardi and James A. Hanson, "The First Venezuelan Coffee Cycle: 1830–1855," *Agricultural History* 44 (1970).

8. John V. Lombardi, *Venezuela: The Search for Order, the Dream of Progress* (New York: Oxford University Press, 1982), 331; Charles W. Bergquist, *Labor in Latin America: Comparative Essays on Chile, Argentina, Venezuela, and Colombia* (Stanford, CA: Stanford University Press, 1986), 203–204.

9. Juan Vicente Gómez and his dictatorship are the source of a large and bitterly contested historiography. Until 1958, a standard narrative of glorification that cast him as a strong steward of national interests at a time of dramatic economic potential and widespread underdevelopment characterized this literature. In the post-dictatorship, Gómez's regime was seen as a pariah by the new democratic leadership, the bulk of whom had formed the opposition to *Gomecismo*, and who now freely castigated the dictator for surrendering Venezuela's subsoil to international companies. More recent studies juxtapose Gómez and the post-1958 leadership and its shortcomings, noting common threads rather than qualitative breaks between both regimes. Daniel J. Clinton, *Gómez, Tyrant of the Andes* (New York: William Morrow, 1936); Pedro Manuel Arcaya, *The Gómez Régime in Venezuela and Its Background* (Washington: Sun Printing Company, 1936); Domingo Alberto Rangel, *Los andinos en el poder: Balance de una hegemonía, 1899–1945* (Caracas: Talleres Gráficos Universitarios, 1964); B. S. McBeth, *Juan Vicente Gómez and the Oil Companies in Venezuela: 1908–1935* (Cambridge: Cambridge University Press, 1983); Yolanda Segnini, *Las luces del gomecismo* (Caracas: Alfadil Ediciones, 1987); Fernando Coronil, *The Magical State: Nature, Money, and Modernity in Venezuela* (Chicago: University of Chicago Press, 1997).

10. An alternative reading of Gómez's neglect of Caracas in this period suggests that, rather than a policy directed at "punishing" the capital and its elites, it was part of the dictator's larger plan to repay Venezuela's enormous international debt by severely limiting public-works expenditure throughout Venezuela between 1920 and 1930. After successful repayment of the debt in 1930, Gómez initiated a national urbanization plan—including Caracas—that was to extend beyond his death, lending credibility to this rational-utilitarian interpretation. John Friedmann, *Regional Development Policy: A Case Study of Venezuela* (Cambridge, MA: MIT Press, 1966), 128–135; David J. Myers, "Caracas: The Politics of Intensifying Primacy," in *Latin American Urban Research*, eds. Wayne A. Cornelius and Robert V. Kemper (Beverly Hills: Sage, 1978), 228; Gerald Michael Greenfield, "Venezuela," in *Latin American Urbanization:*

Historical Profile of Major Cities, ed. Gerald Michael Greenfield (Westport: Greenwood Press, 1994); Arturo Almandoz, "Transfer of Urban Ideas: The Emergence of Venezuelan Urbanism in the Proposals for 1930s Caracas," *International Planning Studies* 4, no. 1 (1999): 81.

11. Almandoz, "Transfer of Urban Ideas," 82.

12. Doug Yarrington, *A Coffee Frontier: Land, Society, and Politics in Duaca, Venezuela, 1830–1936* (Pittsburgh: University of Pittsburgh Press, 1997), 148, 163.

13. Miguel Tinker Salas, *The Enduring Legacy: Oil, Culture, and Society in Venezuela* (Durham, NC: Duke University Press, 2009), 160.

14. Almandoz, "Transfer of Urban Ideas," 81.

15. John Friedmann, *Regional Development Policy: A Case Study of Venezuela* (Cambridge, MA: MIT Press, 1966), 132, quoted in Greenfield, "Venezuela," 490.

16. Almandoz, "Transfer of Urban Ideas," 80, 89.

17. Richard Harding Davis, *Three Gringos in Venezuela and Central America* (New York: Harper, 1896), 221–286; especially "The Paris of South America."

18. Juan José Martín Frechilla, *Diálogos reconstruidos para una historia de la Caracas moderna* (Caracas: Universidad Central de Venezuela, 2004).

19. Greenfield, "Venezuela," 492.

20. Almandoz, "Transfer of Urban Ideas," 93.

21. Rómulo Betancourt, *Venezuela, política y petróleo* (Caracas: Monte Ávila Editores, 2001 [1956]), 345–68, 381–404.

22. Consider the Centro Simón Bolívar (CSB). Founded two weeks after Gallegos was sworn into office in February 1948, the CSB was charged with bringing together the various plans for Caracas that had developed along parallel, sometimes competing, lines in the previous decade. But the CSB's initial efforts were largely limited to completing projects already begun and previously contemplated under earlier plans, and mainly around roads and highways, not directly addressing the capital's burgeoning housing shortage. Martín Frechilla, *Diálogos*, 27–29, 63–66; Juan José Martín Frechilla, "La Comisión Nacional de Urbanismo, 1946–1957 (Origen y quiebra de una utopía)," in *Leopoldo Martínez Olavarría: Desarrollo urbano, vivienda y estado*, ed. Alberto Lovera (Caracas: Fondo Editorial Alemo, 1996).

23. Steve Ellner, *Los partidos políticos y su disputa por el control del movimiento sindical en Venezuela, 1936–1948* (Caracas: Universidad Católica Andrés Bello, 1980); Bergquist, *Labor in Latin America*.

24. Coronil, *Magical State*, 147–150.

25. Acosta and Martínez, interview with the author, Monte Piedad, 2005.

26. Francisco Suárez, interview with the author, Monte Piedad, 2005.

27. "Ordinarily one speaks of the *rancho*, a denomination with which housing along creeks and *cerros* [hills] is characterized . . . [but] it is necessary to make a distinction between individual houses, and housing when considered as part of a neighborhood. . . . This appreciation leads us to conclude that not all housing in *cerros* can be considered *ranchos*. It is true that among those seen as good [housing] some [hygienic and

structural] conditions are absent, but this does not preclude them from being categorized in a class above *ranchos*." *El problema de los cerros en el área metropolitana: Informe preliminar sobre el cerro piloto presentado por el Banco Obrero y la gobernación del distrito federal* (Caracas: Sección de Investigaciones Social, Económica y Tecnológica, Banco Obrero, 1954).

28. Mireya Maldonado, interview with the author, Monte Piedad, 2005.

29. Rafael Gutiérrez, interview with the author, Monte Piedad, 2005.

30. Martín Frechilla, *Diálogos*, 160–82.

31. Carlos Raúl Villanueva and Carlos Celis Cepero, *La vivienda popular en Venezuela, 1928–1952* (Caracas: Banco Obrero, 1953), 115.

32. Francisco López, "Algunos aspectos del problema de la vivienda en Venezuela," *Integral*, May 1957.

33. Coronil, *Magical State*, 174.

34. The Banco Obrero was founded by Juan Vicente Gómez in the 1920s to offer low-interest loans to workers. It was initially assigned to the Ministry of Development and later to the Ministry of Public Works (Ministerio de Obras Públicas, or MOP). María Luisa de Blay, *30 años de Banco Obrero* (Caracas: Banco Obrero, 1959), 103–104.

35. Ibid.

36. Valerie Fraser, "Venezuela," in *Building the New World: Studies in the Modern Architecture of Latin America, 1930–1960* (London: Verso, 2000); Eduardo Pineda Paz, *Urbanismo y vivienda: Aspectos de una acción de gobierno* (Caracas: Instituto Nacional de la Vivienda, 1978), 3.

37. Pineda Paz, *Urbanismo y vivienda*, 3.

38. Sibyl Moholy-Nagy, *Carlos Raúl Villanueva y la arquitectura de Venezuela* (Caracas: Editorial Lectura, 1964).

39. Banco Obrero, *El problema de los cerros*.

40. *La batalla contra el rancho: Urdaneta y Pedro Camejo: Un nuevo mundo para los obreros venezolanos* (Caracas: Banco Obrero, 1951).

41. De Blay, *30 años de Banco Obrero*, 112.

42. *La batalla contra el rancho*.

43. Ibid.

44. Acosta and Martínez, interview with the author, Monte Piedad, 2005.

45. Suárez, interview with the author, Monte Piedad, 2005.

46. Ramón J. Velásquez, "Aspectos de la evolución política de Venezuela en el último medio siglo," in *Venezuela moderna: Medio siglo de historia, 1926–1976*, ed. Ramón J. Velásquez (Caracas: Fundación Eugenio Mendoza, 1979), 167.

47. Meanwhile social-democratic AD and the communist PCV remained, as they had been since 1948, banned. Ibid., 169.

48. Coronil, *Magical State*, 163–165.

49. Velásquez, "Evolución política de Venezuela," 168.

50. Pérez Jiménez quoted in "Skipper of the Dreamboat," *Time*, 28 February 1955.

51. Ibid.

52. Rafael Cartay, "La filosofía del régimen perezjimenista: El Nuevo Ideal Nacional," *Economía* XXIV, no. 15 (1999).

53. Marcos Pérez Jiménez, *Cinco discursos del General Marcos Pérez Jiménez, Presidente de la República, pronunciados durante el año 1955 y obras realizadas por el Gobierno en 1955* (Caracas: Imprenta Nacional, 1955), 37. Quoted in López Villa, "Arquitectura del '2 De Diciembre,'" 149.

54. "Skipper of the Dreamboat." According to David Myers, "the value of investment in Caracas was staggering, approximately 70 percent of the Bs. 24.5 billion spent by the national government between 1952 and 1958." David J. Myers, "Policy Making and Capital City Resource Allocation: The Case of Caracas," in *Venezuela: The Democratic Experience*, eds. David J. Myers and John D. Martz (New York: Praeger, 1977), 286.

55. This figure corresponded to the years 1947–1952. Proportional to the national population, this was the second-highest immigrant intake figure in the world for the same period, behind only Canada. In the main they were "Italian stonemasons, barbers and restaurant keepers, Austrian pastry cooks and opticians, French butchers and dressmakers, Portuguese bus drivers and Spanish carpenters." "Skipper of the Dreamboat." See also: Ermila Troconis de Veracoechea, *El proceso de la inmigración en Venezuela* (Caracas: Academia Nacional de la Historia, 1986).

56. Manuel A. López Villa, "Gestión urbanística, revolución democrática y dictadura militar en Venezuela (1945–1958)," *Urbana* 14/15 (1994): 116–17; Villanueva and Celis Cepero, *Vivienda popular en Venezuela*, 96–101, 128–136.

57. De Blay, *30 años de Banco Obrero*, 126; Guido Bermúdez, "Unidad de habitación Cerro Grande," *Integral*, May 1957.

58. De Blay, *30 años de Banco Obrero*, 150–152; "Unidad Residencial '2 de Diciembre,'" in *Obras Del Banco Obrero* (Caracas: Banco Obrero, 1956).

59. "Unidad Residencial '2 De Diciembre.'"

60. De Blay, *30 años de Banco Obrero*, 153.

61. "Skipper of the Dreamboat."

62. Banco Obrero, *El problema de los cerros*.

63. Eric Carlson, ed., *Proyecto de evaluación de los superbloques* (Caracas: Banco Obrero, 1961), 46.

64. López Villa, "Arquitectura del '2 de Diciembre,'" 169. López Villa describes how of the ten barrios the 2 de Diciembre replaced, three were founded in the late nineteenth century, one in the 1920s (its landowner directed the urbanization process therein), one in the early 1930s (again through an urbanization process directed by its landowner), and three later that decade.

65. The expropriated barrios were, successively: Cerro Belén, Monte Piedad, Colombia, Las Canarias, Cañada de la Iglesia, Cerro San Luis, Los Flores, 18 de Octubre, Barrio Nuevo, and Puerto Rico. De Blay, *30 años de Banco Obrero*, 149–52; López Villa, "Arquitectura del '2 de Diciembre,'" 169. Total surface area is from Carlson, ed., *Proyecto de evaluación*, 28. Pérez Jiménez's decree found in: Marcos Pérez Jiménez, "Presidencia de la República, Decreto No. 115," *Gaceta Oficial de la República de Venezuela* Año LXXXII—Mes VIII, no. 24.462 (1954): 1.

66. See for instance: *La batalla contra el rancho*; Banco Obrero, *Memoria y Cuenta del Año 1956* (Caracas: Ministerio de Obras Públicas, 1957); *Solución al problema de la vivienda: Realizaciones del año 1954* (Caracas: Banco Obrero, 1954); Villanueva and Celis Cepero, *Vivienda popular en Venezuela*.

67. See for instance: "Comunidad '2 De Diciembre'," *Integral*, May 1957; Eugenio Optiz, "Galería de fotos artísticas," *Construcción*, September 1955.

68. Priscilla de Carrero, interview with the author, Monte Piedad, 2005.

69. Acosta and Martínez, interview with the author, Monte Piedad, 2005.

70. Suárez, interview with the author, Monte Piedad, 2005.

71. Acosta and Martínez, interview with the author, Monte Piedad, 2005.

72. So-called *opción a venta* contracts were calculated at a 6% interest rate. Meanwhile rental rates varied dramatically. A later report found rental contracts ranging from Bs. 15 (US$4.50) a month to Bs. 247.30 (US$74) a month. Partly, the wide range was due to different apartment configurations—2, 3, or 4 bedrooms—but the report found wide ranges even among the same types of apartment. Income, rather than apartment type, governed the adjudication of rental agreements. Carlson, ed., *Proyecto de evaluación*, 27, 31.

73. Carrero, interview with the author, Monte Piedad, 2005.

74. Velásquez, "Evolución política de Venezuela," 190.

75. César Acuña, interview with the author, Mirador, 2005.

76. Francisco Chirinos, personal correspondence with the author, 27 September 2003.

77. Angelina Orellana de García-Maldonado, *60 años de experiencia en desarrollos urbanísticos de bajo costo en Venezuela* (Caracas: Instituto Nacional de la Vivienda, 1989), 172.

78. López Villa, "Arquitectura del '2 de Diciembre,'" 169. Crests and troughs in the rate of expropriations attest to the model's cyclical nature. For instance, in the fourth trimester of 1957, so as to accommodate the third and largest phase of the 2 de Diciembre, expropriations spiked 500%. See for instance *Actas del Banco Obrero*, vol. 44 (Caracas: Junta Directiva del Banco Obrero, 1956), 16–19, 206; *Actas del Banco Obrero*, vol. 47 (Caracas: Junta Directiva del Banco Obrero, 1957), 316–17, 418.

79. Juan Martínez, interview with the author, Caracas, 2005. Francisco Suárez, too, remembered how, despite restrictions, his mother and sisters took to selling *empanadas* on weekends in the largely vacant parking area below, where farmers markets would set up on Saturdays. Suárez, interview with the author, Monte Piedad, 2005.

80. Oliveira, interview with the author, La Cañada, 2005.

81. Ibid. According to news reports days later Rivas, a 19-year-old student living in Block 12 of La Cañada, lost his eye from the gunshot wound. Yet he survived. "Balance trágico de la Revolución," *El Nacional*, 26 January 1958.

82. Oliveira, interview with the author, La Cañada, 2005.

83. Coronil, *Magical State*, 204–214; Salas, *Enduring Legacy*, 222–223.

84. Ligia Ovalles, interview with the author, Zona Central, 2005.

85. Ibid. Residents in other blocks experienced similar tensions in the days after 23 January. In Blocks 20–21 in La Cañada, 70 residents organized self-defense brigades keeping watch from "ten at night to five in the morning." It was a response to what they referred to as a "terrorist campaign" by presumed agents of the deposed regime, after two people yelled "bomb" in a bid to sow fear among residents. "Campaña contra terroristas en Bloques 20 y 21," *El Nacional*, 29 January 1958.

86. Velásquez, "Evolución política de Venezuela," 197.

87. "161 muertos y 477 heridos es el balance trágico de la lucha por la libertad," *El Universal*, 24 January 1958.

88. "Murieron trágicamente 93 personas en Caracas," *El Nacional*, 26 January 1958. The figure also included three soldiers and five Seguridad Nacional agents who died at the hands of lynch mobs on 24 and 25 January.

89. "161 muertos y 477 heridos."

90. "Balance trágico de la Revolución."

91. Ovalles, interview with the author, Zona Central, 2005.

92. José Rivas Rivas, *Historia gráfica de Venezuela: Una historia contada por la prensa*, vol. 7 (Caracas: Centro Editor, 1980), 24.

93. Ibid., 60.

94. J. L. Salcedo-Bastardo, *Historia fundamental de Venezuela* (Caracas: Universidad Central de Venezuela, 1996 [1970]), 265.

95. García-Maldonado, *60 años*.

96. "161 muertos y 477 heridos."

97. "Cinco nuevas víctimas enterraron ayer," *El Nacional*, 27 January 1958.

98. "23 de Enero se llama desde ayer la urbanización 2 de Diciembre," *El Nacional*, 29 March 1958.

99. De Blay, *30 años de Banco Obrero*, 149.

100. Steve Ellner, "Venezuelans Reflect on the Meaning of the 23 de Enero," *Latin American Research Review* 20, no. 1 (1985): 246–47. Ellner reviews nearly a dozen monographs, oral histories, and memoirs published around the 25th anniversary of 23 January 1958, covering the events, their antecedents, and their aftermath. Ellner suggests that despite scattered claims of close collaboration between political party activists and military conspirators (claims levied primarily by the former), most agree that "military conspirators acted independently during the first twenty three days of 1958." Contemporaneous accounts by U.S. Embassy personnel likewise understood the conspiracy preceding the 23 January coup as a military matter. Wrote one consular official: "Up to this time, the political crisis has been almost entirely a military affair, and large segments of the public so consider it. This is especially true of the lower classes who have had no opposition leadership presented to it, and who understand little of the implications involved. Shopkeepers and taxi drivers are aware that their business is very slow, and they worry about their economic activity as the government crisis continues, but hope to avoid personal involvement in politics." Glen H. Fisher, "Extent of Civilian Participation in Current Political Agitation, 1958," Foreign Service Despatch, RG 59 General Records of the Department of State, 1955–59, College Park.

2. DEMOCRACY'S PROJECTS

1. "23 de Enero se llama desde ayer la urbanización 2 de Diciembre," *El Nacional,* 29 March 1958.

2. Lourdes Quintero, interview with the author, 2005.

3. "Las nuevas autopistas se inauguraron solas," *El Nacional,* 28 January 1958.

4. Emilia de Pérez, interview with the author, 2005.

5. "Habitantes de los cerros ocuparon los bloques todavía no inaugurados," *El Universal,* 26 January 1958.

6. Pérez, interview with the author, 2005. In fact, according to later BO estimates, as many as 360 apartments were occupied "by two or three families each, with no family ties at all." Eric Carlson, ed., *Proyecto de evaluación de los superbloques* (Caracas: Banco Obrero, 1961), 102.

7. Alfredo Gosen, *El 23 de enero, Caracas toma Caracas* (Caracas: FundArte, 1990).

8. Carlson, *Proyecto de evaluación,* 27–29. By the end of 1958, BO officials continued to work with estimates rather than precise population figures for the 23 de Enero. Upper estimates placed the number of residents at the close of 1958 at 100,000. However, occupancy estimates—which averaged 8.0 people per apartment among the areas seized in January 1958, and 7.7 people per apartment in areas adjudicated during Pérez Jiménez's rule—placed the number closer to 73,000 than 100,000. The difference in part owed to the number of people who had not found apartments in the fray of January 1958, and instead proceeded to occupy schools, commercial spaces, and green areas around the buildings. Some of these people would eventually be provided apartments in five new superblocks built during 1958 in the 23 de Enero. Others would continue to live in the areas around the superblocks, erecting ranchos that over time became more-established neighborhoods in their own right.

9. "Estudiará el Banco Obrero la ocupación de superbloques," *El Nacional,* 31 January 1958.

10. "Una encuesta con 22 mil consultas hicieron los universitarios entre inquilinos del Banco Obrero," *El Nacional,* 17 April 1958.

11. "Estudiarán los problemas de los pobladores de la 23 de Enero," *El Nacional,* 26 February 1958.

12. Surveys found that 67% of those in Monte Piedad, La Cañada, and Zona Central were originally from the capital, while 80% of those who occupied apartments in January 1958 were born in Caracas. The other 40% of apartments consisted of "the nuclear family plus other relatives." Carlson, *Proyecto de evaluación,* 90–91.

13. Rolando Grooscors, *Problemas del desarrollo urbano en Venezuela* (Caracas: Banco Obrero, 1963), 74.

14. Carlson, *Proyecto de evaluación,* 89, 92.

15. "Banco Obrero, Avisos: Denuncios de sub-arrendamientos," *Tribuna Popular,* 26 April 1958.

16. Carlson, *Proyecto de evaluación,* 32.

17. Ibid., 91.

18. "Estudiantes ayudarán en encuesta de los bloques ocupados," *El Nacional*, 3 February 1958.

19. Carlson, *Proyecto de evaluación*, 32.

20. Ibid., 28–29, 59, 145.

21. "Los vecinos de Loma de Viento y 23 de Enero denuncian las irregularidades de los servicios de luz y agua," *Tribuna Popular*, 15 March 1958.

22. Quintero, interview with the author, 2005; "Faltan agua y aseo urbano en bloques 23 de Enero," *El Universal*, 27 January 1958.

23. Carlos Acevedo Mendoza, *La vivienda en el área metropolitana de Caracas* (Caracas: Ediciones del Cuatricentenario de Caracas, 1967), 146.

24. "Pagan 3 bolívares por lata de agua familias del 23 de Enero," *Tribuna Popular*, 18 April 1958.

25. Acevedo Mendoza, *Vivienda en Caracas*, 146.

26. Carlson, *Proyecto de evaluación*, 102.

27. Ibid., 32.

28. Ibid., 101.

29. César Acuña, interview with the author, 2005.

30. "Acusado el pequeño dictador del 23 de Enero de planear el secuestro de Nixon en complicidad con los esbirros perezjimenistas de Cúcuta," *El Nacional*, 15 May 1958.

31. "El caso Diógenes Caballero: Adelantan averiguaciones para pasar el asunto a tribunales," *El Nacional*, 16 May 1958.

32. Acuña, interview with the author, 2005.

33. "En el 23 de Enero piden establecer por su cuenta 'Junta Representativa,'" *El Universal*, 5 February 1958.

34. "Detenido el pequeño dictador de la urbanización 23 de Enero," *El Nacional*, 11 February 1958.

35. "Los desalojados de los cerros ocuparon los bloques de Monte Piedad," *El Nacional*, 30 January 1958.

36. "Faltan agua y aseo urbano."

37. "El Banco Obrero reanudará política de créditos hipotecarios para viviendas," *El Nacional*, 6 March 1958.

38. "Gente de mal vivir y revoltosos: El B.O. comenzó a legalizar la situación de los inquilinos de apartamentos ocupados sin contrato de arrendamiento," *El Nacional*, 29 March 1958.

39. "Constituida junta patriótica en la parroquia Catedral," *El Universal*, 5 February 1958. In fact, all but 5,000 of the parish's residents lived in the superblocks.

40. "Deudores del Banco Obrero solicitan un descuento para pagar los alquileres vencidos," *El Nacional*, 18 February 1958; "Los vecinos del 23 de Enero insisten en la rebaja de alquileres y en un nuevo avalúo de sus propiedades," *El Nacional*, 24 February 1958.

41. "Piden al Banco Obrero rebaja de un 50 por ciento en alquileres de apartamentos," *El Nacional*, 19 March 1958; "Rebaja de alquileres piden al Banco Obrero," *El Nacional*, 8 March 1958.

42. Carlson, *Proyecto de evaluación*, 31.

43. "Estudios para rebajar los alquileres del Banco Obrero," *El Nacional*, 28 March 1958.

44. "Bajó los alquileres el Banco Obrero," *El Nacional*, 27 April 1958; "Con una rebaja de alquileres y de cuotas iniciará nueva política de viviendas el B.O.," *El Nacional*, 3 April 1958.

45. "Piden rebaja de alquileres 500.000 inquilinos del Banco Obrero," *El Nacional*, 9 April 1958.

46. "Que den los apartamentos en venta piden sacerdotes de los sectores residenciales del Banco Obrero," *El Nacional*, 12 April 1958; Arturo Torres, "El problema de los altos alquileres," *Tribuna Popular*, 26 April 1958; "Cortos de las Juntas Pro-Mejoras," *Tribuna Popular*, 16 August 1958.

47. "Los vecinos del 23 de Enero insisten en la rebaja de alquileres"; Arbas, "Altos alquileres en la 23 de Enero," *El Nacional*, 30 March 1958.

48. "Residentes de la urbanización 23 de Enero se entrevistarán con el director del Banco Obrero," *El Nacional*, 27 May 1958.

49. Grooscors, *Desarrollo urbano en Venezuela*, 82–83; "Asamblea en el 23 de Enero," *Tribuna Popular*, 31 May 1958.

50. "Rebaja de alquileres: Acuerdo entre el B.O. y la Junta Pro-Mejoras del 23 de Enero," *Tribuna Popular*, 7 June 1958.

51. "Ampliarán canales de desagüe en la 23 de Enero," *El Nacional*, 4 June 1958. In fact, poorly drained hillsides adjoining the superblocks, especially in theLa Cañada sector, which sat in a natural trough surrounded on all sides by hills, would continue to generate mudslides despite these efforts, and continue for years to come. "Al 23 de Enero: Los cerros se le vienen encima," *Tribuna Popular*, 28 June 1958.

52. "Los inquilinos del 23 de Enero no podrán pagar los cánones de arrendamiento," *Tribuna Popular*, 10 May 1958.

53. "Nombraron Comité Único las Juntas Pro-Mejoras de la Urb. 23 de Enero," *El Nacional*, 6 July 1958.

54. "Se reunirán Juntas Pro-Mejoras de urbanizaciones del Banco Obrero para pedir rebaja de alquileres," *El Nacional*, 19 August 1958.

55. "Se construyen ranchos en varias zonas verdes," *El Nacional*, 31 January 1958.

56. "Venden ranchos en pleno corazón de Caracas," *Tribuna Popular*, 16 November 1958.

57. "En el 23 de Enero: Abandonan apartamentos para construir ranchos," *Tribuna Popular*, 21 June 1958.

58. Ligia Ovalles, interview with the author, 2005.

59. Mireya Maldonado, interview with the author,2005.

60. Eloy Deslances, interview with the author, 2005.

61. Gustavo Parabón, interview with the author, 2005.

62. "Ampliarán canales de desagüe."

63. "Se están anegando los apartamentos de la urbanización 23 de Enero," *El Nacional*, 1 June 1958.

64. Carlson, *Proyecto de evaluación*, 61.

65. "Pide el 23 de Enero mercado libre," *Tribuna Popular*, 2 August 1958.

66. This included 7 daycares, 3 kindergartens, and 2 elementary schools. Carlson, *Proyecto de evaluación*, 116–17.

67. "Creadas tres escuelas para la 23 de Enero," *El Nacional*, 14 June 1958; "Dos meses sin cobrar maestros de escuela del 23 de Enero," *Tribuna Popular*, 22 November 1958.

68. Acevedo Mendoza, *Vivienda en Caracas*, 146.

69. Maldonado, interview with the author, 2005.

70. Ramona Velasco, interview with the author, 2005.

71. Inés Álvarez, interview with the author, 2005.

72. Deslances, interview with the author, 2005.

73. "Medidas inmediatas contra la construcción de nuevos ranchos en el área metropolitana," *El Nacional*, 5 March 1958.

74. "Comenzó la demolición de ranchos construidos en zonas prohibidas," *El Nacional*, 6 March 1958.

75. "Medidas de emergencia para resolver problema de los ranchos," *El Nacional*, 30 March 1958. In August, the measures would extend further as the National Institute for Agriculture moved to relocate recent rural migrants back to their places of origin in the countryside. "Listo el programa del I.A.N. para reubicar familias campesinas que emigraron a centros urbanos," *El Nacional*, 1 August 1958.

76. "Destruidos los ranchos," *El Nacional*, 9 April 1958.

77. "Medidas de emergencia."

78. "Su rancho y 20 cuadros quemó el Banco Obrero a Feliciano Carvallo," *El Nacional*, 22 March 1958.

79. "El grave problema nacional: El rancho," *El Nacional*, 14 July 1958.

80. "Medidas de emergencia."

81. "Informe a la Junta de Gobierno sobre el problema de los ranchos," *El Nacional*, 9 April 1958.

82. "40 mil ranchos hay en Caracas según datos del Banco Obrero," *El Nacional*, 14 April 1958.

83. "Seis edificios para familias obreras," *El Nacional*, 4 March 1958.

84. "6 nuevos bloques en el 23 de Enero costarán 12 millones," *El Nacional*, 13 March 1958; "Aviso del Banco Obrero: Resultados de licitación para nuevos bloques en el 23 de Enero," *El Nacional*, 23 March 1958.

85. "900 apartamentos comenzará a construir esta semana el B.O.," *El Nacional*, 10 April 1958.

86. Félix Ramírez Bauder, "Causas y efectos del éxodo rural," *El Nacional*, 16 June 1958.

87. "Listo el programa del I.A.N."

88. "Dice Sindicato de la Construcción: Destitución de Fortoul obedece a saboteo del Plan de Emergencia," *Tribuna Popular*, 21 June 1958.

89. "Sorpresiva para el Dr. Fortoul noticia de su destitución," *El Nacional*, 18 June 1958.

90. "Destitución del Dr. Fortoul obedece a una reorganización dentro de la gobernación," *El Nacional*, 18 June 1958.

91. "Gran manifestación de los barrios caraqueños para restituir en su cargo al Doctor Celso Fortoul," *Tribuna Popular*, 21 June 1958.

92. "Provocó una manifestación de protesta la destitución del Doctor Celso Fortoul," *El Nacional*, 18 June 1958"; "El Gobernador anunció su renuncia," *El Nacional*, 18 June 1958. By month's end, Col. Marchelli would be replaced by economist Julio Diez. "Julio Diez Gobernador del Distrito Federal," *El Nacional*, 27 June 1958.

93. "Gran manifestación de barrios caraqueños."

94. "Fundan Confederación de Juntas Pro-Fomento más de doscientas organizaciones populares," *Tribuna Popular*, 28 June 1958.

95. These included "housing, the high cost of living, unemployment, education, which will for us be our chief banner, as well as defending street children, the construction of public schools and kitchens, the creation of cultural centers and maternity aid stations, [and the] defense of free education at all levels." "Organizada la confederación de Juntas Pro-Mejoras," *Tribuna Popular*, 19 July 1958.

96. "La Junta visitó El Polvorín," *El Nacional*, 20 June 1958.

97. Andrew B. Wardlaw and William P. Snow, "Background for demonstrations in Caracas against Vice President Nixon," RG59/Records of the Bureau of Inter-American Affairs/Lot File No. 60 D 249, Subject Files Relating to Venezuela, 1955–1958, [Box 2 of 2] Box 2 of 28/Folder 92, Memoranda File, Jan.–June, Chronological, 14 May 1958.

98. Quoted in Alan McPherson, *Yankee No! Anti-Americanism in U.S.–Latin American Relations* (Cambridge, MA: Harvard University Press, 2003), 29.

99. "The Guests of Venezuela," *Time*, 26 May 1958.

100. Carl Bartch, Eduardo Acosta, and William P. Snow, "Memorandum of Conversation: Venezuelan assurances of protection for Vice President," RG59/Records of the Bureau of Inter-American Affairs/Lot File No. 60 D 249, Subject Files Relating to Venezuela, 1955–1958, [Box 2 of 2] Box 2 of 28/Folder 92, Memoranda File, Jan.–June, Chronological, 14 May 1958.

101. Wardlaw and Snow, "Background for demonstrations in Caracas."

102. Bartch, Acosta, and Snow, "Memorandum of Conversation."

103. Ibid.

104. "El caso Diógenes Caballero."

105. "Libertaron a Diógenes Caballero," *El Nacional*, 22 May 1958.

106. Charles R. Burrows and Héctor Santaella, "Memorandum of Conversation," RG59/1955–59/Central Decimal File, Box 2468/Folder 611–31/1–3155, 23 June 1958.

107. Herbert Braun, *The Assassination of Gaitán: Public Life and Urban Violence in Colombia* (Madison: University of Wisconsin Press, 1985).

108. As early as 13 February, Castro León had alerted U.S. Embassy personnel that the military would intervene at the sight of any perceived weakness on the part of the Junta. "Victor C. Algrant to Charles R. Burrows: Meeting with Colonel Jesus Maria Castro Leon," *RG59/Records of the Bureau of Inter-American Affairs/Lot File No. 60 D*

249, *Subject Files Relating to Venezuela, 1955–1958, [Box 1 of 2] Box 1 of 28/Folder 60, Political-General, Feb.–April 1958*, 13 February 1958.

109. Charles R. Burrows, "Transmitting Armed Forces Document Addressed to Junta of Government," in *RG59 General Records of the Department of State, 1955–59* (College Park: National Archives, 1958).

110. According to later press accounts, local party officials had received word of Castro León's full aims after he met on 22 July with Rafael Caldera of the center-right COPEI party and Jóvito Villalba of the centrist URD party in an unsuccessful bid to gain their support. "Caracas: En pie de lucha, obreros, estudiantes, mujeres, y niños en defensa de la democracia," *Tribuna Popular*, 26 July 1958.

111. "Nueva junta Pro-Mejoras en el 23 de Enero destaca su apoyo a la Junta de Gobierno," *El Nacional*, 22 July 1958.

112. "Caracas: En pie de lucha."

113. Robert Alexander, *Rómulo Betancourt and the Transformation of Venezuela* (New Brunswick: Transaction, 1982), 408–9.

114. Herbert W. Baker, "Eyewitness account of incidents before government junta offices on September 7—the day of the latest military coup attempt," *RG59/1955–59/ Central Decimal File, Box 3033/Folder 731.00/8–158*, 19 September 1958.

115. "El bravo pueblo enfrentó sus pechos," *Tribuna Popular*, 13 September 1958.

116. "Barricadas en los barrios caraqueños," *Tribuna Popular*, 13 September 1958.

117. Ramón J. Velásquez, "Aspectos de la evolución política de Venezuela en el último medio siglo," in *Venezuela Moderna: Medio siglo de historia, 1926–1976*, ed. Ramón J. Velásquez (Caracas: Fundación Eugenio Mendoza, 1979), 217.

3. FROM BALLOTS TO BULLETS

1. Emilia de Pérez, interview with theauthor, 2005.

2. "'En Venezuela se está realizando una revolución pacífica, democrática, y Cristiana': Betancourt," *Últimas Noticias*, 10 May 1962.

3. "'Hijo predilecto de Caracas' fue declarado el héroe Fidel Castro al llegar a Venezuela," *Últimas Noticias*, 25 January 1959.

4. "El gabinete ejecutivo brindó un almuerzo al líder revolucionario," *Últimas Noticias*, 25 January 1959.

5. "Cuba y Venezuela unidas en ideales de Libertad y Democracia," *Últimas Noticias*, 25 January 1959.

6. Fidel Castro, "Discurso pronunciado por el Comandante Fidel Castro Ruz, Primer Ministro del Gobierno Revolucionario, en la Plaza Aérea del Silencio, en Caracas, Venezuela, el 23 de enero de 1959," (2009), www.cuba.cu/gobierno/discursos/1959/esp/f230159e.html.

7. "Fidel Castro invitado por urbanización 23 de Enero," *Últimas Noticias*, 13 January 1959.

8. "Hoy se colocará la primera piedra del monumento a la unidad nacional," *Últimas Noticias*, 21 January 1959.

9. "Fidel Castro en el 23 de Enero," *El Nacional*, 25 January 1959; "En la urbanización 23 de Enero fue celebrado el aniversario de esa fecha," *El Universal*, 25 January 1959.

10. "Pagan a 3 y 4 bolívares el agua los vecinos del barrio Sierra Maestra," *Últimas Noticias*, 30 January 1959. In the months prior to and following Castro's visit, several neighborhoods staged similar renamings to reflect affinities for the Cuban cause and the Sierra Maestra mountain range that constituted guerrillas' base of operations. In October 1958, residents of a squatter settlement in the eastern city of Puerto la Cruz had named their budding community after the guerrilla stronghold, at the time still an important front in the struggle against Cuba's Fulgencio Batista. "Sierra Maestra, nuevo barrio de Puerto La Cruz," *Tribuna Popular*, 25 October 1958. In Caracas, too, residents of Los Mecedores in the northwestern edge of the capital, at the foot of the Ávila mountain range, likewise changed their community's name to Sierra Maestra on the eve of Castro's visit to Caracas, taking to the press to solicit "even for a few seconds" Castro's visit to the area. "Barrio Sierra Maestra hay ahora en Caracas," *Últimas Noticias*, 25 January 1959. And in late 1959, in the western city of Maracaibo, capital of the oil-rich Zulia state, a squatter settlement which residents had named Sierra Maestra found itself at the center of a land-rights dispute with Shell Oil Company. "Sucedió en Maracaibo: Atropellos policiales en Sierra Maestra en intento de desalojo por la fuerza," *Tribuna Popular*, 18 December 1959.

11. Pérez, interview with the author, 2005.

12. Ibid.

13. Antonio García Ponte, *Sangre, locura, y fantasía: La guerrilla de los años 60* (Caracas: Editorial Libros Marcados, 2010), 17.

14. "Ametrallados el 23 de Enero, Barrio Unión y Simón Rodríguez," *Tribuna Popular*, 27 October 1960"; "1500 Guardias Nacionales y esbirros de la SotoPol asaltaron el 23 de Enero," *Tribuna Popular*, 28 October 1960; "Disturbios durante todo el día en la urbanización 23 de Enero," *El Nacional*, 27 October 1960.

15. Cristóbal Rodríguez Oberto and Ramón García, "La paz ha vuelto al 23 de Enero, pero el desempleo es su mayor problema," *El Nacional*, 23 January 1965.

16. "La evidente falta de civismo," *Últimas Noticias*, 26 January 1959.

17. "Parlamentarios condenan provocaciones contra la Unidad en los actos públicos," *Últimas Noticias*, 26 January 1959.

18. Larrazábal took 66% of the vote to Betancourt's 13%. Rafael Caldera of COPEI received 18% of the vote, while the remaining 3% were null. "Aplastante derrota de A.D. en el Distrito Federal, pero en la provincia gana ampliamente," *Últimas Noticias*, 8 December 1958; "Escándalo en el 23 de Enero ante creencia de un fraude electoral al encontrar 12 urnas con material sobrante y suponer eran votos," *Últimas Noticias*, 10 December 1958.

19. "Promete el Presidente Larrazábal asistencia a las víctimas de la revolución de enero," *El Nacional*, 6 August 1958.

20. "El Presidente Larrazábal protestó por distribución de llaveros con su efigie," *El Nacional*, 4 July 1958.

21. "Dos comités de barrio anuncian la postulación de Wolfgang Larrazábal," *El Nacional*, 9 July 1958.

22. Ramón J. Velásquez, "Aspectos de la evolución política de Venezuela en el último medio siglo," in *Venezuela moderna: Medio siglo de historia, 1926–1976*, ed. Ramón J. Velásquez (Caracas: Fundación Eugenio Mendoza, 1979), 205.

23. César Acuña, interview with the author, 2005.

24. "Seis edificios para familias obreras," *El Nacional*, 4 March 1958.

25. "6 nuevos bloques en el 23 de Enero costarán 12 millones," *El Nacional*, 13 March 1958; "Aviso del Banco Obrero: Resultados de licitación para nuevos bloques en el 23 de Enero," *El Nacional*, 23 March 1958.

26. "900 apartamentos comenzará a construir esta semana el B.O.," *El Nacional*, 10 April 1958.

27. Dalila Roa, Elka Larío Roa, and Rosa Amelia de González, interview with the author, 2005.

28. The original Spanish reads: *para luchar por sus reivindicaciones*. "Rebaja de alquileres," *Tribuna Popular*, 20 September 1958; "Larrazábal y Eduardo en el 23 de Enero," *Tribuna Popular*, 27 September 1958.

29. Ravín Asuase Sánchez, interview with the author, 2005.

30. *Opción a compra* was a lease program that gave residents the option to purchase their apartments outright rather than rent them indefinitely. Roa, Roa, and González, interview with the author, 2005.

31. Rafael Gutiérrez, interview with the author, 2005.

32. Lourdes Quintero, interview with the author, 2005.

33. "Notas del 23 de Enero," *Tribuna Popular*, 19 July 1958.

34. This interplay between "concrete material aspects" and what may at first glance seem like abstract charismatic appeals also explain the durability of Argentina's Juan Domingo Perón's popularity among working classes, as Daniel James has found. For charisma to be credible, it requires concrete actions. Daniel James, *Resistance and Integration: Peronism and the Argentine Working Class, 1946–1976* (Cambridge: Cambridge University Press, 1988), 21–22.

35. "En el 23 de Enero," *Tribuna Popular*, 3 May 1958. By late 1959, "En el 23" would become a regular weekly column.

36. "La miseria en los rascacielos: El 23 de Enero lucha para sobrevivir," *Tribuna Popular*, 31 May 1958.

37. "El P.C.V. celebrará un acto el domingo en el 23 de Enero," *El Nacional*, 20 June 1958.

38. "El P.C.V. inició campaña electoral," *Tribuna Popular*, 4 October 1958.

39. "Primer acto público de la campaña de crecimiento del PCV en el DF: El gobierno debe tener una participación más activa en el desarrollo económico de Venezuela," *Tribuna Popular*, 28 June 1958.

40. "Primeros candidatos comunistas al congreso," *Tribuna Popular*, 4 October 1958.

41. John M. Cates, "Venezuelan 1958 election: Phenomenon of the Communist congressional vote exceeding the communist presidential vote," *RG59/Central Decimal File, Box 3033/Folder 731.00/1–259*, 8 January 1959.

42. Talton F. Ray, *The Politics of the Barrios of Venezuela* (Berkeley, CA: University of California Press, 1969), 57.

43. "Larrazábal candidato P.C.V.," *Tribuna Popular*, 16 November 1958.

44. V. C. Algrant, "Communist Expectations in case of Larrazabal Victory," RG 59/Records of the Bureau of Inter-American Affairs/Lot File No. 60 D 249, Subject Files Relating to Venezuela, 1955–1958, [Box 2 of 2] Box 2 of 28/Folder 63, Parties-Elections, Nov.–Dec., 3 December 1958. In addition, the Ministry of Public Works (*Ministerio de Obras Públicas*, or MOP) remained one of the most influential in government. According to a 1977 study by David Myers, "Since the overthrow of General Pérez Jiménez, the Ministry of Public Works has administered either the national government's largest or second largest budget, roughly 20 percent of total expenditures." David J. Myers, "Policy Making and Capital City Resource Allocation: The Case of Caracas," in *Venezuela: The Democratic Experience*, eds. David J. Myers and John D. Martz (New York: Praeger, 1977), 292.

45. Forty-four percent, or 71,000 of its nationwide total, came in Caracas. "71 mil votos rojos en el Distrito Federal hacen del P.C.V. el segundo partido de la capital," *Tribuna Popular*, 20 December 1958.

46. The PCV won 18% in working class districts, compared to AD's 14%, COPEI's 13%, and URD's 46%. Cates, "Venezuelan 1958 election: Phenomenon of the Communist congressional vote."

47. "Cerca de 250 mil personas aclamaron a W. Larrazábal," *Últimas Noticias*, 5 December 1958.

48. In the Zona F alone, of 3,130 votes cast, 85% went to Larrazábal. Overall in the 23 de Enero and other Caracas popular sectors, Larrazábal's vote averaged 70%. "Escándalo en el 23 de Enero."

49. Elsewhere in Caracas Larrazábal took 66% of the vote, to Rafael Caldera's 18% (COPEI) and Romulo Betancourt's 12% (AD). In a class analysis of the Caracas electorate between 1958 and 1968, historians John Martz and Peter Harkins found that in sectors they identified as "upper," "middle," and "lower" class, respectively, in 1958 Larrazábal won with all three segments, while Betancourt lost with all three. John D. Martz and Peter B. Harkins, "Urban Electoral Behavior in Latin America: The Case of Metropolitan Caracas, 1958–1968," *Comparative Politics* 5, no. 4 (1973): 543.

50. There were 2.7 million total votes cast in the December 1958 elections. "Aplastante derrota."

51. "Escándalo en el 23 de Enero."

52. "197 menores de edad fueron detenidos en la protesta contra las elecciones," *Últimas Noticias*, 14 December 1958; "Condenables actos antidemocráticos realizaron en manifestaciones ayer," *Últimas Noticias*, 9 December 1958.

53. "Serán suspendidas en Caracas las garantías constitucionales," *Últimas Noticias*, 9 December 1958.

54. "Ya no será necesario suspender las garantías," *Últimas Noticias*, 11 December 1958.

55. "No podemos convertirnos en unos 'tumba elecciones' expresó Larrazábal a manifestantes en su casa," *Últimas Noticias*, 9 December 1958.

56. Fabricio Ojeda, "Caracas merece respeto," *Últimas Noticias*, 12 December 1958.

57. Servando García Ponce, "Que no se desdiga el pueblo caraqueño," *Últimas Noticias*, 12 December 1958.

58. John M. Cates, "Venezuelan elections 1958: Larrazábal demonstrations on two evenings following election day," *RG59/Central Decimal File, Box 3033/Folder 731.00/10–358*, 16 December 1958.

59. Judith Ewell, *The Indictment of a Dictator: The Extradition and Trial of Marcos Pérez Jiménez* (College Station: Texas A&M University Press, 1981), 117.

60. Mercedes Senior, *El Rómulo Betancourt que yo conocí: Políticos y notables, retratos de medio perfil* (Caracas: Editorial Panapo, 1986), 239–40.

61. Robert J. Alexander, *Venezuela's Voice for Democracy: Conversations and Correspondence with Rómulo Betancourt* (New York: Praeger, 1990), 162.

62. Charles R. Burrows, Edward J. Sparks, and Rómulo Betancourt, "Memorandum of Conversation: Conversation with President-Elect Romulo Betancourt," *RG59/Central Decimal File, Box 2468/Folder 611–31/1–3155*, 14 December 1958.

63. John M. Cates, "Foreign Service Despatch: Venezuelan elections 1958 style," RG59/Central Decimal File, Box 3033/Folder 731.00/10–358, 31 December 1958, 11.

64. "'Nada se ha considerado sobre sanción a Wolfgang,'" *Últimas Noticias*, 26 January 1959.

65. "No hay sanción para Wolfgang Larrazábal acordó ayer la junta superior de las F.A.N.," *Últimas Noticias*, 29 January 1959.

66. Luis Peraza, "¿Quiénes quieren anular al Contralmirante?" *Últimas Noticias*, 29 January 1959.

67. "Manifestaciones de desempleados en la tarde en Palacio Blanco," *Últimas Noticias*, 29 January 1959.

68. "Violenta manifestación de desempleados en Palacio apedreó a la policía e incendió varios vehículos," *Últimas Noticias*, 1 February 1959.

69. "Heridas cinco personas, siete vehículos destruidos en las manifestaciones de ayer," *Últimas Noticias*, 1 February 1959.

70. "'El ejercicio de las libertades públicas no puede confundirse con el bochinche,'" *Últimas Noticias*, 6 February 1959.

71. "Los que invocan mi nombre para fomentar disturbios y alterar el orden no son mis amigos ni estoy con ellos," *Últimas Noticias*, 12 February 1959.

72. "El 23 de Enero: Baluarte de la democracia," *Tribuna Popular*, 21 March 1959.

73. "Amenazadas de muerte por pandillas de rateros 4000 familias del barrio Andrés Eloy Blanco," *Últimas Noticias*, 22 January 1959.

74. "Destrozaron los parques infantiles en la Urb. 23 de Enero," *Últimas Noticias*, 28 January 1959.

75. "Ranchos se están construyendo en las faldas de las urbanizaciones obreras," *Últimas Noticias*, 29 January 1959; "Un nuevo barrio tan problemático como los demás está surgiendo en La Cañada en el 23 de Enero," *Últimas Noticias*, 1 February 1959.

76. "Pagan a 3 y 4 bolívares el agua."

77. Robert G. Cox, Foreign Service Dispatch, 20 March 1959.

78. Rómulo Betancourt, *Mensaje del ciudadano Rómulo Betancourt, Presidente de la República, dirigido a los trabajadores en la noche del 30 de abril de 1959, con motivo de la celebración del 1ro de mayo* (Caracas: Presidencia de la República, 1959).

79. Eric Carlson, "Los problemas de gobierno y trazado en los superbloques de Caracas, estudiados por un equipo internacional," *Journal of Housing* 9 (1959).

80. Eric Carlson, ed. *Proyecto de evaluación de los superbloques* (Caracas: Banco Obrero, 1961), 177–80.

81. Ibid., 182–83.

82. Ibid., 8. By November 1958, 70% of all rent delinquency in BO properties emanated from the 23 de Enero, nearly of all it concentrated in the western blocks. Ibid., 59.

83. Ibid., 32.

84. Ibid., 181–82.

85. Ibid., 173.

86. Over the next decade, through two AD administrations, people would continue to flow to the capital, while policy and resources would flow outside Caracas. Alfredo Cilento Sarli, "La visión estratégica del Banco Obrero en el período 1959–1969," in *Leopoldo Martínez Olavarría: Desarrollo urbano, vivienda y estado*, ed. Alberto Lovera (Caracas: Fondo Editorial Alemo, 1996).

87. Carlson, *Proyecto de evaluación*, 102–3.

88. Luis Lyon Pérez and Rodrigo Tovar C., "La voz de los barrios," *Tribuna Popular*, 5 June 1959.

89. Robert G. Cox, Foreign Service Dispatch, 6 August 1959.

90. Ramón Antonio Villarroel, "La suspensión de garantías no va en contra de los enemigos del pueblo sino contra las masas," *Tribuna Popular*, 14 August 1959.

91. Fabricio Ojeda, "La democracia se defiende democráticamente," *Últimas Noticias*, 10 February 1959.

92. "El 23 de Enero," *Tribuna Popular*, 27 November 1959.

93. Alexander, *Venezuela's Voice for Democracy*, 60.

94. "Concejales y congresantes comunistas en el 23 de Enero," *Tribuna Popular*, 16 October 1959.

95. "Rebaja de alquileres exige Sierra Maestra," *Tribuna Popular*, 7 August 1959; "Sierra Maestra clama por agua," *Tribuna Popular*, 21 August 1959; "Voz Municipal: Fumigación para el 23 de Enero," *Tribuna Popular*, 2 October 1959; "Revisión de medidores de luz piden en el 23 de Enero," *Tribuna Popular*, 26 February 1960; "A tres bolívares el kilo de arroz en el 23 de Enero," *Tribuna Popular*, 11 March 1960.

96. Robert J. Alexander, *The Communist Party of Venezuela* (Stanford, CA: Hoover Institution Press, 1969).

97. Steve Ellner, *Venezuela's Movimiento al Socialismo: From Guerrilla Defeat to Innovative Politics* (Durham, NC: Duke University Press, 1988), 43–44; Velásquez, "Aspectos de la evolución política," 243–49; John D. Martz, *Acción Democrática: Evolution of a Modern Political Party in Venezuela* (Princeton, NJ: Princeton University Press, 1966), 176.

98. Senior, *El Rómulo Betancourt que yo conocí*, 240.

99. Alexander, *Venezuela's Voice for Democracy*, 74.

100. Ibid., 102.

101. Luis Lander, interview with the author, 2005.

102. Alexander, *Venezuela's Voice for Democracy*, 73.

103. Senior, *El Rómulo Betancourt que yo conocí*, 246.

104. Alexander, *Venezuela's Voice for Democracy*, 71.

105. "Suspensión parcial de las garantías constitucionales," *Últimas Noticias*, 25 June 1960.

106. "Caracas será de su pueblo aunque Soto Socorro saque sus cascos," *Tribuna Popular*, 24 August 1960.

107. "De pie el 23 de Enero: 180.000 habitantes reclaman al Congreso investiguen el terror policial," *Tribuna Popular*, 1 September 1960; Carlos Del Vecchio, "La batalla de los barrios," *Tribuna Popular*, 29 September 1960.

108. "Barricadas en Caracas en defensa de Cuba," *Tribuna Popular*, 30 August 1960.

109. Historian Ramón J. Velásquez, later analyzing the *popularazo*, called MIR's statement "typically seditious." Velásquez, "Aspectos de la evolución política," 255–58.

110. "Seis heridos durante incidentes anoche ante el Congreso Nacional," *El Universal*, 20 October 1960.

111. "Reprimirá enérgicamente el gobierno todo intento de subvertir el orden," *El Universal*, 22 October 1960; "Gobierno reprimirá con energía subversión para deponer por la violencia el régimen," *Últimas Noticias*, 22 October 1960.

112. Rómulo Betancourt, "El 94% del pueblo eligió y respalda a este gobierno," *Últimas Noticias*, 19 June 1960.

113. "Jesús Faria responde a Uslar Pietri: Si este régimen quiere seguir llamándose democrático, tiene que hacer algo por el pueblo," *Tribuna Popular*, 10 June 1960.

114. Daniel H. Levine, *Conflict and Political Change in Venezuela* (Princeton, NJ: Princeton University Press, 1973), 49.

115. "Patrulla el Ejército la ciudad," *Últimas Noticias*, 26 October 1960.

116. Ibid.

117. "Un muerto y más de veinte heridos en disturbios de lunes y martes," *El Nacional*, 26 October 1960.

118. "Disturbios durante todo el día en la urbanización 23 de Enero."

119. "Persecución contra dirigentes democráticos en todos los barrios de Catia y 23 de Enero," *Tribuna Popular*, 26 October 1960; "Hombres de la 'Cobra Negra' asaltaron dos residencias," *Últimas Noticias*, 1 November 1963.

120. Asuase Sánchez, interview with the author, 2005.

121. Danilo Aray, interview with the author, 2005.

122. "1500 Guardias Nacionales." Official tallies placed the number at nine dead and ninety wounded over four days of disturbances in Caracas. "9 muertos y 90 heridos balance de cuatro días," *Últimas Noticias*, 28 October 1960.

123. "Cómo actúan las fuerzas represivas," *Tribuna Popular*, 28 October 1960.

124. "Gloria al 23 de Enero: Asesinatos, saqueos y violaciones cometen las fuerzas represivas," *Tribuna Popular*, 29 October 1960.

125. "Decomisaron ametralladoras y revólveres en el 23 de Enero," *Últimas Noticias*, 28 October 1960; "Documentos ocupados demuestran plan subversivo de extremistas," *Últimas Noticias*, 28 October 1960.

126. "Dubuc advierte a extremistas: 'Desistir a tiempo de sus descabellados propósitos de popularazo o quedarán definitivamente aislados,'" *Últimas Noticias*, 26 October 1960.

127. "No se justificaría la existencia de la policía si no defiende el orden público y protege la vida y bienes de los ciudadanos," *El Nacional*, 27 October 1960.

128. "Hemos sufrido bajas por ser condescendientes," *Últimas Noticias*, 29 October 1960.

129. "Suspenden al M.I.R. y Partido Comunista y prohíben todas sus actividades," *Últimas Noticias*, 11 May 1962.

130. "Desórdenes en el 23 de Enero, Lídice, Sarria y otros sectores," *Últimas Noticias*, 5 May 1962.

131. "Explosión en el 23 de Enero: Un muerto," *Últimas Noticias*, 19 June 1962.

132. "Suspendidas las garantías: Ultimátum a los alzados," *Últimas Noticias*, 5 May 1962.

133. The original Spanish reads: *la respuesta del gobierno es la respuesta de las armas.* "'Ellos que me están oyendo; que se rindan porque las órdenes son precisas y claras,'" *Últimas Noticias*, 5 May 1962.

134. "La Corte Suprema de Justicia solicitó allanamiento de Eloy Torres y Sáez Mérida," *Últimas Noticias*, 19 June 1962; "Enjuiciar a Sáez Mérida, Eloy Torres y otras 18 personas ordenó Consejo de Guerra," *Últimas Noticias*, 27 May 1962.

135. Carlos Dorante, ed., *Rómulo Betancourt: Ideas y acción de gobierno: Antología de conceptos, 1959–1964* (Caracas: Ediciones Centauro, 1987), 169.

136. Pérez would go on to preside over Venezuela's bloodiest massacre during a second term as president in 1989, in part after drawing on the 1960s-era Plan Ávila to quell massive urban riots over structural adjustment policies. Alejandro Velasco, "'A Weapon as Powerful as the Vote': Street Protest and Electoral Politics in Caracas, Venezuela, before Hugo Chávez" (Ph.D. Dissertation, Duke University, 2009).

137. Antonio Márquez Mata, "El 23 de enero ganó el pueblo otra batalla: Esta vez contra los rojos," *Últimas Noticias*, 27 January 1963.

138. "Las elecciones son del pueblo no de Betancourt," *Últimas Noticias*, 20 November 1963.

139. "Atacan a tiros patrullas y cuatro carros quemados," *Últimas Noticias*, 20 November 1963.

140. "Intenso tiroteo en el 23 de Enero," *Últimas Noticias*, 21 November 1963.

141. "10 muertos y más de 100 heridos en disturbios de ayer en Caracas," *Últimas Noticias*, 20 November 1963; "5 muertos y 17 heridos fue el balance de ayer," *Últimas Noticias*, 21 November 1963; Alejandro Velasco, interview with the author, 2005.

142. Examining presidential and congressional voting patterns in Caracas for the first decade of democratic governance, political scientists John Martz and Peter Harkins concluded that congressional voting represented "a truer indication of political tendency than [did] the vote for president, which [was] considerably more subject to the influence of personality." Martz and Harkins, "Urban Electoral Behavior in Latin America." Accordingly, this analysis draws from congressional vote results as a more accurate gauge of local voting tendencies than national electoral tallies. For congressional vote statistics by parish, see *Las cuatro primeras fuerzas políticas en Venezuela a nivel municipal, 1958–1978* (Caracas: División de Estadística, Consejo Supremo Electoral, 1983).

143. This time, Larrazábal ran as candidate of the upstart Democratic Electoral Front (Frente Democrático Electoral, or FDP), on a platform of reinstituting the Plan de Emergencia and legalizing the PCV and MIR.

144. AD's support in the 23 de Enero neighborhood dropped from 14.1% to 12.5 %. COPEI's drop was even more dramatic, from 10.9% to 5.2%. Combined, AD and COPEI had lost 7% of the vote as compared to their totals in 1958, bringing their electoral presence in the neighborhood to 17%. Meanwhile URD, the third party of the governing coalition under Betancourt, experienced the most precipitous loss of support, from 50% with Larrazábal as its candidate in 1958, to just over 11% without him in 1963.

145. Levine calculated that during Betancourt's presidency constitutional liberties were suspended five times, for a total of 778 days of the 1,847 days of his term, or 42% of the time. Levine, *Conflict and Political Change in Venezuela,* 50.

4. "THE FIGHT WAS FIERCE"

1. Cristóbal Rodríguez Oberto and Ramón García, "La paz ha vuelto al 23 de Enero, pero el desempleo es su mayor problema," *El Nacional,* 23 January 1965.

2. "Disturbios durante todo el día en la urbanización 23 de Enero," *El Nacional,* 27 October 1960; "Decomisaron ametralladoras y revólveres en el 23 de Enero," *Últimas Noticias,* 28 October 1960; "Cómo actúan las fuerzas represivas," *Tribuna Popular,* 28 October 1960."

3. "El 23 de Enero sin agua desde hace mas de 20 días," *Últimas Noticias,* 30 January 1963.

4. Silveria Ríos, interview with the author, 2005.

5. Lourdes Quintero, interview with the author, 2005.

6. Pedro Pablo Linárez, *La lucha armada en Venezuela* (Caracas: Universidad Bolivariana de Venezuela, 2006), 30–31.

7. Quintero, interview with the author, 2005.

8. Colloquial term used in the 1960s to refer to leftist insurgents.

9. Andrés Vásquez, interview with the author, 2005.

10. Rafael Gutiérrez, interview with the author, 2005.

11. Carlos Palma, interview with the author, 2005.

12. Ravín Asuase Sánchez, interview witht the author, 2005.

13. Palma, interview with the author, 2005.

14. Víctor Hernández, "Piden la creación de una escuela en el barrio de Monte Piedad," *Últimas Noticias*, 8 November 1963.

15. Palma, interview with the author, 2005.

16. Asuase Sánchez, interview with the author, 2005.

17. In fact, says Asuase Sánchez, "here in the 23 de Enero, we had groups that weren't known by all of the [guerrilla] leadership," or even to other units in the community. Ibid.

18. Gutiérrez, interview with the author, 2005.

19. Asuase Sánchez, interview with the author, 2005.

20. Dalila Roa, Elka Larío Roa, and Rosa Amelia de González, interview with the author, 2005.

21. C. Allan Stewart, "Personal Correspondence to Robert E. Woodward," in *RG 59 General Records of the Department of State, Bureau of Inter-American Affairs, Office of East Coast Affairs, Records Relating to Venezuela, 1960–1963* (College Park: NARA II, 1962).

22. "Acción para eliminar comunistas que ocupan cargos en el gobierno anunció el ministro," *Últimas Noticias*, 28 June 1962.

23. L. E. Shuck and Edward T. Long, "Joint Weeka no. 16," in *RG59 General Records of the Department of State, Central Foreign Policy Files—1963* (College Park: NARA II, 1963).

24. "Patrulla el Ejército la ciudad," *Últimas Noticias*, 26 October 1960.

25. Ibid.

26. Frank M. Coffin, "Report of Police Assistance Activities for the Period April 15 to August 1, 1963," in *RG306 U.S. Information Agency, P296 Records Relating to Counterinsurgency Matters, 1962–1966* (College Park: NARA II, 1963).

27. Reinaldo Barquero, "Cómo comenzó el fin de las guerrillas urbanas," *Elite*, 8 June 1967.

28. Gutiérrez, interview with the author, 2005.

29. Gustavo Parabón, interview with the author, 2005.

30. Alexis Alzolay, interview with the author, 2005.

31. Gutiérrez, interview with the author, 2005.

32. "Detenido ayer el presunto cabecilla de saqueadores de la Central Madeirense," *El Universal*, 30 October 1960.

33. Elaya de Delgado, interview with the author, 2005.

34. Leo J. Moser and Edward T. Long, "Joint Weeka no. 16 (April 20)," in *RG59 General Records of the Department of State, Central Foreign Policy Files—1964–1966* (College Park: NARA II, 1964).

35. Rodríguez Oberto and García, "La paz ha vuelto al 23 de Enero."

36. Steve Ellner, *Venezuela's Movimiento al Socialismo: From Guerrilla Defeat to Innovative Politics* (Durham, NC: Duke University Press, 1988), 44–49. Some, like Luis Armáquez of Monte Piedad, would go on to join the guerrillas in the mountains. Others, like Trina Urbina, also of Monte Piedad would die there in 1965. "They were people you wondered, how did they manage up there in the mountains, fighting? Very

affectionate, very kind," recalls Gustavo Parabón. For a detailed narrative account of doctrinal tensions within the guerrilla movement, see George Ciccariello-Maher, *We Created Chávez: A People's History of the Venezuelan Revolution* (Durham, NC: Duke University Press, 2013), 22–44.

37. In September 1966, according to U.S. intelligence officials, guerrilla leader Teodoro Petkoff charged in an editorial in the underground PCV publication *Qué* that "the major threat to the Communist movement is the leftist deviation and not 'the right.' He added that this leftist deviation is a 'militarist conception' reflecting 'astronomical ignorance' of fundamental ideological considerations." Kempton B. Jenkins and Francis W. Herron, "Joint Weeka no. 40 (8 October)," in *RG59 General Records of the Department of State, Central Foreign Policy Files—1964–1966* (College Park: NARA II, 1966).

38. "Ciclismo juvenil en el 23 de Enero," *Últimas Noticias*, 22 January 1966; "Equipos de softball femenino organizan en el 23 de Enero," *Últimas Noticias*, 28 January 1964; "Seleccionado nacional de volibol hará exhibición en el 23 de Enero," *Últimas Noticias*, 20 January 1966; "Entregarán premios en el 23 de Enero de concursos navideños," *Últimas Noticias*, 11 January 1966; "Hoy realizan día deportivo en urbanización 23 de Enero," *Últimas Noticias*, 26 January 1964; Mariahé Pabón, "50 mil niños del 23 de Enero carecen de zonas verdes y de campos adecuados para jugar," *El Nacional*, 23 January 1965.

39. "Inaugurado gimnasio en el 23 de Enero," *Últimas Noticias*, 12 November 1963.

40. "Mujeres del barrio La Libertad reclaman luz, cloacas, y agua," *Tribuna Popular*, 25 March 1960. For more details on this sector of the 23 de Enero, see Chapter 5.

41. Carlos Acevedo Mendoza, *La vivienda en el área metropolitana de Caracas* (Caracas: Ediciones del Cuatricentenario de Caracas, 1967), 90. Acevedo Mendoza reports that the value of new constructions in Caracas dropped from Bs. 511 million in 1959 to Bs. 57 million in 1961, before then roughly doubling each year to Bs. 587 million in 1965.

42. Ibid., 149.

43. Asuase Sánchez, interview with the author, 2005.

44. "El 23 de Enero constituida en nueva parroquia caraqueña," *El Nacional*, 20 October 1966.

45. Rodríguez Oberto and García, "La paz ha vuelto al 23 de Enero."

46. Talton F. Ray, *The Politics of the Barrios of Venezuela* (Berkeley, CA: University of California Press, 1969), 155–56.

47. Bruno Scheuren, "La semana roja del 60," *Elite*, 27 November 1970.

48. Mireya Maldonado, interview with the author, 2005; Vásquez, interview with the author, 2005; Lino Álvarez, interview with the author, 2005; Delgado, interview with the author, 2005; Eloy Deslances, interview with the author, 2005.

49. Luis Lander, interview with the author, 2005.

50. Alfredo Cilento Sarli, "La visión estratégica del Banco Obrero en el período 1959–1969," in *Leopoldo Martínez Olavarría: Desarrollo urbano, vivienda y estado*, ed. Alberto Lovera (Caracas: Fondo Editorial Alemo, 1996).

51. Carlos Villegas, "'No sé qué decir quién ha faltado a la palabra, si Leoni o su allegados' declaró Prieto ayer," *Últimas Noticias*, 7 January 1968.

52. Carlos Villegas, "'No sé qué decir,'" *Últimas Noticias*, 7 January 1968; "Prieto en los barrios," *Últimas Noticias*, 13 January 1968; "Prieto hoy al barrio 23 de Enero," *Últimas Noticias*, 18 January 1967.

53. The final results came in at 19.34% for MEP, 22.22% for the URD, 28.24% for AD, and 29.13% for the winning party, COPEI.

54. Jorge Dager, "Los pactos y los partidos," *Últimas Noticias*, 4 February 1969.

55. Wrote political scientist Daniel Levine in 1973: "The 1968 elections marked the first time power had ever been handed over to an opposition party—with a plurality of barely 30,000 votes out of almost 4 million ballots cast. [Venezuela] has one of the longest and bloodiest histories of military dictatorship in Latin America, has spawned a powerful, highly organized, and far reaching system of mass political parties—a system with few parallels in the region." Daniel H. Levine, *Conflict and Political Change in Venezuela* (Princeton, NJ: Princeton University Press, 1973), 3.

56. CCN had been formed in 1966 as a vehicle for Pérez Jiménez to secure representation in the new government, and receive parliamentary immunity, while imprisoned from May 1964 to August 1968. "Iniciado ayer proceso de legalización de 'Cruzada Cívica Nacionalista,'" *Últimas Noticias*, 19 January 1966. Though formally legalized as a party, CCN was barred from presenting Pérez Jiménez as a presidential candidate. However, CCN was permitted to present candidates for Congress. In 1968, 42% of the CCN's total nationwide vote of 400,000 was cast in Caracas. Of CCN voters in Caracas, most were among working classes, who voted 27.6% for Pérez Jiménez's party. Data compiled from *Las cuatro primeras fuerzas políticas en Venezuela a nivel municipal, 1958–1978* (Caracas: División de Estadística, Consejo Supremo Electoral, 1983).

57. For congressional vote statistics by parish, see *Las cuatro primeras fuerzas*, 19.

58. "Anular elección de Pérez Jiménez a senador dictaminó el Fiscal General de la República," *Últimas Noticias*, 7 February 1969.

59. Ricardo Márquez, "No era elegible Pérez Jiménez de acuerdo con la Ley Electoral, decidió la Corte ayer," *Últimas Noticias*, 10 April 1969.

60. "Por nulidad de elección: Manifestaron airadamente ayer los perezjimenistas," *Últimas Noticias*, 10 April 1969"; "Actos en casas de cruzada de apoyo a Pérez Jiménez," *Últimas Noticias*, 13 April 1969.

61. Party opinions were set forth by David Morales Bello (AD), Luis Guillermo Anduela (COPEI), and Eduardo Machado (PCV). Carlos Villegas, "Divididas las opiniones de dirigentes políticos sobre fallo que anula elección de Pérez Jiménez," *Últimas Noticias*, 10 April 1969.

62. "Pérez Jiménez atribuye anulación de su elección a maniobra política," *Últimas Noticias*, 11 April 1969.

63. Carlos Castillo, "'Tres o cuatro han anulado la voluntad de 160 mil electores que votaron por mí': Expresó el General Pérez Jiménez ayer al conocer la nulidad de elección," *Últimas Noticias*, 10 April 1969.

64. John D. Martz and Peter B. Harkins, "Urban Electoral Behavior in Latin America: The Case of Metropolitan Caracas, 1958–1968," *Comparative Politics* 5, no. 4 (1973): 543.

65. URD's candidate, Miguel Ángel Burelli Rivas, edged out Caldera 27.3% to 27.2% in Caracas, although among the working class—including the 23 de Enero—the margin was larger: 28.5% to 24.3%, respectively. Ibid.

66. Ibid., 541.

67. Brian Crisp, Daniel Levine, and José Molina, "The Rise and Decline of COPEI in Venezuela," in *Christian Democracy in Latin America: Electoral Competition and Regime Conflicts*, eds. Scott Mainwaring and Timothy Scully (Stanford, CA: Stanford University Press, 2003), 284.

68. Steve Ellner, *Organized Labor in Venezuela, 1958–1991: Behavior and Concerns in a Democratic Setting* (Wilmington, DE: SR Books, 1993). John Duncan Powell, *Political Mobilization of the Venezuelan Peasant* (Cambridge, MA: Harvard University Press, 1971).

69. In *the* 23 de Enero, COPEI slipped behind not just AD and the CCN, but also the People's Electoral Movement (*Movimiento Electoral del Pueblo*, or MEP), a left-wing AD splinter group. *Las cuatro primeras fuerzas.*

5. WATER, WOMEN, AND PROTEST

1. "Enardecidos por la falta de agua habitantes del 23 de Enero bloquearon las avenidas con barricadas," *El Nacional*, 5 May 1969.

2. Jesús Petit Medina, "Barricadas y disparos: Tomado el 23 de Enero por sus habitantes como protesta por llevar 3 días sin agua," *Últimas Noticias*, 5 May 1969.

3. Ibid.

4. "No se debe llegar a la violencia para pedir regularidad de un servicio," *El Universal*, 6 May 1969.

5. "El barrio La Libertad tuvo agua ayer durante todo el día," *El Nacional*, 6 May 1969.

6. "Consideran represalia contra el sector falta de agua en el 23 de Enero," *Últimas Noticias*, 7 May 1969.

7. Petit Medina, "Barricadas y disparos."

8. "El barrio La Libertad tuvo agua."

9. "Consideran represalia contra el sector."

10. It was the "first time power had ever been handed over to an opposition party—with a plurality of barely 30,000 votes out of almost 4 million ballots cast." Daniel H. Levine, *Conflict and Political Change in Venezuela* (Princeton, NJ: Princeton University Press, 1973).

11. "Las guerrillas un problema de tipo político, no militar, declara nuevo titular de defensa," *Últimas Noticias*, 12 March 1969.

12. Steve Ellner, *Venezuela's Movimiento Al Socialismo: From Guerrilla Defeat to Innovative Politics* (Durham, NC: Duke University Press, 1988).

13. "Hoy se reúne primer Comité Central del Partido Comunista legalmente," *Últimas Noticias*, 29 March 1969; UPI, "Afirma Betancourt: Rehabilitación del P.C.V. responde a disposiciones legales de Caldera," *Últimas Noticias*, 29 March 1969.

14. A recent study of USAID-sponsored police training and assistance programs in Caracas argues that efforts at professionalizing police services in the early and mid-1960s, though considered a success by U.S. officials, in fact overestimated the extent to which policing rather than militarization accounted for the tactical defeat of insurgents. David Romine, "Professional Police Work and Politics Do Not Mix: An Episode in the Alliance for Progress in Venezuela, 1961–1964" (master's thesis, New York University, 2010).

15. See also Decrees 14 and 15. Rafael Caldera, "Presidencia de la República, Decreto No. 16," *Gaceta Oficial de la República de Venezuela* Año XCVII—Mes VI, no. 28.878 (1969).

16. *Exposición, memoria y cuenta del año 1969 presentada por el Gobernador del Distrito Federal Carlos Guinand Baldó al ilustre Concejo Municipal* (Caracas: Imprenta Municipal, 1970), 19–21.

17. Jesús Petit Medina, "Reestructuración de la Policía Municipal anunció Comandante González Medici," *Últimas Noticias*, 16 March 1969; "Tomó posesión nuevo comandante de policía municipal del D.F.," *Últimas Noticias*, 18 April 1969.

18. "Enardecidos por la falta de agua."

19. Petit Medina, "Barricadas y disparos."

20. "Enardecidos por la falta de agua."

21. "Sobre falta de agua interpelarán hoy a funcionarios del I.N.O.S.," *El Universal*, 6 May 1969.

22. "El barrio La Libertad tuvo agua."

23. "Un nuevo sesgo en la manifestación popular," *Últimas Noticias*, 11 May 1969.

24. Jesús Petit Medina, "Tomaron habitantes calle de Propatria en protesta por aguas negras en plena vía," *Últimas Noticias*, 18 May 1969; INNAC, "Protesta pública de habitantes de El Palmar," *El Universal*, 7 May 1969; INNAC, "Protesta contra el Concejo realizaron vecinos de Los Teques," *El Universal*, 7 May 1969; "En emergencia urbanización 'Carlos Guinand' por llevar 18 días sin recibir servicio de agua," *Últimas Noticias*, 8 May 1969.

25. Jose Hernán Briceño, "Caracas alcanzó ayer 2,615,484 habitantes pero no nos alegremos, porque el 44.9 por ciento de esa población vive en la marginalidad," *El Nacional*, 10 August 1973.

26. J. R. Hurtado, "El problema del agua afecta a toda la ciudad," *El Universal*, 7 May 1969; "Si falta agua en el 23 de Enero se debe a que no han hecho la avenida Panteón," *Últimas Noticias*, 16 May 1969; "A largo plazo se resolverá problema de escasez de agua en la urbanización 23 de Enero," *El Universal*, 8 May 1969.

27. "Ausencia de planteles educacionales tiene a diez mil niños sin enseñanza," *Últimas Noticias*, 7 May 1969.

28. Jesús Petit Medina, "La Cañada pide empotramiento de insalubres aguas negras," *Últimas Noticias*, 8 May 1969; Jesús Petit Medina, "Epidemias amenazan el Oeste al continuar falta de agua," *Últimas Noticias*, 9 May 1969; Jesús Petit Medina, "Problema de la basura y aguas negras puede originar epidemias en 23 de Enero," *Últimas Noticias*, 16 May 1969; Jesús Petit Medina, "Se ahogan en basura y alimañas habitantes del 23 de

Enero," *Últimas Noticias*, 13 May 1969; "Salubridad pública en rueda de prensa," *Últimas Noticias*, 23 May 1969; Jesús Petit Medina, "Controlado brote de fiebre infecciosa en carapas de urbanización 23 de Enero," *Últimas Noticias*, 31 May 1969.

29. Jesús Petit Medina, "Nuevos agrietamientos alarman a familias del 23 de Enero," *Últimas Noticias*, 20 May 1969; Jesús Petit Medina, "Barrios del sector Oeste angustiados por la llegada de los aguaceros," *Últimas Noticias*, 8 May 1969.

30. Jesús Petit Medina, "En urbanización 23 de Enero: Actividades sociales, culturales y reivindicativas se propone realizar asociación Juventud en Marcha," *Últimas Noticias*, 12 May 1969.

31. Hipólito Rondón and Sánchez Nada, interview with the author, 2005.

32. "Por orden del Presidente sigue al servicio de la comunidad el Centro Cristo Rey del 23 de Enero," *El Nacional*, 19 June 1974; "Vanguardia musical venezolana ofrecerá concierto popular en la parroquia 23 de Enero," *El Nacional*, 15 May 1969.

33. Comisión Pro-Biblioteca, *Proyecto: Biblioteca 23 de Enero* (Instituto Autónomo Biblioteca Nacional, 1974).

34. Carmen Paiva and Pastora de Guevara, interview with the author, 2005.

35. "Muerto a tiros presunto traficante de marihuana cuando fue sorprendido," *Últimas Noticias*, 14 January 1965; "Descubren sembrado de marihuana frente a un internado religioso," *Últimas Noticias*, 4 May 1962.

36. "Violent crime" here reported as *hechos de sangre*, including assaults, stabbings, and murder—of which there were 8 in 1967 (when neighborhood-level statistics were first reported after the 23 de Enero was formally designated a parish), and 9 in 1968. Between 1967 and 1971, when the series ends, the 23 de Enero reported 106, 122, 109, 129, and 97 yearly incidents of violent crime, respectively, corresponding to 10th, 8th, 9th, 10th, and 12th of 16 parishes in the district. Crime statistics drawn from: *Estadística Delictiva 1971: Policial, Penitenciaria, Criminal* (Caracas: Ministerio de Justicia, 1972); *Estadística Delictiva 1970: Policial, Penitenciaria, Criminal* (Caracas: Ministerio de Justicia, 1971); *Estadística Delictiva 1969: Policial, Penitenciaria, Criminal* (Caracas: Ministerio de Justicia, 1970); *Estadística Delictiva 1959–1968: Policial, Penitenciaria, Criminal* (Caracas: Ministerio de Justicia, 1970).

37. "Pandilla de jóvenes drogados incendió otra vez una vivienda," *El Universal*, 8 May 1969 ; Jesús Petit Medina, "Centro de distribución de marihuana allanó la PTJ en el 23 de Enero," *Últimas Noticias*, 4 May 1969; "En apartamento del 23 de Enero funcionaba un centro de distribución de marihuana," *El Nacional*, 4 May 1969; "Banda de consumidores de drogas capturó la policía en 23 de Enero," *Últimas Noticias*, 9 February 1969.

38. *Detenciones y decomisos por estupefacientes* (Caracas: Ministerio de Justicia, 1973); *Estadística Delictiva 1974: Policial, Penitenciaria, Criminal* (Caracas: Ministerio de Justicia, 1975).

39. Jesús Petit Medina, "Madres del 23 de Enero fundarán centro en memoria de Rosita de Ratto-Ciarlo," *Últimas Noticias*, 23 April 1969.

40. Jesús Petit Medina, "Centro de Madres Rosita de Ratto-Ciarlo será inaugurado en Bloques 23 de Enero," *Últimas Noticias*, 11 May 1969.

41. "Gas directo y teléfonos para el 23 de Enero exige Comité por Unidad de mujeres," *Tribuna Popular*, 7 May 1970.

42. Dalila Roa, Elka Larío Roa, and Rosa Amelia de González, interview with the author, 2005.

43. Ángel C. Rivas, "Tribuna del 23," *Tribuna Popular*, 10 July 1969.

44. "T. P. en Bloques del 23 de Enero," *Tribuna Popular*, 31 July 1969; "El Banco desaloja y la policía atropella en el 23 de Enero," *Tribuna Popular*, 21 August 1969; "El barrio Sucre del 23 de Enero en pie de guerra contra el desalojo," *Tribuna Popular*, 16 October 1969; Héctor Marcano Coello, "Agua para el 23 de Enero," *Tribuna Popular*, 15 May 1969; "Ni agua ni aseo urbano en barrio Sucre del 23 de Enero," *Tribuna Popular*, 16 July 1970; "5 días sin agua y 2 sin luz en el Bloque 45 del 23 de Enero," *Tribuna Popular*, 9 April 1970; "Sin resolver problema de escuela 23 de Enero," *Tribuna Popular*, 28 September 1971.

45. "Células PCV visitan barrios Sucre y Arbolitos," *Tribuna Popular*, 2 October 1969; "Célula Ho Chi Minh del 23 de Enero instaló su conferencia," *Tribuna Popular*, 29 October 1970; "Cena de la Fraternidad Comunista este viernes, auspiciada por el P.C.V. del 23 de Enero," *Tribuna Popular*, 14 May 1970; Rafael Thielen Apitz, "La campaña contra la conferencia del 23 de Enero," *Tribuna Popular*, 9 April 1970; "Gustavo Machado inauguró casa del P.C.V. en Catia–23 de Enero," *Tribuna Popular*, 19 April 1971; "Gran acto en el 23 de Enero," *Tribuna Popular*, 1 October 1971.

46. Roa, Roa, and González, interview with the author, 2005.

47. "Consultorio *Jesús Yerena* en el 23 de Enero," *Tribuna Popular*, 27 August 1970; "En el 23 de Enero: Inaugurado consulturio médico gratuito *Jesús Yerena*," *Tribuna Popular*, 3 September 1970.

48. Carlos Acevedo Mendoza, *La vivienda en el área metropolitana de Caracas* (Caracas: Ediciones del Cuatricentenario de Caracas, 1967), 147.

49. Josefina Hernández de Machado, Pedro Gerardo Cádiz, Diego Carvallo, and Nuria Márquez, interview with the author, 2005.

50. Rondón and Nada, interview with the author, 2005.

51. Ibid.; Francisco Suárez, interview with the author, 2005.

52. Pérez took 48.7% of the vote compared to 36.7% for Fernández.

53. See graph of electoral trends in Figure 26.

54. Briceño, "Caracas alcanzó ayer."

55. Tulio Leyton, "Falta de agua cobra características dramáticas en barrios y urbanizaciones," *Últimas Noticias*, 4 October 1976.

56. Freddy Urbina, "Un joven muerto de balazo, otro herido, y numerosos intoxicados durante disturbios en el 23 de Enero," *Últimas Noticias*, 1 October 1976

57. Jesús Eduardo Brando, "Muertos a tiros dos menores en manifestación de protesta por falta de agua," *El Nacional*, 4 November 1977.

58. Freddy Urbina, "Murió uno de los niños heridos en tiroteo durante disturbios en sector del 23 de Enero," *Últimas Noticias*, 7 October 1978; Francisco Gómez, "Murió el otro joven herido durante disturbios en 23 de Enero," *Últimas Noticias*, 8 October 1978.

59. Coromoto Álvarez, "De 'maniáticos del desorden' califica Mantilla a quienes participan en sabotajes en Caracas," *Últimas Noticias*, 7 October 1978.

60. Coromoto Álvarez, "'Sucesos como los del 23 de Enero hacen más graves las deficiencias existentes en los servicios públicos,'" *Últimas Noticias*, 7 October 1978.

61. Ravin Asuase Sánchez, interview with the author, 2005.

62. "Jefes guerrilleros fueron detenidos al inscribirse en servicio militar," *Últimas Noticias*, 12 January 1968.

63. Gustavo Parabón, interview with the author, 2005.

64. Harassing long-haired men was a nationwide phenomenon in the late 1960s and early 1970s, but testimonies from then-youths in the 23 de Enero also include references to arbitrary shaving by police. "Melenudos acusan a policías de perseguirles injustamente," *Últimas Noticias*, 17 March 1969; "Los melenudos no serán molestados dice prefecto," *Últimas Noticias*, 10 April 1969; "Ofensiva en Estado Bolívar contra hippies y melenudos," *Últimas Noticias*, 12 April 1969; "Batida contra melenudos prosigue la policía en el centro de Caracas," *Últimas Noticias*, 2 July 1967.

65. Andrés Vásquez, interview with the author, 2005; "5 heridos en la balacera: Mataron a liceísta en el 23 de Enero," *Últimas Noticias*, 15 March 1978.

66. Database *El Bravo Pueblo* (Caracas: Universidad Central de Venezuela), accessed 2006.

67. "Desalojados jóvenes del 23 de Enero del único local donde realizaban actividades culturales," *El Nacional*, 1 June 1974.

68. "Por orden del Presidente."

69. Milvia Pacheco, Elba A. Ramos, and Mirian R. Rangel R., "Aproximación al estudio de la parroquia 23 de Enero de Caracas" (Ph.D. dissertation, Universidad Central de Venezuela, 1987), 124.

70. José Manuel Pérez, "Bochinches en el 23 de Enero por falta de agua con participación de encapuchados con armas largas," *Últimas Noticias*, 6 October 1978.

71. Gustavo Rodríguez, interview with the author, 2005.

72. Brian F. Crisp, *Democratic Institutional Design: The Powers and Incentives of Venezuelan Politicians and Interest Groups* (Stanford, CA: Stanford University Press, 2000), 32.

73. Brian Crisp, Daniel Levine, and José Molina, "The Rise and Decline of COPEI in Venezuela," in *Christian Democracy in Latin America: Electoral Competition and Regime Conflicts*, eds. Scott Mainwaring and Timothy Scully (Stanford, CA: Stanford University Press, 2003), 284.

74. All electoral data compiled from *Las cuatro primeras fuerzas políticas en Venezuela a nivel municipal, 1958–1978* (Caracas: División de Estadística, Consejo Supremo Electoral, 1983) and Ezequiel Zamora, ed., *Los partidos políticos y sus estadísticas electorales, 1946–1984*, vol. 1 (Caracas: Consejo Supremo Electoral, 1987). Between 1958 and 1988, Venezuelans cast two ballots every five years, one for president and one for the Congressional delegation, which was selected by voting for a party.

75. According to census data compiled by CEPAL (Comisión Económica para América Latina y el Caribe), in 1970 Venezuela's urban population was 71% of the

national total, increasing to 76% by 1975, and to 79% by 1980. Unless otherwise noted, population data is from the CEPAL online statistical database, CEPALSTAT, available at www.eclac.org/estadisticas/bases/.

76. Briceño, "Caracas alcanzó ayer."

77. Antonio de Liso, "La evolución urbana de Caracas: Indicadores e interpretaciones sobre el desarrollo de la interrelación ciudad-naturaleza," *Revista Geográfica Venezolana* 42, no. 2 (2001): 219.

78. Robert O'Connor, "The Electorate," in *Venezuela at the Polls: The National Elections of 1978*, ed. Howard R. Penniman (Washington, DC: American Enterprise Institute, 1980), 57–58.

79. This was a nationwide face-to-face poll of 1,521 adults. Asked "When did you first have to vote for president?" 26% answered 1947, 23% answered 1958, 11% answered 1963, and 18% answered 1968. Until 1989, voting in Venezuela was compulsory for everyone over age 18. The first direct elections were held in 1947, but the government was deposed seven months into its term by a military coup that would install a ten-year dictatorship. Enrique Baloyra and John Martz, "Baloyra/Martz Poll # 1973-Baloyra: 1973 Pre-Election Poll—Basic Political Attitudes of the Venezuelan People" (Caracas: Universidad Simón Bolívar, 1973).

80. This was a nationwide face-to-face poll of 1,130 young adults between 18 and 22 years of age, conducted in early 1978. In the "index of political participation," 73% reported "passive" participation, 12% reported "very active" participation. "Gallup Poll # 1978-Gm033a: Political Attitudes among the Youth," (Caracas: Gallup, C.A., 1978).

81. Ibid. Among youth responding to the question "If elections were held today, for whom would you vote?" 10% said J. V. Rangel of MAS, 2% backed L. B. Prieto Figueroa of MEP, and 5% backed Américo Martín, a former Marxist guerrilla of MIR. In a separate nationwide face-to-face poll of 2,260 adults conducted in September 1977, for the same voter-intention question, Rangel returned 8%, Prieto Figueroa 2%, and Martín 1%. "Electorate Perceptions on the 1978 Presidential Campaign," (Caracas: Datos, C.A., 1977).

82. In 1968, even as COPEI won the presidency for the first time in elections widely seen as marking the consolidation of Venezuelan democracy, it came in third in the Caracas congressional vote, behind parties nominally to its left (AD) and right (CCN). In elections in 1958, 1963, and 1968, COPEI placed no better than third in the 23 de Enero, returning a high of 12% of the vote in 1968. In 1973, as the political system coalesced around AD and COPEI, COPEI more than doubled its 1968 total to reach 28% of the vote in the 23 de Enero. *Las cuatro primeras fuerzas*, 19.

83. Donald L. Herman, "The Christian Democratic Party," in *Venezuela at the Polls: The National Election of 1978*, ed. Howard R. Penniman (Washington, DC: American Enterprise Institute, 1980), 139.

84. Lino Álvarez, interview with the author, 2005.

85. Ibid.

86. Silveria Ríos, interview with the author, 2005.

87. Robert O'Connor, "The Media and the Campaign," in *Venezuela at the Polls: The National Election of 1978*, ed. Howard R. Penniman (Washington, DC: American

Enterprise Institute, 1980), 181–83. Indeed in 1971, 70% of Caracas households had at least one television; in the 23 de Enero the number was 78%. By decade's end, 88% of households had televisions. República de Venezuela, *X Censo de Población y Vivienda: Resumen por Entidades Federales*, ed. Dirección Nacional de Estadística y Censos Nacionales, vol. 8E (Caracas Ministerio de Fomento, 1976), 10; República de Venezuela, *XI Censo General de Población y Vivienda (20 de Octubre de 1981): Distrito Federal* (Caracas: Oficina Central de Estadística e Informática, 1985), 922.

88. Lyon Pérez, "Vanguardia comunista reafirmó su apoyo a Luis Herrera Campíns para Presidente," *Últimas Noticias*, 22 August 1977; Lyon Pérez, "COPEI se niega a 'acompañar a A.D. en su actitud anticomunista,'" *Últimas Noticias*, 2 October 1976

89. "Electorate Perceptions on the 1978 Presidential Campaign."

90. José Agustín Silva Michelena and Heinz Sonntag, *El proceso electoral de 1978: Su perspectiva histórica estructural* (Caracas: Editorial Ateneo, 1979), 131–33. Michelena and Sonntag's study of the 1978 electoral process describes how corruption and public services were the two main issues on which candidates focused.

91. After falling in the first year of Herrera Campín's administration, investments in water and electric services rose from −2% in 1974, to 31%, 41%, and 77% in 1975, 1976, and 1977, respectively, before falling again to 4% in 1978. *Cuentas Nacionales (Capítulos I-II-III)*, ed. Ignacio Antivero, 6 vols., Series estadísticas de Venezuela de los últimos cincuenta años, vol. 1 (Caracas: Banco Central de Venezuela, 1994), 306–307.

92. Michelena and Sonntag, 127–28.

93. "Faltan agua y aseo urbano en Bloques 23 de Enero," *El Universal*, 27 January 1958.

94. Germán Borregales, "Urbanización 23 de Enero y desaseo dominical," *Últimas Noticias*, 27 January 1966.

95. Diógenes Santander, "Falta de aseo urbano, escuelas, dispensarios y parques infantiles son problemas del 23 de Enero," *Últimas Noticias*, 21 January 1966.

96. Jesús Petit Medina, "Montañas de basura acumuladas en urbanización 23 de Enero," *Últimas Noticias*, 9 January 1970.

97. "Ni agua ni aseo urbano en barrio Sucre"

98. In the 23 de Enero, the program served the Mirador, Alfredo Rojas, La Cruz, Sans Souci, Unido, and Colinas barrios. *Memoria y cuenta del año 1974 presentada por el Gobernador del Distrito Federal Diego Arria al ilustre Concejo Municipal* (Caracas: Imprenta Municipal, 1974).

99. The two barrios were Observatorio and Atlántico. *Memoria y cuenta del año 1975 presentada por el Gobernador del Distrito Federal Diego Arria al ilustre Concejo Municipal* (Caracas: Imprenta Municipal, 1976).

100. "El Instituto Metropolitano de Aseo Urbano recolecta hoy el 47 por ciento más de basura," *Últimas Noticias*, 26 August 1977.

101. J. A. Pérez Díaz, "Bases del Programa de Gobierno del Dr. Luis Herrera Campíns, Candidato Presidencial del Partido Social Cristiano COPEI (I Congreso Social Cristiano Nacional, 19 Agosto 1977)," in *Mi compromiso con Venezuela*, ed. Luis Herrera Campíns (Caracas: COPEI, 1978).

102. Luis Herrera Campíns, *Mi compromiso con Venezuela: Programa de Gobierno para el período 1979–1984*, vol. 1 (Caracas: COPEI, 1978), xv.

103. Asked in early 1977 what issues should be of "immediate" priority for a new administration, respondents answered: (1) reduce the cost of living, (2) fight crime, (3) build more schools, (4) create jobs, (5) support agriculture, (6) improve living conditions for the poor, (7) build more public housing, (8) eliminate corruption, (9) improve medical care, (10) improve public services, (11) help the elderly, (12) improve collective work ethic, (13) improve public administration, (14) improve roads, (15) distribute wealth better, (16) control private industry, (17) promote arts and science, (18) promote decentralization. This was a nationwide face-to-face poll of 2,260 adults. "Electorate Perceptions on the 1978 Presidential Campaign."

104. Herrera Campíns, 197.

105. Ibid., 207.

106. Pérez Díaz, "Bases del Programa de Gobierno," 411.

107. In testimony repeated often among older resident of the 23 de Enero, Emilia de Pérez of Block 27 recalls that during the most intense periods of urban guerrilla conflict in the 1960s, she could hear neighbors screaming "Pérez Jiménez forgive us for we knew not what we were doing!" at the National Guardsmen posted below from their apartment balconies. Emilia de Pérez, interview with the author, 2005.

108. Baloyra and Martz, Poll # 1973. This was a nationwide face-to-face poll of 1,521 Venezuelans. Question 111 asked: "Do you believe people like you have or do not have the power to influence what the government does?" Question 113 asked: "Finally, do you believe that voting is the only way you can influence what the government does?"

109. "Gallup Poll # 1978-Gm033a: Political Attitudes among the Youth."

110. For those wanting to replace democracy, choices included Socialism, military, strong, more-responsive, dictatorship, Communism, and other systems. Out of this group,45% thought a "Socialist" system should follow. The next highest response was "other systems," at 13%. "Electorate Perceptions on the 1978 Presidential Campaign."

111. "Gallup Poll # 1978-Gm033a: Political Attitudes among the Youth."

112. According to Crisp, Levine, and Molina, "subsidiarity refers to the notion that state institutions, state-sponsored initiatives, and state interventions generally should be subordinate to civil society. The basic formations of society, above all family and church but also private economic organizations, are primary." Crisp, Levine, and Molina, "The Rise and Decline of COPEI in Venezuela," 277–78.

113. Steve Ellner, *Rethinking Venezuelan Politics: Class, Conflict, and the Chávez Phenomenon* (Boulder, CO: Lynne Rienner Publishers, 2008), 77.

114. Luis Herrera Campíns, "Promoción popular y Concejo (01–31–69)," in *Palenque*, ed. Guillermo Yepes Boscán (Maracaibo: Fondo Editorial IRFES, 1979), 184–85.

115. Ellner, *Rethinking Venezuelan Politics*, 77–78.

116. Luis Herrera Campíns, "De la democracia representativa a la democracia participativa," in *Seminario de Democracia Participativa* (paper presented at the Seminario de Democracia Participativa, Caracas, Venezuela, September, 1972), 4–15.

117. Donald L. Herman, *Christian Democracy in Venezuela* (Chapel Hill: University of North Carolina Press, 1980), 103.

118. J. Lossada Rondón, "Instalará Herrera Campíns seminario sobre democracia participativa," *El Nacional*, 22 January 1977; "COPEI hará su programa de gobierno con las conclusiones del seminario 'Hacia una democracia participativa,'" *El Nacional*, 30 January 1977.

119. Pérez Díaz, "Bases del Programa de Gobierno," 414.

120. Herrera Campíns, *Mi compromiso con Venezuela*, xii.

121. In Congressional balloting in the 23 de Enero, though it still trailed AD by 2 percentage points, as a party COPEI increased its support from 28% in 1973 to 32%, marking a full 20 percentage-point rise since 1968.

6. "A WEAPON AS POWERFUL AS THE VOTE"

1. Luis Herrera Campíns, *Mi compromiso con Venezuela: Programa de gobierno para el período 1979–1984*, vol. 1 (Caracas: COPEI, 1978), 197.

2. Earles Gutiérrez, interview with the author, 2005.

3. "'Secuestraron' a cuatro camiones del I.M.A.U.," *Diario de Caracas*, 21 December 1981.

4. Gutiérrez, interview with the author, 2005: " . . . *las trabajadoras de la casa, las que sienten más el problema.*"

5. Gilberto Carreño, "Las mujeres del 23 de Enero secuestraron vehículos oficiales y privados," *El Universal*, 22 December 1981; Gutiérrez, interview with the author, 2005: "*[los] que nunca participaban y siempre acusaban de sapo.*"

6. "'Secuestraron' a cuatro camiones."

7. "L.H.C. 'furioso' dio 48 horas a los servicios públicos," *Diario de Caracas*, 23 December 1981.

8. "En el 23 de Enero siguen secuestrando vehículos oficiales," *El Nacional*, 8 January 1982.

9. María Laura Lombardi, "¿Se justifica el secuestro de un camión?" *El Nacional*, 21 January 1982.

10. Daisy Argotte, "El regalo de Caricuao llegó en barriles de basura: Otra parroquia que amenaza con hacer crisis al estilo 23 de Enero," *Diario de Caracas*, 29 December 1981.

11. Lyon Pérez, "Gobierno de concertación nacional propone Betancourt para salvar la democracia," *Últimas Noticias*, 21 February 1981.

12. Desirée Santos Amaral, "Directamente al abismo va la democracia venezolana," *Últimas Noticias*, 2 February 1981.

13. Elisabeth J. Friedman, *Unfinished Transitions: Women and the Gendered Development of Democracy in Venezuela, 1936–1996* (University Park, PA: Penn State University Press, 2000).

14. *Inventario nacional de barrios: Estudio diagnóstico de los barrios urbanos de Venezuela*, 8 vols. (Caracas: Fundación para el Desarrollo de la Comunidad y Fomento Municipal, 1979).

15. Database *El Bravo Pueblo* (Caracas: Universidad Central de Venezuela), accessed 2006.

16. That the President himself appointed the 23 de Enero's *jefa civil* was a highly unorthodox move. Legally, the designation of *jefes civiles* in Caracas parishes fell to the Caracas governor, a figure directly appointed by the President. As a political appointee, the governor of Caracas had customarily also used the appointment of *jefes civiles* to cement political patronage. But in Herrera Campíns's case, he had tapped Delgado for the position on a whim while talking with a local-area resident after attending Mass at the Cristo Rey Church in the Zona Central of the 23 de Enero. According to Manuel Mir, Delgado's father, a longtime COPEI activist and resident of the neighborhood, approached Herrera Campíns and introduced him to his daughter, recently graduated from law school. "You will be *jefa civil,*" the President-elect reportedly said. Manuel Mir, interview with the author, 2005.

17. "Manos criminales incendiaron centro cultural 'Voz del Mirador,'" *Tribuna Popular,* 4–10 September 1981.

18. Lisandro Pérez, interview with the author, 2005. Pérez, a lifelong resident of one of the squatter settlement communities in the 23 de Enero, had been a militant of underground guerilla organization Bandera Roja during his teens in the early 1980s, becoming a cadre by the mid 1980s. He recalls that on at least two occasions between 1980 and 1983 Delgado interceded on his behalf when Metropolitan Police detained him for his political work. In an ironic turn, in 2005 Pérez became *jefe civil* of the 23 de Enero after local groups resisted the appointee of Caracas's pro-Chávez mayor.

19. Juan Contreras, interview with the author, 2005.

20. "La comunidad se unió a la policía para combatir a los delincuentes," *El Nacional,* 31 December 1979.

21. Rafael García, "Hay que tomar en cuenta al 23 de Enero para los Panamericanos," *Últimas Noticias,* 12 February 1981.

22. COPEI took 51% of the vote nationally to AD's 31%; in Caracas, COPEI candidates claimed 49% of the vote to AD's 28%. *Las cuatro primeras fuerzas políticas en Venezuela a nivel municipal, 1958–1978* (Caracas: División de Estadística, Consejo Supremo Electoral, 1983).

23. David Myers, "The Elections and the Evolution of Venezuela's Party System," in *Venezuela at the Polls: The National Elections of 1978,* ed. Howard R. Penniman (Washington, DC: American Enterprise Institute for Public Policy Research, 1980), 240.

24. Terry Lynn Karl, *The Paradox of Plenty: Oil Booms and Petro-States* (Berkeley, CA: University of California Press, 1997), 176, 247–49.

25. In early 1980 a Gallup poll showed that 64% of Venezuelans considered their family's living standards to have increased or stayed the same during the previous year, reflecting the offsetting impact of rising costs and rising wages. "Political Opinion in Venezuela" (Caracas: Gallup, C.A., 1980). Question 10 asked about living standards: "People's living standards are measured by what they can purchase and what they actually do purchase. In general terms, do you believe your family's living standards

have risen (0), dropped (2), or stayed the same (1) in the past year?" Responses: 0: 404; 1: 712; 2: 597; did not know: 11. Venezuelan economist Pedro Palma details six primary reasons for inflation's continued rise during this period, among them "the compulsive rise of wages and salaries in accordance to the Wage and Salary Increase Law in effect since January 1980, which was not met by a parallel increase in productivity." This combination of greater spending power and output levels that were slow to rise resulted in higher competition for a similar numbers of goods, pushing prices up. Pedro A. Palma, "La economía venezolana en el período 1974–1988," in *Venezuela contemporánea, 1974–1989*, ed. Pedro Grases (Caracas: Fundación Eugenio Mendoza, 1989), 194–95.

26. Seventy-four percent considered it among the government's three worst moves. "Political Opinion in Venezuela." Questions 5, 6, and 7 asked about government policy: "Tell us three things the current government did badly or did not do and should have?" Q5: Removing price controls (765); Q6: Removing price controls (353); Q7: Removing price controls (160).

27. Juan de Onís, "Venezuela's Woes Hurt Leader's Image," *New York Times*, 17 March 1980.

28. Warren Hoge, "Oil Wealth Turns Venezuela into Provider of Foreign Aid," *New York Times*, 23 November 1980.

29. "Estamos conscientes de que no basta hablar de participación para evidenciar que tenemos un sistema democrático," *El Universal*, 6 December 1981.

30. "Despite Its Wealth, Caracas Sits in Garbage and Smog," *New York Times*, 17 March 1980.

31. Details of IMAU's restructuring appear in the Natural Resources and Environment Ministry's 1983 yearly report, corresponding to activities undertaken in 1982. José Joaquín Cabrera Malo, *Memoria y cuenta: Año 1983* (Caracas: Ministerio del Ambiente y de los Recursos Naturales Renovables, 1983), 66–68, 345–46, 369.

32. Soon after Buniak's arrest, an informant tipped media about corruption reaching far deeper into the IMAU, casting Buniak as a "lowly operator" thrown out to divert attention from an extortion ring at the highest levels. Portraying the IMAU as a mafia, the informant claimed "many, many people [were] involved," chief among them a high-level "capo" who had collected "tens of millions [of bolívares] . . . for almost a year by authorizing contracts with certain businessmen and by [taking a] cut on everything that the IMAU pays on those contracts." Ricardo Márquez, "'Capo' en irregularidades del I.M.A.U. es un muy alto personaje que permanece oculto," *Últimas Noticias*, 1 February 1981.

33. In mid-February, Arias testified for seven hours before a grand jury. On leaving, he vowed to testify "as many times as needed" to clear IMAU's name and proceed with its restructuring. "I don't just want to clear the trash in the streets," he stressed, "but also all the trash in the IMAU." Ricardo Márquez, "Durante 7 horas declaró presidente del I.M.A.U. ante tribunal que investiga corrupción en ese instituto," *Últimas Noticias*, 14 February 1981.

34. Ricardo Márquez, "Presidente del I.M.A.U. declaró durante 4 horas por presunto pago irregular de un millón a constructora," *Últimas Noticias*, 19 February 1981.

35. De Onís, "Venezuela's Woes Hurt Leader's Image."

36. Herrera Campíns, *Mi compromiso con Venezuela*, 13, 16, 12.

37. Cabrera Malo, *Memoria y cuenta: Año 1983*.

38. Marco Tulio Páez, "El Concejo Municipal descubrió que tiene acceso a la dirección del I.M.A.U.," *El Universal*, 1 December 1981; Florelena López, "Tibio debate en el Concejo sobre la basura en la ciudad," *El Universal*, 1 December 1981.

39. Hugo Colmenares, "Edmundo Arias, presidente del I.M.A.U.: 'No me han pedido la renuncia pero me harían un gran favor,'" *El Nacional*, 2 December 1981.

40. Marco Tulio Páez, "Empresas recolectadoras de basura ratifican al Concejo Municipal del D.F. que Caracas estará limpia en Navidad," *El Universal*, 3 December 1981. Ironically, this episode transpired as Caracas hosted a continental summit on urban waste management, during which participants from throughout the Americas coincided in noting that services were "deficient." "Los servicios de aseo urbano son deficientes en Latinoamérica," *El Universal*, 2 December 1981.

41. Cruz Moreno, "Desde hace 15 días no recogen la basura en el 23 de Enero," *Últimas Noticias*, 18 December 1981.

42. Cruz Moreno, "Un millón de litros de agua potable se pierden diariamente en el 23 de Enero," *Últimas Noticias*, 18 December 1981.

43. José Manuel Pérez, "Río de aguas negras afecta a vecinos del Sector D del 23 de Enero," *Últimas Noticias*, 18 August 1981.

44. José Manuel Pérez, "El drama de un solo ascensor para 5 mil personas de 3 bloques clama por urgente atención oficial," *Últimas Noticias*, 18 August 1981.

45. José Manuel Pérez, "Sigue derrumbándose la calle Real de Monte Piedad," *Últimas Noticias*, 15 September 1981.

46. Gilberto Carreño, "Terrible abandono en el 23 de Enero," *El Universal*, 2 December 1981.

47. "Disturbios en el 23 de Enero," *El Nacional*, 1 December 1981.

48. "No hubo negligencia médica en caso de muchacha abaleada," *El Universal*, 30 November 1981.

49. "Un estudiante se mató al caer de azotea del Liceo Luis Ezpelosín durante disturbios," *Últimas Noticias*, 4 December 1981.

50. "Policía Metropolitana pidió a Fiscalía investigar sucesos del Luis Ezpelosín," *Últimas Noticias*, 5 December 1981; Francisco Gómez, "De un perdigonazo al corazón murió el liceista del Luis Ezpelosín," *Últimas Noticias*, 6 December 1981.

51. Freddy Urbina, "Nuevos disturbios con 3 policías heridos y autobuses, carros y camiones quemados," *Últimas Noticias*, 10 December 1981.

52. Carlos Castillo, "Incendiaron automóviles de 11 profesores," *El Universal*, 12 December 1981.

53. Freddy Urbina, "Saqueado camión cargado de licores por una poblada en el 23 de Enero," *Últimas Noticias*, 15 December 1981; Cruz Moreno, "Saqueado otro camión cargado de alimentos en Zona Central de la urbanización 23 de Enero," *Últimas Noticias*, 16 December 1981; "Una turba saqueó camión de reparto en el 23 de Enero," *El Universal*, 15 December 1981; "Asaltado otro camión cava en el 23 de Enero," *El Universal*, 16 December 1981.

54. "Disturbios estudiantiles en el Liceo Luis Ezpelosín," *El Nacional*, 21 January 1981.

55. "Protesta en el 23 de Enero por la muerte del estudiante," *El Nacional*, 20 January 1981.

56. "La Metropolitana tomó los bloques del 23 de Enero y Pro-Patria," *El Nacional*, 24 January 1981.

57. "Continuaron ayer los disturbios en el 23 de Enero," *El Nacional*, 25 January 1981.

58. "Quemados vehículos por grupos de exaltados," *El Nacional*, 23 January 1981.

59. Coromoto Álvarez, "Nuevos combates entre policías y ultrosos en zona roja del 23 de Enero ayer domingo," *Últimas Noticias*, 9 February 1981.

60. Ibid.

61. Lisandro Pérez, interview with the author, 2005.

62. Carlos Villegas, "Remodelación del 23 de Enero comienza la próxima semana," *Últimas Noticias*, 6 December 1981.

63. "Juramentado Consejo Parroquial de la urbanización 23 de Enero," *El Universal*, 17 December 1981.

64. Pablo Antillano, "Rebelión democrática vs. partidocracia: El país reclama la revitalización de la democracia," *El Nacional*, 3 December 1981.

65. Gustavo Rodríguez, interview with the author, 2005.

66. "'Secuestraron' a cuatro camiones": "*. . . un acto cívico reivindicativo*"; emphasis added in the English.

67. See Chapter 5.

68. Rodríguez, interview with the author, 2005.

69. Gutiérrez, interview with the author, 2005.

70. Cruz Moreno, "Por segundo día consecutivo en el Oeste: Retenidos 3 camiones y un jeep de la basura por habitantes de Sierra Maestra como protesta," *Últimas Noticias*, 22 December 1981.

71. Antonio Martín, "Toneladas de basura en las calles de Catia y 23 de Enero," *El Nacional*, 23 December 1981.

72. Gilberto Carreño, "En el 23 de Enero: La basura causa estragos," *El Universal*, 23 December 1981.

73. "'Secuestraron' a cuatro camiones": "*Los vecinos dijeron que su acción se convierte en una contribución oportuna al cumplimiento de la promesa de los concesionarios de la recolección de basura de 'limpiar a Caracas en Diciembre.'*"

74. Daisy Argotte, "La ira Presidencial sacudió las voluntades: Una 'Operación Cayapa' dejó limpio al 23 de Enero," *Diario de Caracas*, 24 December 1981; "L.H.C. 'furioso.'"

75. "Operativo de emergencia en el 23 de Enero," *El Universal*, 23 December 1981.

76. Gilberto Carreño, "En el 23 de Enero: Las autoridades respondieron al clamor de los vecinos," *El Universal*, 24 December 1981.

77. Cruz Moreno, "190 camiones y 25 máquinas se necesitaron para sacar la basura de muchos meses en El 23," *Últimas Noticias*, 24 December 1981.

78. Argotte, "El regalo de Caricuao."

79. "La marginalidad solo se supera con la participación de la comunidad en la toma de decisiones," *El Universal*, 28 December 1981.

80. "600 ductos destruidos: El I.N.A.V.I. es el culpable de la acumulación de basura en el 23 de Enero," *El Nacional*, 2 January 1982.

81. Daisy Argotte, "No funcionó la cayapa para limpiar el sector: Los habitantes del 23 de Enero 'cayeron por inocentes,'" *Diario de Caracas*, 27 December 1981.

82. Cruz Moreno, "Servicio de ascensores, falta de agua y basura calamidad permanente en el 23 de Enero," *Últimas Noticias*, 31 December 1981.

83. William Rangel, interview with the author, 2005.

84. Contreras, interview with the author, 2005.

85. Frank León, interview with the author, 2005.

86. José Manuel Pérez, "Agoniza dama herida durante manifestación en el 23 de Enero para reclamar solución a problemas," *Últimas Noticias*, 11 January 1982.

87. Desirée Santos Amaral, "Secuestrados otros 3 vehículos y van once por protesta de habitantes del 23 de Enero," *Últimas Noticias*, 18 January 1982; Cruz Moreno, "No ceden habitantes de Monte Piedad y mantienen retenidos 10 vehículos," *Últimas Noticias*, 19 January 1982.

88. Marinela Hernández, "Habitantes del 23 de Enero comprometieron a organismos a solucionarles sus problemas," *Últimas Noticias*, 21 January 1982.

89. Cruz Moreno, "El 23 de Enero llega a sus 24 años en plena lucha porque se cumplan servicios públicos," *Últimas Noticias*, 24 January 1982.

90. All city council quotes from Lombardi, "¿Se justifica el secuestro de un camión?".

91. Mateo Manaure, "El 23 de Enero: Un bravo pueblo," *El Nacional*, 23 January 1982.

92. After spiking at 1,168 in 1971, the number of reported drug-related arrests in the greater metropolitan region of Caracas fell to 558 in 1972 and then oscillated between roughly 600 and 1,000 per year until 1979, when it jumped 125%, from 952 in 1978, to 2,152. The number dropped again, to 843 by 1981, but then it climbed steadily to 1,047, 1,629, 1,747, and 2,240 each year, respectively, from 1982 through 1985. It would then hover near 2,000 each year until 1989. Most arrests in the 1980s were cocaine-related, rather than the largely marijuana-related arrests that make up the 1970s statistics. Data compiled from: *Estadística Delictiva 1989* (Caracas: Ministerio de Justicia, 1991); *Estadística Delictiva 1988* (Caracas: Ministerio de Justicia, 1991); *Estadística Delictiva 1987* (Caracas: Ministerio de Justicia, 1989); *Estadística Delictiva 1986* (Caracas: Ministerio de Justicia, 1988); *Estadística Delictiva 1985* (Caracas: Ministerio de Justicia, 1988); *Estadística Delictiva 1983* (Caracas: Ministerio de Justicia, 1987); *Estadística Delictiva 1984* (Caracas: Ministerio de Justicia, 1987); *Estadística Delictiva 1981* (Caracas: Ministerio de Justicia, 1984); *Estadística Delictiva 1979: Policial, Penitenciaria, Criminal* (Caracas: Ministerio de Justicia, 1982).

93. As early as 1973 the media had begun to report on this dynamic, whereby residents understood both police violence and youth violence as two sides of the same coin of repression in the neighborhood. Luis Buitrago Segura and Gustavo Beltrán, "Atrapados los habitantes de la urbanizacion 23 de Enero entre minorías agresivas y la represión policial," *El Nacional*, 9 May 1973.

94. Valentín Santana et al., interview with the author, 2005; Nelson Santana, interview with the author, 2005.

95. Manaure, "El 23 de Enero: Un bravo pueblo."

96. Alirio Moreno, interview with the author, 2005.

97. Luis Buitrago Segura, "El hampa desafía a las autoridades y las juntas de rescate en los Bloques 42, 43 y 44," *El Nacional*, 23 July 1984.

98. Juan B. Contreras Suniaga, "La Coordinadora Cultural Simón Bolívar: Una experiencia de construcción de poder local en la parroquia 23 de Enero" (postgraduate thesis, Universidad Central de Venezuela, 2000).

99. "Por primera vez en su historia, Inavi pasó un bloque del 23 de Enero a propiedad horizontal," *El Nacional*, 18 December 1984.

100. Criteria included steady employment, sole property, and family need. Prices ranged from USD$1,000 to $1,650. Over 30 years with 10% down payment, monthly mortgage payments would average $15USD. Iris Castellanos, "30 años para pagar menos del 10% de inicial y mensualidades en 180 bolívares," *El Nacional*, 21 December 1984. In 1984, a worker earning Venezuela's legally mandated minimum annual income of USD$1,500, INAVI's mortgage payment would have had to pay 10% of his or her salary. Julio Mora Contreras, "El salario mínimo en la agricultura," *Revista SIC* (June 1990): 206–207.

101. "En el 23 de Enero: Por primera vez en la historia el Inavi pasa un bloque a propiedad horizontal," *El Universal*, 20 December 1984.

102. Ibid.

103. Castellanos, "30 años para pagar."

104. Coromoto Álvarez, "Primer refinanciamiento de deuda del Inavi por 2.408 millones logró Ugueto en el exterior," *Últimas Noticias*, 22 October 1982.

105. Castellanos, "30 años para pagar."

106. Rosita Caldera, "Opina D. F. Maza Zavala: La sexta parte de los venezolanos vive en estado de extrema pobreza," *El Nacional*, 9 January 1982; Douglas Martin, "The Very Mixed Blessings of Pure Liquid Gold," *New York Times*, 23 May 1982.

107. "Venezuela Acts to Avoid Failure of Biggest Bank," *New York Times*, 30 November 1982; "Currency Sale Halted by Caracas," *New York Times*, 22 February 1983.

108. "Los sociólogos exigen un nuevo modelo de desarrollo," *El Nacional*, 10 October 1982.

109. Luis Buitrago Segura, "Heinz Sonntag: El estado clientelista arruinó a Venezuela," *Últimas Noticias*, 2 October 1983.

110. Imperio Rodríguez, "Advierten los economistas: El venezolano debe despertar del letargo de la falsa abundancia," *El Nacional*, 28 February 1983.

111. Miriam Morillo, "Resulta doloroso y vergonzante reconocer que Venezuela es un país en quiebra," *Últimas Noticias*, 21 October 1982; Desirée Santos Amaral, "Altibajos del mercado petrolero golpearán presupuesto del 83 para el D.F.," *Últimas Noticias*, 27 October 1982.

112. Carlos Villegas, "Declarar al país en emergencia y convocar un gobierno de concentración nacional demanda A.D. del Presidente L.H.C.," *Últimas Noticias*, 24 October 1982.

113. Carlos Villegas, "Ha llegado el momento de hacernos una autocrítica, dijo Carlos Andrés," *Últimas Noticias*, 21 January 1983.

114. Carlos Villegas, "Alto Tribunal para que los Presidentes rindan cuentas después de gobernar propuso Senador Larrazábal en la Sesión Solemne por el 23 de Enero," *Últimas Noticias*, 21 January 1983.

115. "Venezuela Units Fight Rebels," *New York Times*, 5 October 1982; "Comisión del Congreso inició investigaciones del encuentro armado en Cantaura," *Últimas Noticias*, 22 October 1982.

116. Warren Hoge, "In Venezuela, Good Times Are Going," *New York Times*, 20 March 1983.

117. Ibid.

118. Coromoto Álvarez, "Día de júbilo el 23 de Enero," *Últimas Noticias*, 15 January 1983.

119. Coromoto Álvarez, "Programa popular de reencuentro con el 23 de Enero: Con cohetes, sermones y flores se celebra hoy el 'Madrugonazo,'" *Últimas Noticias*, 23 January 1983.

120. "Juvenil del M.E.P. llama a rescatar lo positivo del 23 de Enero," *Últimas Noticias*, 23 January 1983.

121. Ernesto Rodríguez, "Los que añoran, los que se quejan, y quienes alaban a la democracia," *Últimas Noticias*, 23 January 1983.

122. Iris Villasmil, "No hay veracidad en versiones cataclísmicas sobre situación nacional," *Últimas Noticias*, 21 October 1982.

123. Hoge, "In Venezuela, Good Times Are Going."

124. Carlos Villegas, "'Pepi' arranca en Caracas del 23 de Enero para buscar su postulación presidencial," *Últimas Noticias*, 10 March 1982.

125. "Obras por 48 millones realiza el Inavi en el 23 de Enero," *El Nacional*, 16 January 1983.

126. Carlos Villegas, "Construirán mercado y remodelarán la Plaza Cristo Rey en la parroquia del 23 de Enero," *Últimas Noticias*, 15 January 1983.

127. "Emotiva celebración del 23 de Enero en la parroquia que lleva ese nombre," *Últimas Noticias*, 24 January 1983.

128. Humberto Álvarez, "En el Bloque 20 y 21 de La Cañada, deben esperar el presupuesto del 83 para ver solucionados sus problemas," *El Nacional*, 11 December 1982.

129. José Manuel Pérez, "El 23 de Enero celebra dentro de 17 días el abandono en que están sumidas sus instalaciones," *Últimas Noticias*, 7 January 1983.

130. Carlos Villegas, "En 15 días pretenden hacer en el 23 de Enero lo que no han podido hacer en muchos años," *Últimas Noticias*, 8 January 1983.

131. José Manuel Pérez, "Que no se quede en limpieza aniversario del 23 de Enero piden sus habitantes," *Últimas Noticias*, 12 January 1983.

132. Francisco Santaella, "La limpieza del 23 de Enero no es solo por los 25 años aclara la Jefa Civil," *Últimas Noticias*, 9 January 1983.

133. Francisco Gómez, "Tarde de disturbios en el 23 de Enero con saqueo e incendio de camión de embutidos," *Últimas Noticias*, 26 January 1983.

134. Desirée Santos Amaral, "El 23 de Enero espera todavía le cancelen la deuda que con ella tiene la democracia," *Últimas Noticias*, 30 January 1983.

135. Alejandro Velasco, "'A Weapon as Powerful as the Vote': Urban Protest and Electoral Politics in Venezuela, 1978–1983," *Hispanic American Historical Review* 90, no. 4 (2010).

136. María Laura Lombardi, "El I.M.A.U. pierde 30 millones de bolívares cada semana," *El Nacional*, 19 January 1982.

137. Cruz Moreno, "Tomadas instalaciones del I.M.A.U. por 5 mil trabajadores despedidos," *Últimas Noticias*, 28 January 1982; Cruz Moreno, "Trabajadores cesaron en toma del I.M.A.U. pero rechazan pagos chucutos de prestaciones," *Últimas Noticias*, 29 January 1982.

138. Esteban Yepes, "Infructuoso operativo del I.M.A.U.," *El Nacional*, 31 January 1982.

139. Desirée Santos Amaral, "Recolección de basura se paralizará en Caracas 'legal o ilegalmente,'" *Últimas Noticias*, 30 October 1982.

140. Desirée Santos Amaral, "Aporte de 100 millones para I.M.A.U. aprobó el Concejo de Caracas con reservas," *Últimas Noticias*, 7 October 1983.

141. María Luisa de Blay, *30 años de Banco Obrero* (Caracas: Banco Obrero, 1959).

142. Manuel A. López Villa, "Gestión urbanística, revolución democrática y dictadura militar en Venezuela, 1945–1958," *Urbana* 14/15 (1994).

143. Alfredo Cilento Sarli, "La visión estratégica del Banco Obrero en el período 1959–1969," in *Leopoldo Martínez Olavarría: Desarrollo urbano, vivienda y estado*, ed. Alberto Lovera (Caracas: Fondo Editorial Alemo, 1996).

144. Angelina Orellana de García-Maldonado, *60 años de experiencia en desarrollos urbanísticos de bajo costo en Venezuela* (Caracas: Instituto Nacional de la Vivienda, 1989).

145. Álvarez, "Primer refinanciamiento de deuda del Inavi."

146. Castellanos, "30 años para pagar."

147. Miguel López Trocelt, "Tito Sidow: Las empresas fabricantes de ascensores traban la entrega de viviendas del I.N.A.V.I.," *El Nacional*, 28 January 1982.

148. Carlos Villegas, "Pide el Concejal Víctor Morillo: Juicio penal contra quienes incumplieron instalación de 56 ascensores en el 23," *Últimas Noticias*, 1 March 1982.

149. "Obras por 48 millones realiza el Inavi."

150. Congreso de la República de Venezuela, "Ley de Propiedad Horizontal," (Gaceta Oficial, 1983).

151. "Los vecinos donaron patrullas a la PM," *Diario de Caracas*, 15 October 1985.

152. Gilberto Carreño and Francisco Seijas, "En el 23 de Enero dan un ejemplo: Cuando se quiere vivir mejor," *El Universal*, 29 October 1985.

153. Ibid.

154. Luis Buitrago Segura and Ramon García, "Liberado el Bloque 37 del 23 de Enero," *El Nacional*, 17 July 1984; Luis Buitrago Segura, "El Bloque 40 se incorporó al territorio liberado del hampa," *El Nacional*, 24 July 1984; Luis Buitrago Segura and Luis Aguilera, "Finalizó la ocupación del hampa en el 23 de Enero: Una isla de paz donde los niños juegan bajo vigilancia armada de sus padres," *El Nacional*, 14 July 1984.

155. Joaquín Ortuño, "Pese a que hemos sido abandonados, la comunidad busca soluciones a sus problemas," *Últimas Noticias*, 17 January 1986.

156. Rafael T. Zamora, "En una dictadura de problemas convertido 23 de Enero," *Últimas Noticias*, 12 January 1986.

157. Rafael T. Zamora, "Millones de cucarachas y miles de armas ocultas en el Viejo Oeste del 23 de Enero," *Últimas Noticias*, 13 January 1986.

158. José Manuel Pérez, "Entre las ratas y los delincuentes se debaten vecinos del 23 de Enero," *Últimas Noticias*, 17 January 1986.

159. José Manuel Pérez, "Un 'maquillaje' para conmemorar su aniversario es lo que recibe el 23 de Enero todos los años," *Últimas Noticias*, 14 January 1986.

160. "Presidente Lusinchi ordenó lavarle la cara al 23 de Enero," *Últimas Noticias*, 22 January 1986.

161. J. Lossada Rondón, "El 14 de este mes, Unidad de Computación inaugura Lusinchi en el 23 de Enero," *El Nacional*, 9 November 1986.

162. "23 de Enero de Caracas símbolo de todos los problemas," *Últimas Noticias*, 23 January 1986.

163. Ernesto L. Rodríguez, "Atropello a los habitantes del 23 de Enero no es propio de una democracia de 28 años," *Últimas Noticias*, 27 January 1986.

164. Marianela Balbi, "El Jefe Civil analiza su parroquia: Los bloques del 23 de Enero sienten el peso del tiempo," *El Nacional*, 23 June 1986.

7. KILLING DEMOCRACY'S PROMISE

1. By 1988, Venezuela's foreign debt had reached a staggering 41% of the national GDP, and the nation's foreign reserves lay depleted. Terry Lynn Karl, "The Venezuelan Petro-State and the Crisis of 'Its' Democracy," in *Venezuelan Democracy under Stress*, ed. Jennifer McCoy et al. (Miami: North South Center, University of Miami, 1995), 42.

2. Carlos Quintana, interview with the author, 2005.

3. Fabricio Ojeda, "Saqueos y barricadas," in *El día que bajaron los cerros* (Caracas: Ateneo de Caracas, 1989), 25.

4. Juan Contreras, interview with the author, 2005; Ojeda, "Saqueos y barricadas," 27. An ongoing strike among the rank and file of the Metropolitan Police, regarding the body's leadership structure, had delayed intervention on 27 February. Margarita López Maya, "The Venezuelan Caracazo of 1989: Popular Protest and Institutional Weakness," *Journal of Latin American Studies* 35, no. 1 (2003): 134.

5. Paulina Gamus Gallegos, *Informe preliminar de la Comisión Permanente de Política Interior sobre los sucesos ocurridos en el país los días 27 y 28 de febrero y subsiguientes* (Caracas: República de Venezuela, Cámara de Diputados, Secretaría, 1989), 12.

6. Contreras, interview with the author, 2005..

7. Julio Ricardo Villaroel et al., interview with the author, 2005.

8. William Rangel, interview with the author, 2005.

9. "Demanda ante la Corte Interamericana de Derechos Humanos contra la República de Venezuela: Caso de Miguel Aguilera, Wolfgang Quintana, Richard Páez y otros," Box: Caso del Caracazo (Aguilera la Rosa), Original, Fondo, Tomo I y II, 6–7 (Organización de los Estados Americanos; Comisión Interamericana de Derechos Humanos, 1999).

10. "Caso del Caracazo vs. Venezuela," San José, Costa Rica: Inter-American Court of Human Rights (11 November 1999): 5.

11. Clodovaldo Hernández, "Copei respaldó decreto de C.A.P. para suspensión de las garantías," *Diario de Caracas*, 11 March 1989. The Movimiento al Socialismo (MAS) and Movimiento Electoral del Pueblo (MEP) both supported the unfolding protests. "M.A.S. y M.E.P. fijaron su posición," *Diario de Caracas*, 28 February 1989.

12. According to Italo del Valle Alliegro, Defense Minister during the *Caracazo*, 65 deaths from 7.65mm-caliber bullets—standard issue for Venezuela's Army at the time—took place between 28 February and 5 March 1989. Of the 65 deaths by high-caliber rifles, as many as 47 took place between 28 February and 1 March. "Demanda ante la Corte Interamericana de Derechos Humanos," 5, 13, 19.

13. J. C., "Caracas recupera una precaria normalidad," *El País*, 5 March 1989.

14. Congress lifted the final restrictions on constitutional guarantees on 22 March. After assembling all reports of deaths during the period 27 February–5 March 1989, local human rights groups PROVEA and COFAVIC placed the figure of casualties during the *Caracazo* at 399. "Demanda ante la Corte Interamericana de Derechos Humanos." In 1991, they added another 69 names after the discovery of mass graves in the La Peste area of Caracas, bringing the total to 468. The most recent official accounting of the dead, conducted during the presidency of Hugo Chávez, places the figure at 348, drawing upon all case files culled from the Attorney General's office. Germán Mundaraín, *A 18 años del Caracazo: Sed de justicia* (Caracas: Defensoría del Pueblo, 2007), 66.

15. Enrique Ochoa Antich, *Los golpes de febrero: De la rebelión de los pobres al alzamiento de los militares* (Caracas: Fuentes Editores, 1992), 11; *Cuando la muerte tomó las calles* (Caracas: El Nacional, 1989), 46; "'Creo que es peligroso desafiar la pobreza,'" *Diario de Caracas*, 9 March 1989, 2.

16. "Caso del Caracazo vs. Venezuela."

17. To date, book-length, comprehensive treatments of the *Caracazo* remain absent from the literature on contemporary Venezuela. Shorter analyses, though more plentiful, likewise remain marked by uneven quality and focus. In the immediate aftermath, two leading social science journals based at the Universidad Central de Venezuela devoted special issues to the *Caracazo*, its political dimensions, and its foreseeable short- and long-term consequences. See *Cuadernos del CENDES* 10, January–April 1989; *Politeia* 15, July 1989. In separate essays, historian Miguel Izard and anthropologists Fernando Coronil and Julie Skurski sought to situate the *Caracazo* within a

broader historical context, tracing the roots of popular discontent to the early 1980s, and the roots of state violence to the El Amparo massacre of eleven peasants by elite military units in the southeastern Colombian border just months prior to the *Caracazo*. Their argument represented an early revisionist perspective to an already standard interpretation of the *Caracazo* as a watershed moment in modern Venezuelan history. See Fernando Coronil and Julie Skurski, "Dismembering and Remembering the Nation: The Semantics of Political Violence in Venezuela," *Comparative Studies in Society and History* 33, no. 2 (1991); Miguel Izard, *El poder, la mentira y la muerte: De El Amparo al Caracazo* (Caracas: Fondo Editorial Trópykos, 1991). Following two failed coup d'état attempts on the government of Carlos Andrés Pérez in 1992, an emerging national and international literature on Venezuela's "crisis" moved away from casting the *Caracazo* as a foundational moment of a new national narrative, and instead marginalized its significance altogether vis-à-vis the now real possibility that a long-touted system marked by institutional resilience might crumble from within rather than from popular pressure. Yet the only sustained analysis of the *Caracazo*'s popular significance suggested otherwise. Five years following the massacre, sociologist José María Cadenas conducted in-depth interviews with children in popular sectors of Caracas most targeted by military forces, in an effort to uncover patterns of "psycho-social trauma" resulting from the acts of state repression. His research revealed surprisingly consistent structures of feeling among children of various ages and from diverse parts of Caracas, for whom memories of the *Caracazo* evoked strong emotions of fear expressed in efforts to forget the events. See José María Cadenas G., *El 27 de Febrero contado por niños y adolescentes* (Caracas: Fondo Editorial Trópykos, 1995). Under the aegis of what may be termed "protest" studies, and influenced by official state policy under the government of Hugo Chávez to cast the *Caracazo* as a moment of popular political catharsis, the 1989 massacre has seen a resurgence in academic attention. This new effort, however, remains rooted in institutional and political analysis and has yet to integrate the social dimensions or the long-developing historical foundations of the *Caracazo*. See López Maya, "The Venezuelan Caracazo of 1989."

18. Elizabeth Araujo, "23 de Enero: Vivir entre balas," in *Cuando la muerte tomó las calles* (Caracas: El Nacional, 1989), 82.

19. Ignacio Betancourt, "El Caracazo," *El Nacional*, 21 February 1999.

20. Margarita López Maya, "La protesta venezolana entre 1989 y 1993: En el umbral del neoliberalismo," in *Lucha popular, democracia, neoliberalismo: La protesta popular en América Latina en los años de ajuste*, ed. Margarita López Maya (Caracas: Nueva Sociedad, 1999), 220.

21. Juan Vásquez, "Venezuela Unrest," *CBS Evening News*, 2 March 1989.

22. Fidel Castro, interview by Noralba Jiménez, *Venezolana de Televisión*, www1 .lanic.utexas.edu/project/castro/db/1989/19890202–1.html.

23. Fernando Coronil, *The Magical State: Nature, Money, and Modernity in Venezuela* (Chicago: University of Chicago Press, 1997), 375–76; Terry Lynn Karl, *The Paradox of Plenty: Oil Booms and Petro-States* (Berkeley: University of California Press, 1997), 179–80.

24. Aldo Lubrano and Rosa Haydée Sánchez, *Del hombre completo a Jaime es como tú: Recuento de un proceso electoral venezolano* (Caracas: Vadell Hermanos Editores, 1987).

25. *Las cuatro primeras fuerzas políticas en Venezuela a nivel municipal, 1958–1978* (Caracas: División de Estadística, Consejo Supremo Electoral, 1983).

26. Compared to Lusinchi's 52% in 1983, the party's candidate had remained statistically even. Ibid.

27. Coronil, *The Magical State*, 372.

28. AD and COPEI combined failed to amass more than 30% of the vote before 1973. In 1958, Larrazábal's URD party handily beat both AD and COPEI; in 1963, Larrazábal's IPFN did the same; and in 1968, it was Pérez Jiménez's CCN party that won in the 23 de Enero.

29. Between 1983 and 1988, AD's vote fell by four percentage points, while COPEI's improved only by two percentage points. Abstention also increased during this time, to 19% of the vote compared to 12% in 1983, mirroring national figures. Heinz Sonntag and Thais Maigon, "Las elecciones en Venezuela en 1988 y 1989: Del ejercicio de rito democrático a la protesta silenciosa," *Revista Mexicana de Sociología* 52, no. 4 (1990): 147–48; *Las cuatro primeras fuerzas*.

30. Julia Reverendo, "Pompeyo Márquez esta mañana en TV: 'Los sectores populares están aterrados con los anuncios económicos del Gobierno,'" *El Mundo*, 13 February 1989.

31. Thamara Nieves, "Una inflación del 80 por ciento creará las condiciones para una explosión social grave," *El Universal*, 16 February 1989.

32. Fabiola Sánchez, "Paralizados hospitales por culpa del 'Paquete,'" *El Mundo*, 16 February 1989.

33. Rubén Darío Albornoz, "Señala el gremio médico: Cierre definitivo de hospitales plantean en comité de conflicto," *El Mundo*, 22 February 1989.

34. Betancourt, "El Caracazo."

35. "En 1990 madurará el plan económico," *Diario de Caracas*, 27 February 1989.

36. Gallegos, *Informe preliminar de la Comisión Permanente*, 11.

37. Manuel Mir, interview with the author, 2005.

38. Ibid.

39. Ibid.

40. Lisandro Pérez, interview with the author, 2005; "Los habitantes del 23 de Enero en lucha contra el abandono oficial," *El Nacional*, 19 January 1982.

41. Pérez, interview with the author, 2005.

42. Ibid.

43. Andrés Vásquez, interview with the author, 2005.

44. Contreras, interview with the author, 2005.

45. José Manuel Pérez, "Comando guerrillero atacó módulo policial de La Cañada en el 23 de Enero con tiros y bombas," *Últimas Noticias*, 15 October 1983.

46. Contreras, interview with the author, 2005.

47. Ibid.

48. Ojeda, "Saqueos y barricadas," 27.

49. Rubén Darío Albornoz, "Llegó la hora en que la PM debe ser conducida por sus directores naturales," *El Mundo*, 16 February 1989.

50. Coronil and Skurski, "Dismembering and Remembering the Nation," 315.

51. Hugo Colmenares, "Facur apoya exigencias de la Policía Metropolitana," *El Nacional*, 15 February 1989.

52. "El Presidente hizo una revisión general de los servicios policiales del país," *El Universal*, 19 February 1989.

53. Humberto Álvarez, "Oficiales de la PM sustituyen en mando a 2 coroneles de GN," *El Nacional*, 24 February 1989.

54. President Pérez offered this statement to the press on 10 June 1990. "Demanda ante la Corte Interamericana de Derechos Humanos," 8.

55. Contreras, interview with the author, 2005.

56. Ibid.

57. Mir, interview with the author, 2005.

58. Contreras, interview with the author, 2005.

59. Mir, interview with the author, 2005.

60. Julián Álvarez, "Sepultado efectivo de la Policía Metropolitana," *Últimas Noticias*, 3 March 1989.

61. "Eduardo Meza Istúriz," *Registro Civil de Defunción*, 1 March 1989.

62. José Luis Rivas, "Plomo cerrado esta mañana en el 23 de Enero," *El Mundo*, 1 March 1989.

63. Contreras, interview with the author, 2005.

64. Mir, interview with the author, 2005.

65. Rangel, interview with the author, 2005.

66. Andrés Vásquez, interview with the author, 2005.

67. Marta Harnecker, *Militares junto al pueblo: Entrevistas a nueve comandantes venezolanos que protagonizaron la gesta de abril de 2002* (Valencia: Vadell Hermanos Editores, 2003), 172.

68. Roberto Giusti, "Italo Del Valle Alliegro: A lo mejor se dispara," in *Cuando la muerte tomó las calles* (Caracas: El Nacional, 1989), 33.

69. Betancourt, "El Caracazo."

70. Corte Suprema de Justicia, República de Venezuela, Sala Político-Administrativa, "1999," p. 30, Box: Caso del Caracazo (Aguilera la Rosa) Original, Documentos Presentados por la República de Venezuela el 10 de noviembre de 1999, en la Audiencia Pública de Fondo, Escrito de COFAVIC Ref/Poder, Fotografías de los sucesos, San José (Costa Rica).

71. Harnecker, *Militares junto al pueblo*, 172.

72. J. M. Rojas, "Pérez descartó guerra civil y negó que sea una acción antigubernamental," *Diario de Caracas*, 4 March 1989.

73. Gallegos, *Informe preliminar de la Comisión Permanente*, 10.

74. The other two areas were El Valle, located next to the Caracas barracks and at the western entrance to Caracas; and Petare, located in the Eastern entrance to

Caracas, connecting the capital to Guarenas and Guatire, where the protests had begun. Roberto Giusti, "Comandante Galué García: A merced de los insurrectos," in *Cuando la muerte tomó las calles* (Caracas: El Nacional, 1989), 24.

75. Betancourt, "El Caracazo."

76. *Informe N. 83/98 Caso 11.455: Miguel Aguilera, Wolfgang Quintana, Richard Páez Y Otros Vs. República De Venezuela* (Washington: Comisión Interamericana de Derechos Humanos; Secretaría de la Organización de Estados Americanos, 1998), 6, OEA/Ser/L/V/II.100 Doc. 54.

77. Julia González, *Levantamiento de cadáveres: Petición de autopsia* (Caracas: Ministerio de Justicia, Cuerpo Técnico de Policía Judicial, División de Medicina Legal, 1989).

78. *Testimonio del Sr. Francisco Moncada* (Washington: Comisión Interamericana de Derechos Humanos, 1997), Transcript.

79. Contreras, interview with the author, 2005. Dorantes Torres's death certificate noted that he died from "internal hemorrhaging following a gunshot wound to the thorax." "Carlos Antonio Dorantes," *Registro Civil de Defunción*, 28 February 1989.

80. "Caso del Caracazo vs. Venezuela," 5.

81. Juan Sará Serrano, "Muchos francotiradores pertenecen al hampa común," *Diario de Caracas*, 9 March 1989, 20.

82. Araujo, "23 de Enero: Vivir entre balas," 83.

83. Serrano, "Muchos francotiradores pertenecen al hampa," 21.

84. Rivas, "Plomo cerrado esta mañana."

85. Contreras, interview with the author, 2005.

86. Araujo, "23 de Enero: Vivir entre balas," 83.

87. Lisandro Pérez, interview with the author, 2005.

88. Régulo Párraga, "Noche de terror," in *El día que bajaron los cerros* (Caracas: Ateneo de Caracas, 1989), 61.

89. Araujo, "23 de Enero: Vivir entre balas," 83.

90. Cristina Marcano Salcedo, "El último toque de queda a bordo de un convoy," *Diario de Caracas*, 7 March 1989, 18.

91. Párraga, "Noche de terror," 63.

92. Erika Hidalgo and Iván González, "José Grillo: En medio del desastre," in *El estallido de febrero: Secuencia escrita y gráfica de sucesos que cambiaron la historia de Venezuela en 1989*, ed. José Agustín Catalá (Caracas: Centauro Editores, 1989), 110.

93. Fabricio Ojeda, "Secuelas de un terremoto social," in *El día que bajaron los cerros* (Caracas: Ateneo de Caracas, 1989), 55.

94. *Informe N. 83/98 Caso 11.455: Miguel Aguilera, Wolfgang Quintana, Richard Páez y Otros vs. República De Venezuela*, 13.

95. "Demanda ante la Corte Interamericana de Derechos Humanos," 72.

96. Párraga, "Noche de terror," 61.

97. Lisandro Pérez, interview with the author, 2005.

98. Juan Sará Serrano, "La violencia se enquistó en el oeste de Caracas," *Diario de Caracas*, 3 March 1989.

99. Marcano Salcedo, "El último toque de queda," 18.

100. José Rojas, "Deportarán a extranjeros detenidos," *Diario de Caracas*, 3 March 1989.

101. J. M. Rojas, "Pérez descartó guerra civil."

102. Araujo, "23 de Enero: Vivir entre balas," 82.

103. José Luis Rivas, "Francotiradores y soldados sostuvieron tiroteo," *Últimas Noticias*, 4 March 1989.

104. Lisandro Pérez, interview with the author.

105. David Gollob, "Troops Hunt for Week's Plunder," *New York Times*, 5 March 1989.

106. "23 de Enero: ¿Francotiradores o víctimas?" *Revista SIC* 52, no. 513 (1989), 111.

107. "Napoleón Soto Vilera," *Registro Civil de Defunción*, 5 March 1989.

108. Emilia de Pérez, interview with the author, 2005.

109. Araujo, "23 de Enero: Vivir entre balas."

110. Anahí Arizmendi and Manuel Guzmán, "Douglas Blanco: 'Y la gente volvería a salir,'" in *El estallido de febrero: Secuencia escrita y gráfica de sucesos que cambiaron la historia de Venezuela en 1989*, ed. José Agustín Catalá (Caracas: Centauro Editores, 1989), 95.

111. "23 de Enero: ¿Francotiradores o víctimas?"

112. Marcano Salcedo, "El último toque de queda." In all, there are 56 numbered superblocks in the neighborhood (with 150, 300, or 450 apartments each, except for Blocks 45–46–47, which have 520 apartments), plus 3 separately numbered blocks in the Atlántico Norte sector, for a total of 59 blocks.

113. In *Empire*, Michael Hardt and Antonio Negri describe the "multitude" as a diffuse social actor that exists in contrast to the politically pliable and ostensibly homogeneous "masses," precisely because "the multitude is a multiplicity, a plane of singularities" that tends toward heterogeneity and thus resists co-optation. Michael Hardt and Antonio Negri, *Empire* (Cambridge, MA: Harvard University Press, 2001), 103. In later work they elaborate the concept further, noting that "the development of the multitude is not anarchic or spontaneous but rather its organization emerges through the collaboration of singular social subjects. Like the formation of habits, or performativity or the development of languages, this production of the common is neither directed by some central point of command and intelligence nor is the result of a spontaneous harmony among individuals, but rather it emerges in the space *between*, in the social space of communication. The multitude is created in collaborative social interactions." Seen in this light, it is possible to consider the 23 de Enero's representation as a hydra in terms of the multitude, as a political subject marked by internal difference rather than uniformity—blocks and barrios, eastern and western sectors, squatters and renters—nevertheless brought into a common identity by the networks of internal communication forged through the shared experiences of living, and struggling, in a symbolically and politically charged environment. Ultimately, as Hardt and Negri write, the "dynamic of singularity and multiplicity that defines the multitude denies the dialectical alternative between One and the Many—it is both and neither."

And so with the 23 de Enero: it is both a common space, a single entity, but also, at once, many spaces, as the experience of the *Caracazos* suggests. Michael Hardt and Antonio Negri, *Multitude: War and Democracy in the Age of Empire* (New York: Penguin, 2004), 222, 225.

114. "23 de Enero: ¿Francotiradores o víctimas?", 111.

115. Ibid., 112.

116. Ibid.

117. José Comas, "Venezuela se recupera lentamente de la revuelta," *El País*, 3 March 1989.

118. V. J. Los Arcos Ayape, "¿Quién cerrará la brecha?," *Diario de Caracas*, 7 March 1989.

CONCLUSION

1. Margarita López Maya, "Refounding the Republic: The Political Project of Chavismo," *NACLA Report on the Americas* 33, no. 6 (2000); Fernando Coronil, "Magical Illusions or Revolutionary Magic? Chávez in Historical Context," *NACLA Report on the Americas* 33, no. 6 (2000).

2. Bart Jones, *Hugo! The Hugo Chávez Story from Mud Hut to Perpetual Revolution* (Hanover, NH: Steerforth Press, 2007), 131–60.

3. Ibid; Gregory Wilpert, *Changing Venezuela by Taking Power: The History and Policies of the Chávez Government* (London: Verso, 2006).

4. Javier Corrales and Michael Penfold, *Dragon in the Tropics: Hugo Chávez and the Political Economy of Revolution in Venezuela* (Washington, DC: Brookings Institution Press, 2011).

5. "Stronghold" and "hard-core" are among the terms used to describe the 23 de Enero's relationship with *chavismo*. Christian Parenti, "Hugo Chávez and Petro-Populism," *The Nation*, 11 April 2005; Larry Rohter, "Officials Say Chavez Wins in Venezuela," *New York Times*, 31 July 2000.

6. For instance, in 2004, during a recall referendum called by opponents, Chávez received 69% of support in the 23 de Enero as voters rejected the recall, the third-highest percentage of support among 22 parishes in Caracas. In congressional elections in October 2004, Chávez's party, then called the *Movimiento Quinta República* (MVR), obtained 90% of the vote in the 23 de Enero, the fourth-highest percentage. Finally, in the 2006 Presidential elections, the 23 de Enero returned 76% for Chávez, again the third-largest margin of support in Caracas. Only Antimano (77%) and Macarao (74%) returned higher totals for Chávez in the 2004 referendum. El Junquito (92%), Catedral (92%), and Macarao (91%) returned higher totals for Chávez in October 2004. In 2006, Antimano (81%) and Macarao (79%) returned higher totals for Chávez. Data available at www.cne.gob.ve/.

7. In April 2003, 53 Cuban physicians arrived in ten parishes in Caracas, including the 23 de Enero. These doctors were the first in a program that would become *Barrio Adentro*, aimed at providing popular sectors with direct access to primary health care.

Yolanda D'Elia, ed., *Las misiones sociales en Venezuela: Una aproximación a su comprensión y análisis* (Caracas: Instituto Latinoamericano de Investigaciones Sociales, 2006), 25. In May 2003, Chávez granted the first urban land titles to Urban Land Committees (*Comités de Tierras Urbanas*, or CTU) from four Caracas communities, including the 23 de Enero. CTUs were organized to help normalize tenancy for squatter communities in Caracas, a program that generated an enormous amount of organizational and electoral support for Chávez. David Coleman, "Venezuela's Chavez Hands Over Land Deeds to Caracas Slum Dwellers," *BBC Worldwide Monitoring*, 12 May 2003. In August 2005, Chávez again provided CTUs in the 23 de Enero with the first funds based on a "communal project" proposal, a project that would set the stage for eventual "communal councils" entrusted with management of community resources. Hugo Chávez, *Construyendo el Poder Popular* (Ministerio de Relaciones Exteriores, 30 August 2005 [cited]; available at www.mre.gov.ve/Noticias/Presidente-Chavez/A2005/Discurso-242.htm.

8. Political parties in Venezuela had held primary elections sporadically in the past, but only at the level of presidential elections. Notably, AD held different types of primary elections to select its presidential candidates in 1973 (indirect primaries), 1988 (electoral college), and 1993 (direct primaries), while COPEI held primaries in 1988. Manuel Alcántara Sáez, *Experimentos de democracia interna: Las primarias de partidos en América Latina*, Helen Kellogg Institute Working Paper Series vol. 293 (South Bend, IN: Notre Dame University, 2002), 28.

9. William Izarra, *La U.B.E. es Poder Popular* (Asamblea Popular Revolucionaria, 12 July 2004 [cited]; available at www.aporrea.org/actualidad/a8899.html.

10. Hugo Chávez, *Aló, Presidente* No. 193 (MINCI, 13 June 2004 [cited]; available at www.minci.gob.ve/alo-presidente/16/6649/alpresidente_n193.html.

11. *Propuesta para la participación popular por la base: Coordinadora Simón Bolívar* (Asamblea Popular Revolucionaria, 7 October 2004 [cited]; available at www.aporrea.org//a10001.html.

12. Alfredo Rojas, "Gobierno negó apoyo armado," *El Universal*, 6 August 2002; Carlos Viloria, "Grupo Carapaica disparó a la P.M.," *El Universal*, 5 August 2002.

13. Joel Capriles, interview with author, 2004.

14. Sujatha Fernandes, "A View from the Barrios: Hugo Chávez as an Expression of Urban Popular Movements," *Latin American Studies Association Forum* 38, no. 1 (2006).

15. In a study of polling data prior to the 1998 presidential elections, Damarys Canache uncovered how the proportion of poll respondents "who expected to vote for Hugo Chávez" drew significantly from working-, middle-, and upper-class backgrounds, with support for Chávez reaching 55%, 44%, and 47%, respectively. Damarys Canache, "Urban Poor and Political Order," in *The Unraveling of Representative Democracy in Venezuela*, eds. Jennifer L. McCoy and David Myers (Baltimore, MD: Johns Hopkins University Press, 2005), 46.

16. Damarys Canache, "From Bullets to Ballots: The Emergence of Popular Support for Hugo Chávez," *Latin American Politics and Society* 44, no. 1 (2002).

17. López Maya, "Refounding the Republic"; Wilpert, *Changing Venezuela by Taking Power*.

18. Allan Randolph Brewer Carías, *Dismantling Democracy in Venezuela: The Cha??vez Authoritarian Experiment* (New York: Cambridge University Press, 2010); Javier Corrales and Michael Penfold, "Venezuela: Crowding Out the Opposition," *Journal of Democracy* 18, no. 2 (2007).

19. Kirk Hawkins, "Populism in Venezuela: The Rise of Chavismo," *Third World Quarterly* 24, no. 6 (2003); Kenneth M. Roberts, "Social Polarization and the Populist Resurgence in Venezuela," in *Venezuelan Politics in the Chávez Era*, eds. Steve Ellner and Daniel Hellinger (Boulder, CO: Lynne Rienner, 2003); Kirk Hawkins, *Venezuela's Chavismo and Populism in Comparative Perspective* (New York: Cambridge University Press, 2010); Kirk Hawkins, "Dependent Civil Society: The *Círculos Bolivarianos* in Venezuela," *Latin American Research Review* 41, no. 1 (2006); Christian Parenti, "Hugo Chávez and Petro-Populism," *The Nation*, 11 April 2005.

20. Daniel Hellinger, "Political Overview: The Breakdown of *Puntofijismo* and the Rise of *Chavismo*," in *Venezuelan Politics in the Chávez Era: Class, Polarization, and Conflict*, eds. Steve Ellner and Daniel Hellinger (Boulder, CO: Lynne Rienner Publishers, 2004); Jennifer L. McCoy, "From Representative to Participatory Democracy?" in *The Unraveling of Representative Democracy in Venezuela*, eds. Jennifer L. McCoy and David Myers (Baltimore, MD: Johns Hopkins University Press, 2004).

21. Francisco Rodríguez, "Why Chávez Wins," *Foreign Policy* (2007); Francisco Rodríguez, "Sharing the Oil Wealth? Appraising the Effects of Venezuela's Social Programs," *LASA Forum* 38, no. 1 (2007).

22. Steve Ellner, *Rethinking Venezuelan Politics: Class, Conflict, and the Chávez Phenomenon* (Boulder, CO: Lynne Rienner Publishers, 2008); Noam Lupu, "Who Votes for *Chavismo*? Class Voting in Hugo Chávez's Venezuela," *Latin American Research Review* 45, no. 1 (2010).

23. Sujatha Fernandes, *Who Can Stop the Drums? Urban Social Movements in Chávez's Venezuela* (Durham, NC: Duke University Press, 2010); Leslie C. Gates, *Electing Chávez: The Business of Anti-Neoliberal Politics in Venezuela* (Pittsburgh: University of Pittsburgh Press, 2010).

24. For instance, Steve Ellner has recently proposed that Venezuela's shifting politics at the level of both state and society may be seen in the context of Trotskyism, with important differences in that the perfectibility of Socialism Trotsky assumed in a context of permanent revolution also, in the Venezuelan case, includes reformist and reactionary elements within the fold of *chavismo*. Steve Ellner, "Does the Process of Change in Venezuela Resemble a 'Permanent Revolution'?" *Dialectical Anthropology* 35 (2011). Meanwhile Javier Corrales and Michael Penfold have approached Venezuela under the rubric of hybridity, considering the currents of democracy and authoritarianism, radicalism and reformism that coincide in the heart of *chavismo*. Corrales and Penfold, *Dragon in the Tropics*.

25. Fernando Coronil, "The Future in Question: History and Utopia in Latin America, 1989–2010," in *Business as Usual: The Roots of the Global Financial Meltdown,*

eds. Craig Calhoun and Georgi Derluguian (New York: New York University Press, 2011), 260.

26. Agustín Blanco Muñoz, *Habla el Comandante* (Caracas: Universidad Central de Venezuela, 1998).

27. As Sujatha Fernandes argues, "to see Chávez as an independent figure pontificating from above, or popular movements as originating in autonomous spaces from below would be to deny the interdependencies that have made possible Chávez's emergence and sustained access to power." Fernandes, "A View from the Barrios," 18.

BIBLIOGRAPHY

Acevedo Mendoza, Carlos. *La vivienda en el área metropolitana de Caracas*. Caracas: Ediciones del Cuatricentenario de Caracas, 1967.

Alcántara Sáez, Manuel. *Experimentos de democracia interna: Las primarias de partidos en América Latina*. Helen Kellogg Institute Working Paper Series, vol. 293. South Bend, IN: Notre Dame University, 2002.

Alexander, Robert J. *The Communist Party of Venezuela*. Stanford: Hoover Institution Press, 1969.

——. *Rómulo Betancourt and the Transformation of Venezuela*. New Brunswick, NJ: Transaction, 1982.

——. *The Venezuelan Democratic Revolution: A Profile of the Regime of Rómulo Betancourt*. New Brunswick, NJ: Rutgers University Press, 1964.

——. *Venezuela's Voice for Democracy: Conversations and Correspondence with Rómulo Betancourt*. New York: Praeger, 1990.

Almandoz, Arturo. "Transfer of Urban Ideas: The Emergence of Venezuelan Urbanism in the Proposals for 1930s Caracas." *International Planning Studies* 4, no. 1 (1999): 79–95.

Álvarez, Rosángel and María Pilar García-Guadilla. "Contraloría social y clientelismo: La praxis de los consejos comunales en Venezuela." *Politeia* 34, no. 46 (2012).

Antivero, Ignacio, ed. *Cuentas Nacionales (Capitulos I-II-III)*. Vol. 1, Series Estadísticas de Venezuela de los últimos cincuenta años. Caracas: Banco Central de Venezuela, 1994.

Arcaya, Pedro Manuel. *The Gómez Régime in Venezuela and Its Background*. Washington: Sun Printing Company, 1936.

Arendt, Hannah. *On Revolution*. New York: Penguin, 1963.

Arizmendi, Anahí, and Manuel Guzmán. "Douglas Blanco: 'Y la gente volvería a salir.'" In *El estallido de febrero: Secuencia escrita y gráfica de sucesos que cambiaron la historia de Venezuela en 1989*, edited by José Agustín Catalá. Caracas: Centauro Editories, 1989.

Auyero, Javier. *Poor People's Politics: Peronist Survival Networks, and the Legacy of Evita.* Durham, NC: Duke University Press, 2000.

Bergquist, Charles W. *Labor in Latin America: Comparative Essays on Chile, Argentina, Venezuela, and Colombia.* Stanford, CA: Stanford University Press, 1986.

Betancourt, Rómulo. *Venezuela, política y petróleo.* Caracas: Monte Ávila Editores, 2001 [1956].

Blanco Muñoz, Agustín. *Habla el Comandante.* Caracas: Universidad Central de Venezuela, 1998.

Blay, María Luisa de. *30 años de Banco Obrero.* Caracas: Banco Obrero, 1959.

Boué, Juan Carlos. *Venezuela: The Political Economy of Oil.* Oxford: Oxford University Press, 1994.

Braun, Herbert. *The Assassination of Gaitán: Public Life and Urban Violence in Colombia.* Madison: University of Wisconsin Press, 1985.

Brewer Carías, Allan Randolph. *Dismantling Democracy in Venezuela: The Chávez Authoritarian Experiment.* New York: Cambridge University Press, 2010.

Brillembourg, Alfredo, Hubert Klumpner, and Iwan Baan, eds. *Torre David: Informal Vertical Communities.* Zürich: Lars Müller, 2013.

Cadenas G., José María. *El 27 de febrero contado por niños y adolescentes.* Caracas: Fondo Editorial Trópykos, 1995.

Canache, Damarys. "From Bullets to Ballots: The Emergence of Popular Support for Hugo Chávez." *Latin American Politics and Society* 44, no. 1 (2002): 69–90.

———. "Urban Poor and Political Order." In *The Unraveling of Representative Democracy in Venezuela*, edited by Jennifer L. McCoy and David Myers. Baltimore, MD: Johns Hopkins University Press, 2005.

Carlson, Eric, ed. *Proyecto de evaluación de los superbloques.* Caracas: Banco Obrero, 1961.

Cartay, Rafael. "La filosofía del régimen perezjimenista: El Nuevo Ideal Nacional." *Economía* 24, no. 15 (1999): 7–24.

Castells, Manuel. *The City and the Grassroots: A Cross-Cultural Theory of Urban Social Movements.* Berkeley: University of California Press, 1983.

Castillo D'Imperio, Ocarina. *Los años del buldozer: Ideología y política, 1948–1958.* Caracas: Fondo Editorial Trópykos, 1990.

Ciccariello-Maher, George. *We Created Chávez: A People's History of the Venezuelan Revolution.* Durham, NC: Duke University Press, 2013.

Cilento Sarli, Alfredo. "La visión estratégica del Banco Obrero en el período 1959–1969." In *Leopoldo Martínez Olavarría: Desarrollo urbano, vivienda y estado*, edited by Alberto Lovera. Caracas: Fondo Editorial Alemo, 1996.

Clinton, Daniel J. *Gómez, Tyrant of the Andes.* New York: William Morrow, 1936.

Conniff, Michael. Introduction to *Populism in Latin America*, edited by Michael Conniff. Tuscaloosa: University of Alabama Press, 1999.

Contreras, Julio Mora. "El salario mínimo en la agricultura." *Revista SIC* 52, no. 525 (June 1990): 206–207.

Contreras Suniaga, Juan B. "La Coordinadora Cultural Simón Bolívar: Una experiencia de construcción de Poder Local en la parroquia 23 de Enero." Postgraduate thesis, Universidad Central de Venezuela, 2000.

Coppedge, Michael. *Strong Parties and Lame Ducks: Presidential Partyarchy and Factionalism in Venezuela.* Stanford, CA: Stanford University Press, 1994.

Corney, Frederick. *Telling October: Memory and the Making of the Bolshevik Revolution.* Ithaca, NY: Cornell University Press, 2004.

Coronil, Fernando. "The Future in Question: History and Utopia in Latin America, 1989–2010." In *Business as Usual: The Roots of the Global Financial Meltdown,* edited by Craig Calhoun and Georgi Derluguian. New York: New York University Press, 2011.

———. "Magical Illusions or Revolutionary Magic? Chávez in Historical Context." *NACLA Report on the Americas* 33, no. 6 (2000).

———. *The Magical State: Nature, Money and Modernity in Venezuela.* Chicago: University of Chicago Press, 1997.

Coronil, Fernando, and Julie Skurski. "Dismembering and Remembering the Nation: The Semantics of Political Violence in Venezuela." *Comparative Studies in Society and History* 33, no. 2 (1991): 288–337.

Corrales, Javier, and Michael Penfold. *Dragon in the Tropics: Hugo Chávez and the Political Economy of Revolution in Venezuela.* Washington, DC: Brookings Institution, 2011.

———. "Venezuela: Crowding Out the Opposition." *Journal of Democracy* 18, no. 2 (2007).

Cox, Robert G. "Conference of Governors Convened by President Betancourt." Edited by State Department, 9. Caracas, 1959.

Crisp, Brian F. *Democratic Institutional Design: The Powers and Incentives of Venezuelan Politicians and Interest Groups.* Stanford, CA: Stanford University Press, 2000.

Crisp, Brian, Daniel Levine, and José Molina. "The Rise and Decline of COPEI in Venezuela." In *Christian Democracy in Latin America: Electoral Competition and Regime Conflicts,* edited by Scott Mainwaring and Timothy Scully. Stanford, CA: Stanford University Press, 2003.

Cruz, Rafael de la. "Nuevos movimientos sociales en Venezuela." In *Los movimientos populares en América Latina,* edited by Daniel Camacho and Rafael Menjívar, 215–246. Mexico: Universidad de las Naciones Unidas, 1989.

Dahl, Robert A. *Polyarchy: Participation and Opposition.* New Haven, CT: Yale University Press, 1971.

Davis, Mike. *Planet of Slums.* London: Verso, 2006.

Davis, Richard Harding. *Three Gringos in Venezuela and Central America.* New York: Harper, 1896.

D'Elia, Yolanda, ed. *Las misiones sociales en Venezuela: Una aproximación a su comprensión y análisis.* Caracas: Instituto Latinoamericano de Investigaciones Sociales, 2006.

División de Estadística, ed. *Las cuatro primeras fuerzas políticas en Venezuela a nivel municipal, 1958–1978.* Caracas: Consejo Supremo Electoral, 1983.

Dorante, Carlos, ed. *Rómulo Betancourt: Ideas y acción de gobierno: Antología de conceptos, 1959–1964*. Caracas: Ediciones Centauro, 1987.

Ellner, Steve. "Does the Process of Change in Venezuela Resemble a 'Permanent Revolution'?" *Dialectical Anthropology* 35 (2011).

———. *Organized Labor in Venezuela, 1958–1991: Behavior and Concerns in a Democratic Setting*. Wilmington, DE: SR Books, 1993.

———. *Los partidos políticos y su disputa por el control del movimiento sindical en Venezuela, 1936–1948*. Caracas: Universidad Católica Andrés Bello, 1980.

———. *Rethinking Venezuelan Politics: Class, Conflict, and the Chávez Phenomenon*. Boulder, CO: Lynne Rienner, 2008.

———. *Venezuela's Movimiento Al Socialismo: From Guerrilla Defeat to Innovative Politics*. Durham, NC: Duke University Press, 1988.

———. "Venezuelans Reflect on the Meaning of the 23 de Enero." *Latin American Research Review* 20, no. 1 (1985): 244–256.

Ewell, Judith. *The Indictment of a Dictator: The Extradition and Trial of Marcos Pérez Jiménez*. College Station: Texas A&M University Press, 1981.

Fernandes, Sujatha. *Who Can Stop the Drums? Urban Social Movements in Chávez's Venezuela*. Durham, NC: Duke University Press, 2010.

———. "A View from the Barrios: Hugo Chávez as an Expression of Urban Popular Movements." *LASA Forum* 38, no. 1 (2006).

Fischer, Brodwyn. *A Poverty of Rights: Citizenship and Inequality in Twentieth-Century Rio de Janeiro*. Stanford, CA: Stanford University Press, 2008.

Fischer, Brodwyn, Bryan McCann, and Javier Auyero, eds. *Cities from Scratch: Poverty and Informality in Urban Latin America*. Durham, NC: Duke University Press, 2014.

Fraser, Valerie. "Venezuela." In *Building the New World: Studies in the Modern Architecture of Latin America, 1930–1960*, 87–144. London: Verso, 2000.

Friedman, Elisabeth J. *Unfinished Transitions: Women and the Gendered Development of Democracy in Venezuela, 1936–1996*. University Park: Penn State University Press, 2000.

Friedmann, John. *Regional Development Policy: A Case Study of Venezuela*. Cambridge, MA: MIT Press, 1966.

García Ponte, Antonio. *La guerrilla de los años 60: Sangre, locura, y fantasía*. Caracas: Editorial Libros Marcados, 2010.

Gates, Leslie C. *Electing Chávez: The Business of Anti-Neoliberal Politics in Venezuela*. Pittsburgh, PA: University of Pittsburgh Press, 2010.

Goodman, Louis Wolf, ed. *Lessons of the Venezuelan Experience*. Washington, DC: Woodrow Wilson Center Press, 1995.

Gordillo, Gastón R. *Rubble: The Afterlife of Destruction*. Durham, NC: Duke University Press, 2014.

Gosen, Alfredo. *El 23 de Enero: Caracas toma Caracas*. Caracas: FundArte, 1990.

Gott, Richard. *Hugo Chávez and the Bolivarian Revolution*. London: Verso, 2005.

Greenfield, Gerald Michael. "Venezuela." In *Latin American Urbanization: Historical Profile of Major Cities*, edited by Gerald Michael Greenfield, 486–509. Westport, CT: Greenwood Press, 1994.

Grooscors, Rolando. *Problemas del desarrollo urbano en Venezuela*. Caracas: Banco Obrero, 1963.

Guevara, Aleida. *Chávez, Venezuela, and the New Latin America*. Melbourne: Ocean Press, 2005.

Hanson, Rebecca. "States Controlling Citizens Controlling the Police: Negotiating Citizen Participation and its Institutionalization within Venezuela's Police Reform." Paper presented at annual meeting of the Latin American Studies Association, Chicago, May 2014

Harnecker, Marta. *Militares junto al pueblo: Entrevistas a nueve comandantes venezolanos que protagonizaron la gesta de abril de 2002*. Valencia: Vadell Hermanos Editores, 2003.

Hawkins, Kirk. "Dependent Civil Society: The *Círculos Bolivarianos* in Venezuela." *Latin American Research Review* 41, no. 1 (2006).

———. "Populism in Venezuela: The Rise of *Chavismo*." *Third World Quarterly* 24, no. 6 (2003).

———. *Venezuela's Chavismo and Populism in Comparative Perspective*. New York: Cambridge University Press, 2010.

Hellinger, Daniel. "Political Overview: The Breakdown of *Puntofijismo* and the Rise of *Chavismo*." In *Venezuelan Politics in the Chávez Era: Class, Polarization, and Conflict*, edited by Steve Ellner and Daniel Hellinger. Boulder, CO: Lynne Rienner, 2004.

———. *Venezuela: Tarnished Democracy*. Boulder, CO: Westview Press, 1991.

Herman, Donald L. *Christian Democracy in Venezuela*. Chapel Hill: University of North Carolina Press, 1980.

———. "The Christian Democratic Party." In *Venezuela at the Polls: The National Election of 1978*, edited by Howard R. Penniman. Washington, DC: American Enterprise Institute, 1980.

Herrera Campíns, Luis. "De la democracia representativa a la democracia participativa." In *Seminario de Democracia Participativa*. Caracas, 1972.

———. *Mi compromiso con Venezuela: Programa de gobierno para el período 1979–1984*. Vol. 1. Caracas: COPEI, 1978.

Hetland, Gabriel. "The Crooked Line: From Populist Mobilization to Participatory Democracy in Chávez Era Venezuela." *Qualitative Sociology* 37, no. 4 (2014): 373–401.

Hillman, Richard S. *Democracy for the Privileged: Crisis and Transition in Venezuela*. Boulder, CO: Lynne Rienner, 1994.

Holston, James. *Insurgent Citizenship: Disjunctions of Democracy and Modernity in Brazil*. Princeton, NJ: Princeton University Press, 2007.

Inventario nacional de barrios: Estudio diagnóstico de los barrios urbanos de Venezuela. 8 vols. Caracas: Fundación para el Desarrollo de la Comunidad y Fomento Municipal, 1979.

Izard, Miguel. *El poder, la mentira y la muerte: De El Amparo al Caracazo*. Caracas: Fondo Editorial Trópykos, 1991.

James, Daniel. "October 17th and 18th, 1945: Mass Protest, Peronism, and the Argentine Working Class." *Journal of Social History* 21 (1988).

———. *Resistance and Integration: Peronism and the Argentine Working Class, 1946–1976*. Cambridge: Cambridge University Press, 1988.

Jones, Bart. *Hugo! The Hugo Chávez Story from Mud Hut to Perpetual Revolution*. Hanover, NH: Steerforth Press, 2007.

Karl, Terry Lynn. *The Paradox of Plenty: Oil Booms and Petro-States*. Berkeley: University of California Press, 1997.

———. "The Venezuelan Petro-State and the Crisis of 'Its' Democracy." In *Venezuelan Democracy under Stress*, edited by Jennifer McCoy et al., 33–55. Miami: North South Center, University of Miami, 1995.

Lazar, Sian. *El Alto, Rebel City: Self and Citizenship in Andean Bolivia*. Durham, NC: Duke University Press, 2008.

Levine, Daniel H. *Conflict and Political Change in Venezuela*. Princeton, NJ: Princeton University Press, 1973.

Linárez, Pedro Pablo. *La lucha armada en Venezuela*. Caracas: Universidad Bolivariana de Venezuela, 2006.

Liso, Antonio de. "La evolución urbana de Caracas: Indicadores e interpretaciones sobre el desarrollo de la interrelación ciudad-naturaleza." *Revista Geográfica Venezolana* 42, no. 2 (2001).

Lombardi, John V. *Venezuela: The Search for Order, the Dream of Progress*. New York: Oxford University Press, 1982.

Lombardi, John V., and James A. Hanson. "The First Venezuelan Coffee Cycle: 1830–1855." *Agricultural History* 44 (1970).

López Maya, Margarita. "La protesta venezolana entre 1989 y 1993 (En el umbral del neoliberalismo)." In *Lucha popular, democracia, neoliberalismo: La protesta popular en América Latina en los años de ajuste*, edited by Margarita López Maya. Caracas: Nueva Sociedad, 1999.

———. "Refounding the Republic: The Political Project of Chavismo." *NACLA Report on the Americas* 33, no. 6 (2000).

———. *Venezuela después del Caracazo: Formas de protesta en un contexto desinstitucionalizado*. Working Paper 287. Helen Kellog Institute, South Bend, IN, 1999.

———. "The Venezuelan *Caracazo* of 1989: Popular Protest and Institutional Weakness." *Journal of Latin American Studies* 35, no. 1 (2003): 117–137.

López Maya, Margarita, and Luis Gómez Calcaño. *De punto fijo al pacto social: Desarrollo y hegemonía en Venezuela, 1958–1985*. Caracas: Fondo Editorial Acta Científica Venezolana, 1989.

López Villa, Manuel A. "La arquitectura del 2 de Diciembre." *Boletín del Centro de Investigaciones Históricas y Estéticas* 27 (1986): 148–172.

———. "Gestión urbanística, revolución democrática y dictadura militar en Venezuela, 1945–1958." *Urbana* 14/15 (1994): 103–119.

Lubrano, Aldo, and Rosa Haydée Sánchez. *Del hombre completo a Jaime es como tú: Elecciones de 1983*. Valencia: Vadell Hermanos Editores, 1987.

Lupu, Noam. "Who Votes for *Chavismo*? Class Voting in Hugo Chávez's Venezuela." *Latin American Research Review* 45, no. 1 (2010).

Martín Frechilla, Juan José. "La comisión nacional de urbanismo, 1946–1957: Origen y quiebra de una utopía." In *Leopoldo Martínez Olavarría: Desarrollo urbano, vivienda y estado*, edited by Alberto Lovera. Caracas: Fondo Editorial Alemo, 1996.

———. *Diálogos reconstruidos para una historia de la Caracas moderna*. Caracas: Universidad Central de Venezuela, 2004.

Martz, John D. *Acción Democrática: Evolution of a Modern Political Party in Venezuela*. Princeton, NJ: Princeton University Press, 1966.

———. "Venezuela's 'Generation of '28': The Genesis of Political Democracy." *Journal of Interamerican Studies* 6, no. 1 (1964): 17–32.

Martz, John D., and Enrique A. Baloyra. *Electoral Mobilization and Public Opinion: The Venezuelan Campaign of 1973*. Chapel Hill: University of North Carolina Press, 1976.

Martz, John D., and Peter B. Harkins. "Urban Electoral Behavior in Latin America: The Case of Metropolitan Caracas, 1958–1968." *Comparative Politics* 5, no. 4 (1973): 523–549.

Mayer, Arno J. *The Furies: Violence and Terror in the French and Russian Revolutions*. Princeton, NJ: Princeton University Press, 2000.

McBeth, B.S. *Juan Vicente Gómez and the Oil Companies in Venezuela: 1908–1935*. Cambridge: Cambridge University Press, 1983.

McCoy, Jennifer L. "From Representative to Participatory Democracy?" In *The Unraveling of Representative Democracy in Venezuela*, edited by Jennifer L. McCoy and David Myers. Baltimore, MD: Johns Hopkins University Press, 2004.

McPherson, Alan. *Yankee No! Anti-Americanism in U.S.-Latin American Relations*. Cambridge, MA: Harvard University Press, 2003.

Moholy-Nagy, Sibyl. *Carlos Raúl Villanueva y la arquitectura de Venezuela*. Caracas: Editorial Lectura, 1964.

Mundaraín, Germán. *A 18 años del Caracazo: Sed de justicia*. Caracas: Defensoría del Pueblo, 2007.

Myers, David J. "Caracas: The Politics of Intensifying Primacy." In *Latin American Urban Research*, edited by Wayne A. Cornelius and Robert V. Kemper, 6. Beverly Hills, CA: Sage, 1978.

———. "The Elections and the Evolution of Venezuela's Party System." In *Venezuela at the Polls: The National Elections of 1978*, edited by Howard R. Penniman. Washington, DC: American Enterprise Institute for Public Policy Research, 1980.

———. "Policy Making and Capital City Resource Allocation: The Case of Caracas." In *Venezuela: The Democratic Experience*, edited by David J. Myers and John D. Martz. New York: Praeger, 1977.

Naím, Moisés. "High Anxiety in the Andes: The Real Story Behind Venezuela's Woes." *Journal of Democracy* 12, no. 2 (2001): 17–31.

————. *Paper Tigers and Minotaurs: The Politics of Venezuela's Economic Reforms.* Washington, DC: Carnegie Endowment for International Peace, 1993.

Ochoa Antich, Enrique. *Los golpes de febrero: De la rebelión de los pobres al alzamiento de los militares.* Caracas: Fuentes Editores, 1992.

O'Connor, Robert. "The Electorate." In *Venezuela at the Polls: The National Elections of 1978* edited by Howard R. Penniman. Washington, DC: American Enterprise Institute, 1980.

————. "The Media and the Campaign." In *Venezuela at the Polls: The National Election of 1978,* edited by Howard R. Penniman. Washington: American Enterprise Institute, 1980.

Orellana de García-Maldonado, Angelina. *60 años de experiencia en desarrollos urbanísticos de bajo costo en Venezuela.* Caracas: Instituto Nacional de la Vivienda, 1989.

Pacheco, Milvia, Elba A. Ramos, and Mirian R. Rangel. "Aproximación al estudio de la parroquia 23 de Enero de Caracas." Ph.D. Dissertation, Universidad Central de Venezuela, 1987.

Palma, Pedro A. "La economía venezolana en el período 1974–1988." In *Venezuela contemporánea, 1974–1989,* edited by Pedro Grases. Caracas: Fundación Eugenio Mendoza, 1989.

Peruzzotti, Enrique, and Catalina Smulovitz. "Social Accountability: An Introduction." In *Enforcing the Rule of Law: Social Accountability in the New Latin American Democracies,* edited by Enrique Peruzzotti and Catalina Smulovitz. Pittsburgh, PA: University of Pittsburgh Press, 2006.

Pineda Paz, Eduardo. *Urbanismo y vivienda: Aspectos de una acción de gobierno.* Caracas: Instituto Nacional de la Vivienda, 1978.

Piñango, Ramón. *El Caso Venezuela: Una ilusión de armonía.* Caracas: Ediciones IESA, 1984.

Powell, John Duncan. *Political Mobilization of the Venezuelan Peasant.* Cambridge, MA: Harvard University Press, 1971.

Przeworski, Adam. *Democracy and the Limits of Self-Government.* Cambridge: Cambridge University Press, 2010.

Putnam, Robert. *Making Democracy Work: Civic Traditions in Modern Italy.* Princeton, NJ: Princeton University Press, 1993.

Ramia, Carmen, ed. *27 de febrero: Cuando la muerte tomó las calles.* Caracas: El Nacional, 1989.

Ramos Rollón, María Luisa. *De las protestas a las propuestas: Identidad, acción y relevancia del movimiento vecinal en Venezuela.* Caracas: Editorial Nueva Sociedad, 1995.

Randall, Laura. *The Political Economy of Venezuelan Oil.* New York: Praeger, 1987.

Rangel, Domingo Alberto. *Los andinos en el poder: Balance de una hegemonía, 1899–1945.* Caracas, 1964.

Ray, Talton F. *The Politics of the Barrios of Venezuela.* Berkeley: University of California Press, 1969.

Rivas Rivas, José. *Historia gráfica de Venezuela: Una historia contada por la prensa.* Vol. 7. Caracas: Centro Editor, 1980.

Roberts, Kenneth M. "Social Polarization and the Populist Resurgence in Venezuela." In *Venezuelan Politics in the Chávez Era*, edited by Steve Ellner and Daniel Hellinger. Boulder, CO: Lynne Rienner, 2003.

Rodríguez, Francisco. "Sharing the Oil Wealth? Appraising the Effects of Venezuela's Social Programs." *LASA Forum* 38, no. 1 (2007).

Romine, David. "'Professional Police Work and Politics Do Not Mix': An Episode in the Alliance for Progress in Venezuela, 1961–1964." M.A. Thesis, New York University, 2010.

Rosenthal, Anton. "Spectacle, Fear, and Protest: A Guide to the History of Urban Public Space in Latin America." *Social Science History* 24, no. 1 (2000).

Roy, Ananya, and Nezar AlSayyad. *Urban Informality: Transnational Perspectives from the Middle East, Latin America, and South Asia*. Lanham, MD: Lexington Books, 2004.

Salas, Miguel Tinker. *The Enduring Legacy: Oil, Culture, and Society in Venezuela*. Durham, NC: Duke University Press, 2009.

Salcedo-Bastardo, J. L. *Historia fundamental de Venezuela*. Caracas: Universidad Central de Venezuela, 1996 [1970].

Segnini, Yolanda. *Las luces del gomecismo*. Caracas: Alfadil Ediciones, 1987.

Senior, Mercedes. *El Rómulo Betancourt que yo conocí: Políticos y notables, retratos de medio perfil*. Caracas: Editorial Panapo, 1986.

Silva Michelena, José Agustín, and Heinz Rudolf Sonntag. *El proceso electoral de 1978: Su perspectiva histórico-estructural*. Caracas: Editorial Ateneo, 1979.

Smilde, David and Daniel Hellinger. *Venezuela's Bolivarian Democracy: Participation, Politics, and Culture under Chávez*. Durham, NC: Duke University Press, 2011.

Sonntag, Heinz, and Thais Maigon. "Las elecciones en Venezuela en 1988 y 1989: Del ejercicio de rito democrático a la protesta silenciosa." *Revista Mexicana de Sociología* 52, no. 4 (1990).

Tarrow, Sydney. *Power in Movement: Social Movements, Collective Action, and Politics*. Cambridge: Cambridge University Press, 1994.

Tennassee, Paul Nehru. *Venezuela: Los obreros petroleros y la lucha por la democracia*. Madrid: Editorial Popular, 1979.

Tilly, Charles. *The Contentious French: Four Centuries of Popular Struggle*. Cambridge, MA: Belknap, 1986.

Troconis de Veracoechea, Ermila. *El proceso de la inmigración en Venezuela*. Caracas: Academia Nacional de la Historia, 1986.

United Nations Global Urban Observatory's Research and Technical Team. *Streets as Public Spaces and Drivers of Urban Prosperity*. Nairobi: United Nations Human Settlements Programme, 2013.

Valecillos T., Héctor. *El reajuste neoliberal en Venezuela: Ensayos de interpretación crítica*. Caracas: Monte Ávila Editores, 1992.

Vegas, Federico. *Falke*. Caracas: Mondadori, 2005.

Velasco, Alejandro. "'A Weapon as Powerful as the Vote': Street Protest and Electoral Politics in Caracas, Venezuela, before Hugo Chávez." Ph.D. Dissertation, Duke University, 2009.

———. "'A Weapon as Powerful as the Vote': Urban Protest and Electoral Politics in Venezuela, 1978–1983." *Hispanic American Historical Review* 90, no. 4 (2010): 661–695.

Velásquez, Ramón J. "Aspectos de la evolución política de Venezuela en el último medio siglo." In *Venezuela moderna: Medio siglo de historia, 1926–1976,* edited by Ramón J. Velásquez, 13–436. Caracas: Fundación Eugenio Mendoza, 1979.

Villanueva, Carlos Raúl, and Carlos Celis Cepero. *La vivienda popular en Venezuela, 1928–1952.* Caracas: Banco Obrero, 1953.

Webber, Jeffrey R. *From Rebellion to Reform in Bolivia: Class Struggle, Indigenous Liberation, and the Politics of Evo Morales.* Chicago: Haymarket, 2011.

Wilpert, Gregory. *Changing Venezuela by Taking Power: The History and Policies of the Chávez Government.* London: Verso, 2006.

Wolford, Wendy. *This Land Is Ours Now: Social Mobilization and the Meanings of Land in Brazil.* Durham, NC: Duke University Press, 2010.

Wood, Andrew, and James Baer. "Strength in Numbers: Urban Rent Strikes and Political Transformation in the Americas, 1904–1925." *Journal of Urban History* 32, no. 6 (2006).

Yarrington, Doug. *A Coffee Frontier: Land, Society, and Politics in Duaca, Venezuela, 1830–1936.* Pittsburgh, PA: University of Pittsburgh Press, 1997.

Zago, Ángela. *La rebelión de los ángeles.* Caracas: Fuentes Editores, 1992.

INDEX

Italic page references indicate illustrations and tables. All locations are in the city of Caracas, Venezuela in the 23 de Enero housing project, unless otherwise specified.